P9-DIF-842

GROWING
UP IN
AMERICA

THE BIG RED SCHOOLHOUSE
by Fred M. Hechinger
AN ADVENTURE IN EDUCATION
by Fred M. Hechinger

PRE-SCHOOL EDUCATION
edited by Fred M. Hechinger

THE NEW YORK TIMES GUIDE
TO NEW YORK CITY PRIVATE SCHOOLS
by Fred M. and Grace Hechinger
TEEN-AGE TYRANNY
by Fred M. and Grace Hechinger
GROWING UP IN AMERICA
by Fred M. and Grace Hechinger

GROWING UP IN AMERICA

Fred M. & Grace Hechinger

McGraw-Hill Book Company

NEW YORK   ST. LOUIS

SAN FRANCISCO   DÜSSELDORF   LONDON

MEXICO   SYDNEY   TORONTO

Book design by Stan Drate.

Copyright © 1975 by Fred M. and Grace Hechinger. All rights reserved. Printed in the United States of America. No part of this publication may be reproduced, stored in a retrieval system, or transmitted, in any form or by any means, electronic, mechanical, photocopying, recording, or otherwise, without the prior written permission of the publisher.

123456789 BPBP 798765

Library of Congress Cataloging in Publication Data

Hechinger, Fred M
    Growing up in America.
    (Aspects of American life and culture; 2)
    Bibliography: p.
    1. Education—United States.   I. Hechinger, Grace,
joint author.   II. Title.   III. Series.
LA217.H43   370'.973   75-2083
ISBN 0-07-027715-X

The publisher is grateful to the following for permission to reprint from copyrighted material:

American Quarterly and Keith W. Olson for "The G.I. Bill and Higher Education: Success and Surprise," from Vol. XXV, No. 5, December 1973, copyright © 1973.

Arno Press and Warren Burton for *The District School as It Was*, copyright © 1928, 1969.

Harcourt, Brace Jovanovich, Inc., and Helen M. and Robert S. Lynd for *Middletown*, copyright © 1959.

Harvard University Press and David Tyack for *The One Best System: A History of American Urban Education*, copyright © 1974.

The *Journal of Pediatrics* and the C. V. Mosby Company for an article by Stendler, "Sixty Years of Child Training Practices: Revolution in the Nursery," from *Journal of Pediatrics 36:* 122–134, copyright © 1950.

Alfred A. Knopf, Inc., and Frederick Rudolph for *The American College and University*, copyright © 1962.

Little, Brown and Company, in association with Atlantic Monthly Press, and Robert Coles for *Children of Crisis: A Study of Courage and Fear*, copyright © 1964, 1965, 1966, 1967.

Macmillan Publishing Company, Inc., and James S. Coleman for *The Adolescent Society*, copyright © The Free Press, 1961.

McGraw-Hill Book Company and Leonard Covello and Guido D'Agostino for *The Heart Is a Teacher*, copyright © 1958.

McGraw-Hill Book Company and Oscar and Mary Handlin for *The American College and American Culture: Socialization as a Function of Higher Education*, an essay written for the Carnegie Commission on Higher Education, copyright © 1970.

McGraw-Hill Book Company and Gunnar Myrdal for *An American Dilemma.*

Pocket Books, Inc., and Dr. Benjamin Spock for *Baby and Child Care*, copyright © 1957, 1968.

The University of Chicago Press and William Leuchtenburg for *Perils of Prosperity: 1914–1932*, copyright © 1958.

Yale University Press and David Riesman for *The Lonely Crowd: A Study of the Changing American Character*, copyright © 1969.

For Paul and John

PUBLISHER'S NOTE

This volume is part of a McGraw-Hill publishing program on Aspects of American Life and Culture.

Editorial Consultants for this program are Harold M. Hyman, William P. Hobby Professor of American History, Rice University, and Leonard W. Levy, Andrew W. Mellon Professor of Humanities and History, Claremont Graduate School.

ACKNOWLEDGMENTS

It would be impossible to cite, and adequately thank, all those who, during the five years of this book's progress, helped with their expertise, advice, and encouragement. Many of those whose writings are listed in this volume's bibliography have also contributed their personal wisdom to our research. There are, however, some—friends, colleagues and experts from many fields—whose counsel and moral support we feel privileged to acknowledge. If such a list could be complete, it would surely include Lawrence Cremin, David Tyack, Carl Degler, Jonathan Messerli, the late Alexander Bickel, Annette Baxter, Clark Kerr, Victor Fuchs, John Hope Franklin, Seymour Martin Lipset, Diane Ravitch, Ruth Elson, and the dedicated graduate adviser to one of the authors, Madelaine Rice. Our efforts to assess the child's place in American society were expertly aided by the late Harry Bakwin, Bruno Bettelheim, Milton Senn, and Edward A. Davies. Gerard MacCauley's experience proved invaluable throughout in moving the book toward publication. The Ford Foundation, in the persons of Harold Howe 3d and Edward Meade, allowed us to update our international perspective. Meredith Wilson, Preston Cutler, and the staff of the Center for the Advanced Study in the Behavioral Sciences provided the ideal setting in which to translate research into manuscript. Our thanks are due the archives of *The New York Times* and the New-York Historical Society, the libraries of Teachers College, Columbia University, and Stanford University, and the invaluable documentation of the past furnished by Arno Press. We owe special thanks to Gladys J. Carr for her expert and sympathetic editing of our manuscript.

CONTENTS

GROWING
UP IN
AMERICA

I
DREAMS AND REALITIES

*T*HE HISTORY OF AMERICAN EDUCATION is the triumph of hope over experience. Yet, in the telling, the benefits derived by an extraordinary percentage of children from the steadily expanding access to schooling have often obscured American education's deficiencies and failures. Like so much commentary on all aspects of American life, portraits of American education have tended to emerge either as heroic tableaux or as vile caricatures—all warts or no warts at all. Euphoric boosters and radical critics have repeatedly fallen into the same trap of assigning to education an impossible role of political omnipotence. The fact is that the schools cannot now, nor ever could, build American democracy in splendid isolation from American life.

It is against such a background that contemporary questioning of American education's goals, values, and achievements must be viewed. Excessive expectations have produced excessive disenchantment. Angry critics reflect the gap between the schools' promise and their performance. What appears to be a fashionable new pessimism about education's potential mirrors the mood about American institutions in general. Doubts about, or confidence in, American education can never be divorced from larger doubts about, or confidence in, the entire American condition.

This inseparable relationship between education and society—the impact of one on the other—constitutes the basis for this book. Each of the succeeding chapters tries to trace and interpret the continuing tension between ideals and realities. Central to this historical inquiry is the startling parallel that exists between growing up in America and the growing up of America.

There seems to us no better vantage point than that of the nation's approach to education from which to gain a broader appreciation of American society. It offers a view of sweeping commitment and often disappointing implementation: Neither tells the full story of American school or society; but an understanding of each is crucial to continued social progress and effective social criticism.

To describe American education merely in terms of what took place inside its institutions, without paying attention to guiding philosophies and ideals is tantamount to a story that is all plot and no meaning. Too often, in the telling of the American story, education's crucial and pervading role is ignored. In too many accounts of American education, the lives of children remain hidden behind the paper curtain of curriculum and statistics. In deciding what to include and what to omit, we have been guided by the need to focus on the shaping of lives—the children's and the nation's—rather than on the chronicle of events.

Most of the available accounts of American education are fragmented history, presented in bits and pieces without being meshed cohesively with the history of the American people. Some of the existing studies and monographs are of high quality, and have often been inspired by a seminal study of distinction, covering a particular person, period, or institution. But these publications generally fail to relate to each other or to the larger scene. The lack of a conceptual framework that marks the great number of specialized studies has given them the appearance of scholarly islands in a large and uncharted sea.

We have, therefore, rejected the conventional periodization of American history, while still following a chronological pattern within each chapter. Except in the beginning chapters, that pattern spans the entire two hundred years of American education's impact on society, thus aiming for cohesion and a panoramic entity in each major area of our concern. The desired effect of this approach is to allow the reader to discern how these areas overlap, affect each other, and, as parallel developments, create a composite that is the larger social fabric.

Conventional periodization was created for a different kind of history. It seemed to us inappropriate because of the time it takes for ideas and policies affecting education, the family, and the rearing of children to enter into the mainstream of popular thinking and to make their impact felt in schools and homes. To aim for precision of timing therefore would be to distort. It is misleading to speak of "the child in the early Republic" or "the Jacksonian child" when the daily lives of these children were little affected by the changes that might be inferred from new thinking and writing produced during these periods. For a meaningful appraisal of the gradual seepage of change into the cultural currents of a developing nation it seemed best to sacrifice the neat and convenient definitions of time and period and concentrate instead on the broader interpretation of trends. For example, it was the aftermath of the great wars, and not the wars themselves, that brought long-term changes—few of them instantly visible or measurable— to school or society.

The American people have followed an uncertain and winding road in their quest for education. Reforms that were billed as new and revolutionary often were, in fact, merely a return to earlier experimentation. Attitudes toward what was right or wrong in pedagogy frequently followed extreme swings in the pendulum of the national mood. Reform movements, almost invariably tended to follow not a straight line of progress or retrogression, but the near-circular path of the spiral, revisiting familiar ground while gradually moving ahead. Time and again, new ideas and arrangements, though intended to liberate from old rigidities, soon became standardized by their proponents' insistence that they had found "the one best way."

Yet it is also strikingly evident that, largely as a result of the nation's huge, continental dimensions, a great variety of different approaches have always continued to exist side by side, often virtually unknown to each other. No one movement has ever swept the country. No earlier reform ever disappears entirely. To speak of the progressive era as of a monolithic entity in time and practice is to overlook the many traditional classrooms which were untouched by progressivism. But to bury progressivism as a failed movement is to ignore the enormous, lasting impact which the philosophy has made, more often by osmosis rather than by design, on American education and culture as a whole.

Specialized accounts exist for nearly every one of education's phases, controversies, and issues. We have sought to synthesize some of the original material available either as "history" or "education" or "history of education." In addition, we have drawn on materials from other areas and works which, while already known, have not previously been considered relevant to a study of education. For the more recent past, particularly for the third quarter of the twentieth century, we relied heavily on current writings on specialized topics as well as on newspapers, magazines, and personal interviews. This is particularly true in our assessment of child-rearing theories and practices, the lives of children in and out of school, the mores and politics of college students, and the experiences of minorities and of women in education.

The picture attempted here is not all-inclusive or definitive; it is meant rather to offer an impressionistic view of American society as much as of American education. Our aim was to show the sweep of American education, in all its facets, across American life and culture. Those who seek a close-up photograph of a particular era or doctrine will ultimately have to look elsewhere, although we hope that our efforts may help make their specialized selection easier. In addition, we hope to have provided a roadmap which gives a sense of direction and a greater capacity for future exploration.

Our orientation has been deliberately national, taking account of the special nature and the great diversity of the American past. We tried to avoid writing from a narrow regional or theoretical point of view—such as that of the Eastern Establishment, the professional educator, or the passionate layman.

There existed, in nineteenth-century America, a cultural pluralism of the kind that is once again desired by contemporary theorists and reformers. It existed then simply because of the still unhomogenized natural differences between geographic sections, between rural and urban districts, between native born and immigrants, between rich and poor, black and white, men and women. It was only in the rhetoric of schoolmen and politicians, committed to the building of a nation, that the goals of unity often overshadowed the reality of diversity. Not until a measure of unity had been achieved—reinforced by urbanization and the impact of the mass media—did the threat of uniformity give rise to the new rhetoric about, and commitment to, a return to cultural pluralism.

In taking account of such trends, we have deliberately stressed what is unique about the American experience—because we believe it to be unique. European traditions and influences are important where they are relevant yardsticks by which to gauge the meaning of the American experience. Without adopting a posture of cultural isolationism, we nevertheless felt that the strengths and weaknesses of the American story, dealing with the problems of growing up in America, should be viewed in American terms.

Chapters 2 and 3 introduce our major themes. Discussions of the colonial and early national periods, with some analysis of that era's viewpoints concerning society and its institutions, is intended to set the scene for a broader understanding of the origins of much that followed.

Many of the misconceptions about the early period of American education stem from what has been called presentmindedness—judging the past by contemporary yardsticks. For example, neither society at large nor educational institutions were then organized as neatly as the complexities of modern life have come to require. Thus, it is misleading to speak of newly founded Harvard as a "divinity school" or to portray the early infant schools or dame schools as the precursors of modern day-care centers. To be sure, higher education was intended for ministers—but it was also a stage in the lives of future lawyers, doctors, businessmen, and occasionally even engineers and artists. The curriculum was not tailored specifically for any of them; it was designed to create the "educated man" and the gentleman. As for the schools, they came in all shapes and types. Depending on where a child lived, he might find good facilities—or none at all.

Chapter 4 examines the partnership and the friction between school and society in building a nation. Until recently, the "Americanization" or acculturation of what Alfred Kazin has called "the first American child" in each generation had been generally accepted without apology, in the belief that the new culture so imposed was naturally superior to what was being stamped out. Neither the pain felt by the older generation nor the loss of the children's roots was seriously considered.

Contrary to folklore, not all immigrants made the transition easily or even successfully. Some failed, slipped into poverty and despair, or even returned to "the old country." The educational process that worked for many nevertheless allowed others to fall by the wayside. It has been our intent to record both success and failure—neither to perpetuate the romantic image nor to replace it with the revisionist myth that, because the schools fell short of their nostalgic legend, education has therefore failed.

We have tried to stress that education is not an independent, self-starting force for progress. It relies for guidance on the politics of the people and the legislatures, as well as on the politics of its own experience and the professional and lay reaction to that experience. Periodically, when conflicts between social goals or human rights became too divisive, education, like other American undertakings, turned to the courts for answers. Since it was the Supreme Court that time and again charted the course at crucial junctions, we were particularly anxious to give to that tribunal its proper place in the chronicle of educational progress.

Such crucial issues as the option to attend private schools, the government's right to compel children to salute the flag or to pray in prescribed fashion, the children's right to demand equal educational opportunities, the question whether even the nation-building priority is sufficient reason to prohibit the teaching of foreign languages and, ultimately, whether the state has the power to compel children to attend school against their parents' wishes —all these questions were left for the courts to decide. It is at the level of the courts, especially the Supreme Court, therefore that the indivisible bonds between education and society—and the constant goals as well as the shifting currents of both—must be examined and understood.

Chapter 5 aims at placing the politics of educational reform in historical perspective. A 1972 Harris poll showed that the proportion of those who profess "a great deal of confidence" in education had declined from sixty-one percent in 1966 to thirty percent in 1972. Viewed in entirely contemporary terms, such a drop in faith might seem catastrophic; a less presentminded assessment, however, shows that questioning of education's value is not a new phenomenon. In the eighteenth century, to cite a random example, Bayard Taylor's "Pennsylvania Farmer" reflected the negative sentiments of his time when he grumbled:

Book learning gets the upper hand and work is slow and slack,
And they that come long after us will find things gone to wrack.

The central message of two centuries of educational politics is contained in the observation of the spiral or cyclical nature of a long succession of reform movements, always under the guiding banner of some widely accepted ideals. If the history of American education often makes it appear that there is never anything new under the sun, it is also evident that little that may be of value is ever completely forgotten or permanently lost. Educational politics, history seems to suggest, are neither as pure as some of the myth makers insist nor as evil or futile as the radical critics charge.

The general course for Chapter 6 was set by the discovery, in the process of our research, that most serious publications on the history of American education ignore the lives and feelings of real children in sharp contrast to the popular folklore which paints a picture of America as a child's paradise. Thus, we were determined that the condition of childhood, in fact rather than in theory, ought to be central to this particular two-hundred-year slice of social and educational history.

It seemed to us equally important to focus on the persistent dichotomy between the two worlds of American childhood— that of the affluent "norm" and that of the deprived poor who tended to be either overlooked or treated as abnormal. To understand the plight of the latter one must be aware of the unpleasant fact that these children were often characterized as "vicious" and "depraved" in the past and are still surreptitiously considered vicious even in a more polite present that no longer allows that characterization to be pronounced out loud. A sensitive view of the American child's history, for example, calls for an understanding that the humane treatment of youngsters in John Dewey's Laboratory School in Chicago existed side-by-side with the cruel exploitation of children in Chicago's stockyards. The former were highly publicized, the latter invisible and ignored.

We are deliberately somewhat imprecise about the children's exact ages. The terms "infant," "child," and "youth" in the seventeenth and eighteenth centuries denoted different numerical ages from the later groupings. "Adolescence" was not regularly acknowledged until the latter part of the nineteenth century. In broad terms, however, our chronicle of childhood deals with the years from birth to the teens, deferring the college-age students for a later chapter.

Our decision to assign a separate place—in Chapter 7—to the Black education experience was prompted by the fact that it represents a part of American history that is at once tragically different and yet in many ways characteristic of a certain blindness in the educational establishment and in the nation at large that has also affected other minorities in varying degree. What has made the Black experience unique is that Blacks did not risk the hazards of an ocean voyage voluntarily in search of a better life. The country that to all others who journeyed there stood as the symbol of liberty was to them a hateful prison.

Even after slavery had been abolished, a more subtle form of enslavement continued to exclude Blacks from the melting pot. Lingering prejudices perpetuated barriers which stood in direct conflict with the American prospectus. A study of Black education moreover affords special insights into the true meaning of education to those who view it as the ultimate liberating force; but it also is essential to an understanding of the wider educational deprivation for Blacks and whites alike in the rural South with its ambiguities of great sectional pride and extended mourning over a lost war in a cause that had to be lost if the nation were to live.

In charting Chapter 8 we felt that the history of higher education was ideally suited to document the impact on American thought of two continuously conflicting currents—elitism and egalitarianism. Buffeted by those currents, colleges and universities have nevertheless moved steadily toward an expansionism that is inseparable from the goal of an open intellectual frontier and an open, or at least fluid, society.

As each expansionist wave hit the campuses, elitist voices were raised against declining academic standards; yet the pressure of those who demanded access proved irresistible. A major reason for this readiness and capacity to accommodate an unprecedented form of educational populism was the fact that rather than being rooted in a separate academic tradition, as were the European universities, American campuses reflected the mind and the will of their communities. The diversity of American higher education is the result, not of a deliberate plan by the academic leadership, but of the society's determination to be served by scholars rather than to be subservient to them.

Just as we felt that an adequate consideration of the child's condition in school and society called for a separate analysis, apart from the institutional history of the schools' curricula and politics, so we were convinced that American students (and post-adolescents) required their own place in the American story. Chapter 9 is an attempt to avoid the charge, often leveled with much justification at historians of higher education as well as at university faculties and administrations, that students are the forgotten or neglected element. It was only as a result of the riotous 1960s that the students moved briefly to center stage, and analysts subsequently tended to overcompensate for past neglect by offering a sentimentalized picture of students as a persistently progressive or even revolutionary force in American history. We have tried to show that the reality of student life and its impact on the shaping of the colleges and the country is far less simplistic and therefore more interesting than might be suggested either by traditionalist or romantic legend.

In our concluding chapter, we have attempted a condensed close-up view of our deliberately impressionistic and panoramic picture of the main currents of educational thought and practice as they helped shape a nation and a society. We have tried to offset the risk of distortions caused by the nature of the subject and the available sources by including as many different views and illustrations as possible, while at the same time deliberately limiting topics and areas of coverage.

The past is a foreign country. History therefore is the original cross-cultural study. A visitor who sees electric lights at night in Deerfield, Massachusetts, in its restored Colonial setting, needs a special imagination to see in his mind how the same scene might have appeared two hundred years ago. The problem came to life for us when, on a sightseeing tour in one of California's replicas of a frontier hotel, we explained to a six-year-old the uses of the chamber pot—only to find him searching the entire building for bathrooms.

Above all, we have tried to humanize the American educational experience. It is an experience that cannot be understood if it is camouflaged by theory. Its chronicle is incomplete if it concentrates on organizational accomplishments and statistical facts, without capturing something of the glow of satisfaction on some children's faces and the sting of pain on other youngsters' hands, black and blue from the blows of the ferule.

Voices from the past will not always convey the "exact" truth, but they can come together to create the mood for a better understanding of the variety in the human and the national experience. Properly recorded, in the context of their time, those voices can speak to the present and heighten contemporary sensitivities to the promise and the limitations of education's service to a free society.

2
SCHOOL ON THE HILL

*I*F A NATION EXPECTS TO BE IGNORANT and free in a state of civilization, it expects what never was and what never will be," wrote Thomas Jefferson. John Jay called knowledge "the soul of a republic." John Adams believed that it was the nation's duty to provide "the instruction of people in every kind of knowledge that can be of use to them in their moral duties as men, citizens and Christians."

Early rhetoric about the importance of education to the newly independent United States was impressive. The establishment of schools and colleges was part of virtually every dream and blueprint in the minds of those early leaders and thinkers who wanted to plant the seeds of popular government and to root out the tyranny of unearned privilege. These founding political philosophers and philosophical politicians were convinced that only an educated populace could check the power of government. In the terms of their time, this meant that all the people had to be literate and a substantial number intellectually competent beyond the level of mere literacy.

Again and again, the men who charted the new nation's future linked the success of the emerging democracy with the dissemination of knowledge, not to the privileged few but to the many. "Popular government without popular information or the means of acquiring it," said James Madison, "is but a prologue to a farce or tragedy, or perhaps both."

In his farewell address in 1796, George Washington appealed to the new leadership: "Promote then, as an object of primary importance, institutions for the general diffusion of knowledge. In proportion as the structure of a government gives force to public opinion, it is essential that public opinion should be enlightened."

And in what was perhaps the most explicit warning against dreams of popular government without popular intelligence, Jefferson wrote in 1820: "I know of no safe depository of the ultimate powers of the society but the people themselves; and if we think them not enlightened enough to exercise their control with a wholesome discretion, the remedy is not to take it from them, but to inform their discretion by education."

How daring these concepts were almost two hundred years ago can readily be gauged by the fact that they are far from secure even now. The people's right to know, and their capacity to comprehend, remains at the heart of every conflict between the sometimes arrogant and often paternalistic attitude of the governmental bureaucracy and the citizens. At the time when these ideas were first propounded they were nothing short of revolutionary. They flew in the face not only of past principles of orderly government but of the then-prevalent uses of education itself.

The brave and prophetic voices therefore continued for some time to cry largely in the wilderness. There was no immediate rush into popular education. Even where specific ordinances were passed, these were more often than not honored only in the breach. Translating a liberal and revolutionary ideal into practice, as local communities struggled toward security and self-sufficiency, was far from easy. Not all the spokesmen of the day shared Jefferson's conviction that the masses really deserved, or could be entrusted with, such unprecedented opportunities. The gap between politico-educational commitment and everyday political realities —never fully closed to this day—was wide.

Determination to use education in the formation of a godly society was strong enough to culminate in the extraordinary achievement of the founding of Harvard College in 1636, less than two decades after the first settlers had secured a foothold in the wilderness. The opening words of Harvard's early history provide a sense of the day's priorities:

> After God had carried us safe to New England, and we had built our houses, provided necessaries for our livelihood, reared convenient places for God's worship, and settled the civil government: One of the next things we longed for, and looked after was to advance learning and perpetuate it to posterity; dreading to leave an illiterate ministry to the churches, when our present ministers shall lie in the dust.

It is easy to overstress religious motivation and conclude, as many past assessments of that era have done, that the commitment to education, if it existed at all, was only a by-product of religious training. Religion was, of course, a vital and pervasive influence on early American society. British settlers had, after all, been steeped in the tradition of a powerful state religion. Quite apart from the political power of the churches, religion had not yet been challenged, much less replaced, as the anchor for family and society. To expect education, whether at Harvard or in the early elementary schools, not to focus attention on religion and in turn be guided by its needs as well as its commands, would be to misunderstand the nature of life as it was then lived. Education's deep and at times overpowering involvement with religion then was as inescapable as the twentieth-century schools' involvement with psychology and sociology.

New England was a deliberate experiment in Christian living. Puritanism, with its strongly religious foundation, was intended, as S. E. Morison put it, to "permeate every phase of living purpose in life and enhance God's glory." Thus it is only natural that these goals were reflected in Harvard's mission. But it would be misleading to conclude that the prototype of the American college was merely a divinity school. In the terms of its day, Harvard was the embodiment of general education for those who were expected to rank high in society.

Harvard's early statutes of 1652 said:

> When any scholar is able to read fully, of such like classical Latin author *extempore,* and make and speak true Latin in verse and prose . . . and decline perfectly the paradigms of nouns and verbs in the Greek tongue, then may he be admitted into the College, nor shall any claim admission before such qualifications.

These requirements were neither particularly religious nor very practical in nature. They reflected the then-established image of the educated man, and they changed very little in the course of the eighteenth century, except for the added prerequisite that the candidate be able to *write* Latin as well.

There was much in the original that has continued to influence both the reality and the nostalgia of American higher education. The college of the Colonial era was small and personal. A single curriculum was shared by all, simultaneously aimed at fortifying character and intellect. The president taught some courses, often in subjects best described under the rubric "moral philosophy."

Undergraduates at early Harvard were given only as much divinity instruction as was considered essential for an educated Christian layman—a good deal, of course, by modern standards. Liberal education of the era was intended to introduce young men to the best thinking and writing of past ages, not to open their minds to the ideas of their own age.

All students, whether or not they were candidates for the pulpit, took prescribed courses in six of the traditional arts—grammar, logic, rhetoric, arithmetic, geometry, and astronomy—and in the three philosophical arts—metaphysics, ethics, and natural science —as well as in Greek, Hebrew, and ancient history. Latin, of course, was already out of the way, having been mastered in grammar school; it was the language of instruction and of most of the major textbooks. Cambridge, England, was the model for Cambridge, New England.

Life at Harvard, in contrast to the high-minded prospectus, was not always as idyllic as might have been expected of a place where Christian gentlemen and ministers were being educated. Affluent students lived in their own quarters outside the college, and not without reason. During John Adams' time as a student, a graduate recalled, the day at the college began at dawn, "the provisions badly cooked . . . the soups were dreadful; we frequently had puddings made of flour and water and boiled so hard as not to be eatable; we frequently threw them out and kicked them about." An earlier verse offers an insight on the realities:

The tutors now instead of being free,
Humane and Generous as they ought to be,
An awful distance dictatorial keep,
And mulcts [fines] and frowns on all their pupils heap.

But the true importance of Harvard to the educational currents of Colonial America was not in any detail of organization; it was rather in the establishment of a pattern of higher education. By the time of the Revolution, nearly every Protestant denomination and sect had its own college, and no major community considered itself complete without it. To some social critics this seemed a dangerous trend—the beginning of the American tendency to be more interested in the proliferation of schools than in the depth of learning. But in the long run, the ready availability of higher education brought with it advantages of educational diversity and social flux which outweighed the greater purity of remote scholarly enclaves. The optimistic faith that peaks of excellence would rise from a plateau accessible to greater numbers was implicit in the establishment of so many early colleges.

It was not, however, the Puritan heritage that encouraged such optimism. In its Old World luggage, it carried a somewhat gloomier view about the creation of a social and moral order. H. L. Mencken later overstated the exuberant pessimism only slightly when he defined Puritanism as "the haunting fear that someone somewhere may be happy." Initially, at least, secular teaching as a means of opening a child's mind to a larger comprehension was thought of as frivolous, if not actually sinful. Church attendance, not school, was compulsory in Old Plymouth, even for nonmembers.

But the new environment and living conditions soon broadened the Puritan concept of education's usefulness. In a pioneering society, more was at stake than to make sure that leading citizens of church and community could read and write to extol the glory of God. Knowledge was essential to insure the success of the divine mission the settlers had set for themselves—to build a city upon a hill, as a shining example for a sinful Europe and free of the corruption of the Old World.

Without education, such a city could not rise. The Puritans' realism told them that, without the power of reason, they could not gain the attention, let alone the respect, of those Europeans who had the advantage of trained minds.

Because Puritanism was aggressively middle-class, it raised the concept of self-improvement virtually to the level of a religious faith. There was less and less room for the old religious belief in predestined fate that had so often and so callously been exploited by the old stratified order. Under the old order, the King's right had been divine, and the masses remained the pawns of their own fatalism, sanctioned by a religion that demanded blind obedience, without much hope for anything more than heaven's mercy. New England Puritanism, conditioned by the leveling experience gained from taming a new land, gave successful laymen a rapidly growing share of worldly power. God, it seemed evident, could be nobly served by building a society that would not be less devout for being successful and prosperous.

In 1642, the general court of Massachusetts Bay passed what was probably the American colonies' first education law. It proclaimed sternly that "this court, taking into consideration the great neglect of many parents and masters in training their children in learning, and labor and other employments" which might be "profitable to the common wealth" would see to it that local communities do their share to provide schoolhouses and teachers. New York State's legislature, at approximately the same time, tried and failed to enact similar statutes, quite possibly because it lacked the support of a unified constituency of the Puritans' strength and determination.

But even in Massachusetts it was easier to issue proclamations than to persuade local townspeople to provide support and money. This may explain why in 1647, Massachusetts passed a second education act with the famous and formidable preamble:

> It being one chief project of that old deluder, Satan, to keep men from the knowledge of the Scriptures, as in former times keeping them in an unknown tongue, so in these later times by persuading from the use of tongues, that so at least the true sense and meaning of the Originall might be clouded with false glosses of Saint-seeming-deceivers; and that learning may not be buried in the graves of our forefathers in Church and Commonwealth, the Lord assisting in our endeavors.

The "old deluder" preamble has been hotly debated by scholars. It has been cited by some as proof that the Puritans' support of education was really a pretext to reinforce not only religion itself, but religious intolerance. Schools, this argument goes, were merely to be the bulwark of Protestant domination, the wall to keep out all other pious or ideological influences.

On the whole, the argument is not convincing, even if it is conceded that some extremists may well have wanted to use the schools in this fashion. Fear of threats to the religious establishment could not justify what was an extraordinary legislative effort to provide public education. It is then far more likely that the preamble was a shrewd political maneuver designed to create a sense of urgency in the community.

All the "reasons" advanced for the passage of this unusual legislation must be examined in the light of seventeenth-century views. Religion was an integral part of everyday life, not confined to churchgoing on Sundays and holidays. Children were taught to read so they would have a first-hand knowledge of the Bible. Salvation was impossible without such knowledge. Thus the main business of education was to instruct children in the moral principles and doctrines of Christianity.

The Puritans' sense of mission convinced them that they would need not only educated leaders and clergy, but an educated populace as well. It was a task too important to be left to chance.

A society whose members would shape their lives by spiritual rigor must take responsibility for training its people. Therefore, principles of English Puritanism which most profoundly affected the social development of New England and subsequently of the United States were not just old religious dogma, but new educational ideals combined with religious goals: a learned clergy and a literate people. That they succeeded remarkably well can be seen by the astonishing literacy rate in the colonies by the 1770s, documented by the rapid growth of newspapers, with a circulation that outdistanced that in the mother country.

In modern terms, the controversial "old deluder Satan" preamble probably represented the original maneuver of effective education lobbying—not very different from the tactics employed by those who, intent on toughening the educational standards of the public schools of the 1950s, saw nothing wrong with stampeding lawmakers into reform action by pointing to the first Russian Sputnik as a major threat to the American Way of Life. The "deluder Satan" can take many shapes and guises, and the National Defense Education Act against the devil of Communism was only a twentieth-century version to spur the faithful into recognizing the benefits to be derived from an educated populace.

There was good reason, in 1647, to use some hard-line persuasion. The law specifically provided that every town of fifty families or more must provide a school where children could learn to read, write, and cipher, and communities of a hundred families or more were to support a master capable of teaching Latin and Greek. Parents remained free to choose between sending their children to those schools or educating them at home, but establishment of the schools was to be compulsory. Most of the population, however, appeared reluctant to make the sacrifices necessary to implement the law, and many communities ignored its provisions unless courts stepped in—apparently not very often—to enforce them.

An important principle had nevertheless been established by allowing the state to make itself the arbiter over so personal a matter as the education of children and a family's obligation to state and child. The seed had been planted for the local control of education, based on local financing. The theory has remained so fundamental to the alternative of a national system of education that it continues to be tenaciously defended two centuries later, when many other major areas of national life have become subject to Federal control.

Typically, New England schooling expected the parents, if they could afford it, to contribute a small fee—three- or fourpence per week for elementary and grammar grades, or six or eight shillings for an entire six-months school year. These payments were used to cover part of the teacher's wage, with the town making up the balance.

Cotton Mather, who symbolized so much of the stern and yet pragmatic character of the Puritan approach to life and society, said in his *Contemplations on The Future State of New England:* "Where schools are not vigorously and honorably encouraged whole colonies will sink apace into a degenerate and contemptible condition and at last become horribly barbarous. If you have any love of God . . . let schools have more encouragement."

And so it was that little Joseph, in the description of diarist Samuel Sewall, toddled off to school at the tender age of two years and eight months of age, carrying his hornbook—another symbol of that day. This basic teaching tool really was no book at all, but a piece of wood shaped like a paddle and on many occasions used as such, when the simple words and sayings imprinted on it did not hold the pupil's attention.

The colonists modeled their secondary schools after the British "Latin" or "grammar" schools whose chief function was to prepare boys for college. The most famous school of this type was the Boston Latin School, founded in 1635. These schools taught mainly Latin and Greek, and it was only later that the curriculum was modified to include English, mathematics, and some other subjects, although there were some parallel models of the private "English school" which offered a less classical and more utilitarian course of study. The latter was intended to prepare some youths for college and others for entry into business careers. Until the beginnings of what much later came to be known as the high schools, academies dominated the education scene, even though they were ill suited to the needs of the emerging new nation.

Moreover, these schools, and indeed virtually all education beyond the Three R's, were intended for boys. Girls, it was still widely believed, were not strong enough to face the rigors of advanced learning. And their assigned place in society was not thought to call for it.

Governor John Winthrop, in his *History of New England,* describes the sad tale of the young woman who "gave herself wholly to reading and writing" and, as a result, lost all of her wits. She could have been spared that terrible fate, Winthrop suggested, had she tended to household affairs.

Such was the conventional wisdom of the time, even though there were some significant exceptions. For example, Henry Laurens, in the eighteenth century, did help to educate his twelve-year-old daughter Martha, by sending her the learning aids she requested, including pencils. Still, he found it appropriate to advise her: "When you are measuring the surface of the globe remember you are to but a part in it, and think of a plumb pudding and other domestic duties. . . ."

Abigail Adams commented: "Female education, in the best families, went no further than writing and arithmetic; in some rare instances music and dancing."

For all who did go to school, the day was long and hard. It often started at 6 A.M. and lasted until six in the evening, with a two-hour break for lunch. There were two weeks of vacation in midsummer and three weeks at Christmas. At age seven or eight, boys could be admitted to grammar school for a seven-year course, mainly aimed at preparation for college.

The basic approach to learning and children was somber, avoiding anything that might be thought frivolous. The most popular textbook, *The New England Primer,* which, in all its many reprints, is estimated to have reached a total edition of over 6 million copies, began with the famous lines:

> In Adam's fall
> We sinned all.
> Thy Life to mend,
> God's Book attend.

These sentiments expressed more than an exhortation of humility before God. It was as much a statement of pedagogy, reflecting

the same attitude with which John Cotton described the content
of his Primer: "Spiritual Milk for Babes in either England Drawn
out of the Breasts of both Testaments for their Souls' Nourish-
ment."

The general assumption that man was by nature corrupt constituted a heavy burden for children, particularly since it was
almost universally believed that they were simply miniature
adults. As such, they were expected to be capable of bearing the
full weight of the masters' heavy-handed efforts to purge them of
evil thoughts and corruption. The only difference between adults
and children was thought to be that the latters' minds and morals
were undeveloped and undisciplined. Cotton Mather called them
"little vipers." John Wesley, over a century after the founding of
New England, urged parents to "break their child's will" to help
save him from doom and perdition. "It should be forced to do as
it is told, even if you have to whip it ten times running," he said.
"Break its will, in order that its soul may live."

The early American schoolhouse, contrary to the nostalgic
legend, was not a very warm and romantic place. In the beginning
of the nineteenth century, Washington Irving described it as "a
low building of one large room, rudely constructed with logs;
the windows partly glazed and partly patched with leaves of old
copybooks." He continued in his *Sketchbook:*

> The schoolhouse stood in a rather lonely but pleasant situa-
> tion just at the foot of a woody hill. . . . From hence the low
> murmur of his pupils' voices, conning over their lessons, might
> be heard on a drowsy summer's day, like the hum of a bee
> hive; interrupted now and then by the authoritative voice of
> the master, in the tone of menace or command; or, peradven-
> ture by the appalling sound of the birch, as he urged some
> tardy loiterer along the flowery path of knowledge.

For some time, during the Colonial period, the so-called "dame
schools" were imported from England and run for small children
by middle-class women generally in "reduced circumstances."
Their quality varied from adequately imparting the rudiments
of the Three R's to the barest of minimal custodial care. Some ob-

servers have viewed them as the day-care centers of their time, and they have often been romanticized as precursors of early childhood education. With a few exceptions, this rosy view is challenged by the records and by a poem of the 1780s by George Crabbe: .

> When a deaf poor patient widow sits
> And awes some twenty infants as she knits
> Infants of the humble, busy wives who pay
> Some trifling price for freedom through the day . . .
> Her room is small, they cannot widely stray
> Her threshold high, they cannot run away. . . .

If the children's lot was hard, so was that of the tutors. Salaries were low, and this came to be virtually a tradition, not only in the Colonies but subsequently in the new nation. In 1837, Walt Whitman taught for about five months at a total salary of $72.20 plus board. For such pay, he was placed in charge of eighty-five pupils from the ages of five to fifteen in Smithtown, Long Island.

Some of the early schoolmasters gained warm personal recognition, such as Daniel Pastorius, who established Germantown Latin School in 1702; Andrew Lamb, an exconvict who immigrated from London and set up a successful school in Philadelphia; and the most beloved of the Colonial schoolmasters, Ezekiel Cheever, who taught in New Haven in the 1640s. Cheever, born in 1614 as the son of a London linen draper, had come to America in 1637. After teaching in New Haven and Ipswich, Massachusetts, he went to the Boston Free School, as the Boston Latin School was then called. Cotton Mather wrote in his "Elegy on Ezekiel Cheever":

> You that are men, and Thoughts of Manhood know,
> Be Just now to the Man that made you so.
> . . . Prais'd, and Lov'd and Wish'd to Life again.
> A mighty Tribe of Well-instructed Youth
> Tell what they owe to him, and Tell with Truth.

And Mather, in his concluding lines, claimed to be setting forth Cheever's own advice to future tutors:

Tutors be Strict, but yet be Gentle too
Don't by fierce Cruelties fair Hopes undo. . . .

These were the giants to be immortalized and remembered; the rank-and-file of tutors of the day rarely resembled them. The typical schoolmaster was young, often between better jobs or studying for the law or the ministry. Ill paid, he often had to do a host of other chores. The grammar school usually had only one teacher, just out of college, perhaps, if not actually still a college student. An account in a New England *Town Book* reports the schoolmaster acting as a court messenger, summons server, and even gravedigger. He might have to conduct ceremonial church services, lead the Sunday choir, and ring the bell for public worship.

Early in his life, John Adams was a schoolteacher in Worcester, Massachusetts, and he complained bitterly about the "large number of runtlings, just capable of lisping ABC and troubling the master." In a dark and bitter mood, he felt sure that teaching school for a long time "would make a base weed and ignoble shrub" of him. And yet, in the midst of his misery and in large measure because he recalled his own dislike for school, he was among those who saw the profession as a potentially noble one, if it could only muster the strength to build on the students' interests. Like thousands of those who followed him, he daydreamed about the pupils' future, and at one such revealing moment he imagined himself, not as a harassed master confronted by "runtlings," but as a powerful potentate at the head of a commonwealth:

"I have several renowned generals but three feet high and several deep projecting politicians in petticoats," he mused. "I have others catching and dissecting flies, accumulating remarkable pebbles, cockle shells, etc., with as ardent curiosity as any virtuoso in the Royal Society."

For good or ill, a beginning had been made in the American people's sometimes enthusiastic but more often halting and grudging support of their children's schools and their schools' teachers. Somewhat later, at the beginning of the nineteenth century,

Washington Irving's schoolmaster was still laboring in his profession's poverty.

> When school hours were over, he was ever the companion and playmate of the larger boys. . . . The revenue arising from his school was small. . . . He lives successfully with different families in the neighborhood of the farmers whose children he taught, [and he went the rounds of the district] with all his worldly effects tied up in a cotton handkerchief.

And it was not, as Irving stressed, that his patrons or employers could not afford to do better by him. It was rather that they "are apt to consider the cost of schooling a grevious [sic] burden, and schoolmasters as mere drones." And so the teacher had to help with the family chores, "making hay, mending fences, taking horses to water, driving cows from pasture and cutting wood for the fires."

Change was in the wind even as the Colonial era drew to a close. There was a curious strength in the American strain of Puritanism. The vigor was not only spiritual. It gave pragmatic and optimistic rise to a new commercialism, and the new version of *The New England Primer* by now contained a verse whose message was to live throughout the growth of American education:

> He who ne'er learns his ABC
> Forever will a blockhead be.
> But he who learns his letters fair,
> Shall have a coach to take the air.

The growth of materialism was not the only new trend. As men dreamed of greater freedoms, they could not help but be troubled about the absence of freedom in the schools. In *Reflections and Maxims,* William Penn wrote of the young people of his day:

> We are in pain to make them scholars but not men, to talk rather than to know, which is true canting. . . . We press their memory too soon, and puzzle, strain, and load them with words and rules to know grammar and rhetoric, and a strange tongue or two that . . . may never be useful to them,

leaving their natural genius to mechanical, physical, or natural knowledge uncultivated and neglected. . . .

Penn's was no lone voice. Powerful forces were stirring. It would not be too long before a traveler from England, Mrs. Harriet Martineau, could report that New Englanders were looking on their educational progress with "just complacency":

"The provision of schools is so adequate," she wrote, "that any citizen who sees a child play during school hours, may ask, 'Why are you not at school?' . . . No control is exercised as to how and where the child shall be educated. It rests with the parent to send him to a public or private school."

And looking beyond the formal machinery, Mrs. Martineau remarked that the children appeared "free and easy and important" and that in private homes "comments slipped in at the table by the children were often the most memorable . . . and most amusing." In Baltimore, she remembered, children would crowd around her, questioning, discussing and speculating, whereas in England it would be "Yes, ma'am, No, ma'am."

3

PRAGMATIC VISIONARIES

*T*HE REVOLUTION THAT WAS TO
change a nation's concern about the purposes of education took
place not on the barricades but in men's minds. Its doctrines
were nothing less than a frontal attack on truths that had long
been held to be self-evident. The fundamental belief on which all
educational thinking used to rest was, as every child was made
to memorize and remember, that "in Adam's fall, we sinned all."

The more dramatic changes were made easier by the fact that
American education, as it emerged from the Colonial era, had
already undergone some subtle shifts made necessary by a pioneering environment. The new nation's leaders agreed about education's importance, but there was far less agreement on how this
recognition was to be translated into national goals or institutional blueprints.

John Adams wrote eloquent but vague observations on education into the Massachusetts Constitution. The Northwest Ordinance of 1787 said: "Religion, morality and knowledge being necessary to good government and the happiness of mankind, schools and means of legislation shall forever be encouraged [by the states]."

What kind of state legislation and how much land was to be provided to make the establishment of schools possible continued to vary from state to state and from year to year. It was characteristic and appropriate that publicly owned land and its real value were—and remained for a long time—the instrument for the national support of schools and colleges. The Federalist Guilian C. Verplanck, as chairman of the Assembly Committee on Colleges, Academies, and Common Schools, in 1821 sketched out the origins and development of the national policy of appropriating such land for educational use.

Originally proposed in Maryland, the plan suggested that a total of more than 9 million acres might be allowed for this purpose. New York was to get approximately one tenth of the total, or 937,076 acres—slightly less than that state was to get later, in 1862, under the Morrill Act, which used the land-grant device for the establishment of a new breed of colleges attuned to the needs of agriculture and to the industrial-mechanical revolution.

New York's Governor DeWitt Clinton, in an appendix to his official message, submitted the Maryland report which concluded with the resolution that "each of the United States has an equal right to participate in the benefits of public lands."

Many other states passed resolutions for the distribution of public lands or of revenues from their sale for the support of education. Even though implementation remained uneven, such legislation was significant as an expression of general interest and of an emerging philosophy.

But it was neither a simple philosophy to shape nor an interest easy to maintain. In 1778, at the age of thirty-five, Thomas Jefferson drafted a "Bill for the More General Diffusion of Knowledge in the State of Virginia." It was never enacted. He drew up a plan which would have built three levels of schooling: elementary education for all children; district schools for the cream of young talent destined for higher education; and the university for the "natural" aristocracy of talent. Such a plan, Jefferson believed, "would have raised the mass of the people to the high ground of moral responsibility necessary to their own safety and orderly government." But, even though some progress was made in the establishment of free public education, Jefferson's hopes for his grandiose scheme were not realized in his lifetime. When his blueprint was defeated in 1817, he said pointedly that the members of the Legislature "do not generally possess information enough to perceive the important truths, that knowledge is power, that knowledge is safety, that knowledge is happiness."

Since republican government made heavy demands of ordinary as well as extraordinary men, the success of the American experiment rested inevitably on the effectiveness of new institutions that would school all men. The faith of those who believed popular intelligence could shape and secure such a republic—a faith by no means universally held—stemmed in large part from the notion that education was not solely a private or religious function.

If the fundamental principles of the American revolution were an outgrowth of the eighteenth-century movement toward freedom of thought and popular government, then a man could no longer look to the past for sanctions of his conduct—any more than he could look to Europe for models of his institutions. If man was truly capable of continuous improvement and advancement then education was the prime instrument.

Because the new American movement was revolutionary in the purest sense of the term, it had to rebel openly and eloquently against the old order. It was a rebellion which had sublime confidence in its virtue and wisdom during that optimistic early stage. The leading minds of the years following 1776 were so certain that the example of man's new freedoms enjoyed in an energetic republic of open frontiers would inspire the Old World that they never considered the need eventually to liberate that world by force. They were far more concerned lest young Americans, in search of education or adventure abroad, might be infected by the virus of the old order's corruption.

"Let us view the disadvantages of sending a youth to Europe," wrote Jefferson to John Banister, Jr., in 1785.

> To enumerate them all would require a volume. I will select a few. If he goes to England he learns drinking, horse-racing

and boxing. . . . He acquires a fondness for European luxury and dissipation and a contempt for the simplicity of his own country; he is fascinated with the privileges of the European aristocracy and sees with abhorrence the lovely equality which the poor enjoys with the rich in his own country. . . . He forms foreign friendships which will never be useful to him. . . . It appears to me then that an American coming to Europe for education loses in his knowledge, in his morals, in his health, in his habits, and in his happiness. . . . Cast your eye over America: who are the men of most learning, of most eloquence, most beloved by their country and most trusted and promoted by them? They are those who have been educated among them, and whose manners, morals and habits are perfectly homogeneous with those of the country.

(Jefferson was pragmatic enough to make an exception in the case of medical students.)

The issue was as much one of new needs versus old habits as it was that of the Old World politics against those of the New. "There is in mankind an unaccountable prejudice in favor of ancient customs and habitudes, which inclines to a continuance of them after the circumstances, which formerly made them useful, cease to exist," wrote Benjamin Franklin in 1789 as part of his observations on the need for a new academy in Philadelphia. Rejecting the old ways of teaching children only Latin and the classics, he concluded: "Thus the time spent in that study might, it seems, be much better employ'd in the education for such a country as ours . . ."

The incipient educational revolution—it has remained an incomplete battle throughout American history—bore the particular imprint of three men: Thomas Jefferson, Benjamin Franklin, and Noah Webster. It would be difficult to think of three more different personalities. But it is because of those differences that their outlook and goals together create a picture that accommodates virtually all the currents and countercurrents that have moved and shaken American education for two hundred years.

Jefferson and Franklin represented the age of enlightened liberalism. Both stood ready to challenge the established order, in education as in politics. Both were out of sympathy with religious domination over state affairs, aristocratic privilege, and all forms of authoritarianism. Both objected to the class-conscious prejudices of their time—and their own classes. In their views and by their actions, they were truly prophetic of the most daring goals American education set for itself and occasionally managed to approach.

Jefferson, the aristocrat, was deeply committed to equality and excellence—two goals which have so often seemed irreconcilable to those who have less faith in the free society. Although the term itself was yet to be coined, "universal education"—at least to the level of effective literacy and citizenship—was to Jefferson an absolute prerequisite. Beyond such minimal attainments, the road to additional and even higher learning would remain open to all who had the qualifications and the ambition. It was imperative, Jefferson wrote in 1779 in his "Bill for the More General Diffusion of Knowledge," for those "whom nature hath endowed with genius and virtue" to be educated for public service so that they might be "worthy to receive, and able to guard, the sacred deposit of the rights and liberties of their fellow citizens." The plan called for scholarships to all able boys, clearly the most democratic blueprint of its day, although Jefferson's belief in individual freedoms made him reject compulsory school attendance.

As was to happen again and again throughout the course of American education, this plan for popular education was defeated by the less lofty, more selfishly short-sighted votes of legislators who had their eyes on tradition, particularly when conservatism was cheaper in immediate tax payments.

Like his personal interests, Jefferson's educational outlook ranged over all of society's activities, mundane and spiritual. They covered agriculture, commerce, manufacturing, the arts and sciences. True education, he felt, would turn people into "examples of virtue to others, and of happiness within themselves."

Jefferson believed that man is free to the extent to which he is self-sufficient. A primary goal of education therefore is to develop the pupil's inner strength and resourcefulness. "The art of life is the art of avoiding pain," he wrote. ". . . The most effectual means of being secure against pain is to retire within ourselves and to suffice for our own happiness." It was probably this trust in the power of the intellect that made this Virginia planter, with his love for land, advocate nevertheless that the University of Virginia follow what was essentially a classical and intellectual course of studies. In all his curricular outlines, there is a blending of the philosophical and the practical—a fusion that might have seemed natural to the Greeks, but that had been overlooked by so many of the Colonial Latin school educators, as it was so often to be overlooked again in the future by the partisans of narrowly vocational and equally narrow academic education.

Like George Washington, Jefferson feared urbanization. He was deeply concerned over the declining values in teeming cities, with their rootless, restless proletariat. His dream was that of a country of small but free farmers, and he was convinced that the land gained through the Louisiana Purchase in 1803 could keep America's frontier and the people's character open for a thousand years.

In 1787, he wrote to James Madison:

> I think our governments will remain virtuous for many centuries; as long as they are chiefly agricultural; and this will be as long as there shall be vacant lands in any part of America. When they get piled upon one another in large cities, as in Europe, they will become corrupt as in Europe. Above all things I hope the education of the common people will be attended to; convinced that on their good sense we may rely with the most security for the preservation of a due degree of liberty.

For fifty years Jefferson kept alive his dream of universally available elementary education, free for anyone who wanted it, without the stigma of pauperism and charity. In theory, at least, he considered schools for the people more important than a university, and it may have been in part a measure of his frustration over the lukewarm political support of this ideal that he later devoted his major efforts to the founding of a university that was to be essentially an exclusive enclave for the privileged.

The weakness of Jefferson's educational leadership may well have been an excessive faith in the people's enlightened self-interest, which he thought sufficient to turn his school plans into reality. Nor did he realistically appreciate the impact of the existing inequalities in the population's wealth—a fact which his Federalist opponents understood and turned into the foundation of their power.

For all his perceptive judgment of the crucial role mass education would eventually have to play if the experiment in popular government were to succeed, Jefferson could not anticipate the political and economic hurdles to be conquered: the sectional rivalries; the slow growth of the states' authority, which, then as now, was hampered further by parochialism and lack of vision in the state legislatures; the antagonism between planters and merchants; the Indian uprisings; and, transcending all the specific problems, the general lag of available tax support for new and unknown public ventures. While the people were pleased with their new power, it was also a time for an emotional relaxation, if not outright letdown, now that the actual fighting was over. Despite all the democratic dreams, the conservative forces and classes still held the reins of power. They were not at all convinced that it was good and proper for their children to attend school with the children of the poor.

Benjamin Franklin represented a different strain in the fabric of American education. While Jefferson was the aristocrat with a social conscience that led him to idealize the potential of the lower classes, Franklin was rooted in the new middle class. His father, a candlemaker, had left England for the colonies to escape religious oppression. The tenth among fifteen children, Benjamin was expected to enter the ministry, following a churchman uncle for whom he had been named.

Self-sufficiency was to Franklin as important a prerequisite for the pride and freedom that made for happiness as it was for Jefferson; but he saw frugality and the bourgeois virtues as the key to all success. Since he could not recall when he had learned to read, it is evident that he had been taught at a very early age. When he was eight, having been selected as the family's emissary into scholarship, he was enrolled in Boston Latin School, where he did so well initially that he was sent to a private school to be tutored in writing and arithmetic. Unfortunately, he seemed unable to repeat the success of the first year, and, while he "learned to write a good hand," he failed in arithmetic. In keeping with the day's stern moral judgments, the boy was denied a second chance. His father, thus judging an academic career to be a poor investment, brought him back home to introduce him to the soap- and candle-making skills.

Thus, Benjamin Franklin's formal education ended at the age of ten. While legend has made much of his subsequent faith and success in self-tutoring and has turned him into a nostalgic proto-type of the ruggedly individualistic self-educated American, an-other aspect of young Franklin's experience is usually overlooked. There is evidence that throughout his life he remembered the cruel finality of his early failure in arithmetic. Since he disliked his father's trade, he turned to reading and self-education as a means of escape from what might otherwise have become his predestined fate.

Fortunately, the elder Franklin, afraid that his son might run away, allowed him to become a printer's apprentice and eventually let him join an older brother who was publishing a newspaper, *The New England Courant,* in Boston.

There was in fact more of the rebel than of the obedient middle-class Colonial in Franklin. He loathed his domineering brother and, having left him before his apprenticeship was over, he later wrote of the experience: "I fancy his harsh and tyrannical treat-ment of me might be a means of impressing me with that aversion to arbitrary powers that has stuck to me through my whole life."

As Franklin became a national myth, his legacy has often been distorted by those who, begrudging the money spent on the educa-tion of the masses, advocated instead the School of Hard Knocks. Actually, there is little in Franklin's writings that suggests his agreement with that philosophy. As a shrewd observer of human nature, he knew that his triumph through self-instruction was the result of one man's genius and could not readily be mass-produced.

In 1749—clearly ahead of both his time and the Revolution—he wrote, as part of his *Proposals Relating to the Education of Youth in Pennsylvania:*

> The good education of youth has been esteemed by wise men in all ages as the surest foundation of the happiness both of private families and of commonwealths. Almost all gov-ernments have therefore made it a principal object of their attention to establish and endow with proper revenues such

seminaries of learning as might supply the succeeding age
with men qualified to serve the public with honor to themselves and to their country.

American youth, he argued, has the capacity; but "the best
capacities require cultivation." Moreover, his hopes for a middle
class propelled to new powers of self-government went far beyond
the earlier demands for schools merely to train a governing elite.
Like Jefferson, he was concerned with the potential of all men,
rich or poor. In 1750, he wrote to Samuel Johnson:

> I think with you, that nothing is of more importance for the
> public weal, than to form and train up youth in wisdom and
> virtue. Wise and good men are, in my opinion, the strength
> of a state; much more so than riches or arms, which, under
> the management of ignorance and wickedness, often draw on
> destruction, instead of providing for the safety of the people.

There was no conflict between Jefferson's and Franklin's goals;
but the latter's personal background made him better attuned to
the postrevolutionary society—its growing commercialism and the
increasing certainty that the aims and needs of the middle class
were to become the dominant American direction. Both Jefferson
and Franklin were inventors driven by insatiable curiosity and an
indomitable faith in the power of man's intellect nourished by
liberty. But Jefferson's inventive genius was used to transmit to a
new and revolutionary era the soundest values as well as the most
enjoyable comforts of an aristocratic past; Franklin's mind was on
the future, and the advantages and comforts he wanted to create
for future Americans relied on originality and utility far more
than on tradition. While still in his early forties, he wrote to his
mother that he hoped, after his death, men would say, "He lived
useful" rather than "He died rich."

The concept of usefulness inevitably clashed with the privilege
of the rich to give their children an education, not for the good of
society but as a luxury for themselves. As a young man of seventeen, Franklin expressed sentiments which dominated his thinking
throughout his life:

> I reflected in my mind on the extreme folly of those parents
> who, blind to their children's dullness and insensible of the

solidity of their skulls, because they think their purses can afford it, will needs send them to the Temple of Learning, where, for want of suitable genius, they learn little more than to carry themselves handsomely, and enter a room genteelly (which might as well be acquired in dancing school), and from whence they return, after abundance of trouble and charge, as great blockheads as ever, only more proud and self-conceited.

But the concept of usefulness was by no means predominantly negative in its assessment of formal education. The influence of the frontier, with its joy in a nation's expansion and a people's pioneering conquest of the continent, and the beginning of what was to become a steady flow of new immigrants turned Franklin toward an urgently positive concept of nation-building and consolidation.

A poor grasp of the realities of those exciting days has led the creators of American folklore and even some historians to treat the author of *Poor Richard's Almanac* as something of a square moralist and the prototype of what was later to be regarded as the American Babbitt. This absurd misinterpretation ignores the shrewdness and the genius of the man who could turn the British-operated post office from bankruptcy into a highly profitable venture; who was as much at home in the applied science of electricity as in the subtleties of diplomacy and the salons of Paris. Indeed, Franklin was the first American to understand and exploit a politically winning image, such as the wearing of a coonskin cap at the court of Versailles. It was this display of a popular trademark of Yankee practicality, knowhow, and shrewdness that, far from being held up to ridicule in its time, gave Franklin the advantage of deliberate novelty that allowed him to bargain effectively with the sophisticated European powers.

To some, Franklin seemed little more than a tinkerer; but in reality his insatiable drive to improve the way men lived and managed their affairs was the mark of the genius experimenter and reformer. Nothing seemed to him so firmly established by tradition that it should not be tested and challenged—not even the language itself. It was precisely because he considered spelling—and the mastery of the art by everyone—to be so important that he became the first of a long line of critics of English spelling. In 1768, he published a proposal for a reformed system of English in which a number of "unnecessary letters" would be eliminated. For example, the letter *c* would have to be abolished, its hard sound replaced by *k* and the soft ones by *s*. The word *deed* would have been spelled *diid*, to distinguish it from *did*.

Franklin moreover had begun to push for a new deal in education nearly a generation before the Revolution. His direction was set, not so much by the politics of the moment as by a remarkably prescient social philosophy. He sensed that the world was moving in radically new directions whose consequences were impossible to predict. He was among those truly radical thinkers who believed that education's new task was to prepare young people for change —the exact reverse of the established purpose of schooling, which was to reinforce customs and traditions and, if possible, to lead the way back to the classics and the godly life of the Scriptures. As one of the first proponents of adult education, he saw learning as a means of keeping open the options for change and self-advancement throughout life.

Franklin's utilitarian as well as moral philosophy of education was tailor-made for the new middle class, with its drive toward upward mobility. Youth, he believed, should be trained to "serve the public with honor to themselves, and to their country, and to fit them for successful careers in business." He had no doubt that with such equipment young men of that rising new class could easily replace the decadent aristocratic leadership. He was not in the least concerned that, in this competition, lack of the social graces might be a disadvantage. In fact, there is evidence that he saw the real contest between the middle and the lower classes. The qualities which seemed essential to Franklin were sound morals, the virtues of temperance, order, industry, and other "useful" habits, along with a command of the English language, mathematics, accounting, natural philosophy, mechanics, and the principles of good health.

His stress on self-education, however, was not—as those who are lukewarm toward universal education have often made it appear— the result of his own doubts about the need of formal education for the many; it was rather the consequence of his own dismal experience and his realistic assessment of the obstacles which continued to stand in the way of adequate education for the lower middle class.

Early in his concern with the future of an American nation, Franklin became deeply involved with another problem which was to remain an almost constant issue throughout the country's educational history: the schools' mission in helping to create a sense of national character and cohesion.

In 1753, Benjamin Franklin set forth what might be called the "nation-building" function of the schools. He was particularly alarmed that the cadre of German settlers in Pennsylvania might endanger the preservation "of our language and even of our government" unless English-speaking schools were established for their children. It was a theme to be repeated over and over again —with the Irish, the Eastern Europeans, the Italians, the Jews, and, more recently, the nonwhite minorities.

Franklin had little in common with Noah Webster—except an abiding belief that the unique qualities of the new nation and the dream of a new way of life called for an efficient instrument to fashion these "new" Americans. Franklin and Webster were convinced—as were generations of liberals and reactionaries thereafter—that this was properly and importantly the function of the schools.

If sophisticated critics tend to be condescending about Franklin's shrewd pragmatism, it is even more tempting to draw the historic image of Webster as that of the jingoistic buffoon, with a dash of the self-promoter. Some of his narrow views of the schools' duty to the American destiny may indeed sound as parochially simplistic as "for God, for country, and for Yale" and as overbearing as the old adage that Britain's battles had been "won on the playing fields of Eton." And yet, just as a college may need the cheerleader's hyperbole to build its spirit, new nations need slogans and myths as a cement to hold the precarious enterprise together. The slogans of smug conservatives and of brash radicals have that much in common: they try, at any cost, to create a shared faith and common understanding.

In 1783, Noah Webster was an obscure Yale graduate who taught school in Goshen, New York. He first achieved public attention as the author of *A Grammatical Institute of the English*

Language, which became famous as *Webster's Blue-Backed Speller.* Eventually, it was followed by his "Reader" and the dictionaries.

Webster's obsession with the creation of a single language for all Americans could easily be put down as cultural chauvinism. "America must be as independent in literature as she is in politics," he said. He was a man of an inflated ego for whom it was not enough to take well-deserved credit for his important and lasting work in the establishment of a truly American language; he also wanted to be known as the father of American education and, beyond that, as one of the Founding Fathers. It was this lack of a sense of proportion that often turned him into a boor and a bore, as when he lectured Alexander Hamilton on how to run political parties, tried to instruct James Madison on how to make the Presidency work, or read pompous lessons to Thomas Jefferson on the nature of democracy—a form of government in which Webster in reality had little faith.

And yet, Webster's abiding belief in the unity and unifying mission of the language turned into a new and truly democratic force in the nation-building effort. It helped to free generations of Americans from a sense of inferiority that had always in the past been the outgrowth of a tell-tale difference between the way the upper and lower classes spoke. If the schools did their job, there was to be no need for a Professor Higgins to turn flower girls into ladies by teaching them genteel speech. Throughout British history, and only to a slightly lesser extent throughout the history of most European countries, the tyranny of class and origin had been reinforced by class-bound speech. Against such a background, Webster's impact on upward mobility was an important social force. He fought against dialects. He wanted to rid Americans of "provincial prejudices" which, he felt, create "reciprocal ridicule" as they did so powerfully in Europe.

Webster's popular success shows that he had hit on a vital need. Versions of his *Reader*—to be followed later by Peter Parley and McGuffey—were used in the nation's classrooms almost until the end of the nineteenth century. William T. Harris, the first United States Commissioner of Education, recalled that during his own school days Webster's speller was studied from cover to cover. Jefferson Davis said on the eve of the Civil War: ". . . Above all other people, we are one, and above all books which have united us in the bond of a common language, I place the good old Spelling-Book of Noah Webster."

The book sold by the tens of millions. It had become the Bible of the spoken word, backed up by the stern rules of the dictionary. The effectiveness of Webster's linguistic crusade may best be measured by the uproar that was created, almost two centuries later, when Webster's Third Edition, abandoning the stern schoolmaster's rigidity, officially introduced a more permissive approach to changing language usage and, in the view of its critics, undermined the foundations which Webster had so carefully laid down. Webster would have agreed with those critics and, as many of them hinted, might well have seen in the new trend a part of a treasonable plot against the values of American life.

Webster often did seem less the intellectual purist than the prude and priggish conservative. Important as the creation of an American unity of expression was to him, the endeavor to purge the language of its "improprieties and vulgarities," which had been introduced by early generations of settlers, seemed often to gain the upper hand. Religion, morality, and patriotism were inseparably linked in Webster's concept of schooling. As Henry Steele Commager put it, religion was for him "a kind of muscular exercise in moralizing." Not even the Bible passed muster; he banished the word "womb" from its pages.

Though zealous in his advocacy of education, Webster had little faith in the young. He was unable to shake the heritage of those Puritan teachers who saw schooling largely as a means of reforming little sinners. He remained representative of that persistent faction in America that sees the school as an essential unpleasantness to save generations of children from themselves and from the possibility of irreverent enjoyments.

His dominant ideology was not personal but national independence. His nationalism was all-pervasive. Nations, he believed, need a common past, which, if it does not exist, must be artificially manufactured, with language the primary tool. Webster's technical proficiency in the use of that tool was a match for the most sophisticated manipulators of words who, as so called communications and public relations experts, later showed how to manufacture consumer needs and even national aspirations where, like the nation's past in Webster's day, these did not exist.

However disparate the strands which Jefferson, Franklin, and Webster wove into the early fabric of American education, the emerging pattern was strong and cohesive enough to establish the concept of schooling on a far more massive scale than had ever been considered possible or even desirable in any previous society. Much political pressure and persuasion was needed to turn these new ideas into the reality of a system. But the remarkable fact is not that the call for such a system still failed to get popular and legislative support but rather that, in the minds of these pioneers, concrete blueprints had emerged. Many of these plans were so detailed and sophisticated that they subsequently—considerably later—formed the basis of the American public school system.

In 1817, Jefferson wrote to George Ticknor that he found himself "entirely absorbed in endeavors to effect the establishment of a general system of education" in Virginia. Such a system would be based on instruction on three levels:

Elementary schools, "which shall give to the children of every citizen gratis, competent instruction in reading, writing, common arithmetic, and generally geography";

Collegiate instructions (in reality the academies or equivalent of the old Latin schools), "for ancient and modern languages, for higher instruction in arithmetic, geography and history, placing for these purposes a college within a day's ride of every inhabitant of the state, and adding a provision for the full education at the public expense of select subjects among the children of the poor, who shall have exhibited at the elementary schools the most prominent indications of aptness of judgment and correct disposition";

A university, "in which all the branches of science deemed useful at this day, shall be taught in their highest degree." Such a curriculum, he went on, would probably require "ten or twelve professors, for most of whom we shall be obliged to apply to Europe, and most likely to Edinburgh, because of the greater advantage the students will receive from communications made in their native language."

These were revolutionary departures from the past—not only because basic education was to be universal and free. Even college-preparatory education was to be freely available to the able poor

—with aptitude rather than accomplishment the criterion. In addition, stress on English as the instrument of instruction clearly labeled as obsolete both the Latin schools and such trend-setting institutions as Harvard.

Less than a year later, Jefferson outlined his educational goals in far greater detail and with full stress on education's expected impact on the citizens' personal freedom and power. In a report to the commissioners appointed to determine the site for the University of Virginia, he set forth among the aims of universal primary education a curriculum that would not only teach every man the "information he needs for the transaction of his own business" and "to understand his duties to his neighbors and country, and to discharge with competence the functions confided to him by either," but also "to know his rights; to exercise with order and justice those he retains; to choose with discretion the fiduciary of those he delegates; and to notice their conduct with diligence, with candor, and judgment."

Jefferson continued:

> To instruct the mass of our citizens in these their rights, interests and duties, as men and citizens, being then the objects of education in the primary schools, whether they be private or public, in them should be taught reading, writing, and numerical arithmetic, the elements of mensuration (useful in so many callings), and the outlines of geography and history.

It was to be left to higher education "to form the statesmen, legislators and judges" and to create a structure of government and of law which, "banishing all arbitrary and unnecessary restraint on individual action, shall leave us free to do whatever does not violate the equal rights of another."

In charting the university, Jefferson set forth the following courses of study:

Ancient languages: Latin; Greek; Hebrew.

Modern languages: French; Spanish; Italian; German; Anglo-Saxon.

Pure mathematics: algebra; fluxions; geometry; architecture (military and naval).

Physico-mathematics: mechanics; statistics; dynamics; pneumatics; acoustics; optics; astronomy; geography.

Physics or natural philosophy: chemistry; mineralogy.

Botany and zoology.

Anatomy and medicine.

Government, political economy, law of nature and nations; and history, "being interwoven with politics and law."

Municipal law.

Ideology ("the doctrine of thought"), general grammar, ethics, rhetoric, belles-lettres, and the fine arts.

Like Franklin, Jefferson never lost sight of the utility of what was to be learned. Thus, for example, he specified that chemistry "is meant, with its other usual branches, to comprehend the theory of agriculture." But when Jefferson applied to the legislature for support of his educational plans, he was adamant that "specific details were not proper for the law. These must be the business of the visitors entrusted with its education."

Franklin, like Jefferson, embraced a modern curriculum, taught in English. In his prototype of the English Academy, children would have moved in six grades from the rules of grammar and speech to the art of reasoning, history, rhetoric, logic, moral philosophy, the study of "the best English authors" and eventually "the best translations of Homer, Virgil" and other classic authors.

In keeping with their new concern for individual differences, Jefferson and Franklin refused to accept the tradition of a curriculum fixed for all students. They brought to American education the revolutionary concept of "elective" courses. In 1823, Jefferson wrote to Ticknor:

> I am not fully informed of the practices at Harvard, but there is one from which we shall certainly vary, although it has been copied, I believe, by nearly every college and academy in the United States. That is, the holding the students to one prescribed course of reading, and disallowing exclusive application to those branches only which are to qualify them for the particular vocations to which they are destined. We shall, on the contrary, allow them the uncontrolled choice of lectures they shall choose to attend, and require elemen-

tary qualification only and sufficient age. Our institution will proceed on the principle of doing all the good it can without consulting its own pride and ambition; or letting every one come and listen to whatever he thinks may improve the condition of his mind.

Details of the proposals matter less than the fact that a movement of liberation—of youth, of the individual, and of the mind—had been unleashed. Its potential effect on society could well be more powerful than the purely political impact of the American Revolution.

These new views were revolutionary—not just in that the people were to be given real powers, but, even more important, in their attitude toward change. Franklin has already been shown to have felt contempt toward unchallenged customs. Even Webster, despite his innate conservatism, saw the need for the creation of new symbols and a new language. Jefferson, in a letter to Madison in 1789, said bluntly that "the dead have neither powers nor rights" over the earth and the living.

"I am not fond of reading what is merely abstract and unapplied immediately to some useful science," Jefferson said in what sounds like the twentieth-century demand for relevancy. This was to be the cornerstone of the practical humanism, with its fusion of the liberal arts and vocational instruction, that first became a powerful influence on American education. More than a century later, these ideas spread across much of Europe and most of the developing nations of Asia and Africa.

For the first time, everything was to be open to question. Although history retained high priority in the new curriculum, nothing that history taught was to be accepted without critical analysis. "History," wrote Jefferson in his *Notes on Virginia,*

by apprising them [students] of the past, will enable them to judge of the future; it will avail them of the experience of other times and other nations; it will qualify them as judges of the actions and designs of men; it will enable them to know ambition under every disguise it may assume; and knowing it, to defeat its views. In every government on earth is some trace of human weakness, some germ of corruption and degeneracy. . . .

In 1814, Jefferson wrote to John Adams that he had been reading Plato's *Republic* and that, "while wading through the whimsies, the puerilities, and the unintelligible jargon of this work," he asked himself how the world could so long have "consented to give reputation to such nonsense as this." The significance is not in what is clearly a debatable critical judgment but rather in the fact that it was voiced so freely. Such an attitude marked the liberation of the mind. Education, Jefferson insisted, "engrafts a new man on the native stock."

In 1787, Jefferson wrote to his young nephew Peter Carr:

> Fix reason firmly in her seat, and call to her tribunal every fact, every opinion. Question with boldness even the existence of a God; because, if there be one, he must more approve the homage of reason, than that of blindfolded fear. . . . Read the Bible then, as you would read Livy or Tacitus. . . .

Jefferson found unacceptable the idea that the human condition was unchangeably decreed by faith or deity or that "we must tread with awful reverence in footsteps of our fathers." Consistent with these views, Jefferson's plan for the University of Virginia made no provision for a professor of divinity and proposed instead that all matters of morality and religion be assigned to the province of a professor of ethics.

New faith in reason was clearly incompatible with the old teaching by autocracy and hornbook paddle. The best way of governing young people, particularly in large groups, Jefferson believed, was not by threat and autocracy. "It may well be questioned," he wrote in 1818,

> whether fear after a certain age, is a motive to which we should have ordinary recourse. The human character is susceptible of other incitements to correct conduct, more worthy of employ, and of better effect. . . . Hardening them to disgrace, to corporal punishments, and servile humiliations cannot be the best process for producing erect character. The affectionate deportment between father and son offers in truth the best example for that of tutor and pupil. . . .

In his "Bill for the General Diffusion of Knowledge," Jefferson urged a new recognition of the difference between children and adults. He wrote:

> There is a certain period of life, say from eight to fifteen or sixteen years of age, when the mind like the body is not yet firm enough for laborious and close operations. If applied to such, it falls an early victim to premature exertion; exhibiting, indeed, at first, in these young and tender subjects, the flattering appearance of their being men while they are yet children, but ending in reducing them to be children when they should be men.

All these practical and lofty goals constituted a reversal of nearly everything that had so long been accepted in the relationships between school and child, between education and society, between freedom and obedience. But lofty and practical though the goals were, not even Jefferson's persuasive leadership nor Franklin's compelling pragmatism could quickly win over the majority of the very people who stood to gain most from these new and liberal views.

Moreover Franklin had raised a question that forced his contemporaries to think what was considered unthinkable. He was convinced that the new nation would not be able to move toward equality, justice, and civic virtue until it removed the unnatural barriers of slavery and racial discrimination. Franklin was president of the Abolition Society, and it was in keeping with his deepest concerns when he warned Congress in 1789, during one of his last public actions, that the issue must be faced. He prayed that the legislators "devise means for removing that inconsistency from the character of the American people."

Franklin helped to establish several committees for the education of Black children and youths. He took a lead in efforts to let free Blacks either be sent to existing schools or to establish schools for them. And, recognizing the important link between school and employment, he created an agency to find jobs and even, if necessary, to establish industries for the employment of educated Blacks.

These were radical prescriptions, and they probably contributed to the doubts which a conservative population already harbored against education as a boon to the poor and the masses. History might have taken a different turn had Franklin been heeded. Because his appeals fell on deaf ears, the record shows that by 1890, when only 13.3 percent of the population was illiterate, illiteracy among Blacks was 56.8 percent. Franklin had known from the outset that to deny equal educational opportunity to any group would eventually hurt—and even threaten to destroy—the new society.

Many of those who struggled on the frontier were too preoccupied to concern themselves with educational and social philosophies. Others, already comfortably established in the growing middle class, had little stomach for the support of other people's children, particularly those of the poor. Conservative forces, including those of organized religion, saw public education as a threat to their own power and to what had in many places remained their monopoly: the control of education as a means of keeping children safely within the fold of the accepted doctrine. Learning could be used as a key to open young minds or to keep them shut to what were thought to be subversive ideas.

Opponents of public, let alone universal, education sensed that the new movement posed a very fundamental threat to the old social order. Although the debate between the elitists and the egalitarians has often been carried on over the more narrow question of academic standards, at the heart of the matter has always remained the deeply political conflict between the open, upward-mobile versus the restricted, stratified society.

In 1830 *The National Gazette,* published in Philadelphia, editorially attacked the concept of taxation to finance public education. Many of its arguments have remained just as much part of the American education debate as Jefferson's appeal to idealism and Franklin's plea for common sense.

Those among the "mechanical and working classes" who have already been moderately successful, the *Gazette* warned, would consider an education tax "evil," since they would be made to feel that "they had toiled for the benefit of other families than their own." Since "one of the chief excitements to industry" is the hope of earning the means to educate one's children, the editorial continued, to provide state-financed schools would destroy all incentive and place a premium on idleness.

"We have no confidence in any compulsory equalizations," said the *Gazette*. "It has well been observed that they pull down what is above, but never raise what is below. . . . A scheme of universal equal education, attempted in reality, would be an unexampled bed of Procrustes for the understandings of our youth. . . ."

But, at the very time when provincialism and conservatism rode high, powerful voices were also raised for the concept of national educational institutions and even nationalized education. Many of the leaders of American independence spoke out eloquently for the establishment of a national university. George Washington, in a message to Congress in 1790, called for the creation of such an institution because "knowledge is in every country the surest basis of public happiness." In his will, he left a bequest for the founding of such a university.

Alexander Hamilton, John Marshall, and Benjamin Rush all advocated a national university which they envisioned as the apex of school systems established in each state. Rush considered such an institution as a unifying force in the new nation—an intellectual armor against foreign aggression and an instrument of reason to quiet internal dissension.

Rush also viewed a national university as a potential training ground for those who would run the new government. He said:

> We require certain qualifications in lawyers, physicians and clergymen before we commit our property, our lives or our soul to their care. . . . We are restrained from injuring ourselves by employing quacks in law; why should we not be restrained in like manner by law from employing quacks in government?

Yet the idea of a national university or of a national system of education was undermined from the outset by serious and fundamental disagreements over education's goals and objectives. Neither on the issue of educational purpose nor on the question of financial sources of support or the manner of governance and control was there ever any consensus—not during the Constitutional Convention in 1787, when the debate began, and not at any time in almost two centuries of American educational growth and development thereafter. Although all the early Presidents favored a national university, the issue became inextricably entangled in politics and sectionalism. By the time Jackson moved into the White House, the momentum had run down. It was reactivated only in the creation of such special-purpose national institutions as West Point and the Smithsonian Institution. On the whole, the opposing strain in the American political dogma—diversity and the supremacy of the states in educational matters—prevailed.

It was not for want of trying by the early thinkers and leaders that the national education concept went down to defeat. Yet, the notion never took root, and it was not until the second half of the twentieth century that Federal legislation for the general aid of public education was finally enacted—over the strong objections of those who, not unlike *The National Gazette* in 1830, considered such an assessment to be an invitation to government control.

Despite all doubts about national patterns of education, however, the drive toward a massive popular involvement in the business of teaching the young was part of the postrevolutionary atmosphere, as it has remained part of the American mythos throughout the years.

In 1795, the American Philosophical Society, of which both Jefferson and Franklin had been presidents, ran a popular contest, offering a prize for the best plan for an education system. The contest was authorized during a meeting that also dealt with ship pumps, vegetable dyes, the longevity of peach trees, and domestic heating systems. The essays submitted had in common the assumption that American institutions would have to be like nothing that had existed elsewhere because a unique new people needed a unique new approach to schooling. Yet, in fact, all contestants were thinking along lines of centralized national education control over a system that was to be free, universal, and open to girls as well as boys—a truly advanced concept at a time when even Jefferson's and Franklin's proposals still talked of boys only.

In the view of most of the participants, the system they recommended was intended as an instrument to instill loyalty for developing American nationalism—hardly surprising in view of the fact that almost two centuries later most pupils begin their day with the pledge of allegiance. At the same time, the nationalism that found expression in these essays tended to be humane and enlightened, with an abiding trust in the perfectibility of men and institutions and with emphasis on the sciences and other "useful" subjects.

Throughout this early period, it is far less fruitful to weigh the specific legislative and institutional gains made in the search for popular education than to appreciate the revolution of ideas and ideals. The doctrine of upward mobility was merely the everyday extension of the philosophical belief in the unlimited capacity of men to improve their minds and their station.

In 1821, Daniel Webster said prophetically:

> For the purpose of public instruction, we hold every man subject to taxation in proportion to his property, and we look not to the question whether he himself have or have not children to be benefited by the education for which he pays; we regard it as a wise and liberal system of police, by which property, and life, and the peace of society are secured. . . . We do not, indeed, expect all men to be philosophers or statesmen; but we confidently trust . . . that by the diffusion of general knowledge, and good and virtuous sentiments, the political fabric may be secure as well against open violence and overthrow as against the slow but sure undermining of licentiousness.

The rejection of inherited privilege could only have the effect of reshuffling society and opening up an unending contest for positions of power and influence. But, unlike so many other revolutionary movements, the original American rebellion against the old ruling class did not seek to replace the established order with rule by the rabble. Jefferson, the aristocrat, and Franklin, the middle-class believer in self-improvement, both placed their faith in the creation of a new and natural aristocracy of merit. In 1813, Jefferson wrote to John Adams:

> . . . I agree with you that there is a natural aristocracy among men. The grounds of this are virtue and talent. . . .

May we not even say that that form of government is best, which provides the most effectually for a pure selection of these natural aristoi into the offices of government? The artificial aristocracy is a mischievous ingredient of government, and provision should be made to prevent its ascendency.

Even Jefferson was too much a creature of his time to look to mass education beyond the elementary skills; but he clearly saw the need for a selective system of free education as "the keystone of the arch of our government."

"An insurrection," he said, had begun—an insurrection "of science, talents, and courage, against rank and birth, which have fallen into contempt." If that insurrection had failed in Europe, he was convinced, it was only "because the mobs of the cities, the instruments used for its accomplishment, debased by ignorance, poverty and vice, could not be restrained to rational action." Whether this judgment was merely the reflection of the agrarian gentleman's natural prejudices or the prophesy of American education's most severe test in a distant future was a crucial question to be answered by the leadership of another age.

4
THE
NEW
AMERICANS

*H*ERE INDIVIDUALS OF ALL NATIONS *are melted into a new race of men, whose labours and posterity will one day cause great change in the world. Americans are the Western pilgrims, who are carrying along with them that great mass of arts, sciences, vigour and industry, which began long since in the East; they will finish the great circle. . . . The American is a new man, who acts upon new principles; he must therefore entertain new ideas, and form new opinions. . . .*

—de Crèvecoeur

From the earliest days the nation-builders—progressives and conservatives alike—assigned to schools the task of Americanization and unification. Even Jefferson, despite his abiding faith in a diversity of views and the right of people to differ, spoke of

Americans as becoming "perfectly homogeneous." So rational a man as Franklin had been sufficiently alarmed by the language of German and Dutch enclaves that his friends—without success—tried to persuade the legislature to suppress their German documents and to make English literacy a prerequisite for the suffrage.

From the beginning, too, the nation-building mission was plagued by a fundamental conflict between the vision of a unified country that would give great powers and equality of opportunity to all Americans and a less attractive view of uniformity attained as the fee toward membership in an "America—love it, or leave it" association.

Three early goals for the schools emerged as part of the process of unification and nation-building: American society is the norm to which all youth must be adjusted; internationalism and cosmopolitanism should be spurned; and, since America is superior to any other country and civilization, the schools must inculcate loyalty to the American way of life.

The process of unification through the schools had begun long before public education, as a system, became a fact. It was initially served largely by the mass circulation of textbooks used in all types of schools. And the key figure in this process of unification-by-book was an earnest, upright, clean-shaven man of wide forehead and bushy eyebrows who had begun teaching in the rural schools of Ohio in 1813 when he was only thirteen years old. His name was William Holmes McGuffey, and it was a name that would become a household word throughout the young nation and was to remain synonymous with traditional American education for more than a century.

Born of Scotch-Irish parents in Pennsylvania, he was taken by his family to the Midwest, where he continued his own largely self-taught education while teaching others in Ohio and Kentucky. Eventually, he earned a bachelor's degree with honors at the age of twenty-six and became a professor of ancient languages at Miami University, in Oxford, Ohio. But his real interest remained the public education of children, and he set up a model school for the training of teachers and education of children in his own home. Later, he became a college president and finally a distinguished professor of "mental and moral philosophy" at the University of Virginia. But his name remains emblazoned on American history as the author of the McGuffey readers, which sold nearly 130 million copies.

The readers combined morality, patriotism, and thrift as the fundamental virtues, while at the same time promising obedient youngsters the reward of material success. This was the codification of those middle-class aspirations which had long captivated men's minds.

In days, when neither radio nor film and television provided children with a universal message, McGuffey was a powerful unifying force. Despite their moralizing, his books were interesting to children. They were filled with brief stories and anecdotes, bits of Shakespeare and exciting tales. And their morality was easy to take: The boy who helped the old man across the street invariably wound up with a good job as an implicit reward for his good deed.

Compared with Noah Webster, McGuffey seems a more relaxed spokesman for the schools' Americanization process. Patriotism, it seems, no longer had to be rammed down the youngsters' throats. Americanism no longer needed to be built on xenophobia or cultural isolationism. McGuffey even included foreign selections, although with a heavy emphasis on the Anglo-Saxon. There was a remarkable absence not only of anti-British propaganda, but of chauvinistic readings about the Mexican War, and the California Gold Rush.

McGuffey—in the absence of a national system of education—gave children across the country a "shared baggage," to use Henry Steele Commager's term, of knowledge and allusions with a popularity and effectiveness that was not to be matched again—until national television, which in 1969 gave American children "Sesame Street." It was entirely McGuffey's doing that youngsters started out on their journey into learning with a shared smattering of familiarity about the Greeks and the Romans, Hamlet and William Tell.

Along with these early, national textbooks, the Bible was enormously important in the development of a national language and a spiritual climate. The King James version was as much a molder of style as of morals. But, along with religiously moralistic teaching, the books of the time moralized on a wide variety of issues. A poem against smoking warned a man that "it robs his pockets, soils his clothes, and makes a chimney of his nose." In another book,

God's punishment for drunkenness is put forth in a poem by J. G. Saxe: "The cole water man tells of a drunk fisherman pulled into the water by a duck on his line."

Not all influences were so moralistic and high-minded. A picture in the famous children's magazine *St. Nicholas,* shows "Miss Pickaninny Snowball," with pigtails, bare feet and parasol, holding an alligator with a muzzle. The caption reads: "I's gwine to have a poodle-dog, same as white folks."

Indians, too, were regularly either held up to ridicule or made to appear vicious by the magazine. A series of articles on Indian chiefs by Major General O. O. Howard, for example, described an Apache warrior: "To look at Sitting Bull one would say that he was always quiet and self-contained. . . . But he was cruel and almost heartless. . . . He was always imperious and insolent toward our generals, the Indian agent, and other friends of the Great Father in Washington, whom he claimed to hate."

And in another chapter, the series described how Geronimo, the last Apache chief on the warpath, was shipped from Arizona to the Mount Vernon barracks in Alabama. "I am a school superintendent now," the tamed chief was quoted. "We have fine lady teachers. All the children go to their school. I make them. I want them to be white children." In the end, the once-proud chief is seen in a Wild West Show on exhibition in St. Louis, and the people—the new Americans—wanted to gawk at him just as they wanted to gawk at the Filipinos from Manila, the Boers from South Africa, or the Eskimos from Alaska. They asked for Geronimo's autograph in return for a fee. He had learned to write his name.

These were the early aberrations in an effort to use the schools to create a nation, with a shared pride—and shared prejudices. The new insiders' sense of belonging was, at times, built on a fiction of the inferiority of all those outside.

It was not an easy road for education. Although the implications of the Northwest Ordinance were that land was to be used to establish schools as the frontier moved westward, actual support provided by these means often proved inadequate. Education usually remained the concern of individual parents or of religious groups. Life was hard, and many people scoffed at the notion that every child ought to be entitled to a free education at the public expense. The general attitude still was—understandable in the midst of a rugged struggle against the forces of nature—that those who want to learn ought to pay for it.

And yet provision of some public financing made possible by grants of public land established the precedent under which at least the facilities for public schools were built, even if the parents still had to pay for the instruction. On the frontier, this trend may have been as important to the future of American education as the more utopian pronouncements that were soon to emanate from the relatively secure Northeast. Increasingly, too, the builders of a frontier society needed the educational foundations necessary to train engineers, mining experts, and agriculturists. A commencement oration, in California, addressed itself to the topic: "The Truly Practical Man, Necessarily an Educated Man."

The remarkable aspect of the development, however slow, was that it took place at all, at a time when learning must have seemed a luxury to those whose preoccupation was the taming of a wild continent.

Life in the frontier schools was far from soft. David Tyack, the educational historian, offers a glimpse of this in his account of the District School in Ashland, Oregon, in the 1860s:

> Housed in a log cabin, a sod hut . . . the district school on the moving frontier symbolized American faith in education. . . . In early Oregon the school belonged to the community in more than a legal sense. Settlers often built the schoolhouse with their own hands. The school building became the focus of many neighborhood activities; there itinerant ministers of various sects met their flocks on successive sabbaths; politicians caucused under the common school's roof; families gathered there to watch lantern slides and to socialize. . . . If the families of a neighborhood were amicable, the school expressed their cohesiveness. If they were discordant, the school was often caught in the middle of warring factions.

Oliver Cromwell Applegate was the district's teacher, and Tyack describes his typical school day on the frontier:

The first bell announcing school rang at 8:20 A.M. Applegate began school with a New Testament reading lesson,
proceeding then to graded readers and geography. At 10:30
came the separate boys' and girls' recesses. After recess until
12 o'clock dismissal, the students recited from their grammars
and spellers, group by group. The afternoon session began
with more Bible reading, continued with their graded readers, and finished after a 2:30 recess with arithmetic and spelling. He dismissed the school at 4. Applegate managed to
squeeze in study of the primer for the littlest children and
recitations in history and natural philosophy for the oldest.

A heavy, and sometimes contradictory, veneer of moralism lay
over these frontier schools. Clarence Darrow recalled the gist of
this moral lesson in his own Ohio schooling:

> We were taught by our books that we must on all accounts
> speak the truth; that we must learn our lessons; that we must
> love our parents and our teachers; must enjoy work; must
> be generous and kind; must despise riches; must avoid ambi-
> tion; and then if we did these things, some fairy godmother
> would come along and give us everything our hearts desired.

In Ashland, too, as Tyack records, these moral tenets shaped
at least the rhetoric. "Pride was a sin and pomp was un-American. . . . Inherited high rank was clearly foreign and undesirable. . . . Christianity was inseparable from Americanism and
morality in the textbooks. . . ."

In 1864, a California superintendent of public instruction, a
transplanted New England Yankee named John Swett, warned
that the state needed a school system because its population is
"drawn from all nations. . . . The next generation will be a
composite one made up of the heterogeneous atoms of all nationalities. Nothing can Americanize these chaotic elements and
breathe into them the spirit of our institutions but the public
schools."

Once started, the growth of education in California was sudden
and explosive. The new Americans of British heritage met with
people of many backgrounds—Latin American, Spanish, French,
German, and others. There were clashes, and there was some vio-

lence. The mining camps were the scene of the first major riots. Greed and suspicion, given free rein during the Gold Rush, found their outlet in antiforeign prejudices.

But if the spirit of the frontier gave American life some of its penchant for violence, it also gave the schools that sense of the open, egalitarian society that was so hard to nurture in the more stratified tradition of the East, with its aristocratic and classical heritage. The explosive, expansionist, unorthodox view of the world that characterized the frontier made schools the cultural centers they had not been before. Moreover, in a society that depended as much on women as on men, women were admitted to learning—shared the rigors of education, just as they shared the rigors of life. Yet, in the East men were still spending much time and eloquence on speeches about women's unfitness for equal education.

Nowhere was the Americanism of McGuffey more triumphant than in the schools of the expanding West. It was there that the children of immigrants from many lands were molded into what Louis B. Wright has called "our inherited Anglo-Saxon pattern," and the second generation of immigrants from Scandinavia, Germany, Poland, Russia, Italy, Yugoslavia, and many other lands "began to look upon traditional English literature as their cultural heritage." Americanization, perhaps somewhat ironically, often meant giving them a custom-built background in English literature. But in reality it mattered little what the chosen fabric was to be, as long as it was generally assumed to be part of the newly woven threads of the new nation. Whatever its past, its future was to be one of unlimited opportunities, the individual's right to self-improvement matching the country's drive across an apparently limitless continent.

Manifest Destiny may, in the hindsight of historical revisionism, smack of imperialism; in the classrooms of the frontier, it expressed the unquestioned confidence of a new people in unchallenged control of their nationhood. If it was understood that "foreigners" had no right to share in the glory, the answer was simply to make Anglo-Saxons of them all. The expansionist engine was stoked by pioneers from New England with their faith in the power of piety and learning.

But while the churches continued to play an important role,

many Americans, looking to the future rather than the past for security and inspiration, were beginning to substitute a new faith in popular education for their former concern with religion.

Horace Mann was the high priest of this new religion. He believed as deeply as Jefferson in the power of knowledge as the engine of Republican government and democratic society. In the tradition of Franklin and Webster, he understood the nation-building force of the school. Joining his vision with his pragmatism, he proclaimed the concept of the universal public school.

Mann admired America's diversity, but he also feared its potential divisiveness. He understood that the newly organized continent's heterogeneity encompassed an almost limitless wealth of different ethnic and national inheritances; but he sensed the tensions which could shatter the precarious unity.

Only a new institution, capable of embracing this diverse humanity, could create a sense of community and mold a new American character based on a shared American philosophy. Since such a unifying enterprise could only succeed by catching the young at a malleable age, it was clear to Mann that the common purpose would have to be achieved through the common school.

But Mann's common school was not the school for the poor nor, in the European tradition, the school for the common people of the lower classes. It was to be the school for all the people. It was to be the institution basic to all American institutions and to the state itself: the place where children of every background would learn together and, in doing so, create generation after generation of Americans who understood and respected each other, whatever their parentage.

Some revisionists of educational history have charged that Mann sought to import the Prussian system of public education as a means of subjecting the masses to the will of the state and to the existing political and economic pattern. Whatever use may have subsequently been made of Mann's ideas, his intent seemed precisely the opposite of what his latter-day critics charged.

Mann's expectation was that education, rather than freeze or even reinforce the status quo of economic power, would become the generator of social and economic equality—or at the very least mobility.

"Now, surely, nothing but Universal Education can counter-work this tendency to the domination of capital and the servility of labor," Mann believed.

> If one class possesses all the wealth and education, while the residue of society is ignorant and poor, it matters not by what name the relation between them may be called; the latter, in fact, and in truth, will be the servile dependents and subjects of the former. But if education be equably diffused, it will draw property after it, by the strongest of all attractions; for such a thing never did happen, as that an intelligent and practical body of men should be permanently poor. Property and labor, in different classes, are essentially antagonistic; but property and labor, in the same class, are essentially fraternal. . . . Education, then, beyond all other devices of human origin, is the great equalizer of the conditions of men—the balance-wheel of the social machinery.

Mann was not so naive as to believe that education alone would suffice to remove from men the drive to dominate others and to keep them down. He was not promising an instant utopia in which the power drives of men would be automatically crushed by universal literacy and the morality of pious primers. But he was convinced that education could give to ordinary citizens the kind of intellectual independence and economic means to enable them to "resist the selfishness of other men." The "war against poverty" was to become a politico-economic remedy of social ills more than a century later; but there already are hints of such a course in Mann's recognition of education as a weapon in that war. "It does better than disarm the poor of their hostility toward the rich. . . . The wanton destruction of the property of others,—the burning of hay-ricks and corn-ricks, the demolition of machinery because it supersedes hand-labor, the sprinkling of vitriol on rich dresses,—is only agrarianism run mad. Education prevents both the revenge and the madness."

This positive concept of Americanization—the reliance on education as a conciliating force—has never disappeared from the national philosophy. At times of prosperity, when social divisions were dormant or the hostilities at least manageable, the generator of cohesion was periodically allowed to run down; but, in moments of social crisis, citizens and politicians still turn to the schools to heal the divisions. And these divisions continue to be primarily between rich and poor. The anger that, in Mann's day, incited the "sprinkling of vitriol on rich dresses," has not changed much either—whether it springs from agrarianism or urbanism run mad. And whether they are expressed in the education component of an urban antipoverty program or in effort to make the agricultural revolution less threatening to the common man, the reformers' hopes remain the same.

Mann knew that nation-building made it essential for schools to teach the meaning of government and politics; but he was also aware of the danger—he called it "catastrophe"—of a political takeover of the educational process, with books and ideologies controlled by the powerful interests of the moment.

The proper course, Mann believed, was to teach to all "those articles in the creed of republicanism, which are accepted by all, believed in by all, and which form the common basis of our political faith."

It is, of course, precisely on this point, with its rather simple view of an inherent unity among all Americans, that the idealistic prescription has periodically run into stormy waters. While few have disagreed that the schools should teach "the creed of republicanism," it was not always easy to get agreement as to the nature of that creed. Time and again, those outside the privileged circle of power have charged that, by reenforcing the views and interests of the insiders, schools became, not the great equalizers as Jefferson and Mann had hoped, but an assembly line manipulated by the wealthy and powerful. Throughout American history, the defenders of cultural pluralism and the nation-builders have repeatedly been at odds with each other.

The need for Americanization became both obvious and pressing whenever large numbers of the poor and underprivileged sought entry into the mainstream or even merely wanted to understand and be understood. Early in the twentieth century when John Finley was president of the City College of New York, one of the first institutions of higher learning dedicated to the education of able but poor students, he was notified of a tragic accident. An undergraduate had drowned in the college's swimming pool.

Finley himself went to the Lower East Side to console the boy's mother. When he found the woman, she understood no English nor any language in which the college president could communicate with her. Finley's diary speaks movingly of the "awful experience" of combing the streets of the neighborhood for some English-speaking friend or relative of the dead student who could translate the terrible news to his mother.

For millions of immigrant children, Americanization was in fact liberation, and not the repressive coercion depicted almost a century later by radical anti-establishmentarians. Mary Antin was a typical example and an eloquent reporter. Born in Russia in 1881, she was brought by her family to the United States as a young teenager.

> There was no free school [in Russia] for girls [she recalled in her book, *The Promised Land*]. . . . At the high school, which was under government control, Jewish children were admitted in limited numbers. . . . There was a special examination for the Jewish candidates, of course; a nine-year-old Jewish child had to answer questions that a thirteen-year-old Gentile was hardly expected to understand . . . and there was no appeal . . . . No, the Czar did not want us in the schools.
>
> Education [in America] was free. That subject my father had written about repeatedly, as comprising his chief hope for us children, the essence of American opportunity, the treasure that no thief could touch, not even misfortune and poverty. It was the one thing that he was able to promise us when he sent for us; surer, safer than bread or shelter . . . . No application was made, no questions asked, no examinations, rulings, exclusions; no machinations, no fees.

But a new rigidity had also begun to affect the schools' Americanization mission: an assumption that there is an American political ideology which must root out any dissenting theory considered objectionable by the rich and powerful—the spokesmen for the American way of life.

Year after year, such views were impressed on the schools by a host of patriotic organizations. Indian children were the first to feel how harsh the policy of Americanization could be. A report by the Commissioner of Indian Affairs in 1881 said bluntly "the American people now demand that Indians shall become white men within one generation." Another report, in 1885, deplores the fact that dayschool had been unsuccessful in teaching Indian children because "the barbarian child of barbarian parents" spends only six hours a day in class. "Here," the report went on,

> he is taught the rudiments of the books, varied, perhaps, by fragmentary lessons in the "good manners" of the superior race to which his teacher belongs. He returns, at the close of the school day, to eat and play and sleep after the savage fashion of his race. In the hours spent in school he has not acquired a distaste for camp-fire, nor a longing for the food, the homelife, or the ordinary avocations of the white man.

Among the rules for Indian schools, published in 1890, was the characteristic provision: "All instruction must be in the English language. Pupils must be compelled to converse with each other in English, and should be properly rebuked or punished for persistent violation of this rule. Every effort should be made to encourage them to abandon their tribal language."

A Hopi Indian boy remembered that, when his little sister first was sent to the new school established for Indian children, "the teacher cut her hair, burned all her clothes, and gave her a new outfit and a new name, Nellie." The youngster—not surprisingly —did not like school and after a few weeks stopped attending. But when, a year later, she was compelled to resume her educational journey, the teachers had forgotten that they had christened her Nellie and now called her Gladys.

"When a Hopi becomes a white man," said a proud Indian, "he no longer has a face. We want to be Hopis, not white men. We want our children to learn Hopi ways and live by them."

To American educators, Indian children were only a sideshow. It was the Americanization of a steady stream of immigrants that became the major concern of the public schools in the hundred years between 1850 and just prior to World War II. Between 1870 and 1890, one American out of every seven was of foreign birth. Eventually, in many sections of the country except the South, aliens made up about one fourth of the population. Moreover, the sources of the influx began to change toward the turn of the century. In 1880, nearly 93 percent of the foreign-born were from northwestern Europe, primarily the United Kingdom and Germany, as well as from Canada. But slowly the tide began to change, and the new arrivals were from Eastern and Southern Europe.

Attitudes toward foreigners began to change, too. The dominant Anglo-Saxon culture had always tended to be less hospitable toward immigrants with different traditions and religions.

In 1851, *The Massachusetts Teacher* commented on the effects particularly of Irish immigration:

> The constantly increasing influx of foreigners during the last ten years has been, and continues to be, a cause of serious alarm to the most intelligent of our own people. What will be the ultimate effect of this vast and unexampled immigration is a problem which has engaged the most anxious thought of our best and wisest men. Will it, like the muddy Missouri, as it pours its waters into the clear Mississippi and contaminates the whole united mass, spread ignorance and vice, crime and disease, through our native population? Or can we, by any process, not only preserve ourselves from the threatened demoralization, but improve and purify and make valuable this new element which is thus forced upon us and which we cannot shut out if we would?

This is a tone quite different from the romantic rhetoric of the nation as the willing recipient of those "huddled masses"— and different, too, from the romanticized vision of public school educators as the joyous guardians of a melting pot in which people of all nationalities and creeds spontaneously adopted the new American flavor and fervor.

At the same time, the Americanizers began to speak in clear and unashamed terms about what they considered to be the differences between the various ethnic groups. Little attention was paid to the central fact that linked all these groups—their one shared experience of having escaped from poverty and oppression in countries where neither the political ideals nor the economic realities had offered them any hope for their own and their children's future. The Irish had come to forget the cruelties of

potato famines and starvation. Germans fled persecution and repression. Scandinavians escaped from harsh farming conditions
and religious intolerance. Russians left the clutches of feudalism,
enforced military service, and starvation and, in the case of
Russian Jews, brutal discrimination with intermittent, violent
pogroms.

It was, of course, true that different groups reacted to school
in different ways. More of the Jewish children—but by no means
all of them—saw in the American school a continuation of their
own tradition of learning, long established by the elders of their
communities and presided over by intellectually demanding rabbis. In the Jewish tradition, success and status had always been
linked, even under the most dismal circumstances of oppression,
with books and learning.

No such traditions existed among the Italians or the Irish.
Jane Addams, in *Democracy and Social Ethics,* describes an Italian immigrant youngster in Chicago:

> The peasant child is perfectly indifferent to showing off and
> making a good recitation. He leaves all that to his school
> fellows, who are more sophisticated and equipped with better
> English. His parents are not deeply interested in keeping him
> in school, and will not hold him there against his inclina-
> tion. Their experience does not point to the good American
> tradition that it is the educated man who finally succeeds.
> The richest man in the Italian colony can neither read nor
> write—even Italian. His cunning and acquisitiveness, com-
> bined with the credulity and ignorance of his countrymen,
> have slowly brought about his large fortune.

Despite the idealistic proclamations by intellectual public
school leaders, such as Horace Mann, men and women who ran
the schools and taught in them never liked the reluctant—or
different—pupils. Since students' failure reflects unfavorably on
teachers, the "professional" tendency has always been to show
contempt for the melting pot's obstreperous ingredients. It is
under such conditions that the Americanization mission often was
viewed as a chore to be resentfully and often autocratically performed. And teachers' frustrations often gave rise to racial and
ethnic theories as excuses for failure.

"Our chief difficulty is with the Irish," said *The Massachusetts Teacher* in 1851.

> The Germans, who are the next in numbers, will give us no trouble. They are more obstinate, more strongly wedded to their own notions and customs than the Irish; but they have, inherently, the redeeming qualities of industry, frugality, and pride, which will save them from vice and pauperism, and they may be safely left to take care of themselves. But the poor Irish, the down-trodden, priest-ridden of centuries, come to us in another shape. So cheaply have they been held at home—so closely have they been pressed down in the social scale—that for the most part the simple virtues of industry, temperance, and frugality are unknown to them; and that wholesome pride which will induce a German, or a native American, to work hard from sun to sun for the smallest wages, rather than seek or accept charitable aid, has literally been crushed out of them.

In actual fact, the public often showed little interest in the education of immigrant children. In New York State, for example, the only reason such education was actually provided appears to have been that the compulsory education law required it. Yet even the law was not always strictly enforced. The records show that in 1906 only 262 parents in the entire state were called to account and only forty-three were subsequently punished for not sending their children to school. A national investigation in 1914, reported by the Federal Bureau of Education, concluded that "chaos existed throughout the nation's schools. . . . There was no real national policy for helping immigrants."

It was the combination of a Puritanical faith in education among the public school philosophers, the sense of obligation among the profession, and—somewhat paradoxically—the superior feeling of many professionals toward the immigrants that continued to press for maximum acculturation. There was a wide gap between the Jeffersonian ideal of equality achieved through the diffusion of knowledge and the dog-trainer approach by many of the actual practitioners to the "inferior" newcomers. It was often the dog-trainer persistence which, devoted to the nation-building mission, prevailed in the classroom and which, despite its objectionable view of the children as "materials" to be molded, nevertheless had the ultimate effect of serving Jefferson's, Franklin's, and Mann's ideal of the open society, though with a heavy overlay of Webster's educational nationalism.

Ellwood Patterson Cubberley, born in the small-town America of Indiana in 1868, combined in his person both the high idealism and the dog-trainer limitations. One of the fathers of educational theory as an academic discipline, Cubberley (who attained nation-wide fame and respectability through his work at Stanford University in California) believed with puritanical fervor that the public school should, and could, take over all the moral, educational, and spiritual functions once performed by the home and the church. "Each year the child is coming to belong more and more to the state, and less and less to the parent," he wrote. The school's nation-building mission to him seemed both sacred and practical.

Cubberley considered it the schools' task to instill in all children "a social and political consciousness that will lead to unity." And to school superintendents, who listened reverently to his teachings, he issued the unambiguous charge:

> Our schools are, in a sense, factories in which the raw products (children) are to be shaped into products to meet the various demands of life. The specifications for manufacturing come from the demands of twentieth-century civilization, and it is the business of the school to build its pupils according to the specifications laid down.

Theories had begun to circulate among educators about the innate differences between certain ethnic groups and about the meaning of certain physical characteristics. Head shapes were often thought to be an indication of mental ability, and these pseudoscientific theories seemed invariably to favor the Anglo-Saxon, Danish, or Swedish physique. In 1912, William E. Chancellor, commenting on the capacity of different types of pupils, said: "The idiot, the imbecile, even the moron cannot compass Americanism. Perhaps with plenty of play and spontaneous occupation, we can save the South Italian and the Hungarian and the

Russian Jew from becoming morons, as they are so strongly inclined to do."

For many children the price of Americanization—even if it ultimately led to material success and a sense of true believing and belonging—often was high. Part of that price was the open hostility of a system that considered them inferior and the attitudes of teachers who often were downright insulting. Elizabeth Stern, in an article on "What It Means to Be a Jewess," in the *Ladies' Home Journal* in 1919, recalled a poignant episode:

> In the opening exercises one morning, the teacher read a selection from the literature book and followed this by a brief talk in which the Jews were designated as "peculiar" people. A number of the pupils discussed the matter in earnest and concluded that even though the teacher knew everything else, she was quite mistaken about them. It hurt to be held up as strange.

Adele M. Shaw, in *The World's Work* of 1913, quotes a teacher asking a pupil: "You dirty little Russian Jew, what are you doing?" She commented that in the majority of the schools she had visited in New York she was embarrassed by the lack of courtesy toward children, who were either treated with contempt or ignored altogether. Miss Shaw felt, however, that the teachers' callousness was mainly the result of their own insecurity—they felt themselves threatened by their insensitive supervisors. Moreover, affluent parents often sent their children to private schools so that these affronts rarely reached the ears of those who might have had the power to demand change and reform. The rank-and-file of the classroom teachers, Miss Shaw observed, were both "non-progressive and non-studious," even though they had been licensed by the Board of Examiners which was considered a body of the highest standards. The drop-out rate among immigrants was high.

For the sake of Americanization the schools applied excessive pressure on immigrant children to disown and abandon their heritage and the ways and the language of their homes.

"We soon got the idea that 'Italian' meant something pretty inferior, and a barrier was erected between children of Italian origin and their parents," recalled Leonard Covello, who later became a respected educator. "This was the accepted process of Americanization. We were becoming Americans by learning to be ashamed of our parents."

Covello remembers the day when his father, having glanced over the grades on his report card, was about to put his signature to the document. Suddenly, he stopped. "What is this?" he asked. "Leonard Covello! What happened to the "i" in Coviello?"

The change from Leonardo to Leonard, the old man said, he could understand—"perfectly natural process." But a family name?

"Mrs. Cutter took it out," the boy explained. "Every time she pronounced Coviello, it came out Covello. So she took the *i* out. That way it's easier for everybody."

"And what has this Mrs. Cutter got to do with my name?" the father now asked in rising anger.

"What difference does it make?" said young Leonard. "It's more American."

It was the first time that Leonard had dared openly to challenge his father, and it was the beginning of a bitter family argument, with his mother also protecting the old Italian name.

"Mamma, you don't understand," the children pleaded.

"Will you stop saying that!" the mother said. "I don't understand. I don't understand. What is there to understand? Now that you have become Americanized you understand everything and I understand nothing."

The school had won, but who was to say at how high a cost?

In school, Leonard learned English in large part through such exercises as writing countless times, "I must not talk"—by repetition, repetition, repetition. He remembered standing at attention as the Bible was read, standing at attention as the flag was unfurled, standing at attention as he sang loudly the important songs whose words he could not understand, standing at attention as he intoned, day after day, *Tree Cheers for de Red Whatzam Blu.*

And yet it is as easy to overdraw the oppressive aspects of the schools' determined, sometimes ridiculous, and often thoughtless effort at nation-building as it is to romanticize their history. Some children hated the process; many parents felt sadly that their children were being taken away from them and from the tradition that had held the families together. Little Esther Oberhein came back from vacation with her name changed to Esther O'Brien—perhaps not quite as dramatic a metamorphosis as Giuseppe Vagnotti, who emerged as Mike Jones. But not all the childhood memories of immigrant children were unhappy. Catherine Brody, recalling school days in New York, wrote in a report in *The American Mercury* in 1928: "But the glamour of the lady teachers, shining on the East Side world, I shall never forget. I see them now, all fused and molded into one symbolic figure."

While some children felt the system to be oppressive, many others stood ready to do anything that was asked of them because they saw this process as the opening door to a better life. To be denied the opportunity seemed to some who were excluded the hardest blow of all. On September 18, 1898, *The New York Herald Tribune* told of a critical space problem in the city schools. There had been several cases, the newspaper claimed, of boys who were denied admission taking their own lives in desperation.

Outside the schools realities were often different from the prospectus, particularly that utopian one drawn up by educational bureaucrats. An early outline by the New York State Department of Education, for example, urged that children be taught "whatever leads them devoutly to wonder at the order, beauty, or majesty of the universe. . . ."

For the poor and struggling immigrants in their urban slums and ghettoes such aims were hardly comprehensible. Such elegant rhetoric could have meant little to many of those immigrant parents, who, suspicious of the authority of the state that had always been their enemy, saw the school authorities in a similar light.

Violence and rioting were not unusual in the city's schools early in the century, although many New Yorkers during the 1960s saw the discord that swept through the system's predominantly Black and Puerto Rican sectors as an unprecedented phenomenon.

Riots, for instance, broke out at Public School 171 on Madison Avenue near 103rd Street in October 1916 in protest against the introduction of the Gary Plan of education—a work-study scheme that had been pioneered in the steel town of Gary, Indiana. To the predominantly Jewish immigrant parents of the neighborhood, the plan seemed a subtle attempt to downgrade their children's education and with it their chances to rise in business and the professions. (Similar suspicions by Blacks concerning educational "tracks" that might freeze their children in low-level employment were to stir up unrest once again almost half a century later.)

In 1916, windows were smashed at P.S. 171, and from the street-corners near schools in Harlem and on the upper East side opponents to the Gary plan tried to promote a general strike against any school that introduced it. Demonstrations and violence spread quickly through much of the system. The protests were joined by those who were angered by a newly lengthened school day which prevented students from holding after-school jobs, as well as others who objected to a new state law that made military training compulsory. A citywide school strike was averted only when the Board of Education's committee on the high schools agreed to meet with delegations of students and teachers—the full board never accepted such negotiations—and the daily school recess was moved back to its conventional hour of 3 P.M.

While many of the protests during the first quarter of the twentieth century were sparked by Jewish immigrants who feared that their children's education was being slighted in the general scheme of an Americanization process that had promised to open wide the doors to equal opportunity, it was the earlier wave of Catholic immigrants that had established the tradition of violent school battles.

The original cause of Catholic parents' anger was the public schools' blatant Protestantism disguised as Americanism, often accompanied by overt anti-Catholicism. A subsequent outgrowth of this fundamental objection, was the Catholics' demand for funds to provide their own schools which would substitute Catholic religious instruction for Protestant indoctrination.

The simple historical truth is that Protestantism as an integral part of early Americanism was firmly entrenched in the original public school concept. It was therefore hardly surprising that the established practice eventually ran head-on against the interests of the growing number of Catholic immigrants. One of the first serious collisions took place in New York during the 1840s when Catholics challenged the use of the Protestant Bible in public schools. The city's schools were run by the Public School Society, which had been formed in 1805 to care for children too poor to attend either religious or private schools. Despite the "public" title, the purpose of these schools was "to inculcate the sublime truths of religion and morality contained in the Holy Scriptures." Textbooks often referred to "deceitful Catholics." They were filled with outright falsifications of history.

Governor William H. Seward (not a Jacksonian Democrat but a Whig), is best known in our history for the Purchase of Alaska —"Seward's Folly"—while Secretary of State in the 1860s. During his early political career in New York, he voiced his concern about the foreign-born and the methods used to assimilate them. He charged that 20,000 Catholic children were being kept out of school to avoid Protestant indoctrination and intolerance. "I solicit their education, less from sympathy than because the welfare of the state demands it, and cannot dispense with it," Seward pleaded.

In 1842, as a result of his courageous insistence, a bill was passed to extend state supervision over the schools to each ward. *The New York Observer* editorialized: "The dark hour is at hand. People must only trust in God to be saved from the Beast." Such public fears led to a spree of window-smashing and street violence against the Irish. Nativists launched campaigns to gain control of the wards and of the school board.

But, despite the fever of emotions, the law eventually prevailed, and by 1844 Bible reading had been abandoned in thirty-one of the city's schools. Similar controversies flared up in many parts of the country, particularly in Philadelphia and in Newark. In 1844, rioting Philadelphians burned St. Augustine's Church. Troops had to be called out to restore order, but not before thirteen persons had been killed.

A severe test of the schools as an instrument, not of coerced homogenization but of honest pluralism came in 1922, when the Oregon legislature passed a law to make public school attendance compulsory. On the pain of fines and imprisonment, parents would have to send their children between the ages of eight and sixteen to public schools only. The effect of the law would have been to eliminate all private and religious schools.

That the test came in Oregon was both ironic and significant. At the time the law was passed almost 95 percent of all children between the ages of seven and thirteen were in school and over 93 percent of these pupils attended public schools. Only 1.5 percent of the state's inhabitants ten years and older were illiterate. Portland, the major city, had few slums and little of the crowding of the Eastern cities. Public and private schools in the state had coexisted peaceably since the early settlements.

The fact that the attack on the private schools, with its strong overtones of anti-Catholicism, xenophobia, and superpatriotism, could occur in Oregon under such circumstances offered added proof of how powerful the undercurrents of intolerant Americanism had remained throughout the country.

Although the statute was generally ascribed to the Scottish Rite Masons, the driving force from the start was the newly revived urban Ku Klux Klan. The paradoxical jumble of fears that Roman Catholicism and Soviet Bolshevism would undermine the republic by destroying public education led to the demand that children in public schools be taught "along standardized lines, which will enable them to acquire a uniform outlook on all national and patriotic questions."

The Klansmen of Oregon, more than half of them city dwellers, were symbolic of a new force—largely blue-collar workers concerned about their own and their children's place in the sun. Many were afraid they had reached a dead end in their jobs and opportunities. They feared change, whether it was embodied in Bolshevism or in a new morality. "Petting parties" and other loose behavior reported among the young alarmed them as much as the threat of foreign influences, and that included Catholicism as much as anything else not categorized as native-born white Anglo-Saxon Protestantism.

There were deep and often ludicrous contradictions in this campaign of fear. Public schools were seen as the only place where love of country and loyalty to constitutional government could be transmitted; yet the coercion implied in the compulsory public education statute actually flew in the face of the freedoms guaranteed to the individual by the Constitution.

Fred Gifford, Grand Dragon and chief sponsor of the legislation, demanded that "these mongrel hordes" be Americanized and charged that the non-WASP population of the crowded cities were like "unpedigreed cats and dogs"—yet somehow he and his followers assumed that, by putting all these "worthless" people into compulsory public school classes, they would emerge purified and "worthy." (The Klan, incidentally, "proved" the inferiority of Southeast European ethnic groups by pointing to the fact that many of them had not measured up to the selective draft requirements of World War I—a "documentation" that segregationists were to apply almost verbatim to Blacks in the wake of World War II.)

Such Klan publicists as Lem Devermade made much of the melting pot function of the public schools where all groups were to be brought together and molded into a harmonious generation of future Americans; yet the same theorists saw nothing wrong with segregated schools for Blacks. They simply ignored both the contradiction and the issue.

Although the compulsory public education law was not to go into effect until 1926, an unprecedented coalition of opposing forces was quickly assembled. Catholics, Jews, and the majority of Protestant church leaders were outraged by the implication that sectarianism was unpatriotic. The private school interests were literally fighting for their lives. Many minority groups, such as recent immigrants and Blacks, who were often at each other's throats, sensed that they faced a common threat at the hands of the Klan with its restrictive concept of who was entitled to full citizenship. Some businessmen simply feared increased taxes if all private school pupils were to be forced to attend school at public expense. But, in a broader sense, the statute challenged the beliefs of all who opposed the tyranny of the majority and the erosion of pluralistic freedoms. Many who opposed the bill said bluntly that the public schools were already exhibiting some autocratic tendencies which would be given free rein by the compulsory attendance law. A mother wrote to the *Portland Journal:* "The parents have precious little to say about their children now. There are teachers, principals and officials of all kinds . . . so high and mighty that you feel like a serf at times."

A public notice quoted former United States Commissioner of Education Philander Claxton:

> I believe in the public school system. It has been the salva-
> tion of our democracy; but the private schools and colleges

have been the salvation of the public schools. These private institutions have their place in an educational system; they prevent it from becoming autocratic and arbitrary and encourage its growth along new lines.

The Society of the Sisters of the Holy Names of Jesus and Mary and the Hill Military Academy jointly filed suits against Governor Pierce and the state authorities. Attorneys for the Governor rested much of their argument on a plea for the populist view of public education: "to require that the poor and the rich, the people of all classes and distinction, and of all different religious beliefs, shall meet in the common schools, which are the great American melting pot, there to become . . . the typical American of the future."

But opposition conceding "the value of compulsory education" and the state's right "to regulate standards in all schools" struck back by asking why Oregon should be the only state, with the exception of the Soviet Union, to "have a monopoly of education, to put it in a straitjacket . . . and thereby to bring their people and their citizens to one common level?"

The attorney for the Sisters went further and actually dared to question whether public schools were, in fact, functioning as a melting pot. He said bluntly—and this view was to become central almost half a century later to the reexamination and criticism of the schools' effectiveness in both racial integration and service to the disadvantaged—that the schools' record fell seriously short of their claim.

"You don't mingle the rich and poor," said Dan Marlarkey.

> You have your schools established in districts; you have your school out here by Riverside, a public school that is as aristocratic an institution as ever existed anywhere. Why? Because the people that live in that neighborhood are people that are well to do. Their children go to the public school. They don't mix with the poor. . . . You go up . . . to the Failing School, and there is where you will find your foreign born. There is where you will find your Italians and your Polish Jews lately over here, and they will be together just as much as they would be in private schools.

On March 31, 1924, a three-man federal court ruled in favor of the plaintiffs, holding that the state's power must not be "exercised arbitrarily and despotically."

On June 1, 1925, the Supreme Court, having heard the state argue that "the moral pestilence of paupers, vagabonds, and possibly convicts" could be averted only by compulsory public school attendance, upheld the ruling of the lower courts that private schools could not be deprived of their property without due process of law under the fourteenth amendment. The court upheld the state's regulatory powers over all schools, including the requirement "that certain studies plainly essential to good citizenship must be taught, and that nothing be taught which is manifestly inimical to the public welfare."

But, what was far more important, the court held that the state had no right "to standardize its children." There were to follow many more efforts—particularly during another phase of anti-Commmunist hysteria during the 1950s—at imposing rigid "patriotic" criteria on public school instruction. What the ruling in the Pierce case, however, established beyond further question was the legitimate role of the nonpublic schools as an integral part of the total compulsory education system.

Almost fifty years later, the Supreme Court was to be asked to rule on a question even more upsetting to those who believed in compulsory public education—whether the state has a right to compel parents to send their children to school, any school, at all. In 1972, the Amish, a Swiss-originated religious and communal group, challenged the right of the Wisconsin school authorities to force their children to attend school beyond the eighth grade.

Committed to a simple life of self-sufficiency through farming, the Amish reject all modern luxuries. They admit the necessity of schooling in the basic skills, but consider the content of secondary education to be in conflict with that life of austerity which, they believe, is the only road to heaven. The worldly, success-oriented curriculum of the high schools to them spelled corruption and alienation from their religious values.

In Wisconsin's test case of Jonas Yoder, the state's Supreme Court, reversing a lower court decision, had ruled that the Amish were indeed entitled to ignore the compulsory attendance laws on religious grounds. But the state, fearful that the precedent might undermine the compulsory school attendance laws, appealed to the Supreme Court. (In other states, notably Pennsylvania, school authorities had shown a more pragmatic and conciliatory attitude, accepting the Amish teenagers' training on their home farms as the equivalent of public vocational education, thus upholding compulsory attendance laws in principle while giving Amish parents what they wanted.)

In arguing their case, the Amish did in fact point to *Pierce v. Society of Sisters* for its affirmation of parents' right to determine the proper kind of education for their children. The state, on the other hand, argued that the previous case had not given approval to the idea that parents could interpret this to mean no schooling at all.

In May, 1972, in *Wisconsin v. Yoder,* the Supreme Court, by a vote of 7 to 0, upheld the Amish parents' right not to send their children to high school because to do so constituted to them an assault on their basic dogma, "Be not conformed to this world." But Chief Justice Warren Burger, who wrote the opinion, deliberately narrowed its impact by stressing that the parents' opposition to high school instruction was based on long-established religiously determined life styles rather than on some new theories of education and child rearing. It was a limitation calculated to prevent the ruling from being used as a battering ram against compulsory education at a time when New Left opinion had begun to depict compulsory schooling as the tool of the conservative establishment and a means of preventing children from breaking with the established order.

In view of such attacks on compulsory education under the mantle of libertarian concern for the children's rights, it was, however, significant that Justice William O. Douglas, who is generally considered the most liberal member of the court, wrote a partial dissent. In it, he expressed concern over court rulings which consider only the views of the parents without probing the children's own aspirations and preferences. The actual rate of defection of a sizable minority of Amish youths from the "simple life" suggests that Douglas's concern was not purely hypothetical —the parents' newly confirmed power to keep their children out of high school may have had the effect, in some instances, of limiting rather than enhancing the children's rights. Or, to put it differently, the end results would be quite different from those sought by New Left opponents to compulsory education.

Perhaps the only conclusion that can be drawn with any certainty from the historic test is that a more flexible school bureaucracy, less singlemindedly bent on the enforcement of "the one best way," could have avoided the confrontation and deprived the opposition to compulsory education of even such a limited victory.

Over the years, as those two cases showed, Americanization had become increasingly defensive and negative. Men who were fearful of what they considered the wrong religions, inferior races, dangerous economic and political philosophies, and heretical dissent no longer felt confident that the diffusion of knowledge alone could protect the state. Their vision of the new America was less clear and less appealing. They were more specific about what an American should not be or think than about the positive virtues and ideals he should represent. They no longer found it as easy as Horace Mann to agree that there could be a "middle course, which all sensible and judicious men, all patriots, and all genuine republicans, must approve."

Language had, from the start, been considered the indispensable cement of a unified nation—and properly so. The experience of older countries where different languages create political and ethnic divisions provided adequate warning. Even strong dialects can create disruptive regional animosities, as they had in the German past, for example, between Bavaria and Prussia. (The South's speech pattern comes closest to being a separate dialect, and it may well have contributed to that region's greater difficulty in taking its place in full equality within the American framework.)

Many hyphenated Americans—German-Americans, Scandinavian-Americans, Italian-Americans, and others—treasured their old language, not as a sign of allegiance to the old countries, but as a bond between generations. But to the nation-builders, the preservation of any foreign-speaking enclaves, even if the foreign language were to be maintained *in addition* to English, had been anathema from the very beginning. As early as 1740, even Benjamin Franklin had been deeply concerned over the influx of Germans into colonial Pennsylvania—a concern admittedly aggravated by the fact that he had failed to gain the support of the German community for his plan to raise an extralegal militia against the French.

"This will in a few years become a German colony," Franklin wrote to his friend James Parker in 1751. "Instead of their learning our language, we must learn theirs, or live as in a foreign country."

By 1911, the *Teachers College Record* reported that American public schools in thirty-seven of the largest American cities counted 57 percent of their pupils as born of foreign parentage. Many of the immigrants moved to the Middle West and lived in small enclaves or in larger colonies of the foreign-born where they preserved their native habits and speech. Before the end of the nineteenth century, Willa Cather wrote about her native Nebraska: "We could drive to a Norwegian church and listen to a sermon in that language or to a Danish or a Swedish church . . . or to a French Catholic sermon or pray with the Lutheran Germans . . . [or watch] a Czech theater where boys and girls gave Czech drama in the original language." She added with sadness that "Americanization has doubtless done away with all this. Our lawmakers have a rooted conviction that a boy can be a better American if he speaks only one language than if he speaks two."

This was the issue when, on April 9, 1919, the Nebraska legislature passed a law prohibiting the teaching of any modern language to any student who had not completed the eighth grade, regardless whether he attended public, private, or parochial school. The fact that the "dead" languages—particularly Greek, Latin, and Hebrew—were not covered by the ban made it clear that the intention of the law was to prevent the perpetuation of any spoken tongue other than English.

Under this statute—and Nebraska was one of twenty-one states which had passed some anti-German legislation in the overcharged atmosphere of World War I—an obscure teacher in the Lutheran Zion Parochial School was found guilty of teaching reading to an elementary school child in the forbidden German language. Robert T. Meyer appealed his conviction, but it was upheld by the state's highest court.

When the case reached the Supreme Court, the national atmosphere was not auspicious for Meyer. Samuel Eliot Morison has written that this period spawned "more hate literature, more nasty, sour and angry groups promoting 100 percent Americanism than any earlier period in our history. . . ." Henry Ford's anti-Semitism, the anti-Catholic attacks on the Knights of Columbus, and the great upsurge in the Klan's popularity made the defense of anything that offended the nativists a difficult undertaking. John J. Tigert, President Harding's Commissioner of Education, was soon to proclaim his determination to eliminate "Communism, Bolshevism, and Socialism from the schools."

The case of *Meyer v. Nebraska* was decided on June 4, 1923, along with issues involving similar statutes in Iowa and two in Ohio. The court, with Justice Oliver Wendell Holmes, Jr., dissenting, declared the statutes unconstitutional, in violation of rights guaranteed by the 14th Amendment. Justice McReynolds, who delivered the majority opinion, held that, "his [Meyer's] *right* to teach and the right of parents to engage him so to instruct their children, we think are within the liberty of the amendment."

The court acknowledged the importance of the schools' role in the Americanization process, but concluded that such goals "cannot be coerced by methods which conflict with the Constitution—a desirable end cannot be promoted by prohibited means."

Indeed, Justice Holmes felt so strongly about the schools' Americanization mission that he ended his spirited dissent with this observation:

> Youth is the time when familiarity with a language is established and if there are sections in the State where a child would hear only Polish or French or German spoken at home I am not prepared to say that it is unreasonable to provide that in his early years he shall hear and speak only English at school.

The wheel came full circle when, in 1974, the Supreme Court upheld the claim of Chinese parents in San Francisco who demanded bilingual instruction for their children. While the use of bilingual teachers might at first glance seem a break with the Americanization concept, it is, in fact, merely the application of new pedagogical means to achieve the old ends. The new method clashes head-on with the conservative belief that the best way to Americanize a foreign-speaking child is to banish the sound of his old language. While experts still debate tactics, the fact is that not only the Supreme Court but increasing numbers of local school districts and state legislatures have actually mandated bilingual instruction as a more humane method of Americanization.

The Supreme Court's ruling in the Meyer case, even though in large part aimed at defense of the property rights of a group of professionals—the foreign-language teachers—marked an important change at the highest level of thought and leadership. In the face of powerful nativist emotions, after World War I, amid panicky fears of radical threats from abroad, it is amazing that the case for the coercive use of school to limit personal freedoms did not triumph. The court appears to have sensed the enormous power a modern state could wield by controlling what children may or may not learn in school. It was testimony of the great distance education in America had traveled. Education was on the way to becoming, as Mann had hoped, "the balance-wheel of the social machinery," and one of the consequences of this success was the increasing need to restrain the state from abusing this powerful device.

As important as language for the creation of a sense of nationhood are the special symbols of nationalism. No government, regardless of its political ideology, has ever dared to dispense with such symbolism. Radicals periodically denounce it. Intellectuals frequently scoff at it. But neither parliamentarian Britain nor Communist Russia nor republican America has been able to free itself of the symbolic trappings of the Union Jack, the Red Flag, or the Stars and Stripes.

A series of lessons called "English for Foreigners," published in Boston in 1909 and designed to Americanize immigrants, included among such topics as how to use a toothbrush and why there must be "law and order" in big cities, a chapter on the American flag.

"The American flag," it said, "means liberty and justice for everybody. . . . All Americans love the Stars and Stripes. Let us all respect the flag and be true to it."

No one successfully questioned such teachings until 1936 when Walter Gobitis of Minersville, Pennsylvania, was shocked to learn that his two children, Lillian, aged twelve, and William, aged ten, had been told by their principal that they could not come back to school unless they agreed to salute the flag together with their classmates, as they recited the pledge of allegiance in the daily compulsory exercise. As a devout member of Jehovah's Witnesses, he believed that saluting the flag was sinful, equal to the making of a "graven image."

When Gobitis appealed the ruling, the Board of Education ordered the Superintendent of Schools to expel his two children. Federal District Judge Albert B. Maris, who had recently been appointed by President Franklin D. Roosevelt, granted "relief" to the Gobitis family, but the Minersville school authorities, considering it their duty to uphold respect for the symbol of nationhood, eventually carried their appeal to the Supreme Court.

It was not the first time that a compulsory flag salute had been appealed to the nation's highest tribunal, but in three prior instances the court had refused to rule, holding that the issue was for the local and state authorities to decide. Over the years, 120 children were known to have refused the salute on religious grounds, but in each case the lower courts had upheld the requirement.

The Gobitis case was different only because the lower courts this time had upheld the children's refusal. When *Minersville School District v. Gobitis* reached the Supreme Court in 1940, the national mood was as unfavorable to Gobitis as it had been to Meyer almost two decades earlier. Nationalism was again running high. Europe was at war, and the United States would surely soon enter the conflict over the very issues of liberty symbolized by the Stars and Stripes. This seemed to most Americans a time for the schools to uphold the sanctity of patriotic ceremonies.

Some of the most distinguished libertarians of the day, including Arthur Garfield Hays, Lloyd K. Garrison, and Charles P. Taft, as well as eminent members of the Harvard Law School, joined the case on the side of the Gobitis children. They saw it as a test of strength between the power of the state and the individual's religious liberty:

> We suggest [said one notable brief] that no American court should presume to tell any person that he is wrong in his opinion as to how he may best serve the God in which he believes. . . . There is no such public need for the compulsory flag salute as to justify the overriding of the religious scruples of children.

Despite such eloquent pleas, the court ruled by a vote of 8 to 1 that the Minersville schools were right in demanding that the children salute the flag.

What lent extraordinary significance to the opinion was the fact that it was written by an eminent defender of civil liberties, Justice Felix Frankfurter, himself an immigrant and the only foreign-born member of the court. "The ultimate foundation of a free society is the binding tie of cohesive sentiment," wrote Frankfurter. And the flag was, in his view, "the symbol of our national unity . . . the emblem of freedom in its truest, best sense." He continued:

> What the school authorities are really asserting is the right to awaken in the child's mind considerations as to the significance of the flag contrary to those implanted by the parents. In such an attempt the state is normally at a disadvantage in competing with the parent's authority, so long—and this is the vital aspect of religious toleration—as parents are unmolested in their right to counteract by their own persuasiveness the wisdom and rightness of those loyalties which the state's educational system is seeking to promote . . . the flag salute is an allowable portion of a school program . . . an exemption might introduce elements of discipline, might cast doubts in the minds of the other children. . . .

Although the Frankfurter opinion undoubtedly expressed the faith of a majority of Americans at the time, the ringing dissent by Justice Harlan F. Stone spoke for a rising new sentiment against governmental coercion, even in the cause of national unity. There are better ways, he said, of inculcating patriotism in a child than forcing him "to affirm that which he does not believe."

"The Constitution," Stone said in his conclusion, ". . . is also an expression of faith and a command that freedom of mind and spirit must be preserved, which *government* must obey, if it is to adhere to that justice and moderation without which no free government can exist."

The decision left the nation troubled and divided. More than 170 leading newspapers in all sections of the country opposed the ruling. But mobs of nativists responded by turning violently against the Jehovah's Witnesses, burning their meeting halls, and disrupting prayer meetings. Several states sent the children of Witnesses who continued to refuse the flag salute to reformatories.

Within less than three years, several of the justices who had joined Frankfurter's majority opinion began to waver, and three of them, in a subsequent, related case, said that, although they had upheld the flag-salute requirement, "we now believe that it was also wrongly decided." After the State of West Virginia passed a flag-salute statute that threatened the parents of disobeying children with imprisonment, the Supreme Court on June 14, 1943, by a vote of 6 to 3 overturned *Gobitis*.

"If there is any fixed star in our constitutional constellation," wrote Justice Robert H. Jackson for the majority, "it is that no official, high or petty, can prescribe what shall be orthodox in politics, nationalism, religion, or other matters of opinion or force citizens to confess by word or act their faith therein."

The reversal—three years after *Gobitis*—was complete. Justices Hugo Black and William Douglas, in joining the majority, went far beyond the issue of religious freedom when they wrote: "Words uttered under coercion are proof of loyalty to nothing but self-interest. Love of country must spring from willing hearts and free minds." Thus, for the first time, the entire concept of the school's or the state's right, in the name of Americanization, to prescribe oaths and ceremonies was seriously questioned. The Supreme Court had given notice to nation-builders that the era of coercive nationalism and enforced patriotism—concepts which clashed with the essence of free government—was drawing to a close.

In 1972, the new freedom from coercion was to be tested on a different level—that of the teacher. Mrs. Susan Russo, a new teacher in the James E. Sperry High School in Henrietta, New

York, whose personal record showed no trace of radicalism or insubordination, stood up, as required, during the daily salute to the flag and pledge of allegiance. (The pledge was piped to all classrooms over the public address system.) But Mrs. Russo neither saluted nor intoned the words of the pledge.

When her actions were challenged, Mrs. Russo said that she felt the existing realities of discrimination made the phrase "with liberty and justice to all" a hollow one. Mouthing it seemed to her an act of hypocrisy that her conscience would not brook.

Although there was no indication that she had ever tried to influence her students to follow her example, Mrs. Russo was fired and her dismissal was upheld in District Court.

In November 1972, a three-judge panel of the United States Court of Appeals unanimously reversed the ruling and upheld the teacher's right to remain silent under the 1st Amendment guarantee of free speech. Judge Irving R. Kaufman (who had imposed the death penalty on Julius and Ethel Rosenberg and was not considered soft on patriotism) held that "patriotism that is forced is a false patriotism just as loyalty that is coerced is the very antithesis of loyalty." He reminded the school board that, since the Supreme Court had already ruled that students could refuse to salute the flag, it would be unreasonable not to grant the same right to teachers.

To many, who still see the schools primarily in their old role of building a nation by assimilating a diverse population to common customs and beliefs, the ruling and what it implied remained odious. Yet it was also clear that much had changed, not only in America's but the world's view of simple national rites. Few other major countries still asked their schools to engage in such daily ceremonial routines, reserving them generally for special occasions of national reaffirmation.

Yet it would be misleading to suggest that greater freedoms for teachers were easily come by or indeed are even today readily available in all communities. One of the most persistent obstacles was the demand for a teacher's higher morality. When a Massachusetts school superintendent in 1898 was fired for an indictment of adultery in another state, the Massachusetts Supreme Judicial Court held that "schools will suffer if those who conduct them are open to general and well-grounded suspicion of this kind." Unmarried teachers have been dismissed for being seen with married men—as recently as 1939. And, well into the twentieth century, smoking in public was taboo for women teachers in many communities—and even riding a bicycle could be considered sufficiently undignified to warrant reprimand or dismissal.

Political restrictions, however, persisted even longer than moral ones. The first case in which the Supreme Court had occasion to consider the impact of a loyalty requirement aimed at teachers was *Adler v. Board of Education* in 1952, when the court upheld the New York Feinberg Law demanding that teachers sign loyalty oaths as a condition for employment. The majority opinion held that teachers were no different from other government employees. "A teacher works in a sensitive area in a schoolroom," the decision said. "There he shapes the attitude of young minds toward the society in which they live. In this, the state has a vital concern. It must preserve the integrity of the schools."

It was the dissent that pointed the way to the future. Justice William O. Douglas, joined by Justice Hugo Black, wrote:

> What happens under this law is typical of what happens in a police state. Teachers are under constant surveillance: their pasts are combed for signs of disloyalty; their utterances are watched for clues to dangerous thoughts. A pall is cast over the classrooms. There can be no real academic freedom in that environment. . . . A "party line"—as dangerous as the "party line" of the Communists—lays hold. . . . Discussion often leaves off where it should begin.

In a subsequent case (*Wieman v. Updegraff*), Justice Frankfurter demonstrated that his instinctive and emotional defense of the requirement to honor the flag by saluting it in no way blunted his fundamental belief in academic freedom. When the court's majority somewhat gingerly moved away from its earlier defense of loyalty oaths, Frankfurter, joined by Douglas, wrote a moving concurring opinion in which he declared teachers "in our entire educational system, from primary grades to the university" are "the priests of our democracy." They cannot carry out their noble task, Frankfurter wrote, "if the conditions for the practice of a responsible and critical mind are denied to them."

And shortly thereafter, in *Sweezy v. New Hampshire* (1957), Frankfurter warned: "Teachers and students must always remain free to inquire, to study and to evaluate, to gain new maturity and understanding; otherwise our civilization will stagnate and die."

The Supreme Court returned to the issue of New York's loyalty oaths in 1967 (*Keyishian v. Board of Regents*), reversing its earlier ruling in *Adler* and striking down key provisions of the loyalty program as vague and overbroad. Justice Brennan, writing for a majority of five, supported his position with an affirmation of academic freedom:

> Our nation is deeply committed to safeguarding academic freedom, which is of transcendent value to all of us and not merely to the teachers concerned. . . . The classroom is peculiarly the "marketplace of ideas." The nation's future depends upon leaders trained through wide exposure to that robust exchange of ideas which discovers truth "out of a multitude of tongues, [rather] than through any kind of authoritative selection." . . .

A long-standing complicating factor in public education's role has been the relationship between the public schools and religion —always a delicate and potentially explosive issue. Jefferson, sensitive to its dangers, had been adamant about the need to build a wall between church and state, lest one dominate the other and diminish its freedom.

In later years, Catholics and other religious minorities—or those who chose not to subscribe to any religious belief—were justified in their fear and occasional anger over the Protestant domination of public school doctrine and instruction. Similarly, proponents of church-state separation were acting in the spirit of Jefferson and the Constitution when they continued to battle against Catholic and other parochial school efforts to gain public subsidy for sectarian schools—a battle that still continues in the courts.

Although the question as to precisely what kind of aid violates the Constitutional prohibition of the "establishment of a religion" by the state has never been fully resolved, the Supreme Court found it easier to speak on the question of prayer in the public schools. The issue was put before the highest tribunal twice, and in each instance the court came down firmly on Jefferson's side.

The first case was brought by five parents—two Jewish, one a member of the Ethical Culture Society, one a Unitarian, and the last a nonbeliever—in the public school district of Hyde Park, New York. The issue was a prayer, written and authorized by the New York State Board of Regents some years earlier—ironically, as an effort to still complaints about sectarian observance.

"Almighty God," the prayer said, "we acknowledge our dependence upon Thee, and we beg Thy blessings upon us, our parents, our teachers, and our country."

On June 25, 1962, the Supreme Court, in a vote of 6 to 1, declared the prayer in violation of the Constitution. Justice Hugo Black, who wrote for the majority, held that "in this country, it is no part of the business of government to compose official prayers for any group of Americans to recite." Speaking from the bench, Black put the case even more sharply: "The prayer of each man from his soul must be his and his alone. That is the genius of the First Amendment."

Many politicians thought otherwise. They sensed that, in the view of many of their constituents, the court's ruling would appear not as a defense of religious freedom, but as an attack on piety and spiritual values. Once again, the specter of the "godless" public schools, conjured up whenever public education is under fire, seemed in the wings. New York's Governor Nelson Rockefeller, lamenting the court's action, said he considered the prayer very important to inculcate in children a belief "in the brotherhood of man and the fatherhood of God." Officials in the State Education Department gave consideration to the substitution of silent prayer.

Though the thrust of the court's ruling seemed fairly obvious, supporters of school prayers chose to take the narrow view that the decision had merely prohibited the state from writing and mandating *its* prayers. Thus, it was argued, real prayers that emanated not from the state but from the church, including the reading of the Bible as a religious exercise, were not directly affected.

Exactly one year later, on June 17, 1963, the Supreme Court eliminated whatever doubts remained about its real intent. The issue this time was the recitation of the Lord's Prayer and of Bible verses, and the court held 8 to 1 that no state or locality may require such exercises in its public schools.

Justice Tom Clark wrote: "In the relationship between man and religion, the state is firmly committed to a position of neutrality." But perhaps in order to anticipate the charges that the public schools deliberately imposed ignorance about the Bible and religion on generations of young Americans, Clark also pointed out: "It certainly may be said that the Bible is worthy of study for its literary and historic qualities." The ruling, he therefore held, does not prohibit such study "when presented objectively as part of a secular form of education."

From the outset, the public school Americanization prospectus contained both promise and threat—the open door to success on the basis of merit rather than parentage, and oppressive standardization in the service of those who controlled power and wealth.

Those two goals were, in reality, not always mutually exclusive. Many immigrants welcomed the promise of having their children prepared to take their places in the economic hierarchy. It was only when that hierarchy became too restrictive or when the schools interpreted Americanization too narrowly and with too little concern for individual and ethnic differences and human dignity that public education's promise appeared to be dimmed.

When historians accept too readily either the ideal goal or the flawed implementation as the main current of American public education, the picture becomes distorted and history turns into propaganda. This is why revisionist swings of the historiographic pendulum occasionally become so persuasive—but only for brief periods. Neither the angel nor the devil theory of the schools' part in nation-building can get to the heart of what is, despite its aberrations, a remarkable story.

Coercive Americanism flared up again in one of its worst and most oppressive forms during the Cold War era of the 1950s when superpatriots tried to rid the schools of the Jeffersonian spirit of free inquiry. Libraries were purged; books burned; teachers fired or cowed in the interest of nationalistic uniformity. American loyalty was measured, not by the yardstick of the New World idealism, but rather in terms of the negative criterion of anti-Communism.

But even during the violent and destructive flare-up of nationalistic fervor there were increasing signs of strong new currents. Revulsion against the jingoistic interlude, growing disillusionment with nationalistic policies symbolized by the war in Indochina and a questioning of the continued viability of nationalism in the thermonuclear age led to a turning away from the rigidities of the Americanization concept.

The civil rights movement of the 1960s served as a reminder that large segments of American children—predominantly the non-whites—had been deliberately overlooked by the acculturation process. They, therefore, understandably resented any heavy-handed efforts at assimilation so late in the game.

In its most extreme reaction, the countermovement of the early 1970s tried to put de-Americanization in the place of Americanization, just as the radical movement of educational politics countered Mann's dream of universal schooling with a new banner of universal de-schooling.

But far more important than such extremes have been recurring efforts at a liberal reinterpretation of the earlier, coercive approach to acculturation. Through the major decisions by the Supreme Court, reflecting both the spirit of the Constitution and changing social attitudes, the interpretation of the schools' nation-building function has become increasingly less harsh and more humane.

It will be argued, probably without end or resolution, whether the system's harsh singlemindedness was its flaw or its virtue—whether that harshness pushed great numbers to success or caused too many to fall by the wayside. It will be argued, too, whether frequent insensitivity actually managed to accomplish an extraordinary degree of acculturation or whether a more sophisticated effort might have made the melting pot less of a pressure cooker—and the product therefore more truly and more lastingly blended.

Let it suffice at this point to say that the experiment was based on high principles. Its problems were staggering. The dreams of the most intelligent and idealistic of men were often placed in the safe-keeping of others who lacked the intelligence and misunderstood the ideals—until their blunders, in turn, gave rise to idealistic reformers who returned to the challenges laid down by Jefferson, Franklin, and Mann.

5

BLACKBOARD POLITICS

*J*EFFERSON CONSIDERED THE "DIFFU-
sion of knowledge" a keystone of popular government. Yet his
hopes that learning and reason would triumph over the old rule of
inherited rank and privilege were based on the vision of an
America untroubled by "the mobs of the cities" which had debased life in Europe with "ignorance, poverty and vice."

Precisely such fears, as urbanization grew in the nineteenth
century, alerted pioneers of educational and social thought to the
need for something more reassuring than voluntary school attendance by the select few. Mob rule seemed no longer a hypothetical
threat—unless education could elevate the poor. The question of
whether schools could assume the role of surrogate parent of the
deprived children in the teeming cities runs with remarkable con-
sistency through the nation's subsequent history.

It was in the urban East that compulsory schooling found most of its original supporters. Massachusetts became the first state to pass a compulsory attendance law in 1852, but the process of mandating nationwide school attendance was not completed until Mississippi joined in the trend in 1918. And, as long as child labor continued, opposition to compulsory education—mainly on the part of conservatives in and out of the education profession—remained strong and articulate. Oscar Cooper, state Superintendent of Education in Texas, called such compulsion evidence of "a drift toward the breakers of socialism, sufficient to arouse concern in the mind of the patriot" and a threat to "the most vital and essential of the institutions on which civilization rests—the family."

Almost a century later, a new attack was to be mounted against compulsory education. The new opponents were not the conservatives but those of the radical left who also wanted to curb the power of the state—not because they feared the trend toward socialism but rather because they saw the state itself as the instrument of conservatism.

Neither the conservatives of the 1870s nor the radicals of the 1970s answered the question of how, under a system of voluntarism, the poorest and most neglected children were to be rescued from their own families' inability or unwillingness to provide for their betterment.

Toward the end of the nineteenth century, however, pressures for compulsory education grew stronger as the atmosphere in the cities deteriorated. The tradition which equated hard work with morality and considered the child virtually the property of its family might well have built an insuperable barrier against the very idea of state-ordered schooling beyond the most essential basic skills, had not the demands and dangers of cities and factories challenged virtually all the old ways of a ruggedly individualistic society.

For a century and a half, the politics of educational planning and reform have tried to find ways of proving that an urban nation could erase the ravages of poverty and ignorance. Theoretically, all the educational forces, though often locked in conflict, believed in political and intellectual freedom, but they disagreed over the means of achieving such freedoms. Nor could they ever reach a consensus as to the extent to which compulsion in education is compatible with, or even essential to, the ultimate attainment of these freedoms. Underlying those ideological battles is the question of how much institutional uniformity is needed—and how much is tolerable—in the creation of an educational system that protects pluralism, the antithesis of systematic uniformity.

Social reform has always been an intrinsic element in American political thinking. But its early manifestations had their roots in a middle-class or aristocratic humanitarianism—sympathy for the less fortunate, including slaves, slum dwellers, and penniless immigrants. It was a moderate rather than a radical movement. Thus the early Federalists' reform spirit was essentially patrician, with deep undercurrents of religious benevolence and philanthropic largesse. The Federalists were the party of the Establishment, and their interest in social betterment was motivated by a feeling of noblesse oblige. They wanted to improve the lot of the common man, but without mingling with him.

Those who gave serious thought to the growing role of the masses under the republican form of government recognized that paternalistic concern for the poor and the ignorant was insufficient, particularly in an urban setting where individual citizens were far more dependent on each other than they had been on the farms. But it was not until the midnineteenth century, when Horace Mann said flatly that "nothing but Universal Education" could prevent the exploitation of labor and the poor by management and the rich, that the course of social and political reform through education was deliberately charted.

During the 1830s increasing numbers of Americans first began to register concern about the educational machinery that up to then had grown essentially without deliberate design.

Abraham Lincoln, while running for the Illinois State Assembly in 1832, had told the voters in his campaign literature that "upon the subject of education, not presuming to dictate any plan or system respecting it, I can only say that I view it as the most important subject we as a people can be engaged in."

Schools had long been springing up, some entirely private and others more or less publicly sponsored and financed. Many states subsidized existing private academies. Cities and towns supported a variety of essentially private charity schools for the poor. Since public schools were decidedly Protestant in their moral and religious approach, states had no qualms about contributing to the support of private schools sponsored by a variety of other sects. Schools and academies were founded in ample number (except in the South and some scattered rural areas) for charity or profit, with a variety of goals, from propagating the faith to fighting crime and delinquency and even advancing the cause of learning.

But it was not a system. Those who were convinced that education was essential to the welfare of the nation became increasingly certain that a more regular pattern of schooling was needed. Originating in the more densely populated East, where the tradition of education reached back to Colonial days and where the urban and industrial changes were most compelling, the common school crusade began to enlist support from virtually every sector and interest group. It brought together many disparate groups who were more often engaged in conflict with each other—Whigs and Democrats, stern Puritans and pragmatically expansionist pioneers and business leaders.

Conservatives and patricians saw the common school as a means of preserving the old verities and keeping the masses, with their growing political power, neatly within the confines of moral and civil law. Trust in the kind of selective access to schooling which Jefferson believed sufficient to create a natural aristocracy of talent and merit no longer seemed enough to conservatives fearful of the Jacksonian upsurge of popular power. The common school to them was a means of taming and domesticating these menacing forces.

Liberal and progressive sectors were equally intent on the growth of the common schools—but for different reasons. They wanted to prevent an establishment of wealth and power from excluding them and their children from the benefits of a changing social order. They were convinced that, if the establishment were to stand in the schoolhouse doors and control access, the educated would maintain political and economic mastery over the ignorant. And, of course, schools seemed to hold out the best hope for the "salvation" of the growing stream of immigrants that followed the Irish potato famines and the liberals' defeat in Germany.

Without these powerful currents stirred up by many disparate forces the educational prophets of the common school—free to all comers and supported, not by tuition, but by the taxpayers—would have had little chance to be heard, let alone heeded. But it would be wrong to suggest that philosophers of public education were merely riding the crest of a new wave. Their faith and philosophy were entirely in tune with the hopes and the convictions of Jefferson, Franklin, and Webster. Their special genius was their sensitivity to the needs of a new age and to the country's growing readiness to replace educational laissez-faire with a comprehensive system that could move from being freely accessible to becoming truly universal.

It is easy, in retrospect, to assign a variety of political motives to these crusaders—to charge, for instance, that they were the lackeys of the Establishment or of political forces which sought to make the individual subservient to the state. Because the common school crusaders, being intelligent and sophisticated, knew that their success depended on their ability to appeal to the rich and poor, employer and employed, native and immigrant, revisionist theories can with relative ease be constructed on the basis of the crusaders' own words. But the facts, born out by a full reading of the early proponents of universal public education, are that these crusaders were both serious and sincere about their goal of making the schools the foundation of popular government and the protector of all the peoples' interests.

School crusaders were interested in more than the creation of a system. They may have found it expedient to make common cause with conservatives in political efforts to move the nation toward acceptance of free and universal education; but they were destined to clash with conservative opinion in their liberal interpretation of education itself.

In the spring of 1843, Horace Mann went abroad for a study tour that took him to the schools of England, Ireland, Scotland, Germany, Holland, Belgium, and France. He returned impressed, not only with the various systems of education but with the way in which the better of the European teachers treated their pupils—"the beautiful relation of harmony and affection which subsisted between teacher and pupils." He commented in one of his famous annual reports that throughout his travels he never saw a blow struck or a sharp rebuke given or a child in tears.

Whether by design or not, Mann had touched a tender nerve. Within months, the masters of Boston's venerable grammar schools issued a stinging rejoinder. Mann, they charged, was clearly soft on the important business of inculcating in children the tough habits of mental discipline. He wanted teachers to pander to the children "by the pleasing manner or amusing speech of their instructor." And they underscored, by way of fundamental doctrine, that "the mere promotion of a child's pleasure should never form the basis of any system of education."

When a child is sick, the masters went on, he cannot appreciate the benefits of taking "disagreeable medicine." Theirs was an eloquent and honest defense of the theory that teaching calls for the dispensing of "disagreeable medicine," which has been at the heart of so much educational thinking and persists to this day among what is usually considered the conservative wing of academic thought. To amuse the child may not, as the Puritans would have put it, be the work of the devil, but it is reversing the natural order: amusement should spring much later from the mastery of difficult subjects.

To the masters—and they are representative of both the early tradition of American education and of a tough strain of popular philosophy that is sometimes dormant but never for long—authority was "the corner-stone of all order . . . discipline is the rule, pleasure the exception." Fear of punishment is essential in dealing with children and savages, two human categories which the stern school of American education has often liked to mention in the same breath.

Actually, Mann's belief that learning and pleasure need not be opposites, though often obscured by the stern Calvinist tradition, has its roots in the instinctive American optimism that shaped the outlook of such men as Jefferson and Franklin. It would be absurd to suggest that any man with Jefferson's delight in his own discovery of knowledge could subscribe to the "unpleasant medicine" school of education. And Franklin was explicit in the heretical assumption that pupils would gladly go to school. He freely used terms such as "delightful" and even "entertaining" in describing the process of learning. When he asked for a school that offered "useful" knowledge, he said flatly that this would be done "to advantage, and with pleasure to the students."

Toward the middle of the nineteenth century, as the common school crusade gathered momentum, new prophets of the Jeffer-

son–Franklin concept of man and society seemed at least temporarily to gain a beachhead against the old pessimism. In 1848,
The Massachusetts Teacher rejected the Boston grammar school
masters. "The teacher," the magazine said, should "devise means
and adopt expedients to excite the curiosity and rouse the energies
of his pupils."

Later in the same year, the magazine was even more explicit in
its support of Mann's–rather than the masters'–view of pedagogy.
The teacher, it counseled, "should labor to inspire his pupils with
the love of knowledge." The burden was clearly shifting from
child to teacher.

The reforms were a reaction to schools which, in their stern
devotion to the idea of children as savages, had become increasingly more oppressive. An editorial believed to have been written
by Walt Whitman in *The Brooklyn Eagle* in the 1840s deplored
the fact that "our Brooklyn teachers" had not had an opportunity
to hear Horace Mann explain his views on education. Teachers
who can think of no other way to establish their authority than
by thrashing their pupils, Whitman said, may prove themselves
"fit perhaps for dog-whipper, or menagerie-tamer, but not for
the holy office of fashioning an immortal human soul."

"As things are," Whitman concluded, "the word school-teacher
is identified with a dozen unpleasant and ridiculous associations–
a sour face, a whip, hard knuckles snapped on tender heads, no
gentle, fatherly kindness, no inciting of young ambition in its
noble phases, none of the beautifiers of authority, but all that is
small, ludicrous, and in after life productive of indignaton."

But these glimmers of reform were several decades ahead of the
time when they would begin to make a larger impact on American
education. Even for public school crusaders, these attacks on the
rigid, authoritarian school were a sideshow. The main event was
still the effort to create a system of universal public education.
The first priority therefore was not so much the reform of
pedagogy as the politics of creating a structure which the reformers could control through their own professional cadre–the school
administrators.

This was not an easy task. The existing decentralization of the
schools pleased many of those in the seats of political power. It

enabled lay school boards not only to tell teachers and principals exactly how to run the schools, but also to manipulate great numbers of desirable jobs and contracts for buildings, equipment, and supplies. Along with political power, this arrangement opened the doors to graft and favoritism.

In some of its worst manifestations, the system was a morass of corruption. A San Francisco school director, quoted in *The Atlantic Monthly* near the end of the nineteenth century, said bluntly that as a native of the city, with many friends who wanted jobs, he merely followed the tradition under which "each director appoints his own friends and relatives, and their names are never questioned by the elementary committee, nor by the full board. . . . That is a courtesy which is extended by every director to each of his fellow directors,—the minority, of course, excepted."

In the worst instances of political domination, as under the heavy hand of Boss Tweed in New York and other politicians like him, corruption went far beyond patronage. Textbooks which offended the bosses were blacklisted. Teachers who valued their jobs were on guard not to teach anything that might cause pupils to question the existing Establishment.

Teachers were selected without regard for their professional qualifications; they were kept in their jobs regardless of their performance as long as they pleased their patrons—or as long as their patrons remained in office. A change in party in power meant dismissal, first, of the top echelon of the school administration and, more gradually, of teachers who had been sponsored by the former bosses. This was less a matter of malice than of the simple political need to pay off loyal supporters. If there were no vacancies, they had to be created.

The cities' ward politics, controlled by bosses, were not created by a political conspiracy; they were the answer to social and economic conditions with which the government of the day had not begun to cope. Great masses of new city dwellers were poor and ignorant, often unable to speak English and to demand the rights which laws theoretically granted them. In the absence of a nonpolitical, trained, and supervised civil service, these foundering millions had no place to turn but to their slightly more sophisticated neighbors who had already learned the ropes. And those ropes led to political bosses, or rather their representatives in the wards and on the blocks.

Corrupt as they were, these representatives filled a vacuum, and, although the supplicants were used for political purposes they usually failed to understand, they were nevertheless provided with services without which they could not have survived. Despite its sleaziness, the system may also have brought into the schools of the turbulent cities a substantial number of teachers who, though lacking in professional skills, were able to establish greater rapport with poor and "foreign" children than such unbending adherents to the old verities as the Boston grammar school masters. Under the circumstances, a little warmth and understanding probably went a long way.

In its haphazard, and often unethical, way the ward and spoils system may have helped accelerate the upward mobility of the immigrants. To rise in the business world, which was in the hands of the established classes, was difficult. A well-organized and carefully supervised civil service, despite its virtues of quality and integrity, nevertheless tends to be something of a closed club into which newcomers, particularly those with a different ethnic and religious past, find it difficult to enter. At a time when immigrants inundated cities, shortcuts provided by political bosses were not the total disaster which latter-day moralizers have pictured.

This system of patronage could not have been considered anything but a temporary expedient—indeed an aberration—if public education was to become professional and stable. Teachers were in constant fear that their employment might come to an end, for political rather than educational reasons. Morale was low.

Prevailing conditions made it easy to argue for change. In mid-nineteenth-century Boston, for example, the elementary school system consisted of 161 one-room, ungraded schools, each with one teacher. Village schools had simply been scattered, virtually unchanged, throughout the city. Those who moved on to grammar school were typically crowded into one large classroom along with some two hundred other students, presided over by one master and several assistants. Few students actually went to high school.

As late as 1892, sixteen of the twenty-eight cities of more than 100,000 population had school boards of twenty or more members, and most of them were elected by ward. Chicago at one time had seventy-nine subcommittees, which dealt with everything from teaching methods to ventilation.

Professional educators, who saw themselves as heirs of Horace Mann in his effort to make public education a cornerstone of a growing, democratic and increasingly urban nation, considered centralization and standardization as the only alternative. Demands for change had been gaining momentum. In 1842, George B. Emerson, co-author of *The School and the Schoolmaster,* had called the "unnecessary multiplication of school districts . . . a sore evil" that not only undermined educational quality but added greatly to the cost of running the schools. A more efficiently centralized approach, he said, would reduce the number of teachers needed, making it possible to increase their salaries "without adding to the burdens of the people."

Superintendents who led the reform movement in the second half of the century moved toward unity and uniformity with a vengeance. The catchphrase of the movement came to be "the one best way" of doing things—the professionally approved solution. The antidote to the chaotic political system seemed to the new managers to be the "scientific" approach to the schools—testing everything with the aim of arriving at the standard operating procedure. John Philbrick, who had been Boston's school superintendent from 1856 to 1878, put it in simple terms: "The best is the best everywhere. If America devised the best school desk, it must go to the ends of the civilized world." Once an answer had been found, whether to the way children should sit in front of their books or to the manner of instruction, the "rational" way was to impose the answer on every classroom. The efficiency of the factory guaranteed the best and most economically designed product: Why not therefore recommend the same royal road to learning? The superintendent of the Worcester schools wrote: "Organization becomes necessary in the crowded school in congested districts, just as hard pavements cover the city streets."

Attempts at standardization were not entirely new. The Lancasterian system of education had enjoyed a brief flurry of popularity during the early nineteenth century. Also called the monitorial system of instruction, its major feature was the collection of a large number of pupils—from two hundred to a thousand was considered possible—in one room. Pupils were seated in rows, and each row of about ten children was assigned to a bright boy who acted as monitor, instructing and disciplining those in his charge.

The youngest children were provided with a sand table on which they could practice writing letters with a stick shaped like a quill pen. Letters to be copied were displayed on boards called "alphabet boards," which were divided into three categories of letters—perpendicular, triangular, and circular. This system, under which one teacher aided by monitors could educate many pupils at small cost, was regarded by many as a panacea for educating the poor and ignorant. The schools were mechanical drill centers, and Lancaster's near-military discipline was thought to be of great benefit to disadvantaged children. By the 1840s, the plan's popularity had begun to wane. But the concept of order and standardization was far from dead.

In 1874, a group of seventy-four prominent educators signed a statement on "The Theory of Education in the United States" that was written largely by William T. Harris, superintendent of schools of St. Louis and subsequently a U.S. Commissioner of Education. "The commercial tone prevalent in the city," the statement said in a concise summary of the goals of the new, centralized thrust, "tends to develop in its schools quick, alert habits and readiness to combine with others in their tasks. Great stress is laid upon (1) punctuality, (2) regularity, (3) attention, and (4) silence, as habits that are necessary in an industrial and commercial civilization."

These priorities which, as subsequent accounts of the reform movement will indicate, were to come under repeated and concentrated fire from those who wanted education to be less rigid and oppressive have remained a powerful ingredient of the American school administrators' thinking. New York City high-school students in the late 1930s—years after reforms which opposed the regimented approach had washed over the schools—could still find themselves confronted by locked gates seconds after the official bell had rung in the morning, compelled to run an obstacle course of administrative sanctions (late passes and demerits) before they were allowed to take their seat in class.

The standardizers had their eyes on the industrial scene, and they were convinced that anything that was considered good for factories, corporations, and railroads was also good for the schools.

They spent a great deal of thought and effort on making the schools run on time.

For the moment at least—and it must be remembered that success was being measured against the chaos that had existed in the ward-dominated schools—educators gloried in the virtues of standardization. Portland, Oregon, had become the ideal system, and its superintendent described a school in which nobody was absent or late as "a grand sight to behold." Attendance records became a matter of towering importance, and statistics were computed to the third decimal point. Children who were a few minutes late for their first class sometimes spent the day hiding in terror of the consequences of their tardiness. Compulsory education became more than the kind of benevolent goal Mann had envisioned; it turned into an obsession.

In 1866, Massachusetts passed a law ordering truant children to be taken from their parents' custody and placed in reform schools. Such stern measures often collided head-on with popular sentiment, and in New York, where similar rules were in force, a truant officer rarely dared venture alone into the slums for fear of being assaulted by angry parents.

But in the main, "the one best way" provided guidelines. Teachers were trained to adhere to the same methods and the prescribed course of study. Children were promoted according to the same criteria. It was the establishment of a professional tradition that survived, often subconsciously, even after the American educators began to cite diversity and concern for individual differences as the main characteristics that distinguished the American school from its European counterpart. It was a tradition that subsequently gave birth to the "lesson plan"—the requirement that every teacher prepare, and file with the supervisor, a detailed plan for each class period in which he set down the aim of the lesson and the road by which that aim was to be attained. Even in the 1970s an editorial attack in *The New York Times* on the lesson plan in the New York City schools was still able to arouse principals to a massive counterattack.

The centralization movement, however, could not have succeeded without powerful support from forces outside the school administrators' rank. Much of that support came from the intellectual and industrial elite, and it included some prominent citizens, particularly in the universities, who subsequently had serious doubts about some methods which the new bureaucracy was to impose. Harvard's president Charles W. Eliot, for example, pointed to the importance of that elite's leadership qualities when he hailed the reduction of the number of Boston School Committee members shortly after the turn of the century. "We used to have 24 men, most of whom were not good," he said in 1908. "Now we have five men, all of whom are good."

Goodness in this "thin layer" of society's elite, as its members described it, meant not only that all five were Harvard men, though this was clearly considered an advantage; the group represented, in addition to school administrators and university scholars, business executives and prominent lawyers. Their concern, in contrast to the old ward politicians, was national rather than provincial. They were the men engaged in building the industrial nation. They were, as speeches to the conventions of the National Education Association of the day kept pointing out, nonpolitical and "neutral" because it was assumed that the interests of business, the professions, and the railroads were nonpolitical and "neutral."

The power and success of that elite were deemed so inseparably linked with the national interest that its policies were not considered politics—at least by them and their followers. In contrast to the separation and even occasional hostility between the schools and higher education that was to develop later, unversity presidents not only led and unified the reform coalition; they themselves had also actually served as school superintendents. Nicholas Murray Butler, who ran Columbia University with despotic power and was one of the king pins of the educational–industrial complex, is credited with wiping out the ward-dominated school leadership and bringing about New York's centralization in 1896. President Eliot and his successor Abbott Lawrence Lowell at Harvard, Daniel Coit Gilman at Johns Hopkins, William Rainey Harper at the University of Chicago, and David Starr Jordan at Stanford were all leaders of the school centralization movement.

An analysis of the Committee of One Hundred—it actually had

104 members—which pushed for centralization in New York showed that ninety-two of its ranks were listed in the Social Register, the overwhelming majority of them lawyers, bankers, leading merchants, and professional men. In a similar reform effort in Los Angeles, a prestigious civic organization picked one hundred leading citizens who, in turn, nominated "seven of the most prominent and busiest men of the city" to create a "nonpartisan" Board of Education.

In 1892, Harris who was now U.S. Commissioner of Education, described the ideal school board members as "business men chosen from the class of merchants, bankers, manufacturers, or professional men who have no personal ends to serve and no special cause to foster. . . ." These men stood in marked contrast to those reformers who were honest and well-meaning but prone to "an unbalanced judgment"—presumably of a more radical bent in matters of education. And finally, there was "a third class of men"—self-seeking or selfish, presumably the old ward politicians.

It is easy to look back on these reformers and characterize them glibly in postindustrial terms as aloof manipulators concerned only with the imposition of their own class-bound views and goals. Their vision of society and particularly their romanticized portrayal of industry, business, transportation, and communications is open to question. But it is unreasonable to expect any leadership group to tower above the dominant institutions and currents of their era. If they seemed calculating about the future mission of children who would be trained in the new standardized schools, they were no more so than the ward politicians who also expected the schools to serve society as they conceived it.

Besides, some of the elitists actually were reformers in a larger sense, beyond the search for schools that ran on time. They had looked at the existing schools and were horrified by the often scandalous conditions of neglect.

When Horace Mann started his crusade earlier in the century, classes often were held in dilapidated buildings. The walls were barren. One town official, asked to describe the condition of the schoolhouse, replied: "inconvenient benches, a clumsy desk, chair for the master, bare walls, no maps, no other apparatus, save school books. . . ." Many town and country folk, reports Jonathan Messerli, Horace Mann's biographer, "even tolerated the absence of that all-important convenience, the outhouse."

Little had changed in many urban schools which the reformers now tackled, except that crowding had been added to the desolation. Buildings were dark, musty, physically unsafe. Masses of pupils were crammed into classrooms where many had no benches. Although not standardized, the lessons, designed by incompetent teachers, were often just as rigid and irrelevant to the children's needs.

Reformers wanted to change all this, and if "the one best way" or the perfectly proportioned desk that would serve children across the nation today seem oppressive in their monotony or comical in their simplicity, they may have looked like the coming of utopia to many children and parents of their time.

More fundamental changes were taking place. It was during the last third of the nineteenth century that the high school became an addition to the public education structure. The extension of secondary education to include poor children represented a dramatic egalitarian advance, equaled only by the expansion of higher education opportunities after World War II.

Secondary education was not new in itself. The Boston Latin School had been founded in 1635, and replicas had sprung up soon thereafter in New Haven and Hartford. The Dutch had established such an institution in New Amsterdam, which survives as the private Collegiate School today. Through the efforts of Benjamin Franklin a high school, incorporated as an academy, had been established in Philadelphia in 1753 where tuition was remitted to those unable to pay. (The school later became the University of Pennsylvania.) The Phillips Academies, at Andover and Exeter, opened in 1780 and 1781 respectively.

But academies at best were part of an uncertain trend that showed no clear pattern. Many were established for profit. Their curriculum ranged from the rigidly classic and college preparatory to the teaching of embroidery and vocational subjects. They were governed by private boards, but often received public funds.

Urbanization brought with it a demand for a different arrangement. Increasing numbers of reformers believed that secondary schooling should not be limited to those who were planning to go to college. Local Latin schools prepared their students for higher education; but those who wanted to go into business or other nonacademic careers had to "go away" to an academy. Moreover, those who lived in the country also were at a disadvantage. In 1890, Eliot complained that three-fourths of the population had no direct access to secondary education.

In an article, "Public High School," attributed to Henry Barnard, important pedagogical reasons were cited why the high schools ought to form a separate part of the public education system. The presence of older students, the paper said, detracted from the proper teaching of the younger ones. On the other hand, high-school students' instruction required "patient application and habits of abstraction . . . time, discussion, and explanation, and the undivided attention of both pupils and teacher."

The author made a special point of the need to offer secondary education to boys and girls alike. "The great influence of the female sex, as daughters, sisters, wives, mothers, companions, and teachers, in determining the manners, morals, and intelligence of the whole community," he explained, "leaves no room to question the necessity of providing for the girls the best means of intellectual and moral culture."

Central to the theme, however, was the promise that the high school would "equalize the opportunities of a good education" and assure a mingling of children from all levels of wealth in each community. "The privileges of a good school will be brought within the reach of all classes of the community, and will actually be enjoyed by children of the same age from families of the most diverse circumstances as to wealth, education, and occupation." This emphasis on democratic integration would remain an important part of the American public school theme.

But the document also established other, more technical guidelines which were to point the way for public education in the future. It stressed the importance of the high schools in setting standards for elementary schools, a typically hierarchical approach that marks the entire system of academic quality control from graduate school down to kindergarten. And while the system occasionally came to seem both arrogant and confining, with each higher level assuming an air of superiority over those beneath, it was in general a more benevolent and less rigid form of determining standards than dictation by a central ministry of education. When, on occasion, domination from above became too severe, it was easier to fight back.

Although the first state high school law was enacted in Massachusetts in 1827, many towns refused for more than a quarter of a century to abide by it. As late as 1850, when seventy-six towns should have established high-school instruction, only forty-seven had actually done so.

In many other states, the high school consisted for decades of a room or two in the local elementary school. In Illinois about 85 percent of the state's 258 high schools were still housed in the elementary school building in 1896.

The Supreme Court of Michigan, on July 21, 1874, upheld the right of the Kalamazoo district to collect taxes for the support of a high school and for the salary of a nonteaching superintendent of schools, both of which had been challenged. This was particularly ironic in Michigan, since its state university had been established in 1837. In general, before this decision, the legal basis for establishing the high school had varied from state to state.

High schools were growing and the words of the decision seemed to reflect the public opinion of the time: "We supposed it had always been understood in this state that education, not merely in the rudiments, but in an enlarged sense, was regarded as an important practical advantage to be supplied at their option to rich and poor alike, and not as something pertaining merely to culture and accomplishment to be brought as such within the reach of those whose accumulated wealth enabled them to pay for it."

Some larger cities began to build high schools. Imposing palaces, often sponsored by private donors, added Gothic or Tudor splendor to the new enterprise. These grandiose structures not only reflected civic pride; they were clearly public education's challenge to private academies. They meant to carry the message that the public high schools, and their graduates, were second to none of the academies, regardless of their traditions and prestige.

After a slow start, high schools became part of the juggernaut that moved steadily toward the ideal of universal education. At the end of the nineteenth century, these schools enrolled only

11 percent of the population between the ages of fourteen and seventeen. By 1930, the total had swelled to 4.8 million or 51 percent of the age group, and by today secondary schooling has become virtually universal.

The establishment of the high school, however, became a powerful factor in the reform movement that had already centralized so much of the education enterprise. More even than the quality and practices of the elementary schools, the high school program was of intensive interest and concern to that coalition of reformers led by university presidents and school superintendents.

Because many high schools simply lacked the competence to prepare their students for college, Eliot charged in 1890, most of the institutions of higher learning were compelled to maintain preparatory departments—the remedial programs of their day—"against their will, and in disregard of the interests of the higher instruction."

Eliot called for more schools, and those schools would have to be "brought to common and higher standards." Another important step in the march toward the upgrading of the schools through standardization was about to be taken.

In 1892, the National Education Association appointed a group of educators, dominated by university professors and presidents and chaired by Eliot, to provide the schools with a blueprint for excellence. The Committee of Ten, as it came to be known, saw itself in the role of a collective philosopher-king as it mapped out subjects to be studied and the "best methods of instruction" for the most appropriate length of time, with results to be gauged by "the best methods of testing." The areas covered, in addition to the traditional college admissions subjects of Latin, Greek, and mathematics, were the "moderns"—English, foreign languages, natural history, physical science, geography, history, civil government, and political economy.

The committee concluded that all subjects should be taught in the same fashion to all students, regardless of whether they did or did not aim for a collegiate career; that students might, however, select some subjects and omit others (even Latin!) and still be admitted to college; and that, at least by implication, there was really no difference between education for college and education for "life."

The report, largely Eliot's work, was in many ways remarkably open-minded—despite its commitment to "the one best way"—and it therefore invited extensive debate and violent criticism. For while the insistence on the same instruction for all students may suggest conservatism, quite the opposite goal was in Eliot's mind. He intended to allow students to postpone as long as possible the choice that might determine the course of their future lives. This was a radical notion then, and it remains radical in many countries and cultures today. It is a powerful device in the battle against hereditary privilege or solidifying class lines.

Similarly, the elimination of fixed college-preparatory subject requirements was nothing short of revolutionary. The classicists understood this at once. They had controlled the college admissions gates. Now they saw their defenses crumbling.

And so the committee was attacked by both the conservatives and the progressives. Eliot stuck to his guns. His argument placed him squarely on the side of the democratization of the school and the universities. The early identification of children as "future peasants, mechanics, trades-people, merchants, and professional people" which was common practice in Europe seemed to him unacceptable in "a democratic society like ours." Like Mann and Franklin, he viewed the task of expanding education with great optimism. Open the doors, and students will rush in and seek to learn.

Perhaps Eliot's optimism was in part the consequence of having viewed education mainly from the august vantage point of Harvard. This may have rendered his expectations, and his estimate of the ultimate difficulties of mass education, unrealistic; but his motivation, at least in this crucial matter, was enthusiastically democratic rather than elitist. True, he had earlier often been critical of the low standards of the elementary schools and the lack of uniformity in high-school quality. But by 1900 he renewed the appeal for joy in learning that had marked Franklin and Mann as daring heretics. Allowing pupils the freedom of humane discipline, he told a meeting of superintendents, should set "the new and happy aim in modern education—joy and gladness in achievement."

What was remarkable at the time—and important to any understanding of the complex and controversial issues that continued to dominate much of the educational debate of the twentieth century—was this Harvard president's belief that there was no inherent contradiction in the establishment of quality controls and the open democratic society.

Eliot's overall view of society was that of the scientist looking at a rock formation. There are, he said, four layers—a very thin upper one that consists of the "managing, leading, guiding class," the "intellectual discoverers," and the organizers; an absolutely indispensable and much more numerous class of skilled workers and artisans; the almost equally indispensable, thick layer of the commercial class—the buyers, sellers and distributors; and finally the "thick fundamental" layer engaged in household work, agriculture, mining, forestry, etc.

While Eliot thus conceived a stratification of functions, based on ability, he considered it an overriding "democratic principle" that "the transition from one of these layers to another must be kept easy."

Some radical critics have typed Eliot as a reactionary guided by this view of a stratified society. They may have been further antagonized because, in the spirit of his day, he considered trade unions as "the most undemocratic agency" since, he thought, they hardened the layers.

But Eliot's criticism of schools, which seemed to him to obstruct social mobility, offers a more pertinent insight into this special breed of reformer, and into a trend of more general reform that was soon to shake the politics of American education.

To keep society fluid, he said, it is "a supremely important function for the teacher throughout the entire school system to discover, recognize, and give ample chance to the remarkable child." Yet it was precisely on that point that he found himself at odds with prevailing practices.

"There has been an actual repression of able children, a holding them back, an averaging of the 56 children that used to sit before a Boston teacher, a marking of time for the quick ones, that the slow ones may be brought up to the march," he wrote in 1909 in *School Review*. "That is the worst sin in education, in my opinion."

It was a sin that was increasingly being committed by those who were implementing the recent reforms. They had put an end to the chaos and corruption. They had replaced meddling school committees with elite boards that gave a free hand to professional educators who sought to turn education into a smoothly functioning machine. They had even found the funds to build the impressive structures in which this orderly, punctual process could take place. They created a system of academic bookkeeping so rational that it has survived to this day—the definition in 1909 of a "standard unit." (It was christened the "Carnegie unit" because the experts of the Carnegie Foundation for the Advancement of Teaching had come up with an all-purpose definition of a "unit" as a course offered for five classroom periods a week during the entire academic year.)

As is the case with most reforms and revolutions, the reformers' disciples tended to lack the masters' sense of proportion. Order became an obsession—the end itself rather than a means to a desirable end. The values of centralized schools became the values of the elite reformers and superintendents—paternalistic in outlook but often despotic in their determination to reshape the parts of the pluralistic society into a conforming sameness.

Central management, partly to enhance its own power but also to reinforce administrative efficiency, greatly increased the bureaucratic structure until Martin Mayer could write in 1961 in *The Schools* that the school system of New York City had more administrators than all of France.

Questions began to be asked about the impact of the new central bureaucracy. The process of centralization itself had not gone forward without some heated argument and stiff opposition. Local politicians were up in arms: it was their power and their patronage that were being cut down. They reacted in the true political campaign style by calling the reformers "anglomaniacs, aristocrats, and anti-Catholics" who wanted to impose Protestantism and stamp out such tools of ethnic identity as foreign languages. But teachers, too, were concerned. Many of them were opposed to the centralization of power in the hands of the superintendent. They saw it as a threat to their own rights.

As central administrations increasingly took over the urban schools, counterattacks increased in volume. One conservative opponent was B. A. Hinsdale, president of Hiram College and later superintendent of schools in Cleveland. Hinsdale conceded that the network of public education had been greatly increased and even that pupils were being taught "more things" than those of fifty or a hundred years ago. But he returned to the question which has been asked over and over again by conservatives throughout the history of American education: "The question is this: Whether we read and write, spell and cipher, better than our ancestors one, two, or three generations ago." It was, in other words, the perennial question of the schools' efficacy in teaching the Three R's—always the touchstone of conservative judgment of all educational success. And Hinsdale's answer was: No.

But Hinsdale's criticism, angrily expressed in 1877, was more than routine conservative carping. As an educator, he pointed to some flaws in the tightly administered, carefully measured, and routinely graded system which were soon also to come under fire from the opposite, progressive camp. The graded school, Hinsdale charged, is "exceedingly rigid and inelastic. Its tendency is to stretch all pupils on the same bedstead." The danger of such schools is "to sacrifice the brightest children to the dullards or to the mediocres," he said. Unless great care was taken to counteract that trend, Hinsdale believed, man's tendency to order his affairs in machinelike fashion would gain the upper hand, as it had in "machine politics, machine religion, and machine education."

Even among the centralizers themselves, some questions began to be asked. Harris, who had been one of the leaders of the reform drive and a very active member of the Committee of Ten, was too perceptive an educator not to sense that the merits were not all on one side. Although he firmly believed in the new graded schools with their "proper classification of pupils," he could not overlook some of the benefits derived by at least some students from the less highly organized village schools of an era that was rapidly passing into history.

Admiration for the precision of a school that moves efficiently like a machine, yes; but still the nostalgic aside that "in the ungraded [village] school a delightful individuality prevails, the pupil helping himself to knowledge . . . and coming and going pretty much as he pleases, with no subordination to rigid discipline."

The problem, however, as Harris and his fellow reformers saw it, was that society in a changing America demanded the sacrifice of some old pleasures. Railroads, great mills, and business houses demanded discipline and punctuality. The rural school, for all its joys of a more relaxed pace, simply "does not fit its pupils for an age of productive industry and emancipation from drudgery by means of machinery. But the city school performs this so well that it reminds some people unpleasantly of a machine."

If the National Education Association was quick to respond to business demands for inclusion into the curriculum of those subjects which business leadership thought useful, it could point to a tradition Franklin had tried to establish as a counterweight to the ephemeral classical teachings of the old elitist school; but the N.E.A. went beyond such pragmatism to support the indoctrination of students in the orthodox economies of laissez-faire capitalism.

Social reformers and Populists were openly attacked by school administrators at their annual meetings. One delegate to such a meeting said in 1885 that "the high school education detects and exposes the fallacies of socialism; the poor learn that they have an interest in respecting the property of the rich. . . ."

Whatever one might think of such political concepts, they came with ill grace from the leaders of a movement that, in its victorious battle against ward politicians, had made so much of the need to take politics out of the schools and the schools out of politics.

For the moment, however, the gathering storm of criticism remained educational rather than political. In 1892, for example, Joseph Mayer Rice, a pediatrician who had taken a careful look at educational developments in Germany, undertook a survey of schools in thirty-six American cities. He was shocked by what the reforms had wrought.

A principal in New York told Rice that children enter school with vocabularies and thoughts so limited as to be "worthless." The school's mission was to provide children with "ready-made thoughts" couched in an equally "ready-made vocabulary." Moreover, while reciting, children should not move their heads since the only proper focus for their eyes was "the teacher in front of them."

In other cities, Rice found the same adherence to the concept of silence, passivity, and unquestioning subservience by teachers as well as pupils to the Bible of the new school, the syllabus. Rice recalled hearing a teacher, who had lined students up at the edge of a floorboard during recitation, tell the docile class: "How can you learn anything with your knees and toes out of order?"

Whether or not the new generation of muckrakers exaggerated their findings and generalized on the basis of the most horrible examples, the "order and discipline" reforms of centralization were in fact turning sour. Examinations became tools of torture, administered to all students at precisely the same time.

Some who had stood in the forefront of the original reforms were alarmed. When Eliot was told by a school administrator that there was no need to treat pupils as individuals, he was shaken. He realized that these interpreters of a movement intended to improve the quality of instruction wanted students "to move together like soldiers on parade."

It was time for change. Reformers had pushed public education a long way, opening the road to universal schooling, establishing the high school as what was then considered "the people's college" but was in reality the transition toward higher education in real colleges for great masses of young Americans. Reformers, also, had broken the stranglehold of the classicists and, by introducing the "modern" subjects, created a link between school and life in the nineteenth century. They had imposed quality controls on the schools, while at the same time gaining the support of those who were able to provide the funds for what was to be the start of continuing growth and expansion.

In the process of this forward march of "democratizing" the schools, reformers had become entrapped by their own enthusiasm and by their patrons' rather one-sided view of the new industrial world and its values. They had become, in the true sense of the word, good soldiers of their time, but, like so many good soldiers, they were marching to an obsolescent tune.

New pressures had been added. Schools were asked not merely to inculcate habits which the industrial and mercantile urban society needed for production; they were urged to offer training for the trades and vocations which had traditionally been provided by way of apprenticeship, and paid for by the business interests rather than by the schools.

Calvin M. Woodward, a Harvard-trained mathematician, during the 1870s launched a campaign to persuade the public that the schools were out of tune with a changing society—as they persisted in training gentlemen rather than men fitted for work.

Woodward was not suggesting narrow vocational training for a specific trade. He wanted manual training to be an equal partner in the broad, general curriculum for all students, and as a prototype he helped found the Manual Training School of Washington University (St. Louis), a three-year secondary school with a program divided equally between mental and manual instruction. In addition to the regular studies of mathematics, science, art, languages, history, and literature, students became proficient in carpentry, iron work, soldering, and so forth. The goal was not to teach what educators later called marketable skills, but to imbue them with an understanding of manual labor as a link to the real world of work.

With a phrase that was to become the slogan for a subsequent educational revolution—the progressive movement that called for the education of "the whole child"—Woodward told educators to "put the whole boy in school" and inculcate in him a sense of overall usefulness. Youths, given an understanding of more than the attributes of academicians and gentlemen, would thus be able to be realistic and mature in ultimately selecting their careers.

Traditionalists—including most of the public school leaders and the N.E.A.—considered the plan a heresy that would undermine the quality and purpose of the public schools. Schools, said one spokesman for the profession, should teach youngsters "how to get information from books." "There is no information stored up in the plow," he sneered.

The debate droned on into the 1880s, but it soon became apparent that Woodward was easily gaining the upper hand. Manual training schools began to proliferate, particularly in the big cities. Moreover, many high schools introduced a new subject named homemaking.

Woodward soon lost control over his creation. Supporters of the new movement were, as might have been expected, businessmen less interested in the improvement of liberal education than in the highly profitable opportunity to let the schools take over vocational training at a time when unions were beginning to impose bothersome rules on the management of apprenticeships.

Many students, too, saw new subjects as a shortcut to better jobs, and they turned away from academic studies, thus scuttling the fusion of intellect and labor. In the end, Woodward, perhaps by then more interested in the statistics of his success than in his original reform plan, appears to have sold out to the commercial interests. "By multiplying manual training schools," he proclaimed, "we solve the problems of training all the mechanics our country needs"—the very goal he had so explicitly excluded from his earlier blueprint.

The die was cast for a course that was never to be reversed and ultimately had the effect of turning vocational education into a separate stream of public schooling, usually with lesser status. By 1910, the National Association of Manufacturers and the American Federation of Labor—in a show of unity that should have aroused suspicion—joined forces in lobbying for Federal support of such schooling. In 1917, the pressure increased. President Wilson linked such support directly with the nation's war effort. The Smith-Hughes Act was passed, providing substantial aid to agricultural, trade, and industrial subjects, along with home economics, the new name for homemaking.

The very dangers Woodward had originally warned against soon began to undermine this intensely political reform. Shortly after World War I, only a few years after the act was passed, Paul Douglas (later to become a senator) found in an extensive survey of its effect that the education it provided had become obsolete—outpaced by the rapidly changing technology.

It was not until the early 1970s that another governmental effort was launched by the Administration of Richard M. Nixon to revive some of the original goals of Woodward's campaign. Now advertised as "career education," United States Education Commissioner Sidney P. Marland, Jr., mounted a major drive to gain support for such training, beginning in the lower grades, in order to give children a better insight into the various vocations, while at the same time providing them with some training. Against the experience of history, the recommendations had tough sledding. Although Marland vehemently denied that the proposals were another effort to place children on an early track toward low-prestige jobs, too many educators remembered Woodward's similar protestations.

Joseph Mayer Rice, the muckraker, had recognized much that was wrong with the schools at the height of the nineteenth century's bureaucratic reforms. He had heard a teacher in Chicago, during a drill, shout at students: "Don't stop to think, tell me what you know!" Several decades later, at the private Deerfield Academy in Massachusetts, Helen Boyden, the wife of the headmaster and a teacher of mathematics, seeing a student struggling with an equation on the blackboard, said to him: "When are you going to stop trying to remember and start trying to think?"

Between those two diagonally opposed admonitions, an educational revolution had taken place.

But revolutionary changes in education were not likely to be made without the prodding from a changing society. Progressive reforms everywhere—in cities and on farms—challenged the old laissez-faire capitalism. Hard questions were being asked whether everything that was good for the establishment in industry, in business and on the farms was ipso facto good for the general welfare. Between the extremes of the autocratic paternalism in the hands of that "thin layer" of business-minded leaders and the totalitarian revolutionaries of the socialist left, there was an American movement of democratic progressives who believed that changes for the better were possible without riding roughshod over the masses.

Rice, who had seen so much that he thought wrong and even scandalous, had also recognized the dark cloud's silver lining. He had watched teachers who devoted their lives to bringing new hope to poor children; teachers who understood the problems of the immigrants and who were trying to make the abstract and forbidding lessons more humane, concrete, and meaningful. He had seen children learn, not by rote, but by establishing the connection between easily understood and familiar daily activities and the process of learning—even learning the Three R's.

Predictably, much professional comment on Rice's criticism and on his call for a new and progressive approach was hostile. The magazine *School* attacked him as an enemy of the public schools who was not to be taken seriously, since he lacked class-room experience and had gained most of his educational knowledge abroad.

Effective change would not have been feasible without some changes in top-level thinking. Eliot and a few other outstanding leaders had recognized the importance of responding to individual differences among children, but the public school enterprise was still dominated by men whose ideology was passed down from the stern Puritan tradition. If they did not actually think of children as basically evil and in need of rescue through hard labor—and this was in fact how they perceived immigrant children from the "wrong" part of the world—these educators still thought of childhood as shapeless neutral clay to be molded by pedagogues.

Horace Mann had been aware of the need to reconcile the apparently conflicting goals of teaching children and inculcating them with the old virtues, while at the same time giving them greater freedom. But in the absence of any new, psychological answers Mann had briefly toyed with a contemporary pseudo-psychological fad, phrenology. It was widely touted as a science based on a picture of the human mind consisting of thirty-seven separate departments or faculties—some evil and others benevolent. Although clearly without basis in scientific fact, it was a useful device to relate teaching and human behavior.

Reformers who followed were more fortunate. Educational experimenters and psychologists by then had developed the beginnings of more rational approaches. Edward Thorndike, an early professor of educational psychology at Teachers College, had engaged in pioneering research, particularly in the methods he devised to measure learning ability.

Thorndike's direct observations constituted an assault on the existing preconceived views of human behavior: the earlier view of man as essentially evil and thus in need of taming and Rousseau's romantic vision of the noble savage who must be left alone lest his goodness be stunted. Based on his research, Thorndike insisted instead that each child brings with him a great variety of "original tendencies," both good and bad, which need to be recognized by those who train and educate. It then would be largely a matter of presenting things in a way to which the child will react in predictable fashion without necessarily understanding his own actions, like an animal to be trained.

This new interpretation of man and education placed much of the burden on school and teacher in precisely the way that had so outraged the masters of Boston's grammar school. "We ought to make an effort . . . to omit the useless and antiquated and get to the best and most useful as soon as possible," Thorndike wrote in *Animal Intelligence.* "We ought to change what *is* to what *ought to be,* as far as we can." In nature, this was evolution; in human affairs, such as education, it was continuing progress and reform. Thorndike had essentially unlimited faith in the capacity of "scientific" experts to solve problems and put an end to disputes, and this faith potentially put great—probably excessive—new powers in the hands of the educational bureaucracy.

John Dewey was less concerned with scientific theories than with the political and social development of society. He understood and mourned the loss of the self-educating force that had shaped people's lives in the farming and pioneering days. Only a generation or two ago, the household had been the center of the world, for child and industry, where most of the goods needed and consumed were also manufactured.

Participation had been the teacher then. Discipline and character were the by-products of this "training in habits" which gave the child a feeling of usefulness. A "sense of reality" was acquired "through first-hand contact with actualities," Dewey said, and "no number of object-lessons, got up *as* object-lessons for the sake of giving information," can fully substitute for the practice of learning from the tasks that have to be done—not for the school but for life.

But, Dewey said, "it is useless to bemoan the departure of the good old days of children's modesty, reverence, and implicit obedience, if we expect merely by bemoaning and exhortation to bring them back." If the conditions of life have changed, then the educational response must also change.

Dewey tried to recapture some of Woodward's original faith in the manual arts, not as vocational training but to broaden the child's understanding of the world around him and of the productive processes that have kept society shod, fed, and sheltered. But Dewey went far beyond those goals. He wanted the school to be "a genuine form of active community life, instead of a place apart in which to learn lessons."

This view of the school clashed head-on with the traditional belief in discipline. Dewey realized that, if the school is to transmit a certain set of lessons to a certain number of children, the only way to accomplish the task is by imposing a fixed set of rules —discipline—and enforce them strictly. But if learning is to grow out of a spirit of community, with every child aware of the goals he is learning to set for himself, then discipline must grow out of the entire community enterprise.

Dewey's vision of the school as an "embryonic society" was more than a challenge to the old pedagogy; it was a daring break with the almost universally accepted view of the school as the generator of industrial and technological society. Under the industrial concept, Dewey said, the child shared in the work, not for the sake of sharing, but for the sake of the product. In the new progressive school, he insisted, the aim must not be the economic value of the product, but the development of the child's social power and insight.

It was inevitable that Dewey would become the center of heated political as well as educational controversy. His theories, constituted a deliberate challenge to conservative institutions. School reform to him did not mean an occasional updating of obsolescent practices but dedication to continual change—not to adjust to society but to improve it. His view of America was that of an "intentionally progressive" society.

Dewey, more than any other educational philosopher, had deep roots in the American tradition. He not only believed that democracy needed a literate and knowing electorate; he considered the school the one institution through which democracy could be continually strengthened and extended. Franklin had written that school could be "delightful." Dewey saw the schools devoted to the creation of a new society "more worthy, lovely, and harmonious."

In Dewey's schools there was no room for rote learning, drill, or sterile discipline which bureaucratic administrators of the previous reform movement had built into the process of education. In planning a curriculum, he said, essentials must come first, refinements second.

Inevitably, this approach created problems and raised questions. What are the essentials? Dewey answered: "The things which are socially most fundamental, that is, which have to do with the experience in which the widest groups share." A democracy, he believed, cannot tolerate a division under which some children are given a narrow, utilitarian education, while others benefit from broadly liberal schooling. He called for a universal education that would allow people to grow and live harmoniously with one another.

Yet, the definition remains evasive. Agreement as to what is "socially most fundamental" or which experiences are shared by the widest groups is difficult to reach, and it was never more difficult than in Dewey's day. Businessmen and union leaders wanted vocational training, urban reformers asked for hygiene and domestic science, superpatriots demanded instant Americanization, and traditionalists urged the retention of the classical subjects.

The conflict that continued to rage over Dewey was rendered more irreconcilable in part by his most serious flaw—his inability to express himself simply and clearly. Yet, the main thread that runs through everything Dewey did and wrote is difficult to miss: it is experimentation, experience, discovery, the inner discipline that comes from active participation in an interesting enterprise rather than external discipline imposed by higher authority.

Unfortunately, not many of Dewey's disciples and mass followers paid attention to the master's devotion to both continuum and order. They cheered the messages of liberation, but overlooked Dewey's basic assumption that scholarship and order are the bedrock from which the liberation must proceed. His own critical discussion of education and society delves deep into Plato, Aristotle, Locke, Rousseau, Kant, Hegel, and Froebel.

Dewey himself became increasingly aware of the dangers inherent in the misrepresentation of his goals by friend and foe alike. He recognized the tendency common to all reformers, to turn successful experimentation into sterile, standard operating procedure. "There is a difference," he warned in 1899, "between working out and testing a new truth, or a new method, and applying it on a wide scale, making it available for the mass of men, making it commercial."

In Los Angeles, in 1913, a school superintendent who thought himself liberated by the master, was able to say: "The principal business of the child is to play and to grow—not to read, write, spell and cipher. These are of incidental importance."

Such misinterpretations made Dewey sigh that "it may perhaps be said that to train teachers in the right principles the wrong way is an improvement over teacher-training that is wrong in both respects. But it is not much of an improvement."

"Anybody can notice today," said Dewey in 1929, "that the effect of an original and powerful teacher is not all to the good. Those influenced by him often show a one-sided interest; they tend to form schools, and to become impervious to other problems and truths; they incline to swear by the words of their master and to go on repeating his thoughts after him, and often without the spirit and insight which originally made them significant."

His conservative and right-wing opponents have blamed Dewey for bringing about what they considered an un-American social revolution. They saw—and still see—concepts that permit the child to explore life in a lifelike school as "permissiveness," the conservatives' code word for progressive education's subversion of the American way of life. And while it sometimes may seem difficult to comprehend the venom with which the rightwing opposition has reviled Dewey—as incidentally did the Stalinist theorists in Russia who even purged his books from the university libraries—one must bear in mind the deep suspicion with which these quarters have always regarded government by the people. In 1928, for example, the official U.S. Army *Training Manual* still defined democracy as "a government of the masses" which "results in mobocracy" and where "attitude toward property is communistic" and the ultimate outcome is "demagogism, license, agitation, discontent, anarchy."

Clearly, such views were destined to clash with Dewey's faith which was derived from the spirit of the Bill of Rights and the heritage of Jefferson, Franklin, and Mann. Democracy to him was not mobocracy but the theory based on "faith in the capacity of the intelligence of the common man to respond with common sense to the free play of facts and ideas which are secured by effective guarantees of free inquiry, free assembly, free communications."

Whatever the political opposition would make of it, Dewey remained the committed heir to that confident, optimistic American strain that unabashedly equated educational expansion with the extension of popular government. Implicit in this faith is the belief that the children must be encouraged to do more than emulate their parents' success, just as society must do more than be satisfied with the maintenance of the old order.

For the educational bureaucracy, doing better also involved organizational questions of being more efficient. Though no longer opposed to progressive pedagogy, professional leadership was not ready to abandon the industrial pattern of successful management. In 1888, Eliot had addressed the nation's superintendents on the topic "Can School Programs Be Shortened and Enriched?" The question of productivity, which was once again to move into the forefront of the reform debate some seventy years later, preoccupied the urban educational establishment at the very time when Dewey addressed himself to his great task of pedagogical liberation.

In 1911, the National Education Association appointed a Committee on Economy and Time in Education and charged it with the elimination of waste from the operation of the public schools. Once again, the search was on for the "one best way"—a way to make certain habits, skills, ideals, and wisdoms "the common property of all," so that each could be "an efficient member of a progressive democratic society." But in contrast to Eliot's original Committee of Ten, which was dominated by university leaders like himself, the new efforts were taken in hand by that newly developed professional hierarchy, the professors of education and superintendents of schools. Academic scholars sat this one out. They were gradually to move toward a growing separatism between the public schools and the university scholars that eventually tore school and campus apart until, after a wave of recriminations and criticism, university scholars, in the 1950s, once again took an active part in the public school reform movement.

For the moment, however, it was the public school hierarchy

that reassessed the success of the enterprise which political reformers had so recently reorganized through centralization and which
the educational reformer, and particularly Dewey, tried to lead
toward a less rigid, future. But while Dewey had tried to leave
the school's part of a continually self-renewing society as open-
ended as possible, the new committee wanted to set down specific
"minimum essentials" to serve society's needs.

The new approach must have seemed intensely practical or
exceedingly narrow, depending on one's expectations of society
and education. The committee's report on arithmetic in 1918,
for example, worked out a syllabus by extracting skills needed in
dealing with a standard cookbook, a factory payroll, newspaper
advertisements, and a hardware catalogue. The committee prided
itself in having isolated the "concrete stuff of which arise the
arithmetical problems of housewives, wage earners, consumers,
and retail hardware dealers." Other disciplines were subjected to
similar treatment. And, although these efforts were carried forward under the progressive, experiential ("learning by doing")
banner of relevancy, the inevitable effect was conservative—freez-
ing the activities and goals of school and society into the mold of
the existing world of home and commerce.

It was not until 1961 that the N.E.A. called a full-scale retreat
from such blatant anti-intellectualism. In a statement on the
"central purpose of American education," it reaffirmed the "rational powers" of each citizen and stressed "the processes of
recalling and imagining, classifying and generalizing, comparing
and evaluation, analyzing and synthesizing, and deducing and
inferring." It was to take the educational establishment almost
seventy years to find its way back to Eliot's views of man and
society.

For the moment, however, the impact of the establishment's
misreading of Dewey was essentially anti-intellectual. Under the
mantle of the new pedagogical "science," the one best "scientific"
way was prescribed by the committee functionaries. "Both fore-
arms should rest on the desk for approximately three quarters of
their length," said the official handwriting prescription.

It was a deliberate attempt to impose administrator-approved
solutions on the teachers. Borrowing increasingly from the professional image of the engineer (scientist) rather than of the artist,

or even the parent, the new efficiency equated the teacher's professionalism with a capacity to apply those approved solutions.

The new reformers had been aroused by the long-entrenched deficiencies of an education that ignored the needs and interests of modern society. At the turn of the century, for example, more than half of all high school students studied Latin, while only half that number studied any modern foreign language. The N.E.A., under the new banner of "social efficiency," was determined to break with the past. In 1918, it issued the "Cardinal Principles of Secondary Education." History and the social sciences (which had seemed so important to Dewey) were replaced by the new discipline of social studies—defined as an investigation of the "social efforts to improve mankind."

Such traditional subjects as algebra came under strong attack. One educator, typical of the mood of the day, charged in a teachers' publication that algebra had "injured the mind, destroyed the health, and wrecked the lives of thousands of children."

In an early draft of the principles, the Three R's were entirely absent, but in the end lip service was paid to them under the rubric "Command of Fundamental Processes."

Dewey himself was disturbed by such extremes. He complained that he discerned something "hard and metallic" in the new efficiency of social engineering. But reform administrators, who thought of themselves as the heirs of his progressive leadership, criticized Dewey for being too individualistic. Smooth management of the schools as well as of society, they warned, would not be made easier by too much latitude for individual goals and differences. The individual, in the view from the superintendent's office, was best served, not by his own peculiarities, but by "the one best way."

Many of those who supported the new wave were motivated not by anti-intellectualism but by an intensely practical response to changing conditions. Mass education had become a reality. Universality of secondary education was rapidly approaching. Horace Mann's dreams seemed to be coming true. Entirely apart from any reformist theorizing, it became evident that standards—whatever their merits and validity—which had served the schools when only a select few attended, simply could not be maintained.

In retrospect, the pseudoscientific enthusiasm of the reformers sounds foolish, largely because it represents the administrators' chronic mania for giving necessity the appearance of high-minded principle and innovative reform. Changes that were brought about, with their deliberate broadening and standardization of the curriculum at the expense of depth and individuality, were. tailor-made to fit the educational logistics of the day.

What weakened, and eventually destroyed, the progressive reform movements was an equal mixture of pedagogical muddle-headedness and lack of political sophistication. The political naivete and arrogance that undermined the reform movement were born of that isolation which educators imposed on themselves through their retreat into a professionalism that excluded the lay world. While progressive politics actually gained in popularity and power, and during the Depression eventually made their way into the triumphant political movement of the New Deal, the Progressive Education Association engaged in dreams of remaking society but avoided contact with real political forces.

Even in the beginning of the movement, when William Wirt had made his plan in the steel town of Gary, Indiana, under the banner of progressive action, its pioneers failed to understand the politics of the day. The Gary Plan tried to make the schools truly an "embryonic community," with libraries, swimming pools, machine shops, neighborhood centers, etc., in operation all day and all year, with different "platoons" using the facilities at different times. Its advocates gloried in instant popular acclaim, but failed to realize that they were being crushed by the embrace of those who saw the program as a way to spend less money. The ultimate failure of the plan was the result of the alliance of the penny-pinchers with those teachers who simply went through the motions of another dimly understood experiment.

In 1932, when George Counts, a Midwesterner who had been one of the leading theorists of the progressive movement, called on teachers to "dare" to "build a new social order," Dewey warned that political realities made it impossible for schools to determine the course of political, intellectual, and moral change.

The Counts "dare" was even more audacious when compared to the attitudes of those urban reformers who, armed with Mann's doctrine of universal education, had set out to find the "one best way" to run schools like, and for the benefit of, factories. They, too, wanted to take the schools out of the hands of the upper-class elite. But they wanted to do so only because they felt the power belonged to the professional administrators who, if left to their own devices, were perfectly satisfied to serve the elite's political purposes and to reinforce the prevailing political doctrine.

The activist leaders of the Progressive Education Association (P.E.A.) wanted to do nothing of the kind. On the contrary, they felt that America had changed radically and that the old forms of capitalism were out of tune with the needs of society. Teachers, said Counts in a dramatic appeal, "owe nothing to any privileged class except to strip it of its privileges." The new battle was to be fought on two fronts—against "the ignorance of the masses and the malevolence of the privileged."

The militant committee could not be faulted for its socio-economic analysis. The nation had faced depression and despair. The old laissez-faire capitalism was indeed bankrupt. But the schools were not then, and would never be, a suitable instrument to bring about political and economic change, although Dewey was quite right in complaining that they had too often been the tool of those who wanted to prevent such change. Schools, dependent as they then were and will probably always be on the support of the people's elected representatives, locally as well as nationally, could not hope to act successfully as a revolutionary force.

Even among their fellow educators, the radical element found little sympathy. This was not surprising because the impatient reformers never paid much attention to the political realities of the world in which the majority of teachers moved.

It was in the midtwenties that the country watched in fascination the trial of John T. Scopes, an obscure biology teacher in Tennessee, accused of violating a state law against teaching the Darwinian theory of evolution. The press gave intensive coverage to the event. Former Presidential candidate William Jennings Bryan upheld the Fundamentalist position; Clarence Darrow defended Scopes and academic freedom. Yet the nation's educational leadership seemed strangely detached, apparently unaware that the token penalty imposed on Scopes was, in fact, a signal that the forces of enlightenment were on the march. Scopes had scored more effectively against the rigidity of the old order than the educational progressives realized or cared to acknowledge.

The movement, which began with Dewey's perceptive efforts to create a new pedagogy, lost its way in a maze of ill-digested economics and politics. Its decline and eventual self-destruction left the schools once again without any philosophical compass. The nation at large had long been preoccupied with other concerns, first with depression and recovery, then with World War II. Toward the end of the war, the public school leadership felt compelled to post some new goals.

It was a fumbling effort. A commission of school administrators and professors of education put together a program on the Life Adjustment Education for Youth which represented another turning away from the college-preparatory functions. Its stated purpose was to "equip all American youth to live democratically with satisfaction to themselves and profit to society as home members, workers, and citizens."

The curriculum that emerged was as vague as the prescription itself. It salvaged much of the Progressives' "learning by doing," but it was clear that, rather than build a new world, the intent now was more modestly to fit children into the old. Thus, from its very beginning, the new approach aroused the hostility of those critics who held the schools responsible for the creation of a conformist organization man—one who easily adjusted to the status quo.

In fairness to the leaders of the life adjustment education movement, which included the United States Office of Education and most of the public school establishment, it should be acknowledged that the schools were in no position to do much more than use their very limited resources to serve a vast number of pupils. The war had not only made education low man on the totem pole of national priorities; it had stopped virtually all school construction, teacher training, and general pedagogical concern. Yet, within a few years after the war's end, the tide of war babies began to sweep into the elementary schools.

As after every major war, the air was awash with simplistic slogans. The nation's drift into the Cold War aroused fears and passions which soon turned to paranoia.

Schools were an easy target. They were desperately in need of funds just to cope with the problems of mass, but they were also intellectually vulnerable to attack. Their own past follies, though politically harmless, exposed them to the wrath of the right wing; at the same time their softness on intellectual rigor aroused the anger of many university scholars who might otherwise have stood in the forefront of the schools' defense against the anticommunist witch-hunters and book-burners.

Throughout much of the 1950s political reaction was running high. Professional anticommunists and excommunists created something close to national hysteria. Vigilante groups demanded a purge of textbooks, charging that existing texts were subversive. If a book mentioned George Washington fewer times than Franklin Roosevelt, it was considered communist-inspired. The political disease that became synonymous with the witch-hunting activities of the late Senator Joseph R. McCarthy seriously undermined the strength and independence of the public schools.

At the same time, the schools came under attack from those who felt that the post-Dewey progressives and the subsequent life adjustment advocates were a threat to the nation's intellectual stamina. In the long run, this was a more serious issue.

The most prolific of the intellectual critics was Arthur E. Bestor, a history professor at the University of Illinois, whose book, *Educational Wastelands: The Retreat from Learning in Our Public Schools,* published in 1953, became the Bible of the counterrevolution. Bestor charged that public schools had become so involved in activities that ought to be the concern of other agencies of society that they no longer had time for intellectual development. He warned that "intellectual training for some of the people, vocational training and life-adjustment for the rest, is the epitome of a class-structured educational philosophy."

Truly democratic education, Bestor said, in a judgment with which Jefferson might have agreed more readily than Franklin, differs from aristocratic education only in the number of persons with whom it deals, not in the values it seeks to impart. To let the ignorant—whether they be pupils or teachers—determine what is to be taught is tantamount to letting a medical patient determine his cure.

Bestor's argument was effective. He was making his case at a time when schools had indeed lost their sense of intellectual values. Even more important, Bestor was riding the crest of a conservative wave. People were afraid—of communism, of subversion, of the future. They were looking for a scapegoat. They had heard so many menacing reports about the schools that they found it easy to make common cause with the new conservative counterrevolution.

In actual fact, the impact of the progressive and life adjustment movements on many classrooms was much less dramatic than the opposition claimed. Paul Woodring, a psychologist and college professor, who had himself often been critical of the progressive movement's excesses, wrote in *Let's Talk Sense about Our Schools:* "The best thing about contemporary education is that a great many classroom teachers ignore the gobbledygook and the pedagoguese and go right ahead and do a sensible job of teaching."

While the profession reeled under the two-front attack from right-wing superpatriots and academic critics, a modern version of Eliot's "thin layer" of the concerned upper class rallied to public education's support. In 1949, the National Citizens Commission for the Public Schools was created to make the nation aware of the school crisis.

The commission carefully affected a neutral posture above the raging ideological battles, concentrating instead on the building of a new grass-roots support. During the seven years of the organization's activities, it was responsible for generating $8 million worth of free public school support newspaper advertising. By the time the commission folded its tent, it had helped in the creation of some 9,000 state and local public school support committees. Membership in the local Parent-Teacher Associations tripled, reaching approximately nine million. In even more tangible terms, school construction which in 1944 had lingered at $55 million reached the $2 billion mark in 1956.

During the same period, support for the public schools came from another quarter. The Ford Foundation and the Carnegie Corporation of New York, sensitive to the danger that the savage attack on public education might drive the school administrators into rigid defensiveness, allocated substantial amounts of money to a reform movement that was to be led by an elite coalition of education specialists within the foundations themselves and the avant-garde of public school educators. Ford's semi-autonomous Fund for the Advancement of Education deliberately exploited the existing spirit of criticism to urge school administrators to concentrate on the reform of educational techniques.

The foundation's appeal to the schools concentrated on new ways to improve educational productivity. It supported the first experiments in the use of semiskilled or paraprofessional support forces as teacher aides. It tried to persuade school administrators to hitch their stalled wagon to the rising star of radio, tape recordings, and television. It subsidized experiments in new approaches to the deployment of teachers, as in "teams" of teachers assuming responsibility for a group of children. It challenged the concept of the orderly arrangement of all children in fixed grades or age groups studying each subject for a fixed number of hours that had been the backbone of all "one best way" reforms. Without putting it that way, the fund borrowed once again from some of the informality of the old rural schoolhouse by reintroducing the mixed classroom, now known as the nongraded school.

The reformers' task was far from easy. They were themselves subject to criticism. Reactionary school critics have always considered foundations as the activist front of the liberal or socialist enemy; the public school establishment, with a complacency no longer supported by the realities of power, tended to lump together all its critics under the convenient all-purpose category of "enemies of the schools." It looked with suspicion and hostility on the new reformers, whom it considered meddlesome lay intruders. Moreover, it suspected that some of the proposed remedies—particularly television and teacher aides—might eventually be used less to improve education than to reduce the amount of money spent on professional salaries. Educators remembered, after all, how such earlier reforms as the Gary Plan had quickly been adopted by the cost-cutting forces.

In addition, teachers resented and feared the inevitable consequence of these new arrangements—the TV camera's probing eye, the teacher aide who is also a member of the lay community, the critical view of a colleague on the teaching team—which would put an end to the concept of the classroom as the teacher's castle. It was bad enough to have the witch-hunters loose on the outside without inviting a new army of potential critics, or critics' allies, into the sanctuary. The profession's generally conservative voice replied to proposed innovations with a demand for more money for more teachers, not for more gimmicks. One response to the threat from the outside was a dramatic acceleration in the teachers' unionization movement.

The reformers adamantly denied that they intended to replace the teacher. They warned that the profession's rejection of change could only shore up the power of the know-nothing opposition. Refusal to use the new technology as an ally, they warned, would not only result in the loss of children's allegiance but would eventually lead to a take-over by other agencies. This prediction was later borne out by the Pied Piper success of public television's creation of "Sesame Street."

Productivity and cost were, despite the reformers' disclaimers, serious issues to be faced. The dramatic increase in enrollments, together with substantial improvements in teachers' salaries, were to put a price-tag on universal education that would probably have been incomprehensible to the early proponents of mass education. Between 1950 and 1970, the elementary school enrollment increased from 20 million to 32.5 million; high school enrollment from just below 6 million to 13.3 million. In the same period, the number of public school teachers doubled to over two million, and teachers' salaries in that twenty-year period increased by approximately 100 percent, in dollars, though not quite as much in purchasing power. Education was a growth industry which reflected the expansion of the nation's population and economy.

Given the strains and stresses of the political inquisition, the intellectual criticism, and the inevitable growing pains of a dramatically enlarged enterprise, it was not surprising that the foundation-sponsored reform movement won few popularity contests within the education establishment.

Yet, the foundation reformers had shrewdly identified the coming phase in the politics of the schools' reform movement. The trend—a reaction to the post-Dewey excesses—was clearly back toward what was then often referred to as academic rigor. The problem was how to move the professional educators toward the acceptance of new goals, without making it appear as if they had surrendered to the very critics whom they had called "enemies of education."

Fortunately for the reformers, an entirely external *deus ex machina* came to the rescue. In 1957, the Soviet Union launched Sputnik, the first successful space rocket. In the past, educational reforms had often been given impetus by external sociopolitical factors—industrialization, urbanization, the Depression, etc.—but they had always been related to domestic needs and aspirations. It was a measure of the country's new role in international affairs that concern over competition abroad for the first time became a spur to educational reform.

Reformers maintained that insufficient attention to such disciplines as mathematics, science, and foreign languages had undermined American technological and scientific power. They bolstered their arguments by pointing to the substantial numbers of European émigré scientists who had performed key tasks in the earlier American atomic breakthrough.

Although the cause-and-effect arguments probably overplayed the relationship between the Soviet space triumph and the lack of educational rigor in the public schools, there was little question that the "hard" academic subjects had been neglected and, in some extreme instances, actually disparaged by those who considered any form of a child's interests and self-expression equal in personal and pedagogical value to any other. The rift between the arts and science faculties and the schools of education had reduced the number of teachers who were as well trained in the disciplines as in educational methodology.

Those who had for years been trying unsuccessfully to persuade Congress that public education could no longer function effectively without federal subsidy skillfully exploited the new mood of the country. Under the prodding of a comparatively conservative President, Dwight D. Eisenhower, the first major Federal education aid bill—other than support for vocational education—was enacted. The National Defense Education Act of 1958 provided funds for the improvement of science, mathematics, and foreign language teaching. It was subsequently broadened to include similar support for the humanities, thus indicating that the reformers were interested in more than Soviet-American competition in space.

At Teachers College, once the pulpit of the progressives, a new wind was blowing. Dr. John H. Fischer, who had just assumed the institution's presidency, called for "a vigorous" academic program. "Schools are established by adults to give young people the advantage of systematic teaching and learning," he said.

Although the new direction seemed unmistakable, who would assume the leadership role? Half a century earlier, the challenge had been answered by Harvard's President Eliot. Now another Harvard president responded to the challenge. James Bryant Conant, a man who believed fervently in the importance of public education, had already established his reputation as a troubleshooter in national crises.

Conant was also a pragmatist with a shrewd understanding of the American psyche and the political process. In 1959, he had observed in *The Child, the Parent, and the State* that few laymen had been fully aware of the revolutionary transformations that had taken place in the American schools since the 1930s. It was not until after the end of World War II, he continued, that large numbers of Americans woke up to the extent of the changes. "And as is often the case with those suddenly awakened from a deep sleep," Conant wrote, "the first exclamations were not too closely related to the actual situation."

What Conant had in mind, of course, was the strident criticism, the witch-hunting, the panic over Sputnik, and the host of other complaints. But the hysteria of the recently awakened, aghast at finding themselves in so strange a situation, did not persuade Conant, as it had so many of the educational establishment, that there was no substance to the complaints. Determined to steer a middle course acceptable to the majority of parents and teachers, he ignored both the charges that education had become a wasteland and claims that schools were better than ever and needed only to be given more money to solve all their remaining problems. Stripping his reform efforts of all the ideological baggage that had so often weighed down both the conservative and the progressive forces, he insisted that the all-important concept of education was "the notion of educating a man to live in any particular time or place."

Schools would have to offer comprehensive programs, aimed at satisfying those who were preparing for college as well as those who needed "marketable skills" with which to earn a living upon graduation. Social democracy, which seemed to Conant the modern mantle of America's republican heritage, called for a "low visibility" of class divisions that would best be achieved by having young people from a wide variety of backgrounds and with greatly different talents mingle within the same school.

Conant conceded, however, that college professors were right in charging that the schools, by trying to satisfy the many, had in fact ignored the needs and the rights of the few—the academically talented, or the upper fifteen to twenty percent in ability.

To correct what had become a critical situation, Conant in 1959 presented the country with a slim volume, *The American High School Today,* which was in fact a do-it-yourself checklist of school improvement and which was soon to become a best-seller as well as the agenda for thousands of school board meetings. Included in the book's "21 points" was a detailed curriculum statement of the minimum number of years for which the academically talented should be required to study the "hard" subjects, such as mathematics, science, foreign languages, history, etc.

With the zeal of the missionary and the pragmatism of a campaigning politician, Conant took to the road to get his comprehensive high-school plan adopted. From coast to coast, he addressed school boards, businessmen's meetings, select luncheons of community leaders, mass meetings of concerned citizens, conventions and rallies of teachers and school administrators. With limitless patience, he answered questions and parried attacks. With incredible stamina, he suffered the lukewarm chicken dinners and watery fruit cocktails in aluminum cups—to no other end than to save American public education from the crossfire that threatened it from without and the academic decline that had eroded it from within.

Given the obstacles of public ignorance and professional arrogance, the Conant crusade chalked up significant victories. Academic rigor once again became respectable in many schools. Encouraged by such a change of mood, colleges again dared to require mastery of the "hard" subjects for admission. Perhaps most important, increasing numbers of university scholars, inspired by the Conant example, worked with the schools instead of merely criticizing them. Such notables as Dr. Jerrold Zacharias, a leading physicist, and Dr. Bentley Glass, an eminent biologist, stepped down from the ivory tower to devise and test new programs of instruction.

Schools began to offer science courses which actually emulated the process of discovery engaged in by scientists themselves. On the level of scholarship—instead of merely on that of the clerk at the cash register or the consumer and the family budget—schools were discovering a higher form of "learning by doing." Dewey would have approved—and so could the professors of education, as well as their colleagues in the liberal arts colleges and the graduate departments.

Only the heirs of the Progressive Education Association, who had seen the schools as a tool with which to bring about revolutionary changes in American society, viewed Conant's efforts to shore up the moderate liberalism of social democracy as reactionary.

Even in strictly academic terms, however, the Conant reforms contained strongly conservative strains. Not unlike Eliot's Committee of Ten in 1893, Conant appeared convinced that a successful democracy requires a constant admixture of the open intermingling of children from all classes in a comprehensive high school with the academic rigor of those traditional subjects crucial to the maintenance of high standards. And it was Conant who, only a few years later, in his book *Slums and Suburbs,* related the "social dynamite" that was building up in the cities' black ghettoes to the failure of the schools to provide the kind of education and skills which the urban poor needed so desperately if they were ever to live in anything resembling the same world as the suburban rich. Some critics have attacked Conant's stress on school-taught "marketable skills," charging that he was trying to preordain poor youngsters for menial tasks, excluding them from the kind of careers to which most middle-class children are taught to aspire. His intent was precisely the opposite.

In the long run, the Conant prescriptions which were addressed directly to the lay public and school boards had an infinitely greater impact than those which demanded dramatic changes of the professional education establishment itself. The requirement of more mathematics and science instruction was no threat to the profession. On the contrary, it promised more jobs all around, not least in the teacher-training institutions. (Only the representatives of music and art instruction grumbled about being left out of the post-Sputnik call for academic rigor.)

But, when Conant began to touch the established order, it was another matter. His proposal to shift the action from teacher-training college classrooms to the schools, with much heavier emphasis on practical experience than on theoretical training, threatened to upset departments, hierarchies, jobs, and routines. When he suggested relatively low, training-level stipends for teachers prior to their full accreditation as professionals, he clashed with existing pay scales and the prerogatives of individual teachers as well as their professional organizations and unions. Like so many before him, Conant ran into that stone wall of resistance as soon as he tried to come to grips with the profession's internal conservatism. Even so moderate and circumspect a critic as Conant said at one point that he found "the establishment's rigidity frightening."

If the Conant reforms fell short of their goals, they nevertheless succeeded in making the point that wide-open, democratic education, symbolized by the comprehensive high school, is not incompatible with a return to those quality controls which had increasingly been sacrificed in the effort to render mass education palatable by making it relatively undemanding. In doing so, he made the school debate once again more rational, taking it out of the hands of the extremists.

Not even Conant's warning about the "social dynamite" that was smoldering in the troubled cities was enough to prepare the educational leadership for the explosive decades of the 1960s and 1970s. Many of the reform efforts of the post–World War II era had been generally on the right track, but they failed in scope and pervasiveness. While reformers sensed the steady build-up of dissatisfaction, they deceived themselves about the ultimate source of discontent.

The educational critics of the 1950s spoke almost exclusively for and to the middle class. They feared that declining academic standards—in the traditional disciplines—constituted a threat to the nation's economic and social effectiveness and values. Reformers of that era were not necessarily callous in their neglect of the forgotten and excluded lower classes; they still believed in the magnetic nature of public education which, if only made universally available, would attract and inspire all children to succeed in school on the same terms. And those terms were, as they had always been, shaped by the middle-class majority.

The Supreme Court's landmark decision, which reversed the doctrine of "separate but equal" schools for black children, was given less public attention than its importance merited. While the South tried for a while to outmaneuver the court's requirement that dual white and black school systems be dismantled "with all deliberate speed," neither Southern nor Northern education leaders recognized the decision for what it so clearly was: legal notice that the American public schools would have to face up to the task of equal educational opportunity for *all* children.

It was in the nation's cities, with their large enclaves of poor, uneducated families, that the new crisis was building up. While efforts at integration monopolized much of the attention during the early 1960s, the real issue, from the outset, was how to educate great numbers of children who, because they were so unfamiliar with middle-class standards and values, failed to respond to middle-class prescriptions.

The problem was far from new. As cited earlier, many urban schools and their teachers had not been sympathetic to the poor of another era—the immigrants from distant lands and cultures, some as uneducated as the nonwhite minorities of the urban ghettoes.

While it is true that many of these earlier urban poor had, in fact, "made it" by conforming to the schools' standards of Americanization and socialization, many others had dropped out. Entire groups—mainly, but not exclusively, the Catholics—had withdrawn from the public education system to set up their own substitutes. For the majority, the demands made by the American public schools, however strange and difficult they were, represented an escape route from the hostile and oppressive societies of "the old country." Under such circumstances, what was new and American seemed inherently desirable. If the schools made you suffer, you felt that there was a reward awaiting those who suffered obediently.

The mood among the dispossessed of the 1960s was quite different. They had been dispossessed, not by malevolent powers abroad, but by an allegedly benevolent society at home. They were not in debt to a nation that promised them unheard-of new rights; they confronted a society that withheld from them rights that they knew should have been theirs. In the end, this new wave of the poor would undoubtedly also have to be inducted into the majority, middle-class culture; but, in the short run, that culture seemed to these children not merely strange but hostile. The schools seemed not an escape route, but a dead end.

The response this time was not doggedness but rage. The urban masses had become more sophisticated in the use of their power. There had been earlier riots by the disaffected poor; but now the tactics of protest often succeeded in bringing the entire system to a halt—not just for the poor but for the middle class as well. Boycotts and strikes managed to close the schools, first, to underscore the demands for racial integration and subsequently to extort the right to control the administration of the schools.

The initial response to the gathering storm concentrated heavily on two related remedies: integration and remedial or compensatory education.

The integrationists followed comfortably in the footsteps of those who, like Mann, believed that the public schools could and must hold a diverse nation together. Confidence that this goal could be accomplished was fundamental to the very meaning of *e pluribus unum* as a national article of faith.

But integration was also a matter of simple justice. In 1849, Charles Sumner, arguing before the supreme court of Massachusetts against "the Constitutionality of Separate Colored Schools," had warned: "Prejudice is the child of ignorance. It is sure to prevail where people do not know each other."

A century later, social scientists added the evidence of their findings to these libertarian sentiments. Dr. Kenneth B. Clark, a psychologist and one of the foremost Black integrationists, helped to persuade the Supreme Court in 1954 that the damage done to the psyche and self-image of Black children by school segregation is such that separate could never be equal.

The second remedy—compensatory education—also was foreshadowed by Sumner in the Boston school case of 1849. "If the colored people are ignorant, degraded, and unhappy," he told the court, "then they should be the special object of our care. From the abundance of your possessions you must seek to remedy their lot."

Lyndon B. Johnson, the Southern President who adopted the Black civil rights movement's pledge, "We Shall Overcome," translated compensatory education into national policy. On June 4, 1965, at Howard University, Johnson pledged that "the task is to give 20 million Negroes the same chance as every other American to learn and grow, to work and share in society, to develop their abilities—physical, mental and spiritual—and to pursue their individual happiness."

Out of such pledges came a variety of new strategies, all designed to give the disadvantaged a foot up on the educational ladder. Project Head Start was the most visible symbol of the new approach. It was a preschool effort to give poor children those advantages—greater verbal competence, health care, and improved nutrition—with which middle-class children grow up to school age as a matter of course.

The new educational theorists no longer assumed that the mere equality of being allowed to go to school at the same age gives to all children the same opportunity to learn. Sociologist James Coleman had shown the overriding impact of the home environment on success in school. But he had also discovered, as part of his study of the effects of racial integration, that placing a minority of disadvantaged children among a classroom of middle-class youngsters improves the performance of the poor children.

If learning is actually contagious in the proper environment, as the new research suggested, then the creation of a favorable preschool environment would help to overcome class- and poverty-imposed handicaps.

New research and ideology were moving steadily away from the notion of schools that had long been considered all-powerful in splendid professional isolation. The school was no longer seen as an independent engine that could improve society virtually singlehandedly. It had become evident that society and school must be improved simultaneously, if the one is not to drag down the quality of the other. Dr. Martin Deutsch, one of the early supporters of preschool education, reported in 1965 that children from fatherless homes had been found to have significantly lower IQ scores by the time they reach the fifth grade. Deutsch concluded from these findings that the children's retardation "was a consequence not so much of the absence of the father, as it was of the diminution of organized family activity."

What all these investigations demonstrated was that an intellectually and physically retarding environment means that the children actually accumulate a deficit during the years before they enter school. Simply opening the school doors to them is not enough. Something needs to be done to wipe out the deficit.

For several years, during Lyndon Johnson's Presidency, the nation's legislative strategies were shaped by these concepts. Substantial amounts of government funds were channeled into preschool programs. Even greater amounts were allotted to the new Johnsonian education measures which called for distribution of funds on the basis of the number of poverty-level children enrolled in each district's schools.

It was not surprising that so revolutionary a concept—special education for the poor instead of the same education for all—should arouse opposition. It is, of course, true that the rich have, by virtue of their financial resources, frequently enjoyed the privilege of special education, not only in selective private schools but, as Conant stressed, increasingly in the posh facilities and almost exclusively college-preparatory suburban public schools. Yet, the extension of such privileges to the poor seemed, at least in political terms, quite a different matter. In the American mind, poverty has never been able to shake completely the stigma of being the fault of the poor, not a personal misfortune or the consequence of social and economic policies.

President Johnson was the exception rather than the rule among twentieth-century politicians in that he saw his populist measures as essential to the health of the entire nation. Whatever its administrative flaws, Johnson's War on Poverty—educational as well as fiscal—was clearly an extension of the early public education pioneers' conviction that a self-governing republic must find ways of educating all its people. It was also an effort to find an answer to Jefferson's gloomy forebodings that the grand scheme of a free society might not stand the test of urbanization.

Like most American reform movements, the compensatory education drive soon suffered the consequences of its supporters' excessive zeal and of its opponents' conservative objections.

The basic claims of integrationists or of advocates of compensatory education had not been proven false. Yet, neither integration nor compensatory education could quickly and relatively inexpensively wipe out large accumulated deficits, and do it in the face of continuing segregation in housing. Nor was it practically feasible to create those ideal conditions prescribed by Coleman—the distribution of relatively small numbers of minority children among classrooms whose learning pattern would be determined by the middle-class majority. Social and political realities blocked the way to such utopian solutions.

President Johnson's success in gaining temporary acceptance for his proposals had depended in large measure on the national mood of guilt and repentance that followed the assassination of President John F. Kennedy. But idealism born of remorse—along with fear of riotous insurrection in the Black ghettoes—soon began to evaporate and give way to conservative counter-pressures.

The countermovement was aided by Black impatience with the liberal reforms that had held out such high hopes, but seemed to deliver only limited gains. As the white majority turned against integration, or at least failed to bring it about in many urban Black ghettoes, militant Black leadership turned back to earlier demands for separatism and community control—meaning Black power control—of the schools.

It was in New York City that the major battle was fought. The prelude to that historic clash over school control was written in central Harlem in 1967. The symbol of the gathering storm was Intermediate School 201, a brand new structure—massive, windowless, and air-conditioned. To the Board of Education planners, it was a model of modern technology; to the angry and suspicious community it was a monument to old segregation in a new shell. Local wags said its cement overhang that covered most of the sidewalk like a stone umbrella was ideal for all-weather picketing.

Community forces, taking the board's earlier integration pledges at face value, opposed the construction of a new school deep inside a Black ghetto. Forced into the defensive, the board pledged that it would make the new school so superior that it would attract white children from distant attendance zones. To give credibility to the pledge, the board sent out invitations to white parents in other districts to enroll their children.

Predictably, these invitations to send youngsters deep into a ghetto area found no takers. When the school opened to Black children only, parents proclaimed an effective boycott and demanded community control over I.S. 201. The first casualty was the white principal.

But I.S. 201 proved to be only an initial skirmish in a war that challenged virtually all the assumptions made by urban school reformers at the turn of the century. Those assumptions had been based on centralization of the schools as an antidote to the chaos, corruption, and favoritism that had become the mark of ward politics.

Once again, the reform movement had come full circle. The charge against the centralized system and its bureaucracy was that it had lost touch with the children's needs. Although dissatisfaction had been building up steadily for some time and had occasionally been shared by teachers, who complained about unreasonable headquarters policies, and by field administrators, who resented the central board's imperious attitudes, matters were ultimately brought to a head by Black parents over the board's inability to deliver on the promises made to them and their children. The policy statements had pledged "quality integrated education." Since masses of Black children were failing in predominantly Black schools, parents joined the new reformers who sought a remedy either in decentralization or, in more extreme instances, total community control.

The collision came in 1968 over an experimentally established Demonstration School District in Brooklyn's Ocean Hill—Brownsville, a depressed Black and Puerto Rican area. Supported by the Ford Foundation and somewhat reluctantly certified by the Board of Education, the Black leaders of the experiment flexed their muscle by ordering the involuntary transfer of some twenty white teachers.

Although similar transfers had long been quietly accepted by all parties as a means of preventing local dissatisfactions from bursting into the open, the deliberate provocation on the part of Ocean Hill–Brownsville was seized upon by the United Federation of Teachers, the union which represented the city's teaching staff of 60,000, as an opportunity to man the barricades against any future encroachment by the community control forces on the teachers' rights and job security.

Union president Albert Shanker, insisting that an attack on teachers' rights in any district represented a threat to similar rights in all districts, escalated the conflict into a citywide strike. The ensuing confrontation not only pitted liberal reformers against the conservative establishment, but raised the specter of an open break between Blacks and the predominantly Jewish ranks of teachers and school administrators and their frightened white middle-class allies. Early apostles of the public schools as the cornerstone of American society might have found grim irony in the fact that the schools had indeed become so fundamental to urban life that the 1968 school crisis may well have come closer than any previous civic confrontation to tearing the city asunder.

The two forces that faced each other, often literally on the barricades, were equally convinced of the justice of their cause. Blacks, feeling betrayed by the system and prevented by the rules of the game from rising within its power structure, ascribed to primitive racism many of the consequences of mere bureaucratic conservatism. White professionals similarly interpreted all Black demands as antiwhite and, where the whites were Jewish, as anti-Semitic. In the heat of battle, few of these professionals chose to recall that each successive wave of newcomers to the system had, in fact, experienced very similar frustrations as outsiders. In a moment of quiet retrospection shortly after the crisis, Dr. Nathan Brown, then Acting Superintendent of Schools, recalled that when he had entered the system as a young teacher in the 1930s "there were only seven Jewish principals, and four of them had converted to Catholicism" in order to get their appointments.

In terms of the future of urban education, however, community control was only a deceptive sideshow. With funding of public education clearly dependent on the larger, more distant units —the city, the state, and increasingly even the Federal government —those who seriously believed that total, or even greatly increased, power could be shifted to local communities were indulging in naïve dreams. Ultimately, such an arrangement might well have locked the poorest communities into their own misfortune of independent poverty, while affluent districts would enjoy their own riches in splendid isolation. History provides little evidence that political power will ever be financed by someone else's money, without strings of political control.

The drive toward decentralization was quite another matter. Centralized governmental power had enjoyed favor among liberal reformers for more than a century in the schools and for close to half a century in American society at large. "There is great need of some one mind," the Boston School Committees had warned in 1852, "to take a survey of the whole system and of all the schools and to suggest such improvements as the good of the whole requires." A central system, the reformers then insisted, would have to replace the existing decentralized chaos in which each unit "is a sort of petty kingdom in itself and perhaps somewhat jealous of its own rights."

And so the reforms of "the one best way" had taken their course. Systematic efficiency and professionalism came to the schools, and over the years this trend raised the standards of American public education, just as the political centralization that gathered momentum under Franklin D. Roosevelt's New Deal raised the standard of living in an industrialized nation. It is inconceivable that either the American people's journey into an urbanized social democracy or the American schools' journey to mass education of unprecedented magnitude could have been accomplished peacefully and without revolution, except for increasing reliance on centralization.

But a cycle was ending. With centralization's gains had come its penalties. Increasing numbers of Americans felt that the centralized power of government and the centralized power of the school bureaucracies were either overreaching themselves or were ineffective in responding to local needs and desires. Sincere but excessive promises by central planners left localities disappointed and eventually disaffected. Centralization had accomplished much; but it was only natural that, where it failed to respond to urgent new crises, a disappointed populace would give less thought to the system's past achievements than to its present deficiencies.

Original advocates of centralization had hoped to do more

than eliminate the corruption of the wards. They envisioned their reforms as a triumph of professionalism, with a hierarchy of highly skilled experts applying the new scientific knowledge they hoped would bring order and wisdom to the enterprise.

But, amid the urban turmoil and alienation of the 1960s, critics of the system—i.e., the advocates of a new reform of decentralization—challenged not only the centralized structure but even the claim that those who administered and worked in the system were professionals in the true sense of the word.

Herbert Kohl, one of the most articulate critics of education in urban slums, described his experiences in 1962 in an East Harlem school's sixth grade in his book *36 Children*. He found that "the myth of children as 'animals,' the fear that they may be uncontrollable, hangs over all the ghetto schools," adding that for a while it hung over his own classroom, too.

Moreover, the centralized system was chronically inefficient. When the books arrived, there were twenty-five arithmetic texts from one publisher and twelve from another, and in the entire school there was no complete set of sixth-grade arithmetic books. The social studies texts, to be used in this setting of poverty and deprivation, "praised industrial America in terms that ranged from the enthusiastic to the exorbitant."

"Those phony books?" asked one child. But when Kohl suggested that they get through them fast and then turn to better things, "the class understood and accepted the terms."

In general, the decentralization movement fits neatly into the seesawing pattern of the American history of public school politics. David Rogers, one of the harshest critics of the old system, decried the schools' organizational models of "the Prussian military, the Roman Catholic Church, and the Industrial Corporation." These models—specifically the first and the last—were precisely the organizational prototypes to which the reformers of a hundred years ago had aspired in their search for an efficient "best way."

Those who considered their own, and the schools', well-being intimately and perhaps inseparably linked to the system and to the internal rules created to perpetuate it were understandably alarmed by the prospect of decentralization. The United Federation of Teachers, the urban schools' powerful union, had created a slogan—"Teachers Want What Children Need." It soon became a banner under which teachers marched in cities across the nation whenever they either saw their rights and prerogatives in jeopardy.

Albert Shanker, the union's president and unquestionably the most influential spokesman for the urban teaching establishment, expressed the doubts of organized education about decentralization and local community control. Instead of returning to small units and the grassroots, he suggested quite the opposite—a gradual drive in the direction of metropolitan school systems which would include urban and suburban districts, as well as a move toward state and even interstate school systems. The goal, Shanker said bluntly, "is heavy Federal financing and Federal control."

This would inevitably mean more rather than less power for the system. Opponents of such a trend might ascribe the union leader's enthusiasm for such a course to his conviction that the union had become so powerful an instrument that it had far less to fear from the governmental and the educational bureaucracy than from a local citizenry dissatisfied with its schools. Over the years unions had been able to become secure within the Establishment. Unionized teachers saw little advantage in reducing the power of an Establishment in which, after years of battle as exploited outsiders, they had at last won a large, and perhaps even a controlling, share.

Shanker—not unlike the centralizing reformers of the previous century whom the then weak and vulnerable teachers' unions had adamantly opposed—returned to the example of industry. "Large motor companies, with highly centralized boards," he said, "can develop forms of administrative decentralization within highly centralized systems."

This was the heart of the issue over which the unions and much of the profession clashed with the reformers. Those who charged that the profession had failed to respond to their specific needs wanted something quite different from the model of General Motors whose central headquarters allowed its Plymouth or Cadillac divisions a certain amount of token independence. They questioned whether what is good for General Motors is, in fact, good for the country. They suspected that in centralized education, as in centralized industry, the criterion of success would increasingly be—not the quality of the product or the satisfaction of the consumer—but the affluence of the producer. As long as Shanker's and the profession's views seemed to echo Nicholas Murray Butler's pronouncement of some seventy years earlier that it makes no more sense to democratize the control of the schools than to democratize appendicitis, the forces of decentralization would reject the proposition that teachers wanted primarily what children needed. (By way of historic irony, Butler had made his original blustering defense of centralized school control in specific reply to the early teachers' union demands for a voice in school policies.)

Opponents of decentralization found much fruitful data in accounts of the corruption and waste that had brought the original ward control of education into disrepute. As New York City moved into its reenactment of local school control, there were indeed enough instances of hands in the till and of questionable appointments to give substance to such warnings. Yet it had also been demonstrably true that corruption, occasionally on a grand scale, had occurred in the centralized system. Ghettoes and slums were not averse to a little overflow of the gravy in their direction. Moreover, the central bureaucracy, despite its codified merit system, had not been singularly successful in making its standardized licensing and appointment system a model of the highest professional quality, when measured in responsiveness to changing needs.

Liberal and left-wing opinion had soured on the unions. Gone were the days when, as during the 1930s and the New Deal, labor represented the liberating force, an engine of social justice. In the view of the 1960s reformers, unions had become part and parcel of the basically conservative establishment, more secure with the status quo than with social change. The aspirations and demands of the poor, nonwhite minorities were more often than not seen as a threat to organized labor and its leaders.

Education was no exception. The liberal reform movement pushed for decentralization, and the radical fringe either demanded community control or wanted to dismantle the organized school system altogether. Teachers' unions, having originally fought the central school bureaucracy as their enemy, had now learned to enjoy the fruits of its victories. Collective bargaining had given the organized teachers great power.

In one area, however, liberal reformers and organized teachers were moving in the same direction: school financing. Both advocated a new centralism, though for different reasons. Unions saw in the prospect of state-financed, and perhaps ultimately Federally financed education, an opportunity for even greater union power at increasingly higher levels of bargaining and a more sharply focused concentration of lobbying.

Liberal reformers, to whom such a growth of union power was ordinarily anathema, nevertheless began in the early 1970s to push for central school financing because they considered it essential to the equalization of educational opportunity.

The issue moved to the center of the national stage in 1971, when the California Supreme Court ruled in *Serrano v. Priest* that the state's reliance on local property taxes for school financing violates the equal protection clause of the Constitution in that it "invidiously discriminates against the poor because it makes the quality of a child's education a function of the wealth of his parents and neighbors. . . . Affluent districts can have their cake and eat it too: they can provide a high quality education for their children while paying lower taxes. Poor districts, by contrast, have no cake at all." Although the court stopped short of ordering the state to take over the financing of the schools on the basis of equal allocations for every pupil, it demanded that the school authorities submit a more equitable plan of equalization.

Courts in other states, among them Michigan, Minnesota, and New Jersey, moved in the same direction. But the issue was joined at the highest level when the Texas case of *San Antonio Independent School District v. Rodriguez* reached the Supreme Court.

On March 21, 1973, the court observed that "The method of financing public schools in Texas, as in almost every other state, has resulted in a system of public education that can fairly be described as chaotic and unjust." Still, the court shied away from a radical solution.

"No scheme of taxation," the court said ". . . has yet been devised which is free of all discriminatory impact. . . . It is inevitable that some localities are going to be blessed with more taxable assets than others." Moreover, citing Coleman's sociological observation, the court continued: "The history of education since the industrial revolution shows a continual struggle between two forces: the desire by members of society to have educational opportunity for all children, and the desire of each family to provide the best education it can afford for its own children." The Texas system of school finance, the court added, is responsive to these two forces:

> While assuring a basic education for every child in the State, it permits and encourages a large measure of participation in and control of each district's schools at the local level. In an era that has witnessed a consistent trend toward centralization of the functions of government, local sharing of responsibility for public education has survived.

Would the liberal Warren Court, with its emphasis on social justice, have ruled differently? The dissenting views of the minority of justices suggest that it might indeed have come down on the side of equality. "Discrimination," the dissent warned, "falls directly upon the children whose educational opportunity is dependent upon where they happen to live." But the majority insisted, "Ultimate solutions must come from the lawmakers and from the democratic pressures of those who elect them."

It is nevertheless important to note that even in the context of this essentially conservative ruling, the majority added what it called a "cautionary postscript":

> We hardly need to add that this Court action today is not to be viewed as placing its judicial imprimatur on the status quo. The need is apparent for reform in tax systems which may well have relied too long and too heavily on the local property tax. And certainly innovative new thinking as to public education, its methods and its funding, is necessary to assure both a higher level of quality and greater uniformity of opportunity. . . .

Reformers who had hoped for a court-ordered equalization of school financing were generally in the vanguard of the battle against centralized power, both by school authorities and unions.

Yet the move toward centralized financing would almost inevitably lead to increased centralization, possibly with a subsequent leveling of expenditures to a point between the admittedly inadequate financing of poor districts and the lavish spending of affluent ones.

The push for equal expenditure, moreover, was often led by the very reformers who at the same time questioned the schools' capacity to improve the lot of the deprived in any case and who expressed doubts that money spent on education made much difference, except to increase teachers' salaries.

What nevertheless gave *Serrano* and *Rodriguez* extraordinary significance was the fact that the courts had begun to confront a situation of intolerable inequalities which had been allowed to develop by irresponsible legislatures in direct contradiction to the hopes and intent of public education's founding fathers. Legal challenges of these inequalities, and the fact that even a conservative court found school financing to be "chaotic and unjust," amounted to a warning that time was running out on the status quo. The political establishment was given notice that drastic remedies could be averted only by a more effective voluntary effort at equalization.

By the beginning of the 1970s the politics of American education were in a state of chaos. A tide of conservatism had swept over the nation. An uncertain economy and an accelerated rate of inflation, along with a growing sentiment against expenditures supportive of the poor, caused President Richard M. Nixon to turn his back on the Johnsonian commitment to fight educational poverty and deprivation. Spokesmen for the new Administration gave maximum public exposure to reports which questioned the success of compensatory education programs and called for the reduction in their support.

Some of those who had been leading the compensatory education movement challenged the research basis of these unfavorable reports. Dr. Deutsch, who had pioneered the preschool research and development, had always insisted that, even at the height of the movement's popularity, the amounts allocated per child had remained inadequate and the follow-through by the regular schools had been spotty.

Yet even the reformers themselves looked back on their optimism of the 1950s and 1960s and admitted that things had not gone as well as anticipated. The Ford Foundation, in a moment of introspection rare for social and political institutions, reviewed its own earlier efforts during the days when the new technology, along with more money, more buildings, and more teachers, were thought to have moved the nation to the threshold of a happy society built by better schools.

The report, entitled *A Foundation Goes to School,* concluded that many of the hopeful innovations had failed—not to produce results where they were given an honest chance—but to "catch on" in a significant, systemwide way. The new technology was never truly given a fair chance by a school establishment that, not unlike many intellectuals, considered all technological gadgets something of a threat. "In far too many instances," the report said, "equipment of all kinds is gathering dust."

An even more fundamental weakness was that the reforms could simply not respond fast enough to changes in society. Too much of the successful experimentation was carried out in well-to-do suburbs—because they were most sophisticated and therefore more hospitable to change. Their experience could not be adapted quickly or massively enough to what was not yet fully understood —the gathering storm in the inner cities. Foundations' hopes that selected districts would become lighthouses of change were disappointed by the reluctance of conservative educators in other districts to imitate even a demonstrably successful program. Communities and teachers often reacted negatively to any unconventional form of freewheeling experimentation. They considered it a threat to established practice, job security, and discipline.

With political conservatism in the ascendency and the liberals in the doldrums because they had sponsored most of the by now discredited idealistic school reforms of the 1950s, American public education suddenly found itself exposed to yet another assault from a novel and therefore unexpected quarter—the revisionist New Left.

The attack had its origin in two movements of quite distinct historical and political antecedents. The first took its ideological inspiration from Rousseau's view of the child and humanity and from Thoreau's view of the individual and the state. It considered the school an oppressive obstacle to the child's natural search for his identity through the expression of the good within him. It was a movement that longed for a return to a simpler age and a less complex society whose children would be taught, as they once were on the farms, by sympathetic adults around them, rather than by organized professionals.

Adherents of this nostalgic cult took much of their inspiration from such modern social and educational philosophers as Paul Goodman who, being opposed to compulsion of any kind, naturally looked with disapproval on compulsory education.

Goodman, a freethinker with unlimited faith in the potential of free men, was not an extremist. He admitted reluctantly that "the conditions of modern life are far too complicated for independent young spirits to get going on their own." They need, he conceded, "some preparation, though probably not as much as is supposed; but more important, they need various institutional frameworks in which they can try out and learn the ropes." He fervently believed, however, that education needed less rather than more rigid organization, and he said flatly that he "would not give a penny more to the present school administrators."

The second wave of the New Left attack on the established schools came from a more radical and less conciliatory quarter. It was revolutionary in political rather than in educational terms. Its home base ranged from old-fashioned Marxism to various adaptations of Maoism. Its extreme goal, as outlined by Ivan Illich, was "the de-schooling of society." The aim was literally to reverse and undo the long history and the accumulated works of builders of the American public education system, from Jefferson and Franklin to Mann, Dewey, Eliot, and Conant.

Although these revisionists differed in their critical approach to public education, they had in common the belief that the only way to change the American political and economic system was to change the schools—or at least to reduce what they considered the schools' stranglehold on American youth.

To some extent, this was a return to those who, in the brave rhetoric of Counts, had wanted to enlist the schools in the creation of a new social order. But since the new revolutionaries were far more political than Counts had been as a mere social reformer, they tended to rely on the more pragmatic strategy of undermining or dismantling the system rather than entrusting the revolution to it. Advocacy of complete deschooling suggests the historic parallel of Lenin's utopian promise that the state would wither away, leaving the people free to govern themselves without interference by institutions and Establishment.

Not all the new voices from the left joined Illich's call for total deschooling as the road to social change. The most highly publicized of these voices, in effect, recommended simply that the schools be bypassed. In the view of Christopher Jencks, an educational sociologist at Harvard, public schools had failed to achieve the social goals set for them by their founders and claimed by their boosters. In his book, *Inequality: A Reassessment of the Effect of Family and Schooling in America,* which was to become the most controversial educational publication during the early 1970s, Jencks charged that the schools had failed to close the economic inequality gap and concluded that this could only be accomplished by way of socialism and the redistribution of income.

While the schools did not, in Jencks's view, really matter, he did not ask for their abolition. Let them continue, he seemed to say, to do the best they can for the children. Let them moreover be pleasant places in which youngsters may be taught and enjoy themselves. But expect no great social reforms to emerge— none of the equalizing miracles that Horace Mann had forecast as the consequence of rich and poor rubbing elbows on the same school bench.

In many ways, the Jencks doctrine tends to be politically less dangerous for the schools than the earlier progressives' appeal to use the schools for the creation of a new social order. If the schools seemed to Jencks ineffectual as instruments of social reform, let alone revolution, they could at least be spared the ire and the counterattack of the right. Jencks' efforts to usher in socialism could, after all, be fought on nonschool grounds.

Criticism of the public schools' failure to reach a sufficient percentage of the urban poor was obviously justified. In fact, the public schools had, throughout their history, often failed many of the children of the poor, unless parents themselves made extraordinary efforts both to demand effective schooling and to inspire in their children a lust for learning. Many children had fallen by the wayside in the past. What makes such "dropping

out"—a mark of the schools' failure to reach, serve, and inspire—
infinitely more serious in this postindustrial society is that jobs
for the uneducated have dwindled. Whatever low-level jobs remain provide so little reward and incentive that failure in school
paves the way for alienation and despair.

Although revisionists have been sensitive to that alienation and
despair, the question remains whether their solutions—downgrad-
ing or abolishing the schools and breaking with the concept of
compulsory education—will help or hurt the disadvantaged. Will
the greater freedom of choice—whether or where to go to school
—once again give the advantage to the affluent, who would send
their children to school with or without compulsion?

Critics were quite right in exposing the puffery of those
who had proclaimed public education the cureall of society's ills.
Neither in the United States nor in any other country have the
schools been able to bring about social or political revolutions,
although they have often been used by revolutionaries as a powerful auxiliary force—usually *after* the revolution's political
triumph. Neither in Germany nor in Russia, for example, did
the schools play an important part in the National Socialist or
the Bolshevist victories. Yet it is likely that, if the schools in
those countries had been more successful in preventing their
societies' stratification, the radical revolutions and the subsequent
establishment of totalitarianism could have been prevented.
Moreover, in the wake of the revolutions, schools became major
instruments for keeping totalitarian regimes firmly entrenched.

In such a historical framework, then, the question is not
whether the schools failed because they were unable to eliminate
inequality, but rather whether they have achieved some measure
of success in helping substantial numbers of children rise on the
material and social scale of affluence, influence, and status in relation to what Mann called their "natural capacities." Whether, at
the same time, a country opts for the gradual or drastic redistribution of incomes, regardless of achievement or natural capacities,
is not an issue to be decided by the schools.

The danger inherent in the collective voices of the New Left
was that, by chanting the refrain that the schools had failed, that
they did not really matter, that they could never solve the problems of poverty, they would swell the ranks of those who wanted

to reduce the schools' budgets and relieve the taxpayers' burden.

The revisionists' significance is not in their capacity to affect public education policies by virtue of their own power or persuasiveness. It is rather that, for the first time, a vocal attack against the public schools had been launched simultaneously by the political left and by conservative right-of-center forces. At a time of the schools' grievous failure to cope with serious urban problems, symbolized by the reading retardation of ghetto children, the New Left and the Old Right, albeit for entirely different reasons, questioned in quite similar terms whether the investment in educational reforms is worthwhile. To be sure, Jencks emphasized repeatedly that he favored higher expenditures for the schools not because he expected them to succeed in improving American society, but simply because—in Goodman's terms—children have the right to expect pleasant surroundings. But in practical terms this vague appeal does stir general uneasiness among taxpayers.

Whatever the cause, in 1974 the Education Commission of the States, an organization of governors, legislators, and educators from forty-five states, acknowledged that support for public schools had been declining. Education's priority was seen as being displaced by concern for environmental protection, mass transportation, and health care. Governor Reubin Askew of Florida, the commission's chairman, reported that "taxpayers in state after state are demonstrating their unwillingness to impose added property tax burdens upon themselves to support education."

For the first time in a decade, the commission said, the portion of state revenues allocated to schools and colleges had fallen below the 50 percent mark, reflecting a softening of state legislatures' attitudes toward the schools. (Disturbing as such a trend would inevitably appear to educators and many concerned citizens, it is nevertheless worth recalling the battles that had to be fought by the original proponents of public education. That someday half of the states' expenditures might be devoted to education would have seemed to them nothing short of an impossible dream.)

For a brief period during the 1960s, the pendulum of American school reform had been swinging once again away from the standardized, rigid approach and toward greater freedom of options and concern for individual differences. The Open Classroom movement, the so-called "free schools" without any fixed curriculum and standard requirements, the alternative schools offering children a choice of different educational goals and methods—all these were a return to Dewey's search for a school environment in which children discovered spontaneously and grew as they found themselves socially, psychologically, and intellectually. Liberal political currents, along with distaste for an Establishment that had led the nation into the morass of Vietnam, swept education in the same direction.

But once again, the combination of a conservative Establishment and the frequently inept implementation of the reforms soon deprived the new movement of its initial momentum. A new wave of political conservatism, fed by inflation and recession, raised questions about the less structured school. Many of the urban poor, moreover, believed the improvement of their children's education depended on conventional instruction in the Three R's which, they were convinced, had brought success to the affluent middle class. As in the past, reformers had failed to establish adequate rapport with those they wanted to help.

It was a failure reminiscent of the days during the 1920s, when the reformers tried to persuade parents that giving children "group-mindedness" was more important than teaching them the traditional lessons. Parents in an Italian ghetto then had rejected the experiments, saying that their children, in contrast to the sheltered rich, had plenty of group activity in the streets. What they needed was the capacity for letters and numbers that so clearly had pointed more affluent youngsters toward success—and even greater wealth.

The schools' failures to respond to the different needs of individual children, and even of specific groups of children, are not difficult to identify. They are serious failures. They spring in large measure from the mass education system's still heavy reliance on "the one best way"—the scientific method applied, like an army manual, to the mass of teachers and pupils. These failures spring, too, from the unresolved dilemma of how to make a compulsory activity desirable and attractive. And they spring from the tendency of any organized Establishment to stress its admittedly im-

portant mission to create societal cohesion, continuity, stability—
frequently at the expense of innovation and individualism.

Again and again, the seesawing battle between the education
establishment and the reformers was fought over those issues and
conflicts. At moments of grave social discontent, the politics of
public education tend to resort to the same excesses in rhetoric
and dialectic as do the politics of the nation. Failure to attain the
ideal then is increasingly mistaken for failure of the ideal itself.

Under such circumstances, the politics of American education
come to be judged by their radical critics as being corrupt in concept and beyond redemption. Such judgments overlook the achievements of a system which, by any yardstick of comparison with other
industrial societies, has kept the population upwardly mobile
and the society fluid. It has not been able to wipe out poverty or
eliminate inequality; but it has made an identifiable contribution
to the process of allowing the children of the poor to climb on the
ladder of income and success.

The nineteen-nation study by the Institute for the International
Evaluation of Educational Achievement (IEA), completed in 1973,
showed that the academic elite among high-school seniors (the top
9 percent) in the United States contained the largest percentage of
children from lower-class (unskilled and semiskilled workers')
homes of any of the nations surveyed. Specifically, the American
lower-class segment constituted 14 percent of the entire group,
compared with only 1 percent in West Germany. To that statistic
must be added the fact that 75 percent of the age group finish
high school in the United States, the highest percentage of any
nation in the survey and probably in the world today.

Despite these accomplishments, public schools still fall far short
of their goal. The number of children whom they fail to reach and
to teach is far too large, and those children today are concentrated
in cities where too many of the uneducated are condemned to a
life of poverty and crime. Thus, Jefferson's fears that the free
society would run afoul of "the mobs of the cities" remain a matter
of real concern.

And yet the capacity of public education to act as a counterweight against the natural tendency of all societies to become stratified has been consistently proven and remains a powerful factor.

The spiral movement of the public schools—from central control to decentralization and back, or from traditional to progressive thought—may not appear the most efficient way to move forward. But, costly as these circuitous movements are, they offer greater safety than a rigid commitment to an approved and accepted course. And, whatever their shortcomings, these gyrations reflect the way of American society.

6

AMERICAN CHILDHOOD: THE UTOPIAN MYTH

O UR POST-REVOLUTIONARY YOUTHS are born under happier stars than you and I were," Thomas Jefferson wrote to his friend John Adams in 1814.

Such reveries may have reflected an aging man's normal envy of the pleasures enjoyed by youth. But, beyond the classic lament of the older generation, there is in Jefferson's musing something of an instinctive realization that the traditional views of childhood were bound to change, however slowly, in a changing society.

And yet it would be misleading to draw from such romantic visions an idealized picture of childhood in America. Contrary to the persistent myth, America provides no history of a child-centered society. As a civilization, America has not always cared deeply about all its children. The facts of American children's lives tell a different story for the children of the poor—who are often neglected or exploited. For reformers and idealists, the cause of children's rights, including the right to a good education, has been an uphill battle.

The Colonial view of life had made little allowance for the idea of childhood, particularly after age six or seven. Once out of diapers and past infancy, children were regarded as miniature adults, as even their dress indicated.

Children shared fully the era's physical and psychological hardships. Their health, and their very lives, remained precarious. Only a strong and lucky few could expect to live to maturity. Those not so fortunate were widely thought to be the victims of demons, and medical advice, sometimes by ministers, was in keeping with that philosophy. Physicians were virtually unavailable, and the science of pediatrics was years in the future.

Parents and children alike lived constantly with the intimate knowledge of death. Infant mortality was high, and, though it was subsequently to decline, it was not brought under control until well into the twentieth century. But in 1711 Cotton Mather could say fatalistically: "'Tis a frequent thing for parents to bury their children. Else we could not see, as they say we do, at least half the children of men dying short of twenty." Epidemics of yellow fever, smallpox, and "throat distempers"—scarlet fever and diphtheria—were principal killers of the young.

Mather himself was survived by only two of his fifteen children. During a measles epidemic in 1713, three of his children died, as did his wife, within less than two weeks. His diary contains these poignant entries:

NOV. 17–18. About midnight, little Eleazar died.
NOV. 20. Little Martha died, about ten o'clock A.M.
NOV. 21. This Day, I attended the Funeral, of my two: Eleazar and Martha. Betwixt 9h and 10h at Night, my lovely Jerusha Expired. She was two years, and about seven Months. . . . Lord, I am oppressed; undertake for me!

Both in the treatment of children's illnesses and in the care for healthy youngsters, the standard fare was quackery and moralizing. Two eminent men of their day, William Cadogan and John Locke —both physicians as well as philosophers—advised parents to harden their children as a means of adjusting them to their environment. "Children in general," wrote Cadogan, "are over-clothed and over-fed," and he offered the comforting information that "there are many instances, both ancient and modern, of infants exposed and deserted that have lived several days." Locke added that "most children's constitutions are either spoiled, or at least harmed, by cockering and tenderness."

Such advice—based, as so much that was to follow in dealing with children, on intellectual theory rather than fact or observation—did little to alleviate parents' problems for years to come. John Jay, the first Chief Justice of the Supreme Court, rejoiced in the birth of a beautiful and healthy baby girl, only to see her grow sick and die a few weeks later. Thomas Jefferson buried two infant sons as well as a daughter who lived into her twenties. So did John Adams. Abraham Lincoln buried one son before he went to the White House and another while he was President.

In Colonial America, parents were ignorant in the matter of their children's physical health. As for their youngsters' intellectual and personal development, the harsh Puritan ethic prevailed. One minister's prescription of discipline was quite typical: "And surely there is in all children a stubbornness, and stoutness of mind arising from natural pride, which must in the first place, be broken and beaten down. . . ."

Yet there is much evidence that the Puritans' stern approach to children was not inherently cruel. It simply reflected a fundamental misunderstanding of childhood. Although Cotton Mather is usually remembered for his view that a child is better whipped than damned, such maxims should be understood as a matter of last resort. The Puritans, in fact, believed that it was better for a child to be "puresuaded" than whipped. They did not grant a child a will of his own, but neither did they belittle the power of a parent's affection and understanding in administering the child's will.

New currents were beginning to disturb old patterns of thought. The Age of Reason had begun to make its impact on once sternly untouchable religious articles of faith. Locke compared the formation of children's minds and attitudes to the "fountains of some rivers, where a gentle application of the hand turns the flexible waters into channels that make them take quite contrary courses."

In terms of twentieth-century enlightenment, this view may seem excessively manipulative; but compared to the then-prevailing concept of original sin and the need to root out evil by breaking the child's spirit, Locke's gentle optimism about human nature represented a radical turn toward a humane respect for a child's soul and mind.

Locke believed that adults should respect, rather than merely tolerate, children's "innocent folly, playing and childish actions" as the natural ways of "their age." Most of all, Locke believed in the flexibility of human nature, which reacts to practical training, humane treatment, and experience. It was through experience rather than dogma that man (and the child) learned. There is a distinctly modern note—to be sounded two centuries later by Dewey—in the idea that education takes place in all actions and observations at all times rather than as a narrow, formal, occasional exercise.

Moreover, Locke brought to his ideas of education the physician's concern with physical health. *Some Thoughts Concerning Education* begins with the call for "a sound mind in a sound body" and continues with advice on children's health, food, and shelter. It is only after his discourse on the essential attention to a child's physical well-being that he turns to the cultivation of the mind.

Although Locke believed in discipline and punishment, his was the first insistent voice against the old "Spare the rod and spoil the child" concept that persists in the authoritarian crevices of the popular and even the professional mind to this day. To both the philosopher and the physician in search of rational answers to human development, the rod seemed a lazy way of punishment. The rod, "the only instrument of government that tutors generally know, or even think of, is the most unfit of any to be used in education," he warned. "Constant observation," rather than moral theory, had led him to conclude that beating does "little good." And the boy whose spirit has been broken will grow up, not as a God-fearing man, but as "an useless thing to himself and others."

Locke, too, however, must be understood as a man of his age. It would be misleading to portray him as an avant-garde egalitarian whose benign prescription for the upbringing and education of the young was intended to revolutionize the treatment of all the world's children. In reality, his concern was limited to the education of English gentlemen. The rights of the children of the lower classes were as remote from his kindly thoughts as the rights of Black children were from the thoughts of otherwise enlightened minds in nineteenth- and even early twentieth-century America. Locke's prescriptions for the children of the poor were harsh, not excluding the workhouse and whippings—and it was this separation of humanity into two distinct worlds of class and caste that carried over into America, despite the subsequent Constitutional pledges of equality. It was a concept, once deeply ingrained in the ancient Athenian idea of democracy, that has been difficult to eradicate, perhaps in part because the privileged sector is always intent on securing its powers at the expense of the underprivileged. In many subtle and covert ways, the exclusion of poor children from the concerns afforded the children of affluence has persisted well into the twentieth century. It has been responsible for most of education's accumulating problems. It constitutes much of its unfinished business.

Nevertheless, the rays of enlightenment which fell into the established pattern of Colonial life must be understood in the terms of a society whose guiding light had been religion narrowly described. Religion was an integral part of the children's experience and expectation. Original sin was no fairy tale to keep little children in line; it was, as historian Edmund Morgan defined it, "an unpleasant but inescapable fact, and the sooner children became acquainted with it, the better." The Puritans' only hope was that, despite their natural wickedness, a stern regimen of mind and soul could save them.

But the children's future, and the continuity of true religious faith, were also powerful motivating forces in the Puritans' move to New England. One-third of the *Mayflower*'s passengers were children. And, if the modern student of Puritan days is appalled by the hardships suffered by children, it is well to remember that they may often have been better off than their contemporaries in Europe.

Life in the Colonies was harsh, but its benefits, as well as its hardships, were fully shared by all members of the family, regardless of age. As soon as they were able to sit up, children attended church with their parents—one of the few social activities of the time. The books children read, such as *The New England Primer*,

Foxe's *Book of Martyrs,* and, of course, the Bible, dealt with the terrifying themes of hellfire, death, and damnation. There was a community of awe among the generations, as in the verse:

> Here lie both the young and old,
> Confined in the coffin so small,
> The earth covers over them cold,
> The grave-worms devour them all.

The sense of sin pervaded children's literature. Even infants were "by nature sinners . . . they go astray as soon as they are born," wrote a minister in an "Essay on the State of Infants." Children's schoolbooks were filled with the same intimidating religious ideology. Most of the textbooks, moreover, had to be imported from England, and it was therefore hardly surprising to find a "Protestant Tutor" which, in addition to teaching spelling, reading, and writing of "true English," also was devoted to exposing to the children "the notorious errors, damnable doctrines, and cruel massacres of the bloody Papists. . . ."

Those who could afford it, especially in the South, frequently sent their children to school in England. William Byrd the Elder, who served on the building committee of the College of William and Mary, dispatched his children to his in-laws in England because he felt that they "could learn nothing good here in a great family of Negroes." A friend of John Winthrop's expressed the prevailing sentiment among the well-to-do when he said: "How harde wyll it bee for one broughte up amonge bookes and learned men to lyve in a barbarous place where is no learnying and lesse cyvillytie."

No people in search of a new identity could long remain within the confines of such a self-imposed sense of inferiority. The Colonists had come to America to find a new Utopia, however ill-defined, and, although they had hoped that their children would grow up in the true and pure religion, they had become receptive to new ideas about the worlds they intended to conquer. The social order they had inherited was dominated by religious doctrine. But the wilderness and the vast expanses of land that now confronted them called for more flexible views of life.

The promise of the frontier and of what seemed like an unlimited abundance of land and resources would be better served by Locke's rational reliance on a sound mind in a sound body. This was not an environment for broken spirits but for bold and confident men and women.

Old established legal customs were giving way to a dramatically different concept of the family, property, and inherited wealth. Formerly, power had been thought inherent in some, just as it was withheld from others, as a matter of natural law. English landholding practices and limitations such as the law of entail confined the passing on of an estate to a specific preordained line of heirs, much as in the royal succession; and primogeniture had long provided for the succession of the oldest son to complete ownership, and with it the ultimate power over the family, and of the father's possessions.

Primogeniture was abolished in all the Southern states by 1791, though its effects on land distribution had been limited to instances where there was no will after a landowner's death. Entail was also abolished soon after the Revolution. The elimination of these laws is not nearly as important as the fact that they had never really taken hold of American social development because they ran counter to American views of society.

Thus, family wealth could be broken up and distributed among each new generation. As a result, a new system of property disbursal brought an important change in the traditional family power structure that previously had been dominated by the ruling father and the oldest son as "crown prince." The changes pointed to more equality for all family members, with a far greater impact on American life than is generally realized. The radical nature of these changes may best be gauged from the fact that primogeniture in Britain was not abolished as the prevailing custom until the 1920s.

Children became both a promise and a threat. They could help conquer the new continent, but they could also strike out on their own if home and family became too limiting or too oppressive. There was no place for a dissatisfied son to go in the old country; but by the middle of the eighteenth century the frontier, in America, had become an alternative to the restrictions of a conservative home.

In the New World, too, the challenges and dangers of reality tended to be more relevant than the terror and threats of the fire-and-brimstone sermon and of Hell. Parents and children faced the hazards and the promise of the wilderness together. And, while this created new bonds and a new sense of equality between the generations, it also deflated the authority of the elders. The father's problem was not only that his sons could, and frequently did, leave for greener pastures; the new situation also reduced the value of his experience. In fact, in the new environment, the advantage was often on the side of the young, who could learn faster and were less rigidly bound to what historian Bernard Bailyn has called "prescriptive memories."

"They, and not their parents," wrote Bailyn, "became the effective guides to a new world, and they thereby gained a strange, anomalous authority difficult to accommodate within the ancient structure of family life." Here, then, was the faint beginning of that generational conflict which later was to become so significant in the shaping of American society—a conflict that continues to affect the often contradictory goals of those who control the processes of American education and those who are processed by it.

Even before the American Revolution, the seeds were planted for a new society in which the absolute power of the family would soon be a past memory and where the eternal verities would ultimately find themselves confronted by the very opposite—the youth culture. When the Declaration of Independence was written, its author's age—in his early thirties—symbolized youth's new position in the New World.

The increasingly important new role of youth and childhood in America cannot be simply defined as a more humanitarian view of children. More hands were needed to till the new land and to roll back the wilderness. Adam Smith wrote of America: "Labor is there so well rewarded that a numerous family of children, instead of being a burden, is a source of opulence and prosperity to the parents. The labor of each child before it can leave their house, is computed to be worth a hundred pounds clear gain to them." Marriage, too, Smith observed, is an economic asset under these circumstances, and "the value of children is the greatest of all encouragements to marriage."

An indication of the rather utilitarian view of children was the fact that American farmers soon sought recourse to the law in their efforts to keep the young tied to the farm. As it became difficult and costly to keep hired help, some Colonists tried to solve the problem by supporting the passage of harsh laws requiring filial obedience. Even though enforcement of these laws was to prove irregular and difficult, their very existence offers the first indication of the future contest between children's greater freedom to climb above their parents' station and conservative traditions reinforced by economic need. Mobility, with its prerequisite of the child's open road to opportunity, was not to be achieved without a battle. The rights of children would continue to clash with, and be contested by, the will and the interests of their elders.

In 1657, a Massachusetts minister voiced an age-old complaint: ". . . I find greatest trouble and grief about the rising generation. Young people are little stirred here; but they strengthen one another in evil, by example, by counsel." Worried about the future, he continued: "I tremble to think what will become of this glorious work that we have begun, when the ancient shall be gathered unto their fathers. . . . Methinks I see little godliness, but all in a hurry about the world; everyone for himself, little care of public or common good."

The early *Massachusetts Records* include a resolution which, upon finding that "there is much disorder and rudeness in youth in many congregations in time of the worship of God," the court was ordered to segregate children and youths in church and to "appoint some grave and sober person or persons to take particular care and inspection over them. . . ." Irreverent youths, the resolution continued, were to be scolded on first offense, while repeaters would be fined "and if incorrigible" whipped "with ten stripes" or sent to the house of correction for three days.

Much as the traditionalists may have deplored such developments, there was for many philosophical and detached observers of America a joyous satisfaction in the promise of a new order. The experience, moreover, gave practical support and confirmation to the theoretical optimism inherent in the eighteenth century's faith in reason and the nineteenth century's espousal of romanticism. To many Europeans, America was the land of the "noble savage" in its most admirable incarnation. For those who took to heart Wordsworth's conviction that the child is the father of the man, it was in America that the doctrine and the poetic wish were visibly turning into tested reality.

These were the conditions and the attitudes that made possible a marked change in the new nation's regard for its children, preparing the ground for new philosophical underpinnings. Although belief in infant depravity faded slowly, Locke's view of the child's potential fitted far better into the optimistic assessment of the nation's potential. A rational vision of humanity gave support to the political rebellion against irrational and oppressive governmental powers.

Jefferson, it will be remembered, had been remarkably specific in asking for a new awareness of the difference between children and adults. He had warned that, both physically and intellectually, children and youths between the ages of eight and sixteen were not prepared for the kind of exertions which were often expected or even demanded of them. To ignore these fundamental differences in human development, Jefferson believed with an insight far ahead of his time, was not only hard on children but might indeed prepare the way for an immature and presumably maladjusted adulthood. Children—"these young and tender subjects" —required protection, both for their own sake and for their future health and capacity.

Here, then, was an instinctive and truly revolutionary departure from the traditional view of children as miniature adults. Indeed, Jefferson anticipated the views, tested and documented by empirical evidence a century later, when child psychologists began to plead against the persistent habit of pushing children beyond the innate restrictions of age and immaturity.

By twentieth-century standards, the softening of attitudes toward children would have seemed minimal. Children's lives continued to be harsh. Corporal punishment, still legal in many school districts even today, remained severe. Efforts to "understand" children on their own terms remained little more than a pious wish on the part of the Romantics.

Yet, in the context of the day, these changes were significant. Children's books were becoming more lively and less frightening. If morality still remained always within sight, it no longer was entirely based on fear of damnation. In fact, it began to be coupled with a new and quite worldly materialism that made service to God and economic success on earth readily compatible.

During the 1830s Samuel Griswold Goodrich created the fictitious pedagogue Peter Parley and provided a new formula which mixed easily assimilated facts and opinions with tales of Parley's adventures. Increasingly, textbooks and children's tales made the repetition and moralizing more palatable, a method that would have been scorned as coddling of young minds by earlier generations. The inclusion of fairy tales in children's literature acknowledged the need for entertainment that might have been considered a sinful deviation from God's purpose by the early Puritans. In 1822, as a symbol of changed attitudes, a New York educator named Clement Moore, seeking to delight his own children, wrote: " 'Twas the Night Before Christmas: A Visit from St. Nicholas."

The new respectability of materialism alarmed some thoughtful observers and educators who did not see it as a sound alternative to fire-and-brimstone moralizing. The Transcendentalists—American disciples and theoretical adapters of the European Romantics—sought a world guided by the esthetic and philosophical concepts of truth, beauty, and natural goodness, and these ideas clashed head-on both with the earlier gloomy view of child depravity and with the rising modern adoration of material success. In March 1831, Bronson Alcott, father of Louisa May, the author of *Little Women,* began what was one of the first infant diaries when he recorded the early days of his children, Louisa, Anna, and Elizabeth. Thoughts about his children, as reflected in these chronicles, showed a mixture of philosophic idealism, romantic imagery in the Wordsworth tradition, and religious sentiment. Far from the traditional view of the child as a miniature adult to be modeled after superior adult ways and standards, what emerges is closer to the reverse hope that "a little child shall lead ye." Simple, innocent, and guided by natural goodness and idealism, the child seemed to Alcott able to point the way to a natural moral standard free of, and therefore ideally suited to expose, the adults' materialism and hypocrisies—a view of the world that was to become increasingly the mark of America as a "young" civilization. Eventually, it became the underlying doctrine of the youth culture of the 1950s and the youth revolt of the 1960s. In Alcott's day, however, the impact of his ideas, often expressed in ponderous prose, remained far more modest. Yet the transcendental image of the child led increasingly to an expectation that the family was duty bound to "protect" the children from the ills and the materialism of society rather than merely from the traditional threats of immorality.

Transcendentalism was the ideal philosophical preparation for a new nation's break with oppressive authority and inhibiting traditions. The spirit of independent men, walking proudly toward a new future of self-government, called for a different self-image, and the transcendentalism of Ralph Waldo Emerson provided it. For the new nation that believed God had created all men as equals, there was comfort in Emerson's view of every individual as a unique expression of the Creator. Self-reliance was no longer sinful arrogance but a reflection of true morality. "Whoso would be a man must be a non-conformist," wrote Emerson in his *Essay on Self-Reliance*. "Nothing is at last sacred but the integrity of your own mind."

As Emerson looked at the schools and the teachers of his day, he was appalled by their oppressive approach to the child. His self-reliant man of the future could simply not emerge from an education that stressed passivity, obedience, and conformity. The only way to serve God, he was convinced, would be by the originality in thought and action that alone could bring to full flower the divine gifts of brain and heart. Far in advance of a later American trend toward an education of independent inquiry and study, Emerson said in his address on *The American Scholar:*

> Of course, there is a portion of reading quite indispensible to a wise man. History and science he must learn by laborious reading. Colleges, in like manner, have their indispensible office—to teach elements. But they can only highly serve us, when they aim not to drill, but to create; when they gather from far every ray of various genius to their hospitable halls, and, by the concentrated fires, set the hearts of youth on fire.

In practical terms, back on the farm and on the frontier, the new nation was faced, not with philosophy, but with the problem of reconciling the new freedoms and mobility with the traditional morality—to prevent the children from being irresistibly drawn away from home and the family into a world of highly tempting materialism. Autocratic attempts to force the young to stay at home and do service under the stern patriarchical rule had not worked. And so the American family looked for new ways of rearing children, in an effort to make a virtue of necessity.

These new concerns were reflected in the appearance, between 1820 and 1860, of the first child-rearing manuals. Even though the idea of breaking the child's will, not unlike the taming of a wild horse, was slow to give way, there were signs of a search for more gentle ways of leading the child toward obedience and redemption. A new image of the child was conjured up—"an immortal bud just commencing to unfold its spotless leaves . . . a beautiful flower opening to the sunshine," as reported in an early manual.

Some of the ideas about child rearing, which were to become staples of American women's magazine fare in our time, were making their first appearance. Foremost among these was the role of the mother. With increasing industrialization and a steady trend toward urban living, fathers were moving more and more away from the daily routine in the home. Mother's influence and responsibilities rose in direct proportion to father's diminished presence. Many of the romantic chroniclers of that day painted a picture of mother's voice speaking always within the child, even after the youth had left home for the "wicked" city. It was, of course, flattering and comforting for mothers to be told that "a happy childhood is a boy's safeguard."

But, in addition to the romantic bolstering of mother's image, the new movement provided advice on such mundane matters as nutrition and the dangers of overfeeding or drugging children, on their motor development, on the problems of sexuality, toilet training, cleanliness, and virtue. Dr. William Dewees became noted for his advice, medical and otherwise, to parents, given in his book *A Treatise on the Physical and Medical Treatment of Children.* But in general, such information was still in short supply.

Elizabeth Cady Stanton, later a famous feminist leader, commented in the 1840s: "I had been thinking, reading and observing, and had as little faith in the popular theories in regard to babies as on any subject. I saw them, on all sides, ill half the time, pale and peevish, dying early, having no joy in life. . . ." After the first of her seven children was born, she felt that, "having gone through the ordeal of bearing a child," she was "determined if possible to keep him." Mrs. Stanton searched in vain for literature on babies.

"I was entirely afloat," she wrote, "launched on the seas of doubt without chart or compass. The life and well-being of the race seemed to hang on the slender thread of such traditions as were handed down by ignorant mothers and nurses."

Despite some advances, harsh old ways in dealing with children were firmly entrenched and far from easy to change. When Horace Mann proposed that the use of the rod be limited, he was subjected to vicious attacks for his softness and radicalism. His compassion for children led to an angry exchange between him and leading Boston spokesmen for the teachers' and society's conservative views.

And yet, slowly and steadily, during the middle of the nineteenth century, a rational approach to bringing up children was making its impact felt. Despite the continuing admixture of religious and moral preachings, the child was increasingly seen as an extension of the parents and as the standard bearer of society's expectations. In keeping with the ever-present goals of building a new country and extending man's mastery over the wilderness, there was the growing faith in man's capacity to influence the environment. Young minds and bodies could readily be molded, if only parents and teachers would apply the proper methods and approaches. Parents expected much of children, but they also wanted them to be happy, if for no other reason than to keep them at home. In a reversal of the doctrine of child depravity, Emerson wrote: "Infancy is the perpetual Messiah, which comes into the arms of fallen men and pleads with them to return to paradise."

Henry Barnard, who represented the humane current, wrote: "[Children] must be taken at the earliest opportunity, if the seeds of good are to be planted before the seeds of evil begin to germinate. . . . Here by kindness, patience, order . . . groups may enjoy the sunshine of a happy childhood at school and be bound to respectability and virtue, by ties which they will not willingly break." And Horace Mann urged that "children must actually [see] the eternal laws of justice, as plainly as we can see the sun in the heavens. . . ."

The most telling proof of the changes which, however minimal they might appear in comparison with twentieth-century ideas, were affecting childhood in America was in the reaction by European observers of the day to the relationship between children and adults in America. Quite understandably, the recurring refrain was that children were "precious" or "spoiled," undermining adult authority. Captain F. Marryat, a British naval officer recorded the following exchange he had overheard during a visit to the United States in 1837:

> Father: Come in, Johnny.
> Son: I won't.
> Father: I tell you, come in directly, sir—do you hear?
> Son: I won't. (Running away)

Was the father furious? Quite the contrary, reports the captain. " 'A sturdy republican, sir,' says his father to me, smiling at the boy's resolute disobedience," recalled the British observer.

A sampling of similar foreign comments, usually stressing the uninhibited egoism of American children, includes frequent observations about parents who have "no command over their children," youngsters whose faces were dirty and whose hair uncombed, all of it in a setting where "all members of the family, from the boy of six years of age up to the owner (I was going to say master) of the house, appeared independent of each other."

"The lad of fourteen . . ." said another distressed foreign observer, "struts and swaggers and smokes his cigar and drinks rum; treads on the toes of his grandfather, swears at his mother and sister and vows that he will run away."

But not all European observers were so upset by what they saw. In the 1860s another Englishman watched a father and his fourteen-year-old son chatting and singing together on a train. "There was no attempt," he commented "at keeping up the dignity of a parent as might have been considered necessary and proper with us. There was no reserve. They were . . . already on an equal footing of persons of the same age."

It would be easy (and misleading) at this point to accept the portrait of the lives of native-born American children in relatively comfortable homes—the progeny of the middle and upper classes

—as the full picture of childhood in early America. The dichotomy that had allowed even Locke to lead the way toward a humane turn in the treatment of children, while fully accepting the harsh and often violent handling of the children of poverty, had also begun to govern American standards of judgment, behavior, and policy. The double standard along the divisions of class and economics was an inheritance that was blithely adopted, ignoring the American mandate that ought to have rooted out such distinctions on moral as well as on politico-ideological grounds.

Poor immigrant children, who came to the United States during the first half of the nineteenth century enjoyed few of the benefits of the new concept of childhood. Together with their parents, they experienced the stinging pains of poverty and physical suffering that began with the crossing of the Atlantic itself.

Efforts by U.S. government inspectors to eliminate the most inhumane conditions of such crossings were largely ignored. In 1868, such officials reported that on the ship *Leibnitz,* which had carried 544 passengers, 108 had died of sickness during one single journey. "During the voyage," said the report, "some families had died out entirely; here, a husband had left a poor widow, with small children; and there, a husband had lost his wife. We spoke to some little boys and girls, who, when asked where were their parents, pointed to the ocean with sobs and tears, and cried, 'Down there!' "

Nor was life easy for those who survived the crossing. *The New York Daily Times,* in a story on "Walks Among the New York Poor," gave this account:

> It is a new world to them. . . . They may have the vaguest idea of it all—still to the dullest some thoughts come of the New Free World. . . . Very many of these, who are arriving, will start tomorrow at once for the far West. Some will hang about the German boarding houses in Greenwich Street, each day losing their money, their children getting out of their control, until they at last seek a refuge in Ward's Island, or settle down in the Eleventh Ward, to add to the great mass of foreign poverty and misery there gathered. From there, you shall see their children sallying out these summer mornings, as soon as light to do the petty work of the City, rag-picking,

bone-gathering, selling chips, peddling, by the thousands, radishes, strawberries and fruit, through every street.

Some solid upper-class citizens were alarmed by those conditions and their impact on the cities—perhaps more than on the children themselves. In 1821, Josiah Quincy, who later became president of Harvard, looked at the hordes of poor children in Boston and commented in an official report that he felt they had "a right to require from society a distinct attention and more scrupulous and precise supervision." It was important, he thought (as leading citizens were to think again and again when they saw the violent consequences of poverty endangering the tranquillity of their cities) to provide "for those idle and vicious children, of both sexes and different ages, which often under the command and always with the permission of thoughtless and abandoned parents, are found begging in our streets, or haunting our wharves, market places . . . thus beginning a system of petty stealing. . . ."

And, in an account reminiscent of some of the conditions of the Black ghettoes of the 1960s, John H. B. Latrobe, son of the architect Benjamin Henry Latrobe, thus described the behavior of the "street boys" in 1840:

> If there is tumult of any kind in the streets, they swarm like bees around the spot. . . . If a fire takes place, there is always one or more of them certain to be in the vicinity; and their wild and elfish shreiks are echoed by the whole tribe throughout the streets until the entire city is alarmed. . . . They dare danger with the boldness of older spirits, and when the fire is extinguished they are to be seen prowling among the blackened ruins, turning over the smouldering fragments of beams and rafters and seeking among them for the spoils that the conflagration may have spared. They jostle and fight, too, for their plunder, like the foul birds whose feasts are made of the leavings of decay and death.

There was precious little suggestion of any comprehension that these children's scavenging may have been caused, not by any inherent wickedness or some evil qualities characteristic of foreigners, but by poverty, hopelessness, and neglect. In the persistent myopia of the affluent looking on the ways of the poor, Latrobe worried less about the causes than about the consequences of these children's antisocial acts, voicing the universal fear of the time that these children would join together in mob violence and ultimately create political turmoil. "When the demon spirit of the mob is aroused," he wrote,

> these boys form the nucleus upon which gather all the malignant elements of incendiary violence; theirs is the loudest shout; their hands are the first to hurl the missile and apply the firebrand; and nameless and irresponsible, but numerous and bold, they often succeed in giving to the suggestions of a few discontented spirits the character of a general outbreak. . . .

The double standard in the attitude toward rich and poor children—along with all the prejudices toward what is strange and foreign—is illustrated in Frances Trollope's "history" of Nick the Chicken Boy. Mrs. Trollope, mother of the British novelist Anthony Trollope, visited the United States in the early 1830s. She saw Nick's house surrounded by an air of "indecent poverty," although she seemed content to do business with the little chicken vender.

After bargaining over the price and the conditions of the chickens, Mrs. Trollope concedes that "he brought them at the time directed, extremely well fixed," and as a consequence she "often dealt with him afterwards." Her curiosity, she said, was excited, "and though I felt an involuntary disgust towards the young Jew, I repeatedly conversed with him."

When Nick talked about his hard-earned cash, he seemed to Mrs. Trollope to sneer "with a most unchildish expression." She reluctantly marveled at his shrewdness when he revealed how he bought lean chickens and, after fattening them, probably with food scrounged from his own meager fare, sold them at double the original price. When he admitted that he did not return his profits to his mother, Mrs. Trollope reported the "sharp glance of his ugly blue eyes."

"How Nick got his first dollar," with which to start his business, Mrs. Trollope hinted darkly, "is very doubtful." And then she embarked on what may well be the classic illustration of the sad and ironic paradox in the judgment of children's behavior with which the traditions of the Old World infected the views of the New. "The spirit, activity and industry with which he caused [his first dollar] to increase and multiply," Mrs. Trollope wrote,

> would have been delightful in one of Miss Edgeworth's [a nineteenth-century British novelist] dear little clean bright-looking boys, who would have carried all he got to his mother; but in Nick it was detestable. No human feeling seemed to warm his young heart, not even the love of self-indulgence, for he was not only ragged and dirty, but looked considerably more than half starved, and I doubt not his dinners and suppers half fed his fat chickens.

Mrs. Trollope's little saga cannot be saved from its essential insensitivity toward poor children by the upbeat and inappropriate ending that suggests Nick may some day be very rich and perhaps become President—possibly less a humane commentary on the boy's potential than a political aside concerning the primitive standards of nouveau riche America. What matters is the classic demonstration of the upper class lacking a compassionate understanding of the conditions and the handicaps that confront children of poverty. Nick's lack of manners and grooming seemed evil rather than sadly natural. His truculent speech seemed insolent and hostile, with never a thought given to the boy's insecurity and embarrassment, a consciousness of his inability to put his feelings into the words of a limited—and to Mrs. Trollope, strange, incomprehensible, and offensive—vocabulary.

Time and again, the approaches made to the children of poverty by society and the schools were governed by the belief that these children lived only in a somewhat less fortunate corner of the same world and that they could easily enter into the mainstream, if they only worked hard and imitated the ways of their more affluent contemporaries. Little allowance was made for the numbness that paralyzes the poor in the face of their own, and their families', deprivations and tragedies.

Few of even the more compassionate upper-class observers had any true measure of the burden of the poor. A man could not afford to miss a day's labor, even in the face of a child's death, for

fear of losing his job. Funeral costs added to the grief and desperation because there was not enough money to feed the living. In
1883, a factory worker from Fall River, Massachusetts, testified
before a Senate committee:

> And another thing that helped to keep me down: a year ago
> this month, I buried the oldest boy we had, and that brings
> things very expensive on a poor man. For instance, it will cost
> there, to bury a body, about $100: [Fall River textile men, the
> record showed, earned $1.50 a day, and many worked only
> nine months and were laid off for the rest of the year. Chil-
> dren were given only 60 cents a day.] Now, we could have that
> done in England for about $20. . . . Doctors' bills are very
> heavy—about $2 a visit; and if a doctor comes once a day for
> two or three weeks it is quite a pile for a poor man to pay.

"They charge you as much as they charge people of more
means?" asked the interrogator.

"They charge as much as if I was the richest man in the city,"
the worker replied.

It was hardly surprising that the poor and their children were
overcome by the burden of economic hopelessness, and their
numbness was mistaken for insensitivity and lack of feeling.

Native myths about childhood differed only slightly from Mrs.
Trollope's. Horatio Alger's *Ragged Dick* shared some of Nick the
Chicken Boy's problems and attitudes, but his poverty was
romanticized, his character susceptible to reform and redemption.
"Our ragged hero," the story went, "wasn't a model boy in all
respects. I am afraid he swore sometimes [swearing in Alger's accounts consisted of an occasional "By gracious"] and now and
then he played tricks upon unsophisticated boys from the country
or gave a wrong direction to honest old gentlemen unused to the
city. . . . Then I am sorry to add that Dick had formed the habit
of smoking."

In contrast to Nick, who seemed to Mrs. Trollope so shifty and
detestable, Dick is a lovable poor scoundrel who merely waits for
some genteel ladies or gentlemen to set him on the right course
with a bit of lecturing and sermonizing.

"Nobody ever talked to me so before," says Dick when he has
the fortune to meet such a person of "Good Influence." "They

just called me Ragged Dick and told me I'd grow up to be a vagabond and come to the gallows."

"Telling you won't make it turn out so, Dick," says Good Influence. "If you'll try to be somebody, and grow up into a respectable member of society, you will. You may not become rich—
it isn't everybody that becomes rich, you know—but you can obtain a good position and be respected."

"I'll try," replies Dick, earnestly. "I needn't have been Ragged
Dick so long if I hadn't spent my money in goin' to the theatre,
and treatin' boys to oyster-stews, and bettin' money on cards and
such like."

This was a different, far more benign, and easy-to-shake kind
of poverty. Its sentimental optimism and moralizing were part of
most of the day's literature for and about children. Schoolbooks
and children's magazines moreover reflected all the class consciousness and racial prejudice of society. They were replete with references to people "of a different rank" or a "different station in life."

These attitudes were still evident at the end of the nineteenth
century in *St. Nicholas* magazine, a superb old-fashioned combination of education, moralizing and entertainment. It contained
stories by Frank Stockton, Louisa May Alcott, Thomas Bailey
Aldrich, Helen Hunt, and Bret Harte. There were articles by
Thomas Wentworth Higginson and poems by William Cullen
Bryant. Since this was long before the day when children's literature became a specialty for writers skilled in children's vocabulary
and interests, such contributors constituted an unusual array of
talent for a children's magazine.

Equally interesting was the magazine's "ungraded" approach to
different age levels, with puzzles and stories for the older ones and
special stories for beginning readers, featuring simple words and
printed in larger type. Dick and Jane were still to be invented, but
there were elements of their simplicity in such sentences as "Will
you try to be kind and good, too? I am sure you will. It is the best
way to live."

Children's diaries in *St. Nicholas,* moreover, no matter how
saccharine, had a ring of truth and even an occasional child-
oriented criticism of adults that would have been considered
highly improper a generation or two earlier. "I love Effie," went
one of these, "and I love my mother and father, and Gramma

Blummer. I don't love Aunt Debby. Aunt Debby does not love little girls. When little girls have a pudding pan, Aunt Debby says it is all nonsense for them to have them."

In the days long before movies and television with little opportunity to travel and get to know unfamiliar places and people, *St. Nicholas* was typical of the best entertainment available for children. If it was long on moralizing and if it perpetuated some of the prejudices and class consciousness of the era, it also constituted a major concession to the right of children to be amused and entertained—as children.

Yet these signs of change and progress which improved the lives and the lot of many children among the more secure middle and upper classes should not obscure the dismal conditions in which poor children, particularly among the immigrants, found themselves. They still existed in that grinding poverty that had seemed to Mrs. Trollope so "indecent." A member of the Children's Aid Society, after visiting New York tenements in the 1850s, reported: "Of all the many children who come under our operations, very seldom, indeed, is ever one an American or a Protestant. The Irish emigrants are generally more degraded, even, than the Germans. They rise more slowly, and are cursed with that scourge of their race—Intemperance."

Even the children's books of those days sometimes included references which suggested that poverty was the fault of the poor youngsters, and particularly of the immigrants. "They (young criminals) are mostly children of foreigners who live in garrets and cellars, who are themselves thriftless and indolent . . ." said *The Youth's Companion,* a publication for the entertainment of the more fortunate children of affluent homes.

In a nation whose agricultural and industrial power was expanding rapidly, material and spiritual concerns became scrambled and confused. As the century wore on, Americans were busy building factories, mills, railroads, a country. Few in that hectic era saw, or concerned themselves with, the devastation wrought upon the Indians, or the continuing injustice toward Blacks, or the corruption rampant in industry and politics. It was an era marked by the ascendancy of Boss Tweed and Big Jim Fisk, the exploitation of the workers, the creation of new wealth by the toil and the sweat of the poor, natives and immigrants alike. The earlier dream of continental conquest had almost been fulfilled, and the country now was faced with the promises and problems of industrial growth and urbanization—changes that Jefferson had dreaded as a menace to the republican freedoms.

These were cruel days for poor children in America. Sympathetic observers who visited the orphan asylums and the shelters for the poor were appalled by the conditions they encountered. Children of poor soldiers who had died for their country in the Civil War suffered the double hardship of being penniless and without parents. Some provisions were being made for blind or otherwise severely handicapped youngsters, but those who were merely poor were often left unaided. The stigma of their parents' poverty was visited on them—objects of contempt rather than of pity. And, as always, the poor were feared as the cause of violence.

In July 1863, claiming that children were the leaders of the New York Civil War draft riots, *Harper's Weekly* had reported:

> The affair of Monday last bore a closer resemblance to a European riot than any thing we have ever had here. The leaders and principal actors in the affair were boys—beardless youths of fifteen to eighteen. Behind these, and seemingly operating as a mere reserve force, was a body of men—operatives in foundries and factories, laborers, stablemen, etc.— who did the murdering of policemen, the gutting of houses, the firing of dwellings, etc. after the boys had opened the battle with volleys of stones.

In the same vein, Charles Loring Brace maintained in the *Eleventh Annual Report* to the Children's Aid Society in 1863 that the riots had been carried out by "street-children grown up." He went on:

> . . . There are no dangers to the value of property or to the permanency of our institutions, so great as those from the existence of such a class of vagabond, ignorant, ungoverned children. This "dangerous class" has not yet begun to show itself. . . . They will vote. They will have the same rights as we ourselves, though they have grown up ignorant of moral principle as any savage or Indian. . . . They will perhaps be

embittered at the wealth, and the luxuries, they never share. Then let society beware, when the outcast, vicious, reckless multitude of New York boys, swarming now in every foul alley and low street, come to know their power and use it.

Fear of alienated children unleashed from the discipline of home and society is not peculiar to the American experience. In 1920, in the wake of the Bolshevist revolution, the Soviet authorities expressed very similar alarm about the "wild children," bands of youngsters who had been set adrift by the upheaval and the uncertainties of the day and were seen as a threat to the countryside and the cities in much the same way as the "vagabond" children during and after the Civil War in New York—and one might add the hippies and street people of the 1960s.

What made nineteenth-century America something of a unique historic setting was the confluence of a physical and attitudinal expansion with the pouring into the country's ports of wave after wave of immigrants. Land was still plentiful, and there were jobs for most. Underlying it all was a sense of mobility, the opportunity to move on, without any stigma of defeat.

In a setting that made dependence of children on their families both undesirable and difficult, it became part of the spirit of the time to expand the public schools. Increasing enrollments, however, were more a reflection of practical needs than of political egalitarianism. It has long been a myth that all American children attended the same cozy and comfortable little red schoolhouse where they had the same, unifying experience that eliminated all marks of privilege. The reality of most children's experience was not so uniform. Much depended on whether the pupils were rich or poor, immigrants or native born, urban or rural.

Mary Payne Beard, the mother of historian Charles Beard, recalled her school days in 1849 to 1859 in the Midwest:

> Our school would commence at 8 A.M. We had 15 minutes at 10 o'clock to exercise. Then one hour at noon. The drinking water was carried in an old wooden bucket from a farmer's house a quarter of a mile away, then passed around once a day. We all drank out of an old tin cup, snot nose and all. We had 15 minutes recess in the afternoon. School closed at 4 P.M. . . . Every scholar played together. Black and white . . .

I have not mentioned that there were lice by the millions—
and often the Itch would break out in school.

Another school story is recorded by an Italian immigrant boy of
the same era.

> Every day before receiving our bowl of soup we recited the
> Lord's Prayer. I had no inkling of what the words meant. . . .
> I learned arithmetic and penmanship and spelling—every
> misspelled word written ten times or more, traced painfully
> and carefully in my blankbook. . . . Most learning was done
> in unison. You recited to the teacher standing at attention.
> . . . Repetition. Repetition until the things you learned beat
> in your brain even at night when you were falling asleep . . .
> Lord help you if you broke the rule of silence. I can still
> see a distant relative of mine . . . who could never stop
> talking, standing in a corner behind Mrs. Cutter throughout
> an entire assembly with a string-type clothespin fastened to
> her lower lip as punishment. Uncowed, defiant—with that
> clothespin dangling from her lip.

In another account, Hamlin Garland wrote in *Son of the Middle
Border:*

> . . . It was always too hot or too cold in our schoolroom and
> on certain days when a savage wind beat and clamored at the
> loose windows, the girls humped and shivering, sat upon their
> feet to keep them warm and the younger children with shawls
> over their shoulders sought permission to gather close to the
> stove.
> Our dinner pails (stored in the entry way) were often
> frozen solid and it was necessary to thaw out our mince pie
> as well as our bread and butter by putting it on the stove.
> I recall, vividly, gnawing, dog-like, at the mollified outside of
> a doughnut while its frosty heart made my teeth ache. . . .

In urban schools in the East, and throughout most of the South,
segregation of the sexes was considered desirable well into the
middle of the nineteenth century. A report by New York City's
Board of Education said in 1853: "The considerations of propriety
are so obvious that they need not be enumerated much less dwelt

upon." The pattern prevailed in the city as late as 1890, when there were only fourteen coeducational elementary schools out of a total of 108. (No such "considerations of propriety" prevented the resort to coeducation in the West and most of the newly settled regions where the economics of numbers simply made separate schooling for boys and girls impractical.)

American reformers knew there was much room for improvement. They looked on the haphazard approach to public education with intense concern. Horace Mann had studied a great variety of town reports in the late 1830s and found many of the schools small and shabby. One school in Massachusetts was reported to stand in the middle of the road. Many schools lacked even an outhouse. Mann sadly concluded "that in most of these particulars which contribute to the common comforts and conveniences of life . .   the convicts are better provided for than the children."

Teacher's pay was as low as the esteem in which teachers were often held throughout the nineteenth century and well into the twentieth. Women were paid less than men; rural teachers less than those in the cities.

Nineteenth-century reformers who urged that more women be employed as teachers bolstered their appeal with an interesting and revealing rationale. Women, they argued, had higher innate moral character. A woman was thus "constitutionally fitted . . . by her Creator for the duties of a teacher." Horace Mann reflected this view in his statement: "Females govern with less resort to physical force, and exert a more kindly, humanizing and refining influence upon the dispositions and manners of their pupils." Henry Barnard echoed these sentiments with his observation that the "introduction of a large number of female teachers, in winter as well as in summer, has greatly improved the discipline, moral influence, and manners of the Rhode Island public schools."

Mrs. Hale of *Godey's Lady's Book* stated that women teachers were "fast becoming the fashion" in midcentury—a trend that was probably due as much to men's not flocking to a profession that offered them so little money and status, as to women's supposedly higher moral fiber. For men or women, teachers' lives were often dismal. Their role in the classroom tended to be an adversary one. An observer in Kentucky recalled a teacher who "ruled despotically" and another who was "too sweet to be spoiled by the drudgery of the classroom." Few teachers were college-educated; their major function was to maintain order and to listen to recitations. "Teachers," said one report, "did the janitor work, but often when one was well liked, boys would be early at school to help the teacher."

The cumulative effect of the teachers' low prestige and spotty education plus children's greater assertiveness was an excessive reliance on physical force. Throughout the nineteenth century, corporal punishment was still almost routinely considered a mark of proper teaching. Henry Thoreau had quit the classroom after two weeks because he refused to whip his pupils, even when their parents demanded it. Herman Melville lasted through one winter in a school in Pittsfield (Massachusetts) before he left in disgust over the brutality.

In his memoirs, Reverend Warren Burton wrote: "I . . . heard our Ben tell of the direful punishments of the winter school; of the tingling hand, black and blue with twenty strokes, and to be closed for a fortnight from soreness." One of his own teachers had left him with these memories: "She kept order; for her punishments were horrible, especially to us little ones. She dungeoned us in that windowless closet for a whisper. . . . If we were restless on our seats . . . a twist of the ear, or a snap on the head from her thimbled finger, reminded us that sitting perfectly still was the most important virtue of a little boy in school. . . ."

Not only pioneer children or immigrants were beaten. The sons of Boston's elite got their share. Charles Francis Adams recalls, in a biography of Richard Henry Dana: "How often did our hearts sicken at the sight of that chest and that ferule. The boys were then called out, one at a time, and the blows were given upon the flat of their hands, from two or four up to one or two dozen, according to the nature of the offence and the size of the boys." Thomas Wentworth Higginson recalls a Mr. Wells who "carried always a rattan in his hand and it descended frequently on back and arm."

A schoolmaster summarized contemporary thought: "The truth is, that it seemed to be the prevailing opinion both among teachers and parents, that boys and girls would play and be mischievous at any rate, and that consequently masters must punish in some way or other. It was a matter of course, nothing better was expected."

William Dean Howells, recalling rural schools as late as the 1870s, spoke of children whipped, not only for misconduct but also for academic failure. Thrashing, he suggested, is "one of the most efficient agencies of education." Similarly, many parents were apprehensive if their children's teacher spared the rod or failed to augment corporal punishment with the humiliating use of dunce caps and special dunce corners. The ministerial spirit of punishing the sinning child for the good of his own soul died slowly—if at all. Well into the twentieth century, parents felt they were expressing the proper school spirit by singing:

> Schooldays, schooldays,
> Dear old golden rule days,
> Readin' and writin' and 'rithmetic,
> Taught to the tune of the hickory stick . . .

More than three hundred years have passed since Harvard enacted a statute in 1656 that called for the punishment of "all misdemeanors of the youth in their society, either by fine or by whipping in the Hall openly. . . ." And more than a century has passed since the Indiana Supreme Court in 1853, after noting that it had been made illegal for a husband to beat his wife or a master his apprentice or even an officer in the Navy a sailor, asked: "Why the person of the schoolboy should be less sacred than that of the apprentice, or the sailor, is not easily explained."

The question remains yet to be answered. The majority of states still either specifically allow or do not prohibit corporal punishment. New York's penal code states that parents, guardians, and teachers "may use physical force, but not deadly physical force," when they "reasonably" believe it necessary to maintain discipline or promote the welfare of minors.

Even though New York City does have a statute prohibiting corporal punishment in the public schools, it was nevertheless discovered in 1974 that administrators in some of its junior high schools had routinely used paddles and belts to beat children. Public reaction, however, was generally one of indifference, and many persons approved outright. Even many of the parents in the school's predominantly Black neighborhood—the administrators charged with the illegal beatings were also Black—seemed to support that form of discipline. *The New York Teacher,* official publication of the United Federation of Teachers, headlined its report, "U.F.T. Upholds Due Process in Corporal Punishment Charges," thus giving the defense of the administrators accused of doing the beating priority over concern for the students who had been beaten. The district's school superintendent complained of a "double standard" that permitted school officials in suburban and upstate New York to apply corporal punishment whereas the city's bylaws prohibited such discipline.

Yet, even though the stern and cruel myth about the beneficial rod was still very much alive, there were signs of progress. The city's school authorities this time came down hard on the teachers and deans who had ignored the ban.

In the past, the harsh treatment of children may actually have become aggravated by the very fact that a new spirit of independence among the young and the first signs of a generation gap had begun to make pupils less docile than had traditionally been expected by home and society.

A superintendent in Pennsylvania, during the 1850s, described this scene:

> I found between 30 and 40 pupils of every grade of size from mere infants to young women. . . . The floor was literally covered with shavings, chips, apple cores, etc. . . . One little chap was sitting in the middle of the floor busily engaged stuffing the chips with which he was surrounded into his shoes. Others were stretched at full length on the benches enjoying, if not a siesta, at least a comfortable lounge.

The treatment of children, and the beginning efforts by a minority of humanitarians and progressives to render it less cruel, was not to be an issue to be resolved exclusively in the schools. With industrialization, the child's "usefulness" had begun to shift from the farms—where the earlier bonds of quasi-indenture on the family plot had long been loosened by the open opportunities of the frontier—to the urban sweatshops. Better than any other chapter in the history of American childhood, the uphill battle against child labor and the exploitation of the young for economic reasons illustrates the country's often contradictory attitudes toward children.

Throughout the Colonial period, children had been an integral part of the labor pool, exactly as they had been an inseparable part of the family. In the middle of the seventeenth century, the Massachusetts General Court had decreed that "all hands not necessarily imployd on other occasions, as woemen, girls, and boyes, shall, and hereby are enjoyned to spin according to their skill and abillitie; and that the select men in every towne doe consider the condition and capacitie of every familie, and accordingly to assess them, as one or more spinners." William Penn's charter for Pennsylvania prescribed in 1682 that all children in the province, on reaching the age of twelve, should be taught some skill or trade. Many of those who came to the Colonies as servants were children and youths who entered into voluntary agreements to serve, in return for their passage which allowed them to escape from the orphanages and workhouses in England. The line between servitude and apprenticeship was thin.

Colonial apprenticeship had grown out of the medieval practice, as articulated in the Elizabethan Statute of Artificers; but there was an important difference: the American system emphasized responsibility for general education. Between 1642 and 1731, several colonies passed laws that reflected at least theoretical concern for the education of apprentices. Masters who were unwilling or unable to tutor their apprentices were expected to send them to school.

Although some children began to work as early as age six, it was usually at about fourteen that their fathers chose a permanent calling for them. According to the Puritan ethic, such a calling was more than a means of earning a living—it was the father's way to carry out God's plan and also to be certain that the child's occupation would be of service to society.

As the power of religion declined during the seventeenth and eighteenth centuries, the concept of the innate value of work became increasingly harnessed to worldly and personal gain rather than to God and community. But this did not alter the widespread belief that to make children work was to do what was "good for them." Idle hands continued to be a lure for the devil.

The Puritans' treatment of their children was often harsh, but there is little evidence of deliberate and cruel abuse. Then as now, "battered child" cases occurred, but they were punished by law. The Records of Plymouth Colony Court Orders, for example, show this summary of a case in 1655: "The said John was put forth in the extremity of cold, though unabled by lameness and soreness to perform what was required; and therefore in respect of cruelty and hard usage he died." His master was punished. The case was the exception; the rule was for children to work alongside the adults on their parents' farms, in the workshops and in the home.

Toward the latter part of the eighteenth and well into the nineteenth century, the growth of the cotton industry and other similar developments led to a diversification of, and need for, labor that made the employment of children a key to industrial expansion. The Slater textile factory in New England at first intended to maintain the apprentice system, but it was soon concluded that this "did not suit the American temperament" and was quickly abandoned. Children became labor—at a low and profitable price.

Two systems had been developed for recruiting children as factory labor. The first placed the entire family within a compound owned by the mill; the other relied on a boarding house arrangement for children and youths only, while their parents resided elsewhere. Families who lived in the mill or factory compounds were compelled to buy all their provisions at the company store, leading to a continuous struggle to stay out of debt. More and more of these families found themselves locked into a vicious circle of work plus poverty. Their own and their children's status was akin to that of indentured labor and to the system that kept sharecroppers the subservient property of the land owners.

Advocates of child labor for developing industries in need of cheap and plentiful manpower built their case on the fear of idleness and the sanctity of work. George Washington, in the spirit of his time, had noted in his diary that he was favorably impressed with the work of young girls in a cloth factory, referring to them as "the daughters of decayed families" who were nevertheless "girls of character." The work they were doing seemed to him "of public utility and private advantage."

Alexander Hamilton, in his report on the advantages of manufacturing, in 1791 had expressed the conviction that, "in general,
women and children are rendered more useful, by manufacturing
establishments, than they would otherwise be."

Tench Coxe, a Philadelphian who was president of the Society
for the Encouragement of Manufacturers, in assessing the conditions and potential success of "emigrators," thought that their
children could be "kept from idleness and rambling, and of course
from early temptations to vice" if they were placed in "manufac-
tories" for a time, increasing thereby also their parents' capacity
to "clothe, feed and educate them."

Boosters of industry painted an idyllic picture of manufacturing, not as the breeder of urban congestion, but as an enclave of
the work ethic. The image created by one such advocate's prospectus was that of factories located "on chosen sites, by the fall
of waters and the running streams, the seats of health and cheer-
fulness, where good instruction will secure the morals of the young,
and good regulations will promote . . . the exercise of civil duties." This public relations statement of high purpose wound up
by suggesting that "the best educated of the poorer class" would
owe their chance at being educated at all to the benevolence of
the factory system. The recurrent theme of the day was that what
was good for the manufacturers was good for the poor.

The first law requiring the schooling of children in "manufac-
tures" was passed in Connecticut in 1813. But, as with so much
social legislation, and particularly with legal education requirements, the statute continued to be honored more in the breach
than the observance. To be sure, some Sunday schools were established for the factory children. They were, however, reflections
of the paternalism that dominated philanthropic thinking rather
than of genuine concern for either the children or their education.
These practices were copied, as Samuel Slater, the cotton manufacturer of Massachusetts, made clear, from such European establishments as the cotton mills of Derbyshire, England, where they
had been "shown to be useful and applicable to the circumstances
of an American population."

After the pieties are brushed aside, there remains one overriding reason for the popularity of child labor: it was cheap. But the
price paid for it by the children was exorbitant, to their health,

their education, and their future, and to the families whose human bonds were being destroyed as surely as the children's own lives. When children and parents were members of the same labor pool, subject to the same authority of "bosses," dependent on the same paternalism, if they were fortunate, or the same autocratic rule, if they were not, parental authority was eroded and the family unit dismantled.

A few voices cried out against such lack of humane concern. The children's pinched faces spoke more eloquently than the industry-boosters' rhetoric. In 1801, Josiah Quincy, who was subsequently to become president of Harvard and who was to speak with little sentimentality about "those idle and vicious children" in the streets, was taken on a tour of a factory. He listened to the guide's eloquent praise of the opportunities to earn a living offered to so many poor children. Quincy wondered. "An eloquence," he said, "was exerted on the other side of the question more commanding than this, which calls us to pity those little creatures, plying in a contracted room, among flyers and coggs, at an age when nature requires for them air, space and sports. There was a dull dejection in the countenance of all of them."

By the middle of the nineteenth century child labor had grown to become an integral part of industrialization. No humanitarian force was strong enough to eliminate a system on which the profits of the new factories depended in such large measure. Although many of the Eastern states passed laws requiring the laboring children to attend school, these measures were little more than legal window-dressing.

Thus, Horace Mann was able to say six years after the passage of Massachusetts' compulsory school attendance law in 1836:

> It is obvious that children of ten, twelve or fourteen years of age may be steadily worked in our manufactories, without any schooling, and this cruel deprivation may be preserved for six, eight, or ten years, and yet during all this period, no very alarming outbreak will occur to arouse the public mind from its guilty slumber.

And parents—out of necessity, timidity, and greed—cooperated with employers in the wholesale violation of the laws which aimed at improving their children's chances for a better life.

The early nineteenth century saw some sporadic efforts to improve the children's lot in the factories. A report to the Assembly of the New York Legislature in 1835 said that the number of hours which children were required to work was "altogether too great a proportion of their time . . . they . . . are required to labor from 12 to 14 hours each day, being several hours more labor than is exacted even from the convicts in our State Prisons." In 1850, Horace Greeley called for a ten-hour work day for children under twelve, but to no avail.

The public, not wanting its conscience troubled by reality, continued to pretend that nothing had changed since the days of the apprentice system, when the young workers had had a far more personal relationship with their employers. The distortion of the Protestant work ethic, with its benefits to employer and worker alike, persisted and bolstered the moral rhetoric about the value derived by the children from their labor. Any suggestion to limit the hours of work, even for the very young children, was adamantly opposed as an improper interference with the parents' natural rights.

And so children suffered. Harriet Robinson, who later became a pioneer in the battle for women's rights, looked back on her own drudgery in a Lowell, Massachusetts, mill in the mid-1830s. She had been fortunate, as so many of her fellows were not, to attend school until the age of ten, when her widowed mother was forced to send her to work. The working day, Miss Robinson recalled,

> extended from five o'clock in the morning until seven in the evening, with one-half hour for breakfast and for dinner. Even the doffers were forced to be on duty nearly fourteen hours a day. . . . We were obliged to be in the mill at just such a minute, every hour, in order to doff out full bobbins and replace them with empty ones.

Spinners and weavers were not allowed to read books openly in the mill. But, the account went on, "they brought their favorite 'pieces' of poetry, hymns, and extracts, and pasted them up over their looms or frames, so they could . . . commit them to memory."

The gap between rich and poor widened. As industry expanded, so did the variety and scope of child labor. Its spread became particularly rapid in the South after the Civil War and the end of slavery. By 1900, one third of the workers in Southern mills were children. Whatever feeble efforts at reform were occasionally launched, they generally aimed at providing some schooling for working children rather than protecting them from exploitation. Child labor itself was still considered both financially necessary and ethically sound.

In 1860, a Special Commission on the Hours of Labor and the Condition and Prospects of the Industrial Classes heard the following testimony from John Wild, a worker in Fall River, Massachusetts:

> I have two little boys, one eleven and the other about eight and a half. I am no scholar myself, because I have always been working in the mill, and I am sorry for it. I don't want my children to be brought up in the same night school. I want, if it is possible, to get a law so that they go to school, and know how to read and write their names.

Asked if his youngest boy was getting any schooling at the time, Wild replied: "When he gets done in the mill, he is ready to go to bed."

> Question: Do you know that your children are working contrary to the law?
> Wild: I didn't know there was any law.
> Question: Did you know that if I should go to Fall River and prosecute their employer, he could be compelled to pay a fine for employing your children?
> Wild: No sir, being no scholar.

Another witness recalled these conditions:

> Five days of the week, at the outer edge of winter, I never stood out in the daylight. I was a human mole, going to work while the stars were out and returning under the stars. . . . The mule-room was kept at 85 to 90 degrees of heat. The hardwood floor burned my bare feet. I had to gasp quick, short gasps to get air into my lungs at all. The tobacco chew-

ers expectorated on the floor, and left little pools for me to wade through. . . . There are few prison rules more stringent than the rules I worked under in that mule-room. . . . There was a rule against looking out of a window. . . . There was a rule preventing us from talking to one another. . . . We were not supposed to sit down, even though we had caught up with our work. . . . There was a rule that anyone coming to work a minute late would lose work.

The shame of child labor extended from coast to coast. The Fourth Annual Report of the California Bureau of Labor Statistics of 1890, describing conditions in a jute mill in East Oakland, not only duplicated all the horrors found in Massachusetts, but added that "some of the unnatural parents live off the earnings of these overworked toilers." The Third Annual Report of the Illinois Factory Inspectors in 1895 painted an equally dismal picture of the Chicago stockyards where "in several places a boy has been found working at a dangerous machine because his father had been disabled by it."

Although some of the official and upper-class moralists tended to scorn parents for exposing their children to these hardships, they cavalierly overlooked the practice engaged in by many manufacturing companies that virtually compelled ignorant, poor, and unskilled parents to enter into agreements, usually oral, to commit their children to the factories at an early age.

Neither laws nor human compassion compensated the children for the consequences of injuries sustained on their often dangerous jobs. An investigation by the National Child Labor Committee in 1913 recorded this tersely:

> Joseph Alski, aged 14, injured at Jane Mills Fruit Packing Company. Injured while coring apples. The knife slipped and stuck him in the eye. The accident caused complete blindness, also affecting sight of the other eye. He lost two months and about $24 pay. No financial relief was given. May 17, 1913.

Only gradually, public opinion began to come face to face with the grim realities. Reformers and muckraking journalists had taken up the crusade. Upton Sinclair's *The Jungle* exposed the exploitation of Polish children in the Chicago stockyards. John Spargo published *The Bitter Cry of the Children*. Magazines such as *Survey* and *McClure's* detailed with increasing frequency the atrocities committed against childhood in the sweatshops, the mills, and the mines as well as in the cotton fields of Texas and in the migrant labor camps of the Northwest.

In its February 1903 issue, *McClure's* Magazine laid bare the horrors of life in a coal mine. "The boss," the article said, "is armed with a stick, with which he occasionally raps on the head and shoulders a boy who betrays a lack of zeal. . . . The report makes no classification of miners by their ages, but I am convinced that . . . a total of . . . nearly one-sixth of all the employees of the anthracite coal mines are children."

Then the article offered the following exchange:

> Union official: How old are you?
> Boy miner: Thirteen going on fourteen.
> Union official: On the level now. This is union business. You can speak freely, understand?
> Boy: Oh, dat's a diffurnt thing altogether. I'm nine years old. I've been working since me fadder got hurted in the explosion in No. 17 a year ago. . . .

At the time of the coal strike of 1902, boys constituted twenty percent of the membership of the United Mine Workers of America.

Reformers were diligent and compassionate in describing the children's harsh lot. They did much to debunk the importance of child labor to the survival of poor widows. They wanted to enact laws to prohibit children from working, but they failed to comprehend that all this was only half the battle—that the children and their families needed help that could only come through positive social and economic action.

As long as the government lacked the power to "interfere" with the "free contract" between children, or their parents, and factory owners, it was practically impossible to prevent exploitation and cruelty. Courts of that era, accepting the supremacy of laissez faire, bent most of their efforts to the citation of judicial excuses for the exploitation of children. In 1885, for example, the

New York Court of Appeals struck down a law forbidding cigar manufacture in tenements on the grounds that the "hallowed associations and beneficent influence" of the home could best protect the health and morals of the child. Clearly, the judges had not bothered to look at conditions in the tenement sweatshops which they adorned with all the sentimentality of a "Home, Sweet Home" sampler.

Huge fortunes were made in factories, mines, and mills precisely because children toiled in semistarvation. Labor unions, whose interests clearly called for action against such exploitation, were not yet strong enough, and the governmental repression that was invoked against the strikes of the era had left them almost as powerless as the children themselves. Under such conditions, nobody was able to take effective steps when, for example, poverty-stricken youngsters in New York manufactured artificial flowers in slum tenements at a wage of 6 cents for twelve dozen or 144 flowers which were sold for 7 cents apiece.

Against such practices, reformers established the National Child Labor Committee in 1904, with the support of such prominent figures as Felix Adler, the founder of the Ethical Culture Society, Florence Kelley, Jane Addams, and Lillian Wald. But it was not until 1914 that the committee, which had sharply divided over the question of federal legislation, agreed that this was in fact the only way to obtain uniform and enforceable standards. Joining forces with the U.S. Children's Bureau, which had been established in 1912, the committee worked successfully for passage of the Keating-Owens Act in 1916. Regarded as a progressive triumph, the measure had been in effect for 275 days, when the Supreme Court declared it unconstitutional on June 3, 1918.

By a vote of five to four, the court held in *Hammer v. Dagenhart* that the act exceeded the authority given to Congress in matters involving interstate commerce and assumed "power as to a purely local matter to which the Federal authority does not extend." If Congress can thus restrict the local authority's powers, the majority held, "all freedom of commerce will be at an end, and thus our system of government be practically destroyed." Clear proof, if it were needed, that the right to exploit children was considered fundamental to the nation's economic and political stability.

Justice Oliver Wendell Holmes, in a historic dissent, wondered why it was proper to translate popular moral outrage into the prohibition of alcoholic beverages under the Volstead Act, but impermissible to prohibit the evil of child labor. "If there is any matter," Holmes wrote, "upon which civilized countries have agreed— far more unanimously than they have with regard to intoxicants and some other matters over which this country is now emotionally aroused—it is the evil of premature and excessive child labor."

Conservatives continued for twenty years thereafter to argue successfully that federal child labor legislation would be in violation of states' rights, and they thus prevented such a federal law from being enacted until the 1930s. Although new and progressive pedagogical ideas had begun to seep into the schools of that era and far-reaching psychological reassessments of children, emanating from the work of Freud and Gesell, promised to revolutionize child rearing, the lives of those "other" children of the invisible minority of poverty continued to be governed by economic and political primitivism.

Since the 1920s were a time of "normalcy" rather than of national concern, the American people's attitude toward children— at least to those children who, because of their low station, were exposed to the consequences of public policy—assumes special significance. In 1924, a joint resolution proposing a child labor amendment passed both houses of Congress by large majorities. But powerful forces were at once set in motion to block ratification by the states. During the same year, the Louisiana and Georgia legislatures refused to approve the amendment, and voters in Massachusetts rejected it in a referendum. Yet it had been in Massachusetts that the nation's first compulsory school legislation was enacted in the previous century.

Conservative publications and business journals denounced the proposed amendment in terms typified by the *Manufacturer's Record*, which editorialized on September 4, 1924:

> If adopted, this amendment would be the greatest thing ever done in America in behalf of the activities of Hell. It would make millions of young people under 18 years of age idlers in brain and body, and thus make them the devil's best

workshop. It would destroy the initiative and self-reliance
and manhood and womanhood of the coming generations.

Using the presidency of Columbia University as his pulpit,
Nicholas Murray Butler intoned: "Surely no true friend of childhood can wish to support a measure which will make possible the
substitution of Congressional control of childhood and youth for
the natural relationship of parent and guardian."

And, with what was to become the predictable lever of American policy-making by popular fear, the threat of subversion was
invoked in an editorial in the Catholic *Boston Pilot* that warned:
"For the parental control over children [the amendment], would
substitute the will of Congress and the dictate of a centralized
bureaucracy, more in keeping with Soviet Russia than with the
fundamental principles of American government."

It was only when the reforms of the New Deal swept across
the nation's socioeconomic landscape during the Depression that
a federal child labor law was also enacted. After specific legislation prohibiting child labor was finally passed, Franklin D. Roosevelt said: "That makes me personally happier than any other one
thing which I have been connected with since I came to Washington."

Even then, not all children were freed from exploitation and
drudgery. Although pressure from by now powerful labor unions
and school attendance laws, which had at long last come to be
enforced in the majority of states and communities, kept children
out of factories and barred them from most of heavy labor, much
farm work and harvesting continued to depend on the cheap
manpower of minors. *The New York Times* reported in April
1971 on the dismal conditions under which such children continued to toil. The American Friends Service Committee, in
March 1971, described child farm labor of the 1970s in terms
reminiscent of industrial child labor prior to 1938. Although
twenty states have enacted laws to restrict field work for children
during school hours, enforcement remains as erratic as it had been
in the days of child labor in the factories and mills in the 1890s.

In Louisiana, a federally supported special school program
for out-of-state, migrant harvesters provides for classes that start
at noon, after the berries have been picked. The children thus re-

join their families at 6 P.M., at the end of a twelve-hour day of labor in the fields and in school. The parents collect the children's pay to supplement the meager family income. It is a compromise, with a nod to the children's right to an education, but with little concern for the children's welfare and development. Clearly, too, it is a policy that would be rejected out of hand for the nation's majority of more fortunate children, thus keeping intact the dichotomy that has governed the Establishment's approach to children's rights ever since Locke made his distinction between the humane new concern for the sons and daughters of the privileged classes and the progeny of the poor.

Economic policy continues to be a powerful persuader, and arguments to prevent reforms remain what they had been a century earlier. A high-school principal in a Louisiana school readily conceded that the youngsters who come to school at noon are tired from a hard morning in the fields. But, he added, the families simply could not survive if the children were not allowed to work. Howard T. Juji, director of research and legislation in Oregon's Farm Bureau, said that, "if children were kept out of the fields, they could lose the opportunity to earn," and that, at any rate, working taught them a sense of responsibility. In Aroostook County, Maine, where school recesses for the potato harvest in September and October and children pick thirty-five percent of the crop, the State Commissioner of Agriculture called this an opportunity to learn "self-reliance."

A school superintendent in the Southwest said: "We have tried to make the best of a bad situation. The youngsters are an economic asset to the parents, and if they were forced to leave for school at 8 [in the morning], daddy's little helpers would have to pick [berries] and not go to school at all." A farmer, asked if this was an accurate appraisal, looked up from his loading of berry crates and replied in Spanish: "Then, in the future, they could think about doing something else besides going out on the farms." For some children, what was a right and a reality for so many others still remained a dream.

The same forces which, at the turn of the century, were trying to protect children against exploitation in the mills, mines, and factories, were also campaigning for a new reliance on experts with specialized knowledge, in changing the public view of children's place in society. Many of the reformers had become convinced of the need for a Federal Children's Bureau. Lillian Wald and Florence Kelley had been campaigning for it, and in 1909 President Roosevelt urged its establishment in a special message to Congress.

It was an uphill fight. Despite the President's endorsement, the bill failed to reach the floor of Congress in 1909. Critics of the proposal challenged its constitutionality, charging that such an agency would usurp jurisdiction over child welfare which by rights belongs to the states and localities. The New York Society for the Prevention of Cruelty to Children opposed the measure adamantly for exactly the same reasons.

Others fought the Children's Bureau, not on such alleged principles, but on bureaucratic grounds. They insisted that the Bureau of the Census or the Bureau of Education could readily take over whatever new duties the supporters of the Children's Bureau had in mind, without adding a new agency. Spokesmen for the South, who were bitterly opposed to all proposals to limit child labor, reacted against the idea of a Children's Bureau simply because the National Child Labor Committee was among its principal sponsors.

Despite such a powerful coalition of the conservative forces and the vested interest groups of the existing—though chronically ineffective—child welfare agencies, the bureau was approved, after eighty hours of heated debate, in 1912. The bill's supporters attributed its passage largely to the last-minute support of Elihu Root of New York. "I wept (and felt like an idiot!)," Lillian Wald wrote, "when Root came forward and fought for it. For it meant the tide had turned and we had won."

Although the legislative victory was indeed an indication that the tide was turning, opponents to a more generous attitude to children continued to fight a powerful rearguard action. Once established, the new bureau faced starvation by appropriation. In 1914, only $25,640 were allocated to the new agency, and each time the question of renewal reached the floor of Congress, Southern Democrats, aided by some New England traditionalists and mill interests, fought adequate funding by raising again and again the issues of constitutionality and governmental efficiency.

After a slow and troubled start as little more than a fact-finding office, the bureau eventually grew into a significant force for the improvement of the lives and rights of children throughout the nation. Grace Abbott, who headed the bureau from 1921 to 1934, provides this description of its early problems and its philosophy in *The Child and the State:*

> It was originally wholly a research organization and information center as were the scientific bureaus in the Department of Agriculture, the Interior, and Commerce and Labor. While scientific research in animal husbandry, foods, minerals, or fish was accepted without question as a function of the government, the proposal to study the physical, mental and social problems of childhood was opposed as socialistic.

Questions of home, school, and society were only part of the new concern for children. The very subject of children's health as distinct from adult medical care had not even been defined until after the Civil War. Fatalism, orthodoxy, and ignorance, among the lay public as well as within the health professions, posed as much of a threat to progress as the attack by germs and infection itself.

In 1890, Abraham Jacobi, who is generally credited with the founding of modern pediatrics, wrote: "There never was any systematic instruction in the diseases of children, by a teacher appointed for that branch of medicine exclusively, until (in 1860) I established a weekly children's clinic in the New York Medical College, at the time in East Thirteenth Street."

In the training of a medical student, Jacobi pointed out, "a single hour weekly [is reserved] . . . for the special study of the diseases of children, who will, in his future practice, form the majority of his patients."

Abraham Flexner, in his classic exposé of the low estate of medical education, published in 1910 by the Carnegie Foundation, reported that pediatric education was virtually nonexistent and instruction in obstetrics in a dismal state.

Breaking down the walls of indifference and ignorance was a laborious task. Campaigns had to be waged for mandatory birth registration and the compulsory pasteurization of milk. School buildings needed to conform to minimum health and safety standards. The Children's Bureau had begun to disseminate information about infant care, but state and municipal agencies continued to administer most programs; and they did so with a wide range in effectiveness.

In 1906, *The Journal of the American Medical Association* called for the establishment of a National Department of Health. "Thousands have been expended," the editorial said,

> in stamping out cholera among swine, but not one dollar was ever voted for eradicating pneumonia among human beings. . . . The states' rights doctrine can be applied against the Department of Agriculture as effectively as against a National Department of Health. It is not then, a question of constitutionality, but rather, of whether or not such a department is needed by the nation.

A measure of the historic progress in efforts at raising the nation's consciousness of children's needs is provided by themes and goals of the early White House Conferences on Children. The first such meeting, to which Theodore Roosevelt invited 216 child welfare workers in 1909, merely dramatized the plight of "dependent" children—orphans, abandoned, and destitute youngsters—without calling for any concrete action or funds.

The second White House Conference in 1919 went about setting minimum standards for child welfare. Its general statement said in a tone of hope and idealism:

> Every child should have a normal home life, an opportunity for education, recreation, vocational preparation for life, and for moral and spiritual development in harmony with American ideals and the educational and spiritual agencies by which these rights of the child are normally safeguarded.

At about the same time, the Supreme Court still held child labor laws to be unconstitutional; yet it is of considerable significance that "the rights of children" were for the first time being cited at the very summit of the American government.

The third White House Conference was called in 1930, in the midst of the depression which had brought untold suffering to the nation's children. About 3000 delegates were in attendance to discuss "Child Health and Protection." A Children's Charter was issued "recognizing the rights of the child as the first rights of citizenship." It was a charter that sought to offer "for every child a home and that love and security which a home provides. . . . For every child health protection from birth through adolescence . . . protection against labor that stunts growth."

But outside the conference rooms, many children faced gloom and deprivation. Although the Children's Bureau had provided every possible documentation of the desperate need for relief and food in many severely depressed areas, a bill sponsored by Robert LaFollette and Edward P. Costigan that would have empowered the bureau to administer unemployment relief was blocked by the Hoover Administration. President Hoover, who had personally led relief efforts abroad and organized food shipments to alleviate human suffering in Russia after World War I, nevertheless scuttled legislative efforts to allow the Children's Bureau to mobilize a similar humanitarian mission in the United States.

Independent of the politico-economic conflicts, but increasingly related to them, important theoretical and philosophical changes were taking place. During the second half of the nineteenth century there had begun to be a steady growth of "expertise" regarding the treatment of children, dominated by a search for "scientific" answers. To be sure, popular advice books and pamphlets still stressed moral goals to the virtual exclusion of specific practical proposals, let alone any regard for individual differences. But slowly a new, liberal readiness to face the realities of childhood started to seep into literature.

Horace Bushnell, a concerned minister, in his book at mid-century, urging parents to be more relaxed, suggested the virtues of play. He wrote: "One of the first duties of a genuinely Christian parent is to show a generous sympathy with the play of his children; providing playthings and means of play, giving them play times, inviting suitable companions for them . . . They will enjoy no other playtime so much as that, and it will have the effect to make the authority, so far unbent, just as much stronger and more welcome as it has brought itself closer to them. . . ."

In *The American Woman's Home,* Harriet Beecher Stowe and

her sister Catherine Beecher expressed their firm belief that the
old verities could readily be preserved in the New American environment. The Beechers rejected privilege based on the accident
of birth, wealth, or occupation, but they felt that much of the old
order could nevertheless be preserved, simply because different
roles required different prerogatives. Thus, the Beechers com-
forted worried adults, it would remain natural and even essential
that "children be subordinate to parents, pupils to teachers, the
employed to their employers, and subjects to magistrates."

A popular "how-to-do-it" home manual, *The Universal Self-
Instructor*, contains a section on children titled, "Confidence Between Parents and Children." It reflects a new view of the child's—
and the country's—potential. Physical punishment is repudiated.
Close and easy personal relations between the generations are
recommended. "The grim old-fashioned stateliness that keeps
[children] at arms' length will never do with this independent generation," the book counsels as a foretaste of things to come. The
first intimations of permissiveness are clearly visible in the simple
piece of advice: "You cannot expect your future explorer, who
will one day make his way to the North Pole or the interior of
Africa, to abstain from excursions into the city or the woods, even
if he loses himself." Not only does this sort of indulgence suggest
that children's action should no longer be harshly classified as
right or wrong, but there is also a matter-of-fact expression of
faith in the child's unlimited future accomplishment, unrelated
to the parents' station. In an intensely practical way, the influence
of the children's peers is openly acknowledged. "When you see
a girl anxious to tell your daughter something she must not repeat
to mother," the book warns, "check the intimacy at once."

There were signs of a new effort to strike a rational balance
in the relations between the generations that was subsequently
to fall victim to the extreme pressures of the youth culture of the
1960s, with its reliance on peer models. At this early dawning of
a new relationship, Emerson, in his essay on "Education," commented on this balance:

> Would you leave the young child to the mad career of his
> own passions and whimsies, and call this anarchy a respect
> for the child's nature? I answer,—Respect the child, respect

him to the end, but also respect yourself. Be the companion
of his thought, the friend of his friendship, the lover of his
virtue,—but no kinsmen of his sin.

New currents brought with them some uneasiness about their
meaning to American life. A nagging moral confusion is reflected
in the home and child-care literature of the day. The editors of
Childhood Magazine, for example, noted the timidity and confusion among parents that might be traced to the clash of new
ideas with old traditions.

Kate Wiggin, best known for the book *Rebecca of Sunnybrook
Farm,* also wrote *Children's Rights,* in which she called life too
hectic for the middle-class child. "He was always on edge, dressed
for show like some pet animal," she wrote. Children, she felt, were
always "over-clean." She warned parents against aiming for "hothouse virtue" in children. Similarly, Henry James suggested that
the lives of middle- and upper-class children were not always
smooth and happy. When he described these affluent youngsters
as "hotel children" who were often left alone or remanded to the
care of strangers, while the parents went on their social rounds,
he challenged the very same practices that are still criticized in
the second half of the twentieth century. Indeed, those who today
complain about child neglect often find little difference in the
unhappy consequences between the modern version of the "hotel
children" of the rich and the "door-key kids"—the children of the
slums who, at an early age, are sent to school or on the streets with
the door key to their tenements dangling around their necks.

Contradictions between American ideals and contemporary
practice, which had become sharper toward the end of the nineteenth century, were still largely ignored. Professed faith in the
ethical imperatives of freedom and equality was increasingly at
odds with the era's gross materialism. Scientific progress was,
moreover, still thought of as an unalloyed social and even moral
asset. Most Americans remained convinced that high moral standards and material benefits could live side by side, without inherent conflict.

In the schools, such textbooks as McGuffey's and moralizing
entertainment on the Horatio Alger model tried to create the
belief that the highest moral principles would make children, not

only morally good, but healthy, wealthy, and wise. If youngsters only worked hard, they would get ahead in life, grow rich and respected, and might even become President of the United States or, at any rate, famous. It was still assumed that some children were more equal than others, but the idea that ambitious goals might be attained through hard work and morality was a far cry from the earlier submission to God's and the parents' will.

The implications of evolution shattered the more sentimentally optimistic concept of easy human perfectibility. New philosophical forces were at work together with the shift from faith in religion to an almost similarly blind faith in science. The new science of psychology was to become a major influence on the child and his education.

Many outstanding names were associated with the early years during which psychology declared its independence from philosophy. One of those most closely linked with the application of the new science to children's lives was G. Stanley Hall. Borrowing both from Darwin and from the English philosopher Herbert Spencer, Hall propounded the thesis that an individual's development proceeds in stages which correspond roughly to those of civilization. Normal growth was described as an orderly progression from one stage to the next.

Hall's first work to gain widespread recognition, *The Content of Children's Minds,* published in 1883, is of major significance because it states flatly that the growth of urbanization calls for the recognition that children were growing up with a different set of concepts and experiences than their predecessors, who had grown up on farms. Thus, the entire arsenal of devices and teachings in dealing with children, in the home and in the schools, required reexamination and change.

Most previous educational thinking—and much of it still prevails in Western Europe today and is time and again revived by conservatives in the United States—held that the child must be fitted to the school. Hall insisted that the school must be fitted to the needs of the child. He rejected the time-honored, stern view that the burden of proof in the educational process was on the child—that the pupil must perform or get out. Through Hall's pioneering vision, the schools would soon be opened wide to an infinite variety of studies and subjects, instead of the traditional fare. Every kind of activity could legitimately be introduced into the curriculum, trivial as well as serious, provided only that it met some of the new needs of children of a different age in a changing society.

Above all, Hall—not unlike the Romantics—approached children with love and sympathy. "The guardians of the young," he wrote in *The Forum* issue of 1901–1902, "should . . . feel profoundly that childhood as it comes fresh from the hand of God, is not corrupt, but illustrates the survival of the most consummate thing in the world; they should be convinced that there is nothing else so worthy of love, reverence and service as the body and soul of the growing child."

In 1909, Hall invited Sigmund Freud to lecture at Clark University. Already something of an impresario of the new stardom of psychology, Hall counted among his disciples such men as Arnold Gesell who first defined the stages of a child's development, and Lewis Terman, the testing pioneer. Hall thought it time for the Viennese psychiatrist to be introduced to the American world of education.

Freud's initial appearance and impact were disappointing. His ideas seeped only slowly into American educational thinking and child-rearing practices. In 1909, America was not quite ready for Freud's thinking.

The intellectual world had not yet fully come to terms with Darwin. At a time when the latest psychological theories were still considered by many Americans as heresy and a threat to established religion and morality, Freud's theories constituted an even greater threat. Many of his early critics thought him immoral, and many professionals in medicine and education looked on him as a charlatan. His theories were based on the observation of sick minds, the reasoning went. How could they therefore be applied to healthy citizens in a democratic society?

But, during the forty years that followed Freud's introduction by Hall, his ideas gradually began to sink roots, and Freud—via Hall and Dewey—profoundly affected countless millions who had never read or understood his words. The most pervasive American use of Freud's concepts in education was in their role of creating a means of "adjusting" the individual to the demands of society.

The American adaptation of Freud's theories gave them a national envelope. For better or worse, the new science was used to help individuals conform to generally accepted American cultural behavior. For children, this meant specifically getting along with their peers, engaging in productive activity, and developing a sense of responsibility toward their family and friends. Those were "mature" actions which therefore were to be considered "healthy" and "normal." Any behavior that did not fit these descriptions was labeled "neurotic" or "abnormal." In other words, a new yardstick was being introduced for the kind of judgment of children's behavior that had earlier been assessed largely by rigid standards of morality. The new judges were not ministers or moralists, with their strong religious bias, but the psychologists and the psychologically oriented educators.

The new goal was—at least in theory—the development of relaxed, well-adjusted persons whose minds and psyches were functioning harmoniously and promised a productive and "normal" response to the environment. In fact, this American interpretation contained a strong dose of pragmatism which co-opted Freud to serve the American work ethic—productivity being equated with morality. It was an interpretation that formed an easy bridge over which educators could move toward what was to become a dominant new theme—the life-adjustment curriculum.

Actually, the way for the gradual introduction of Freud's ideas into American education had been prepared by Hall's teachings and, even more effectively, by John Dewey's new emphasis on the child rather than the curriculum, with its deliberate shift from the old view of the school as a preparation for life to the new effort to make school a satisfying experience in its own right.

Early in the twentieth century, progressive educators were indeed bending their efforts to the narrowing of the gulf between the American practice and the American ideal, and they were doing so by making the child the center of their, and the schools', concern. John Dewey, progressive education's patron saint and foremost philosopher, worried about children in the concrete rather than the abstract. He searched, for example, for child-sized desks as part of his crusade to turn society's and the educators' attention to the real conditions of childhood.

Dewey believed that children entered school with a desire to learn, but much of his observation had convinced him that adults—and professional educators no less than others—allowed their insensitivity about children to destroy that desire. He considered the curiosity the child brings to school as "uninvested capital," to be "invested" in the growth of the child to stimulate further growth. The job of the school was to guide the child toward participation in the collective wisdom of the race.

For Dewey, the child and the curriculum (the title of one of his books) were two ends of a single process in which the child would see the relationship between what he already knows and the exploration of the still largely unknown world around him. Unlike Hall, Dewey believed teachers must do more than get out of a child's way. He called for positive steps to connect the child's experience with the world at large. To Dewey, the curriculum was a map. It was needed, but looking at it was no substitute for actually going to the places shown on it.

The fact that Dewey's concept of the child-centered school was considered revolutionary is in itself proof of how much the child's interests and prerogatives had previously been ignored or misunderstood. If schools were established to educate the child —rather than to serve primarily the goals and interests of adult society or the state—then to consider the child the center of the schools' mission and purpose ought never to have been viewed as either radical or surprising. And yet, Dewey's new definitions (they were soon to become slogans emblazoned on the progressive education banner) were deeply unsettling to those who had traditionally subordinated the child's prerogatives to those of adult society. The term "child-centered" seemed an affront to those who felt that the school, like the rest of society, ought to be adult-centered. The "whole child" theory similarly was an affront to those educators who felt their professional dignity and superior status—as well as their teaching effectiveness—impaired by the demand that they concern themselves, nursemaid fashion, with the nonintellectual behavior of their pupils.

These conservative objections to Dewey's view of the child ought not to obscure the fact that in later years many of the master's overzealous disciples misinterpreted and abused his theories. It was in their hands, rather than in Dewey's mind, that "child-centered" came to describe a school in which the child, instead of being the center of the adult's concern, was placed in the position of central authority. And it was in their anti-intellectual minds, rather than in Dewey's prescription, that attention to the whole child often was translated into an education that downgraded the intellect and favored the child's physical and social needs at the expense of academic rigor.

Dewey's vision was as different from those interpretations as it was from the traditional view of child, school and society. He was troubled by the isolation of the school from the life of the child. Once, during a classroom visit, a superintendent told him that many children "were surprised to learn that the Mississippi River in the textbook had anything to do with the stream of water flowing past their homes." Dewey wanted education to become intimately related to the facts which the children "see, feel, and touch every day."

A mother, after visiting Dewey's Laboratory School at the University of Chicago, had been astonished to see, not books, but a live alligator, an Indian blanket, fruit, and sandwiches. Some children were speaking in Latin. Was this, she asked, preparation for Tolstoy's socialism? Dewey assured her that no such subversion was planned, that the traditional subjects were merely being taught through practical activity.

At the heart of Dewey's new approach was his effort to humanize the school. When he looked at traditional desks, he was told by an equipment salesman: "You want something at which the children may work; these are all for listening." Dewey insisted that teachers listen to the children, instead of merely trying to be listened to as they poured knowledge into little heads.

Like all efforts at school reform, Dewey's impact was not as effective nor as instant as his disciples boasted or as his opponents charged. At least two decades passed before his ideas and recommendations filtered down into education practice in the nation's schools. It was only during the 1930s that a growing folklore of parody began to indicate that progressive education had made its mark in the popular consciousness. It was then that Mr. Dooley, Finley Peter Dunne's mythical humorist and social critic, offered this "description" of progressive education at work:

I dropped in on Cassidy's daughter, Mary Ellen, and her kindygartnin'. The childher was setting around t' flure and some was moldin' dachshunds out iv mud an' wipin' their hands on their hair, an' some was carvin' figures iv a goat . . . an' some was singin' an' some was sleepin' and a few was dancin'. One child was pullin' another's hair. The visitor asked the teacher "Why don' ye take t' coal shovel to thát little barbaryan?" The teacher replied that "We don't believe in corporeal punishment" and that school should be made pleasant for the child. Then she explained: "The child who's hair is bein' pulled is larn' patience an' th' child that's pullin' th' hair is discoverin' th' futility iv human indeavor."

Despite the parodies and the actual excesses, the historic fact is that Dewey's view of the child gradually brought about fundamental changes in the nation's schools—changes which may in the long run have had a greater impact on the atmosphere than on the curriculum. However slowly, society's attitudes toward children were changing, though (as the history of the battle against child labor indicated so clearly) against stubborn opposition. Children were being viewed from a new perspective. Thus, for example, juvenile courts began to be established around the turn of the century to deal with youthful offenders in a more understanding way, and by 1912 legislation to that effect had been enacted in twenty-two states.

In its early stages, reforms brought about by Dewey's vision of the child-centered school resulted in only spotty and inconclusive changes in actual classroom practice. These were merely the halting first steps toward a new philosophy about children. The boastful description of the twentieth century as "The Century of the Child" remained a long way from fulfillment.

But the changes that were being advocated and would subsequently affect the lives of increasing numbers of children and the practices of increasing numbers of schools were aided by socioeconomic developments of the era. Such reform proposals were ideally suited to the changing aspirations of a growing middle class for itself and its children. Even as poor immigrants continued to crowd into the cities' slums between 1870 and 1910, the new middle class was growing in numbers and in influence as the model for the American future.

It was for the upward mobile new class that progressive education as well as the idea of life-adjustment education had its greatest appeal. Instead of being threatened by the emancipation of its children, it stood to rise in stature and prestige as its children were encouraged to make the best of an environment favorable to their future advancement.

It was only as the middle class became more securely established and thus more conservative that the progressive and life-adjustment movements were to be widely discredited and saddled with the blame for virtually every social and educational ill and failure. Conservatives charged that, by simply adjusting the child to whatever might be the prevailing trends of behavior, life-adjustment education was the instrument of the immoral perverters of youth. Academic purists were equally critical, on the grounds that old yardsticks of academic excellence and intellectual priorities were being sacrificed on the altar of crass pragmatism—a later generation called it "relevancy." And as always, when schools appeared to depart from the traditional role of Americanization and indoctrination, the new approach was denounced as subversive of the American way of life, a tool in the hands of the socialists and communists.

Since life-adjustment education eventually fell victim to such a torrent of scorn, ridicule, and abuse, the question must be raised how and why it had ever managed to take hold of the educators' imagination. The answer is clearly in the new mission the schools of that era had been asked to accept—the admission of an ever-larger number and broader spectrum of children for longer and longer periods of time. There was a vast difference between the traditional task of educating limited numbers of children in order to fit them into a relatively stable social order, as the schools had been expected to do in Europe, and the new challenge of opening the doors to schools which were, in fact, to become the engines of social mobility.

Yet that was precisely what American social and political philosophers expected of the school between the 1880s and the Great Depression of the 1930s. The process of acculturation, which to conservatives meant simply molding youngsters to conform to custom and tradition, had become quite the opposite: fitting children to a civilization in a state of flux, change, and growth. The capacity to cut loose from the past, once considered a sin, had become a necessity, even at the cost of repudiating many of the values of one's own parents.

Given such an unprecedented, broad, and inevitably controversial mandate, educators needed all the help they could find in the new theorists. Reliance on Freud (often only dimly understood) and on life adjustment (often misinterpreted by mediocre minds to mean the value-free acceptance of all prevailing mores) became a rational, perhaps even essential, development during the 1940s and 1950s as mass education shifted into high gear.

Superficial attention to counterattacks during the late 1950s and the 1960s, which forced the life-adjustment forces into retreat, would make it appear that the entire movement, with its radically new concept of the child's relationship with the school, had been nothing but a brief aberration. In reality, its impact on the American schools was immense and irreversible. Psychological concern about children's total personality and behavior and the need to adjust their learning to future needs rather than only to past custom has infiltrated the entire structure of American education and given a new texture to the schools' fabric. Where passivity had been seen as a child's proper attitude, curiosity and independence of mind were now the new virtues. Progressivism opened windows on new educational and child-psychological ideas, just as the commitment to mass education had opened the doors to the multitude. The new movement was an effort to find ways through education to make democracy work in an urbanized mass culture.

The question whether these strategies were in themselves sufficient to reconcile the contradictions between the proponents of quantity and the guardians of quality has never been fully answered. Educators themselves remain at odds over what are in the end ideological issues as much as educational ones. The clash between those who see the authority of the school threatened by the introduction of flexible standards and those who view authoritarian school administrators and teachers as the source of youthful alienation and ultimately of insurrection has never been resolved. In the 1970s it flared up as part of the pupils'—and the radical educational theorists'—insistence that the school's relevancy could be assured only by the pupils' active participation in educational policy-making.

While new educational and psychological philosophers brought a fresh understanding to the physical, intellectual, and psychological development of children in a radically changed and still changing social environment, a new science was being developed in efforts to quantify and predict the speed and intensity of such development. Edward L. Thorndike, at Teachers College, Columbia University, wrote in 1903 that "the science of education, when it develops, will, like other sciences rest upon direct observations of and experiments on the influence of educational institutions and methods made and reported with quantitative precision."

Thorndike's faith in quantification was almost limitless, and he is credited with saying that whatever exists, exists in quantity and can be measured. He was convinced that as the science of education came to be the equal of the established sciences, educational institutions would be able to make decisions and determine methods of instruction based on scientific observation "with quantitative precision." Scientific methods and the logic of statistics would provide answers that had remained elusive. Educational measurement became an increasing preoccupation, and the use of intelligence tests to classify children in school was slowly gaining acceptance.

It was during this period that Lewis Terman and others at Stanford University had revised and adapted the Binet-Simon intelligence tests, which had originated in France, to the standardized "mental tests." The idea of a scale of intelligence emerged from a series of problems or puzzles of graded difficulty, which American educators quickly (perhaps too quickly) embraced as a scale that could be applied to measuring both ability and achievement.

Somewhat ironically, the popularization of, and enormous interest in, intelligence tests was sparked by their use for the classification of Army recruits during World War I. In 1917, after America entered the war, the Army needed a fast system to classify recruits, to weed out the incompetents and to identify the most intelligent men to be trained as officers. Unfortunately, the psychologists who administered the tests assigned to the soldiers mental ages derived from tests basically designed for children. The results were a disaster—made more so because, purported to be "scientific," they were given wide publicity.

By 1919, the tests had been given to more than 1,700,000 men, and their dismal results began to leak out before an official report was published in 1921. The data pegged the average mental age of Americans at fourteen. Specifically 47.3 percent of the white draftees and eighty-nine percent of the Black draftees scored at a "mental age" of twelve years old or under. An adult with a "mental age" under twelve was supposed to be "feeble-minded." Was half the American population really feeble-minded, as suggested by the military tests?

A bitter and intense controversy over these findings raised doubts about the feasibility of mass-education if so many Americans allegedly lacked minimal intelligence. Colgate University President George Cutten argued that only fifteen percent of the population was intelligent enough to be admitted to college and to benefit from it. Henry Pritchett of the Carnegie Foundation went on record with the claim that too many children were going to school and that most of them were ill-equipped to benefit from much formal education. Dean Christian Gauss of Princeton proclaimed that one sixth of the college population should not have been admitted, and a report from the University of Michigan suggested that the bottom twenty percent of the students could have been denied admission without any loss to the institution.

The testing controversy became a burning issue and was hotly debated in the press during the 1920s. A note of cool reason was struck by the columnist Walter Lippmann in a series of articles devoted to the testing debate. He warned in 1922 that,

> if the impression takes root that these tests really measure intelligence, that they constitute a sort of last judgment on the child's capacity, that they reveal "scientifically" his predestined ability, then it would be a thousand times better if all the intelligence testers and all their questionnaires were sunk without warning in the Sargasso Sea. . . .

Tests continued to be abused. An analysis of one of the Army tests had been based on the scores of immigrants from various European countries. In 1917 and 1918 it was discovered that immigrants from southeastern Europe in general had lower scores on intelligence tests than immigrants from Northern Europe. Many studies by psychologists of the era insisted these Southern Europeans, since they had done poorly on the tests, were therefore "proven" to be genetically stupid. It was believed that if such people were to enter the United States in large numbers they would depress the nation's intelligence level. Leon Kamin, a Princeton psychologist, later pointed out that the work of the Army intelligence testers during that period was influential in persuading the public that immigration from the Eastern European countries should be stopped. Testimony before the House Committee on Immigration and subsequent restrictive legislation of the 1920s are proof of the impact of such ill-conceived "scientific" theories based on misapplied and misinterpreted tests.

Schools, too, accepted the I.Q. tests with amazing speed and lack of caution, ignoring Lippmann's warning that "the claim that we have learned how to *measure hereditary intelligence* has no scientific foundation" and that, if the psychologists recognized this fact, they could "save themselves from the humiliation of having furnished doped evidence to the exponents of the New Snobbery."

The issue over the discriminatory aspect of I.Q. tests exploded again in the 1960s when it was charged that the tests discriminated against Black and Puerto Rican children in the same fashion and for the same reason that they had discriminated against Southern and Eastern Europeans almost half a century earlier. Symptomatic of the controversy, New York City's Board of Education decided to abolish group I.Q. tests in 1964, substituting for them tests of the children's actual achievements in school, particularly in reading. Simultaneously, the Board commissioned the Educational Testing Service in Princeton, New Jersey, to try to design "color-blind" tests.

The conservative wing of the education Establishment represented by the New York High School Principals Association, raised objections to the change, charging that the "test ban" was "another instance of impulsive and precipitate action—a decision in a professional matter that seems to be prompted more by social and even political pressures than by disinterested educational considerations."

Opponents of the tests were adamant. Kenneth Clark, the psychologist whose testimony had played a key role in the Supreme Court's 1954 desegregation ruling, had analyzed the I.Q. issue and declared: "These scores, and those of similar examinations, cannot be used as a basis for predicting the academic success of Negro students in general."

Before the end of the decade, the debate was to take a new and even more controversial turn when several social scientists came forward with claims, based on what they said was new statistical research data, that heredity might be more important than environment in determining a child's I.Q. The leading proponent of that theory was Arthur Jensen, a professor of educational psychology at Berkeley, who presented his findings in a 123-page article in the Winter 1969 issue of the *Harvard Educational Review.*

After reviewing the history of tests "evolved to predict scholastic performance in largely European and North American middle-class populations around the turn of the century," Jensen claimed that, according to his investigations, "the heritability of the I.Q. . . . comes to about 80 percent. . . ." In other words, he suggested that the low scores among certain groups—racial, ethnic, or socioeconomic—may be caused by genetic inheritance to a larger degree than had been assumed, with the environmental factors contributing less.

Jensen's theories were not entirely new. Alfred Binet had written more than half a century earlier,

> . . . our personal investigations, as well as those of many others, have demonstrated that children of the poorer class are shorter, weigh less, have smaller heads and slighter muscular force, than a child of the upper class; they less often reach the high school; they are more often behind in their studies. . . .

It is not clear, however, why such findings ought to come as a surprise to anyone aware of the consequences of a limiting environment—in nutrition, verbal stimulation, intellectual encouragement, creature comforts, etc.—on all the measurable criteria of physical, intellectual, and economic well-being.

The instant response to Jensen, and to similar statements by Dr. Richard Herrenstein, a psychologist at Harvard, was one of political anger rather than scientific dialogue. The attacks launched against Jensen and Herrenstein on their own campuses were so vitriolic that they amounted to academic persecution. The two scholars were denounced as racists; their lectures were disrupted and speaking engagements canceled under duress; even in the scholarly community efforts were made to suppress publication of their views.

Although defenders of academic freedom were shocked by such resort to repression and censorship from within the academy itself, there nevertheless remained serious questions about the validity of Jensen's claims. The statistical approach to determine the relative influence on the I.Q. by either heredity or environment remained subject to challenge. To what extent, for example, could the two factors contributing to intelligence be meaningfully distinguished? If a group had been subjected to poverty and intellectual deprivation for generations, would not the deficiency in physiological as well as in intellectual nutrition, which are essentially environmental, also appear to be hereditary—at least until such a time as a drastic and long-term reversal of such handicaps could in turn register its impact on successive generations? Jensen himself wrote, in answer to charges of racism leveled against him: "I believe that the cause of the observed differences in I.Q. and scholastic performance among different ethnic groups is scientifically still an open question, an important question, and a researchable question." But Jensen also said:

> I believe that official statements, apparently accepted without question by some social scientists, such as "It is a demonstrable fact that the talent pool in any one ethnic group is substantially the same as in any other ethnic group" (U.S. Office of Education, 1966) and "Intelligence potential is distributed among Negro infants in the same proportion and pattern as among Icelanders or Chinese, or any other group" (Department of Labor, 1965) are without scientific merit. They lack any factual basis and must be regarded only as hypotheses.

While the argument, with its intensely political overtones, appeared in no way to move toward any scientific resolution, what remained an assumption—and a still highly debatable one—on both sides of the controversy was that an individual's I.Q. is fixed at a predetermined and easily definable level. Yet a number of experiments seemed to challenge, if not outright contradict, such a view. For example, Albert Upton, a professor of English at Whittier College, in California, had announced in 1960 that, after eight months of "exercises" involving the comprehension of words and analysis of ideas, the I.Q.s of a class of freshmen had been raised by an average of 10.5 points, with the largest individual gain a phenomenal 32 points.

The turn to the quantitative measurement of children's individual intellectual capacity thus did not necessarily disprove the Romantics' earlier faith that children's potential could be nurtured and brought to full flower by a loving and understanding environment; but it did introduce the notion of a ceiling on such development. And, since that ceiling differed with individual children, the I.Q. theory did amount—as cited earlier—to a challenge to the literal interpretation of absolute equality.

While the proponents of the new scientific measurements were devoted to the liberation of children from unreasonable demands and oppressive expectations, the new tools were subject to future abuse and the danger of rigidities which, during the 1960s, were to lead to the persistent charge that I.Q. tests had come to tyrannize rather than to free generations of children. Because the tests were attuned to the capacities and experience of middle-class children, they tended to misdiagnose the potential of minority children, thereby switching them at an early age to a track of lower expectation—and diminished opportunity. Moreover, the critics of the I.Q. measurement added, the test scores were often used by teachers and school administrators as a self-serving justification of children's disappointing achievements.

In other words, the considerable advances promised by the scientific application of measurements to the child were jeopardized when professional educators made use of them without sufficient understanding and sophistication. Instead of focusing on the original promise to free the child from the system's frustrating lockstep, educational administrators, impressed as always with the prospect of a more orderly process, created a new set of rigidities. The I.Q. test, at best a delicate indicator that should be carefully interpreted by experts with an intimate understanding of the

tested child, became a mass-sorting device responsible for the mis-
diagnosing and misplacing of great numbers of children—particularly those who were unable to conform to the middle-class
norm. And so, new tools, which, properly applied, might have
made it easier to combine mass education with greater responsiveness to the individual child's potential, threatened instead to
push American education in the direction of class-dominated
European systems which had always determined a child's educational course, and thereby his socioeconomic status, at an early age.

These dangers were not fully recognized until several decades
after the tests had been introduced. In the interim, their influence
over the profession that had embraced them as a scientific solution to the sorting of children remained virtually unchallenged.

By the 1920s child care, along with formal education, had become professionalized. The educators' persistent belief in "the one
best way" had now invaded the entire realm of child rearing. The
"well-adjusted" or "normal" child, parents were told, would inevitably result if certain practices were conscientiously followed
"by the book." When things went wrong, it was implied, the parents were at fault. Perhaps some of the prescribed methods and
applied measurements might occasionally need refinement; but
nobody questioned the infallibility of the established norms and
standard procedures.

The dramatic nature of these changes may be gauged from the
advice given to mothers by popular magazines. Celia B. Stendler,
reporting on these changes in *The Journal of Pediatrics* (January–
June 1950) points out that during the 1890s mothers had been
given such relatively relaxed counsel as "love, petting and indulgence will not hurt a child if at the same time he is taught to be
unselfish and obedient. Love is the mighty solvent." The mother
was still the exalted model from whose imitation good habits and
strong character were derived. Mother love would overcome most
problems.

As an example of the relaxed attitude toward children's behavior, *Ladies' Home Journal* published this poem in 1891:

> If a babe sucks his thumb
> 'Tis an ease to his gum:

A comfort, a boon, a calmer of grief
A friend in his need affording relief;
A solace, a good, a soother of pain;
A composer to sleep, a charm and a gain.

By the 1920s such indulgence was branded old-fashioned, senti-mental, and harmful. Faith in "science" had replaced faith in cuddling. Instead of soothing a child's screams with the gentle motion of the rocking chair, new trust in rigid schedules called for an efficiently "professional" response—"let them cry." Parents, according to Stendler, "were told that if baby were to be picked up just once when he cried, he could be 'conditioned,' that is, he would learn that the stimulus of crying produced a particular re-sponse, being picked up, and a bond between the two would be set up in his nervous system."

The scientific approach became dominant. Every up-to-date mother was expected to know all about calories, vitamins, and nutritious food that was "good for the baby," even if he loathed it.

Although Woodrow Wilson proclaimed the first Mother's Day around 1914, the power and prestige of motherhood had by that time come under heavy siege by experts who considered mother too unscientific and unprofessional to be left in charge.

One of the most widely read pamphlets of the day was *Infant Care*, published by the Children's Bureau in 1914. Frequently revised to keep pace with theoretical changes, it became the Gov-ernment Printing Office's best-seller. In the spirit of the time, *Infant Care* upheld the importance of the "scientific" and sys-tematized approach to children.

"The care of a baby is readily reduced to a system unless he is sick," the pamphlet told the nation's mothers. A sample "schedule" suggested the one best way of establishing a routine. Parents were to be kept at arms' length. "The rule that parents should not play with the baby," the pamphlet said,

> may seem hard, but it is without doubt a safe one. A young,
> delicate, or nervous baby especially needs rest and quiet, and
> however robust the child, much of the play that is indulged
> in is more or less harmful. . . . It is a regrettable fact that
> the few minutes of play that the father has when he gets

home at night, which is often almost the only time he has
with the child, may result in nervous disturbances of the baby
and upset his regular habits.

Such an arrogant "professional" conviction that mother and
father never know best was tinged with a strong element of "discipline" which, though wrapped in scientism, seemed almost derived
from the old Puritan view that the child's will needs to be broken.
Parents were forever warned about the danger of allowing bad
habits to develop. "When a baby cries simply because he has
learned from experience that this brings him what he wants,"
indulgent mothers were told, "it is one of the worst habits he can
learn, and one which takes all the strength of the mother to
break."

The importance of a routine and correct system for training the
child was impressed on pediatricians who relayed the message to
mothers. One influential book, *The Diseases of Infancy and Childhood* by L. Emmett Holt, M.D., warned that "playing with young
children, stimulating to laughter and exciting them by sights,
sounds or movements until they shriek with apparent delight" may
amuse parents but "it is almost invariably an injury" to the child.
"It is the plain duty of the physician to enlighten parents upon
this point . . . and that all such playing and romping as has been
referred to shall, during the first year at least, be absolutely prohibited."

Holt continued: "The importance of training young children
to regular habits regarding evacuations from the bowels can
hardly be over-estimated. It should be impressed upon every
mother and nurse by the physician, and especially the necessity of
beginning training during infancy." Bladder training, he suggested, is "not quite so important. . . . Before the end of the first
year most intelligent children can be trained to indicate a desire
to empty the bladder."

Of particular interest are Holt's observations on crying:

> The cry of habit is one of the most difficult to recognize.
> These habits are formed by indulging infants in various
> ways. . . . The extent to which this kind of crying may be
> indulged in, even by very young infants is surprising, and it

explains much of the crying of early childhood. The fact that the cry ceases immediately when the child gets what it wants is diagnostic of the cry of habit. The only successful treatment of such cases to allow the child to "cry it out" once or twice and then the habit is broken.

The importance of imparting good habits to children by bringing them up by a strict routine approached an obsession during the twenties and thirties. It was believed that such a "scientific" course would keep children healthy and lower the still appalling infant mortality rate. These rigidities were not the result of deliberate cruelty; they stemmed instead from a scanty knowledge of child development and from excessive faith in scientific methods.

By the end of the thirties, some voices were raised for moderation. The 1942–1945 edition of *Infant Care,* for example, no longer stated that crying was "a bad habit." Parents once again were told that "a baby sometimes cries because he wants a little more attention. He probably needs a little extra attention under some circumstances just as he sometimes needs a little extra food and water. Babies want attention; they probably need plenty of it." It was a rediscovery of the magic of mother love that had temporarily fallen victim to the cult of efficiency.

During its heyday, the expert approach to conditioning and rigid routines was reinforced by the burgeoning schools of the psychological behaviorists. John B. Watson, in *Psychological Care of Infant and Child,* published in 1928, and in his influential book *Behaviorism,* strongly supported the idea of unbending schedules, prohibition of thumb-sucking, and absolute adherence to the sterilization of everything the baby might touch. In contrast to the Romantics, who hoped to bring childhood to flower with love and affection, behaviorists were convinced that they had found the scientific key to the shaping of children's lives. Watson is credited with having said that, if he were given a number of healthy infants, he would know "how to make each into an artist, a scientist, or a thief, at will." It was not until some thirty years later that B. F. Skinner, a leading behavioral psychologist, created the Skinner Box, a terrarium-like, glass-enclosed, controlled-atmosphere crib in which the baby's growth, actions, reactions, and general behavior would be regulated to conform to the one best way of scientific expertise.

By comparison, the "scientific" approach of the 1920s and 1930s seemed primitive. It concentrated on prescriptions to "let the baby cry," rigid feeding schedules, a strict regimen of toilet training, and the like. It was also emphatically middle class in its norms.

"Tenements with dark rooms are not fit homes for children," warned the early *Infant Care* reverting to the earlier "moral" belief that poverty is the fault of the poor. "Suburban homes, or those in the outskirts of cities or close to public parks, give to city children of the average family the best chance for proper growth and development," parents were told.

Under the thumb of disapproving experts, it was hardly surprising that mothers' confidence was going into steep decline. A pediatrician noted as early as 1905: "A troublesome obstacle that the pediatrist encounters today is the general ignorance and helplessness of the young mother. She may be skilled in letters, arts and sciences as a college graduate, but know little or nothing regarding the essential hygiene of early life."

Helen and Robert Lynd, in their study of *Middletown*, which described the changes brought to Muncie, Indiana, by industrialization and urbanization, showed the helplessness of parents caught between new needs and bewilderment over the new practices.

"Life was simpler for my mother," said a thoughtful woman. "In those days one did not realize that there was so much to be known about the care of children. I realize that I ought to be half a dozen experts, but I am afraid of making mistakes and usually do not know where to go for advice."

The children's own words, too, indicated the parents' dilemma, as in the following exchange recorded by the Lynds:

> Boy: Parents don't know anything about their children and what they are doing.
> Girl: They don't want to know.
> Girl: We won't let them know.
> Boy: Ours is a speedy world and they're old.
> Boy: Parents ought to get together. Usually one is easy and one is hard.

Eventually Dr. Benjamin Spock would lead a counteroffensive against the arrogant and rigid professional rule and give American mothers an infusion of self-confidence and common sense. But during the early days of the professionalization of child care, such reassuring comforts seemed a long way off. As late as the 1920s, one observer still complained that parents were becoming "the willing instruments of a public mania for standardization which tries to make every human soul into the image of a folded pattern."

If the newly dictated relationship between parent and child was puzzling to native-born, middle-class mothers, the implications were nothing short of tragic for many poor immigrants. Suddenly and cruelly, they were told by the experts that it was the parents' duty to encourage their children to grow away from them. The cold, official prose of a report published by the Americanization Division of the Bureau of Education in the United States Department of the Interior, hints at the plight of an immigrant mother. "The foreign woman is timid, made so in many instances by the strangeness of the new surroundings," the publication said. "She knows how different she is from her neighbors, and she often lacks her children's chance to learn the new language."

"One result of this situation," the report concluded, "is that the mother, the center of the household, is neglected and looked down upon by husband and children who have outstripped her in the acquisition of the tools of citizenship."

One of the long-term benefits of the professionalization of child-rearing was its translation into institutional policy—the extension of schooling to an earlier age. The move toward kindergartens and nursery schools represented an important educational advance. It acknowledged the fact that, particularly in an urban setting, reliance on the home alone was not enough. Except for the very rich—who had their nurseries and nursemaids—institutionalized preschool child care and education also implied a measure of parental liberation, particularly for mother.

For the educational leadership, the trend opened up new avenues of standardization. "It is proposed," wrote William T. Harris, a prominent school superintendent, that the child be trained in school, for three hours or more daily (between the ages of 3 and 6), in the company of his fellows, by thoroughly competent teachers, to form habits of personal neatness and cleanliness, courtesy, and deference toward others, punctuality and regularity; to use proper language; to become familiar with the elements of numbers and geometric form. . . .

All classes of children, Harris felt, would benefit from such training, and in the elitist idiom of his day he nevertheless foreshadowed what the proponents of Operation Head Start and other compensatory education for disadvantaged children were to advocate in the 1960s. "If the children of the vicious and improvident can be trained from the age of three years in kindergartens," he wrote, "they will be saved for constructive work in our civilization, instead of drifting into our penal institutions." On the other hand, the children of affluent parents "who have built up fortunes by their great directive powers, are often left to the home training of ignorant or weak servants, by reason of the fact that their parents are absorbed in large enterprises." Such children, Harris advised, must be trained early in "habits of self-control and industry" as a means of saving them from frittering away their parents' fortunes.

Fortunately, the development of the American kindergarten—by the 1920s an estimated twelve percent of the nation's children of the pertinent age group were enrolled in such preschool classes— coincided with the growing influence of Dewey and Freud. Thus, some of the worst excesses of the professional drive toward standardization were counteracted by a more humane approach. Yet, as the ranks of the early childhood professionals grew, their power and their tendency to impose standardized views and goals became more assertive. Many of these practitioners seemed to take their cue from Richard W. Gelder, who wrote in 1903:

You cannot catch your citizen too early in order to make him a good citizen. The kindergarten age marks our earliest opportunity to catch the little Russian, the little Italian, the little German, Pole, Syrian and the rest and begin to make good American citizens of them. And our little American-born citizen is often in quite as much need of early catching and training.

Like most new approaches to the American child, the preschool movement was caught up, from its very beginning, in the fundamental controversy between those who wanted educational institutions to shape the child in conformity with society's needs and expectations and those who welcomed an opportunity to liberate children and to open new horizons to them.

Earlier, Elizabeth Peabody, Horace Mann's sister-in-law, had seen in the kindergarten a chance to apply the transcendental theories of early childhood, preached and tested in Germany by the disciples of Friedrich Froebel. Miss Peabody's sister, Mary Mann, and Kate Wiggin set down the guidelines for a "well-regulated" kindergarten in which "there should be no punishments" and whose major role would be to teach the child "to take his place in the company of his equals . . . and still later to learn wider social relations and their involved duties."

A kindergarten, wrote Miss Peabody, "is children in society—a commonwealth or republic of children—whose laws are all part and parcel of the Higher Law alone."

But as public school educators, such as Harris, realized that preschool education would become an effective mass service, they once again tended to put the search for "the one best way" ahead of more romantic hopes. Early training in "self-control and industry" began to vie with the vision of the Children's Republic.

A combination of the growing professionalization of child care and the effort to keep as many children as possible in school from infancy past adolescence downgraded the parental role. Both intentionally and unintentionally, the influence of the family was undermined. Generations were drifting apart and the young were growing up isolated from the adult world.

The change was fundamental and far-reaching. The road toward it had led from the concept of the child as a miniature adult, subject entirely to the will and the aims of adult society, via the new companionable relationship between sons and fathers that had so astonished foreign visitors, to the increasing independence of the young. The ultimate phenomenon was the youth culture of the 1960s which on occasion threatened to be as tyrannical as the adult establishment had been two centuries earlier.

The trend did not become recognizable until well into the

twentieth century—not until the dream of getting virtually all children into school was realized and until the technical capacity and the material means of rapidly transmitting a new popular culture had become available.

It was in the 1920s—in the midst of general prosperity and optimism, when American youth felt it had rescued the democracies of the Old World—that the image of "flaming youth" had emerged as a social and cultural force. It was the sign of a new world, promising to the young, threatening to the old, and although its exuberant and often irresponsible and iconoclastic spirit was soon to be dampened by the Great Depression, it was the prelude to irreversible social changes.

An American mother described the problem poignantly when she spoke to an English visitor in 1933:

> We mothers are rapidly losing all influence over our children. . . . We have little or no control over them, whether boys or girls. The schools and the colleges take them out of our hands. They give them everything for nothing, and that is what the children expect when they come home. Their standards and their ideals are formed in the school atmosphere, and more by their companions than their teachers. They become more and more intractable to home influence and there is nothing for it but to let them go their own way.

After World War II, the changes in American society which were to affect the condition of children had been phenomenal. The middle class rushed from the cities to suburbia. Hitherto undreamed-of demands made on mass production—60,000 war planes a year—in response to the military crisis gave to industry and research a new, seemingly limitless power. The corporate structure, which now served an expansionism in industry comparable to that of the old frontier, once again made a virtue of mobility. The G.I. Bill of Rights which sent onto the university campuses unprecedented numbers of children of previously non-college-going families opened the gates to opportunity. A spirit of exuberant optimism and youthful impatience made early marriage the prelude to the postwar baby boom. Children were born to parents barely out of their own adolescence; babies were raised by parents who were themselves closer to the ways and attitudes of childhood than of adult maturity.

As families moved restlessly from home to home, young mothers were faced with three or more children under the age of six, without Grandma's aid and comfort except via long-distance telephone, and with little experience in dealing with the children's problems.

Much of the expert literature was as out of tune with these new conditions as the white-gloved books of etiquette were in the social setting of the new suburbs. Most of the books, full of rigid do's and don'ts, were as impractical as they were in conflict with the teachings of Dewey and Freud. This was no longer a time for rigid child-care "schedules"—not psychologically and not in simple terms of housekeeping realities.

Like the idea whose time has come, Dr. Benjamin Spock arrived on this troubled scene. He brought to these harassed young mothers, not the stern, cold professional expertise of the old government pamphlets but the easy reassurance of a calm sense of humor and a matter-of-fact approach to children.

"I want to urge you not to worry or decide that you've made a mistake with your child on the basis of anything that you read in this book (or anywhere else for that matter)," Spock told these mothers, in violation of the entire code of earlier professional self-importance.

"Trust yourself," he said to worried and diffident parents. "Don't take too seriously all that the neighbors say. Don't be overawed by what the experts say. Don't be afraid to trust your common sense." Earlier manuals had made a fetish of going by the book, of conditioning baby's behavior by feeding him on schedule and letting him cry if he wanted to eat at any other time. To give in was to "spoil" the infant.

Spock, when asked whether a baby can be spoiled, said bluntly, "not by feeding him when he's hungry, comforting him when he's especially miserable, being sociable with him in an easy-going way." Spoiling, he added, comes only from "a chronic situation." The essence of Spock was an effort to give control over child-rearing back to mother and the family. Respect for the child, once thought so important by Emerson but subsequently given less attention by order-oriented experts, was high on Spock's list. Like

Emerson, he wanted parents to stay in control by means of a loving heart and a gently guiding hand.

Eventually, Spock too was widely misinterpreted. Where he was relaxed in dealing with children, his disciples abdicated to total permissiveness. Where he warned against heavy-handed discipline, his followers abandoned all restraints. Where he urged adults to respect children, Spock-inspired ideologies demanded that adults genuflect before childhood and youth.

Children, moreover, had now become consumers with a considerable influence in telling adults how to spend their money. As they moved toward adolescence, they collectively had huge amounts of their own cash to use as they pleased. The youth market became a substantial slice of the economy. Such wealth—and those who controlled it—were fair game for exploitation. As potential customers and spenders, America's children were placed into a dangerous driver's seat of financial and social power.

The era of permissiveness and the gradual drift into the Youth Culture would not have been possible without the general aura of affluence that shaped American life in the post–World War II years. Children had long ceased to be the economic asset they once were in agrarian America. But, even if they had come to be a fiscal liability, children were one of a growing number of luxuries that a well-to-do middle class could afford and indulge.

Medical progress had taken most of the risks out of childbirth and child care, making it much easier to bring up well-fed and healthy children. Keeping children in school for longer and longer years became less and less of a sacrifice. The cost was justified by the facts that society needed more highly educated workers and that school attendance provided, in addition to the necessary skills, a greater promise of status—along with the safety that comes with being sheltered from the real world which had no need for children's labor.

In the classic study, *The Lonely Crowd,* David Riesman, et al., described the new isolation of children and adults from each other. About the anxiety and confusion of parents, Riesman said: "Increasingly in doubt as to how to bring up their children, parents turn to other contemporaries for advice. . . . They cannot help but show their children, by their own anxiety, how little they depend on themselves and how much on others."

In an affluent society, children learn to "consume" early and in an adult manner. "Today there is no fast line that separates these consumption patterns of the adult world from those of the child, except the consumption objects themselves," Riesman wrote. "The child may consume comics or toys while the adult consumes editorials and cars; more and more both consume in the same way."

Written in 1950, before the added impact of television, the study took into account the influence of the mass media of movies, radio, and comics. Riesman concluded:

> No longer is it thought to be the child's job to understand the adult world as the adult sees it. . . . Instead, the mass media ask the child to see the world as "the" child—that is, the other child—sees it. . . . The media have created a picture of what boyhood and girlhood are like . . . and they force children either to accept or aggressively resist this picture of themselves.

The advent of television constituted a quantum jump in the relationship between the child and the world at large. Children learned by absorbing lessons that were not taught in the conventional way in school—a new reality to which educators found it difficult to adjust. Traditionally, the implicit assumptions by parents and educators alike had been that children could only learn through formal schooling. It took the phenomenal success of *Sesame Street* to drive home the fact that these assumptions were obsolete. Television had become a teaching tool, whether educators themselves used it or not. Neither good nor bad in itself, its influence is inescapable.

For better or worse, some of the most effective "teaching," in terms of sheer impact, takes place through the "institution" of children's peers. The importance of peer pressure and the isolation of high-school students in their own private world is described by James Coleman in his 1961 study, *Adolescent Society*. Coleman found adolescents "cut off, probably more than ever before, from the adult society," and under growing pressure to conform to the expectations of their peers.

In an upper-middle class school, Coleman reported, not one of the girls "in the top leading crowd" said she wanted to be remembered as a brilliant student. In addition, "the boy who is named as the best scholar does not want to think of himself as a brilliant student nearly so much as the best athlete wants to think of himself as an athletic star." But a boy scholar, the study found, was more likely to accept the image "than . . . the girl scholar who is presumably repelled by the culture's negative evaluation of this image."

The compelling pressure of conformity—and the sexist standards—in American high schools of that period was documented by the finding that during a four-year-period the best girl student became strikingly less likely to want to be remembered for scholastic success, while the boys became more eager for such a reputation.

Dr. Coleman also discovered that, in every school he studied,

> the average girl's grades cluster together more closely than do those of the average boy. This suggests strongly that the girls are motivated to "do well" in everything, whether it is something at which they excel or not, while boys are less constrained by parents' demands and the demands of the adolescent culture to be "good" in those things they care less about. The girl apparently stays subject to constraints to be good but not aggressively brilliant, while a boy's grades in later years come more and more to be a function of his own variable interest.

It was hardly surprising that the isolation of the Youth Culture would eventually lead to a revolt against adult institutions, such as the colleges and schools (the institutions naturally most exposed to attack), and against rules which those institutions still tried to enforce.

In the wake of the college riots of the 1960s, Bruno Bettelheim analyzed the sources of children's alienation and revolt. No longer, he suggested in 1969, was childhood a phase that was routinely terminated by an orderly transition to the life of work, responsibility, marriage, and parenthood. Instead, childhood and adolescence were now prolonged, creating a large, restless, hostile population sector, not too different in its explosiveness from the intellectual, unemployed proletariat that, in an earlier era, had in some European countries become the nucleus of social revolt.

What this youthful army lacked, according to Bettelheim, was the slow growth which had traditionally been fostered, first by parental teachings and, later, by the schools and society at large. In a reversal of the old Puritan view that any childish expression that did not reflect the moral precepts of adult society was wrong and sinful, the misinterpretations of Freud and Dewey had led parents and educators to applaud anything a child did and said as a valuable, if not sacred, expression and a sign of creativity.

The inherent problem with this stormy and disturbed era of America's relationship with children and childhood, Bettelheim felt, was the adults' own confusion of goals and values which left children confused and ultimately enraged. "Many middle-class families," he concluded, "chose to follow Freud where it suited their convenience, and were as demanding of conformity as the worst Victorian parent where it did not. In either case, they evaded their adult responsibility."

One of the sins committed by middle-class parents and many educators, ignoring the warnings of those who had urged greater respect for the capacities and interests of individuals, was the steady and often coercive manner in which they pressured their children to enter college and academic careers. Extensive new research had been conducted throughout the 1960s by psychologists who had come to believe that children are capable of learning such skills as reading, writing, and the use of numbers at a far earlier age than had been thought—possibly at the ages of three and four. More important, these experimenters, and Harvard's Jerome S. Bruner was foremost among them, considered it possible to introduce logic and ethics long before the traditional age for such studies, provided that such teaching be conducted on a level of sophistication suitable to the children's age.

Bruner's interest was not in speeding up children's education but rather in exploring the mysteries that have always excited and confounded educators and parents—how children learn. While these explorations promised to open new windows on the human mind, and particularly that of the child, they were instantly seized upon and abused by those—parents as well as teachers—who saw them as a means of rushing the children's development. Here, in the race for success, was another way to speed the children to college and greater social status.

Among those who sensed the high risks of this hothouse approach was Jean Piaget, the eminent Swiss child psychologist who, next to Dewey, may be the most influential pioneer in efforts to improve children's lives as well as their education. Piaget had long felt that the children's true interests tended to be lost in adults' preoccupation with their own goals. Educators, he complained, were more interested in teaching than in children. They concentrated on methods and materials, with only a sketchy knowledge of psychology and even less of scientific research.

Not unlike Dewey, Piaget criticized teachers who want to teach and have children listen passively, an arrangement that seemed to him the very antithesis of learning. Like Dewey, too, Piaget insisted that "knowledge is derived from action." A baby learns as he crawls to retrieve a toy. By the same token, children do not learn to swim by sitting in rows of chairs watching an expert swimmer. (The extent to which educators have allowed themselves to be ensnared by the passive approach to learning may be gauged from the fact that many physical education teachers actually do attempt to teach sports, such as tennis or golf, literally "by the book," having pupils follow the rules and the illustrations rather than teaching them through action.)

Piaget believed ardently in the "action school" and the "discovery method." These views, deeply rooted in a respect for the child's natural growth and development, clash head-on with American impatience over biological or genetic limitations on growth, ignoring the normal timing of growth. Indeed, Piaget called it "the American question"—the recurring query why, if there are certain stages in a child's development, American know-how should not be able to make children pass through them at an ever faster pace. If a task can be done in an hour, can it not, with improved efficiency, be performed as well in half the time? Instead of savoring, or at least understanding, a child's natural growth, Piaget complained, "the American question" asks incessantly how the process can be speeded up.

Damaging as such pressure can be to the natural growth and psychological well-being of the "normal" child of the middle-class majority, it could also aggravate that perennial dichotomy between the affluent mainstream and the separate world of the deprived and excluded. And yet it was precisely because of the new insights into children's development provided by the rediscovery of Dewey and new research by such men as Piaget that efforts were made at last to free the disadvantaged children from the lockstep of the administrator-dominated school. Although educational and political conservatives once again echoed the Boston Latin masters of Horace Mann's day in their charges that children were being coddled and standards diluted, increasing numbers of teachers, and even schools, relaxed the tyranny of tests and grades.

Children crippled by poverty would, most reformers conceded, have to be prepared to compete in the middle-class society after they complete their education; yet, in the course of such preparation, the reformers insisted, schools would have to be fitted to children, in attitude as well as pace, instead of molding the children to "the standards" of the school.

Such a child liberation movement has a long way to go. Strong conservative currents still threaten to stem the tide. But, more emphatically than at any earlier time in the nation's history, advocates of a humane and realistic response to the problems of poor children are making their case. Pedagogy has come a long way from the patronizing approach to poor and "vicious" children that characterized even some of the best-intentioned urban reformers' efforts in the past. There now are growing indications that the more humane and rational reshaping of the education of the deprived is beginning to exert a liberalizing influence on the education of all children.

More adults who deal with the problems of childhood today are ready to consider the lesson first preached by Locke: "Children are travelers newly arrived in a strange country of which they know nothing. We should, therefore, make conscience not to mislead them. . . ."

7

THE BLACK ORDEAL

*I*F THE DOUBLE STANDARD AS APPLIED to American children made the affluent more equal than the poor, the most stinging pain of inequality was reserved for the nonwhite minorities, particularly Blacks. For a substantial part of American history, the Black child was not just discriminated against, he was invisible. Black education was an issue left to Supreme Court decisions; it was not part of any systematic review of American education.

In the South, moreover, where so much of the pattern for Black education had been established, the lot of Black children was submerged in the educational deprivation suffered by severely neglected poor white youngsters. In a society that could characterize the poor white as "white trash," the cruelty of neglect toward the even poorer Blacks becomes comprehensible. It was no doubt reinforced by the poor whites' fear that they would sink even lower if any Blacks were allowed to rise on the overall scale of status and success.

Compared to the North, moreover, public education in the South before the Civil War was barely operative. Most of the common schools that did exist were for paupers, although apprentices were given some schooling. The region's scattered farms and plantations made it considerably more difficult than the concentrated population pattern of the compact New England towns to plan and provide public education.

Wealthy plantation owners, who were the trend-setters of the area, hired private tutors for their children or sent them to England for their education. Even though the earliest recorded endowment of a free school in the Colonies—two hundred acres of land and eight cows—was provided in Virginia through the will of Benjamin Syms in 1634, schooling opportunities in Colonial Virginia nevertheless remained scanty.

The beginnings of Black education thus must be viewed against the region's poor record in general. Whatever little opportunity was offered to Black children was carried on by missionaries intent on recruiting converts for the Church of England. One such group was the Society for the Propagation of the Gospel in Foreign Parts, and the work of these religious colonizers aimed at reaching Blacks as well as whites. They were to learn soon, however, that even to carry God's message across the color line was a dangerous challenge to local mores and traditions.

Many slave owners were afraid that, once their Blacks were baptized, they would claim the right to be free. If slaves learned to read and write, it was feared, they would be increasingly difficult to control. The problem of baptism was readily resolved when assemblies of Southern Colonies, and eventually the British government itself, declared officially that baptism did not offer any claim to freedom. No such easy legalistic way out was available in the matter of education and literacy.

In 1724, a minister insisted that

> both the children of Negroes and Indians undoubtedly ought all to be baptized . . . and go to church, and not accustom themselves to lie, swear and steal, though (as the poorer sort in England) be not taught to read and write; which as yet

has been found to be dangerous upon several political accounts, especially self-preservation.

Another contemporary observer reported that the planters "urge
it a sin . . . to enlarge the understanding of their slaves, which
will render them more impatient of slavery."

After the Revolutionary War, the Northern states, one by one,
made provisions for the freeing of the slaves. In most instances,
these measures included plans for gradual emancipation; freedom
was usually granted after slaves reached a certain age. Educational
provisions for Black children, however, remained haphazard.
Manumission societies in the North offered education for the
emancipated. These philanthropic organizations, usually directed
by wealthy and influential citizens, occasionally even managed to
obtain public support for such schools.

The Philadelpia Society for Free Instruction of Colored People—perhaps inspired by the example of Anthony Benezet, a leading Quaker, who had taught Black students until his death in
1784—encouraged and organized Quaker efforts to teach Black
children in several mid-Atlantic cities. But compared to the task
at hand these actions barely scratched the surface, and great numbers of Black children grew up without the benefit of education.

Despite occasional exceptions, it is doubtful that Black children
of the pre–Civil War era were able to attend school comfortably
alongside white children, even in Massachusetts. In the case of
Sarah C. Roberts v. the City of Boston, Charles Sumner argued
that the five-year-old Black girl should be allowed to attend a
white school. He lost. Chief Justice Lemuel Shaw, speaking for a
unanimous court, held that prejudice "is not created by law and
probably cannot be changed by law. . . . Whether this distinction and prejudice, existing in the opinion and feelings of the
community, would not be as effectually fostered by compelling
colored and white children to associate together in the same
schools, may well be doubted. . . ."

The Massachusetts legislature reversed the Roberts case decision through the enactment of new laws. But it is reasonable to
conclude that a "separate but equal" approach was the actual
practice, even if it was not formally supported by the statutes.
Indeed, Chief Justice Shaw's belief that racial prejudice cannot

be solved by way of legislation continued to be deeply imbedded in American folklore.

The climate that prevailed in much of early America may be illustrated by an episode in the lives of Mary and Horace Mann. It was in the late 1840s, when a Black woman named Chloe Lee was admitted to a teacher training school in West Newton, near Boston, where the Manns lived at the time. When nobody in town offered a room to Miss Lee, the Manns opened their home to her. Underscoring the general disapproval of this act of compassion and justice, even Mary's sister Sophia, wife of Nathaniel Hawthorne, wrote: "All that I question is your right to *oblige* your guests to tolerate her presence if it be distasteful or disagreeable to them."

Many whites in the North were ostracized by their former friends and neighbors when they espoused the abolitionist cause. Regardless of the laws, schools and churches in the North were generally segregated. Ohio, in a pattern adopted by many states, in 1849 passed a law authorizing the establishment of separate schools for the education of Black children. The Ohio Supreme Court subsequently upheld the exclusion of these children from white schools.

In the South, the substantial increase of Blacks throughout the eighteenth century came at a time when farmers relied heavily on slaves for the tasks that used to be performed by their own families and by paid servants. Restrictions placed on Blacks grew in direct proportion to their increasing numbers. While the South had always been ambivalent about educating Blacks—as early as 1740, a law had actually prohibited the teaching of writing to slaves—the antagonisms and fears increased by the beginning of the nineteenth century. Cheap labor had become crucial to the South's efforts to build an economy on cotton and tobacco, while the North increasingly turned to industry where machines replaced the need for slaves. Against a worldwide trend of growing disapproval of the slave-trade and the gradual abolition of slavery everywhere, the South fought desperately to uphold the status quo.

During the 1820s attitudes were hardening into what came to seem an unbreakable mold. After Nat Turner's rebellion early in the 1830s, some Southern states passed laws forbidding the teaching of reading to slaves. Although these laws were sometimes evaded, their overall effect was devastatingly powerful in keeping the tools of self-improvement out of the hands of each new generation of Blacks. The Black historian Carter Woodson has concluded that approximately ten percent of the adult Negroes knew how to read prior to the Civil War, but other historians consider that estimate high.

With the majority of poor whites also still illiterate, whatever proposals were forthcoming at the time to improve the education of the indigent usually made it clear that Black children were to remain excluded. George Fitzhugh, a prominent exponent of the Southern point of view, said: "The abolitionists taunt us with the ignorance of our poor white citizens. This is a stigma on the South that should be wiped out. Half of the people of the South, or nearly so, are blacks. We have only to educate the other half. At the North, they educate all."

Against such oppression by custom as well as by law, the Blacks' struggle toward the forbidden fruit of learning constitutes a heartbreaking and inspiring chapter in the nation's educational history. It would have been difficult to make a stronger case for the importance of education than either by the conservative South's confidence that lack of schooling would continue to make Blacks the docile fuel of its economic machine or by the Blacks' firm conviction that education would lead them to a better life and eventually to freedom.

Frederick Law Olmsted, in his *Journey in the Back Country*, reports on some slaves on a Mississippi plantation who had learned to read. His informant told him that "Niggers is mighty apt at larnin'," and, when Olmsted suggested that this was contrary to prevailing popular belief, the local man sought to prove his point by citing the plantation's own experience. One slave had come there, he said, who had learned to read, and he in turn taught others. With their own meager savings, they had managed to get some books from a peddler. Asked about the legal prohibition against teaching Blacks or selling them books, the fellow said he had never heard of such a law. Yet it is clear that for the few Blacks who benefited from such lack of enforcement of laws intended to keep them ignorant, it was a tremendous struggle to gain even the barest rudiments of an education.

There were, to be sure, some schools "for free children of color" even in the South. On April 22, 1830, an editorial in *The Raleigh Register* patronizingly described such an institution:

> We have seldom received more gratification from any exhibition of a similar character. To witness a well regulated school, composed of this class of persons—to see them setting an example both in behavior and scholarship, which their white superiors might take pride in imitating, was a cheering spectacle to a philanthropist.

But, despite such occasional exceptions, it is fair to say that Black education was virtually nonexistent prior to the Civil War, and indeed even those whites who had to rely on the public schools were pretty much abandoned to charity and luck in the South. Chancellor William Harper of South Carolina expressed the South's majority view in defense of keeping the slaves in ignorance, when he wrote: "A knowledge of reading, writing, and the elements of arithmetic, is convenient and important to the free laborer, who is the transactor of his own affairs, and the guardian of his own interests—but of what use could they be to the slaves?"

Tocqueville, the perceptive reporter of social currents, commented: "The Americans of the South, who do not admit that the Negroes can ever be comingled with themselves, have forbidden them, under severe penalties, to be taught to read or write; and as they will not raise them to their level, they sink them as nearly as possible to that of brutes."

And the life of brute animals it was for many Blacks. When Olmsted's travels took him to a slave nursery, he was shaken. "Very few of the babies were in arms," he wrote. "Such as were not, generally lay on the floor, rolling about or sat still sucking their thumbs. The nurse was a kind-looking old Negro woman, with, no doubt, philoprogenitiveness well developed; but she paid little attention to them, only sometimes chiding the older ones for laughing or singing too loud. I watched for half an hour, and in all that time not a baby of them began to cry; nor have I ever heard one, at two or three other plantation nurseries which I have visited. . . . I make note of it, as indicating how young the little twig is bent. . . ."

Freedom and education had become inseparably intertwined

in the minds of those Blacks who wanted to break the chains in which their ignorance, poverty, and brutal conditioning had kept them. Even before the Civil War had ended, the prospect of sharing the secret of knowledge that appeared to have given to the white masters such power and superiority seemed to make the instruments of learning the grail that was now within reach.

"You have no idea of the state of things here," wrote the Reverend Thomas Calahan, a missionary from the United Presbyterian Church, in 1863, while serving among the freedmen in Louisiana.

> Go out in any direction and you meet negroes on horses, negroes on mules . . . cart and buggy load, negroes on foot, men, women and children . . . all hopeful, almost all cheerful, every one pleading to be taught, willing to do anything for learning. They are never out of our rooms, and their cry is for "Books! books!" and when will school begin? Negro women come and offer to cook and wash for us, if we only teach them to read the Bible. . . .

The hunger for learning among the newly freed slaves was insatiable; it had been denied food for so long. "It was," Booker T. Washington summed up as he later looked back on his own childhood, "a whole race trying to go to school."

During the twelve years after the Union victory, the states of the former Confederacy sent thirteen Blacks to the House of Representatives and two to the Senate. These men varied in temperament, ability, and personal background. Some had been slaves, while others had been free from birth; some were virtually without education, others were highly sophisticated. They came from a variety of sectors and activities, and they differed on many issues, but they all agreed on one point: Education was the first priority for their brothers and sisters.

The white South, too, had become conscious of the importance of schooling. Despite the chaos and widespread poverty of the era, Southern states undertook the establishment of public education systems—for whites. Laws to that end were passed along with others setting aside funds for the starving.

But old prejudices had survived the war and were aggravated

by defeat. Even as the Southern states pushed themselves hard in efforts to catch up with the North's public education progress, they groped for new ways to maintain white supremacy and to block the Blacks' road to equal rights and opportunities. In violation of both the spirit and the letter of the emancipation, Southern politicians enacted the Black Codes which placed severe limitations on the freedmen's lives and status. The rationalization of these statutes was that the Black was too ignorant to be fit for the full and demanding role of a free citizen—a role which had not been denied by any corresponding legislation to the equally ignorant poor whites. Indeed, the remedy for the poor whites' unfitness was openly acknowledged to be the provision of public education.

There were other signs of continued Southern resistance to the policies of equal rights imposed by the North. Clearly, even after the guns had ceased firing, the spirit of the old South remained at war with the North's determination to bring about fundamental social changes in the vanquished region.

It was quite naturally in the matter of education for Blacks that the two rival philosophies clashed head-on. Southern whites were angered by the very fact that the Freedman's Bureau had been established, and they continued to be outraged by its activities in support of Black education, along with its mission to aid and protect Negroes freed by the Emancipation Proclamation. General O. O. Howard, the bureau's first commissioner, whose name Howard University was to bear, assured it of military backing, thus rendering it one of the Reconstruction's most powerful instruments.

Over the years, Southern-inspired folklore has given the bureau a reputation for graft and corruption as well as for high-handed and unscrupulous methods—charges which more than a century later were to be leveled, often with more prejudice than documentation, against virtually every local, state, and federal agency created by Lyndon B. Johnson in support of Black economic rights. In fact, modern scholarship, emancipated from the tradition of Southern myth-making that had long dominated the historic record of the era, gives full credit to the bureau for its efforts to nurse Black education in the postwar South through its embattled infancy.

At the time, however, public education, Black and white, suffered setbacks because it came to be associated, in the Southern mind, with the aims and works of Yankee carpetbaggers. A Texas newspaper editor, reacting to the use of Northern textbooks by Southern children, swore: "Now we would rather see two hundred thousand vipers unfold themselves and crawl over the face of our country than some numbers of Messrs. Appleton and Messrs. Barnes textbooks."

Many of the most dedicated teachers in the new Southern schools were indeed former abolitionists with crusading missionary zeal. As a result, these Northern teachers often found themselves ostracized and harassed in South communities. Local inns refused to serve them. Churches barred them from services. Some teachers were driven out by threats of violence, while others actually were tarred and feathered or flogged. White Southern resentment sprang from the same sources and followed the same course then as it did much later, in the 1950s and after, when federal laws pressed for the desegregation of the schools. States' rights advocates resented all federal action as "outside interference," just as they subsequently denounced all civil rights spokesmen as "outside agitators." Conservatives viewed the changes that were to be imposed on Southern laws and customs as a direct threat to their way of life.

Above all those fears and suspicions hovered the ultimate horror of having to accept the Negro as a political, economic, and social equal. Even those Southerners who had abandoned the earlier stand against any and all schooling for Black children, now tended to fear and resent a loss of control over the kind of education that seemed to them proper for "their" Blacks. Blacks, they felt, ought to be educated in a special Southern style that would serve to make them better workers and assure that they would be rendered "moral" in the sense of being obedient and submissive.

During the height of what has been called Radical Reconstruction, as Southern Blacks made their entrance on the political scene, white hostility was fed by the fact that much of this activity was indeed supported by federal bayonets. But objective reviews of actual conditions, shorn of post–Civil War propaganda and legend, indicate that neither the persecution of former Confederates nor the "domination" of the political scene by Blacks was as powerful, as long-lived, and as corrupt as earlier accounts had maintained.

Contrary to the politically inspired myths, according to Carl Degler's historical analysis, Blacks did not dominate the Southern states' legislatures. "Perhaps," he concludes, "if there had been Negro domination, Reconstruction . . . would have been milder, for in both the conventions and the legislatures, the Negro members were the opposites of vindictive toward the whites." Although Southern resistance made much of the carpetbaggers', the Blacks', and the army's graft and corruption, they generally overlooked the fact that the postwar political scene in the Northern cities, where none of these forces were at work, was no less graftridden and corrupt.

The double standard that was carefully developed as a means of keeping the Southern Blacks in line shrewdly and unscrupulously used the argument that only a literate and responsible electorate could legitimately claim the franchise—at the very moment when Blacks had gained the right to vote. Those who advanced this view were little bothered by the widespread illiteracy of poor white voters. Moreover, as John Hope Franklin, the Black historian, has pointed out, millions of Europeans who "poured into this country in every post-war decade and who muddied the political waters considerably" were not similarly disenfranchised. Indeed, in a number of states, during these periods, immigrants had actually been allowed to vote before they attained citizenship, an important factor in the big-city bosses' rise to power.

None of those rational arguments were to prevail. In the long run, deep-seated Southern racial fears and prejudices triumphed. New legal hurdles were successfully thrown up to keep Blacks from voting, and deliberate policies aimed at keeping Blacks uneducated made it impossible for the overwhelming majority to clear those barriers and become a political force. It was not until the passage of the Voting Rights Act, during the Johnson Administration of the 1960s, that the political stranglehold was broken.

Despite acrimony and plotting during the Reconstruction years, the momentum of the new drive toward public education proved irresistible. As a result, the one enduring monument to the era was the accomplishment, however limited by modern standards, of laying the foundations for free public education, for Black as well as white children. Resentment that the philosophy of universal instruction carried the stamp of the New England crusaders' zeal could not stop the tide. Schools were built. For the first time, the South had entered the area in which the rest of the country had, with varying degrees of enthusiasm, been engaged for some time.

When federal programs and good intentions gave way to Southern-dominated compromises, Congress, under the leadership of Charles Sumner, made one last effort to bolster Black rights with the passage of a Civil Rights Act that was originally intended to prohibit the establishment of segregated public schools among its provisions. When the new law in fact sanctioned segregated schools, the Blacks' faith was shaken. Until then the freed Blacks had believed that, if only they could be educated like white men, they would also be treated like white men. Their despair was reflected in declining school enrollments. Yet, for those Blacks who continued their children's schooling, even under conditions of segregation, education still seemed the most tangible hope for equality to which to cling.

Even in its diminished form, the Civil Rights Act seemed to segregationists too radical in the protection of Black rights. In 1883, the Supreme Court struck down the act eight years after its approval. The Black, the court said, must stop being "the special favorite of the laws" and become a "mere citizen"—an attitude that was to surface every time a minority asked to be assured of its normal rights by way of special laws which were enacted, in fact, precisely because such groups had been denied their normal rights. In this specific instance, conservative reaction to the Civil Rights Act was to deny Congress the power to protect Black claims to equal treatment. The matter was not to be taken up again with the full weight of federal enforcement until the passage of the Civil Right Act of 1965.

The court's action demolished the fragile coalition of progress that had consisted of federal guarantee, public enlightenment, and Black protest which had begun to make some real progress in many areas of racial integration in the South. By calling a cautious retreat, the court prepared the way for the tragedy of segregated schooling which was to create some of the nation's most serious social and economic problems and threaten, more directly than any other issue, the ideological basis of the American dream of the casteless, open, and just society.

Although much Southern maneuvering concerned the issue of school segregation, the region's far more real problem was financial. An impoverished South was unable to foot the bill for public education, regardless of color. In an effort to cope with the problem—long before federal aid to education was finally enacted under the Eisenhower Administration—a major bill was introduced during the 1880s as a proposal to provide a federal subsidy to the nation's schools by way of ten annual appropriations to be distributed among the states in proportion to the number of their illiterates. It was a formula that was not again to be discussed seriously in Congress until the 1960s. At that time, however, the bill, having been approved by the Senate several times, never came to a vote in the House, despite the fact that it clearly allowed the operation of segregated schools.

The sanctity of states' rights was still too deeply embedded in the national consciousness, and it would not bend to the obvious needs of the era, even though an agent for the powerful Peabody Fund—a man named J. L. M. Curry—found it possible to stretch his belief in the states' prerogatives to allow for support of the aid bill. "Through no fault of their own," Curry said, "the emancipated Negroes were too poor to pay taxes, and the South too impoverished to provide the necessary education to keep them from succumbing to the false ideas of demagogues."

By the end of the 1870s, as the last federal troops were leaving the area, poverty engulfed the entire South, Black and white. Political power drifted into the hands of the Redeemers—the landed gentry who, although they also had suffered great losses, approached economic policy from the point of view of the relatively privileged kind of conservatism that tends to seek salvation in belt-tightening and retrenchment rather than in progressive action.

Public education was to suffer first, particularly since it bore the stigma of a carpetbag measure. And so the great hopes of the South's Blacks that equality in education would open the road to equality as citizens was to last little more than a decade after Appomattox.

Retreat from the commitments of Reconstruction would inevitably shape the attitudes of American Blacks toward all subsequent promises of reform. It was to be a crucial factor in the Black leadership's fear that history would repeat itself when, within less than a decade of Lyndon Johnson's civil rights efforts and within less than two decades of the Supreme Court's 1954 antisegregation ruling, the new conservatism of the Nixon Administration once again clashed with the Blacks' demands for equal rights and opportunities.

During the period between the withdrawal of federal troops and the end of the nineteenth century, economic and political developments in the South became steadily more threatening to Blacks, and particularly to their chances for true access to public education. In addition to legally emancipating Blacks, the Civil War had created the beginnings of a new social order. The lower-class "poor whites" had also been emancipated and, as they vied for new powers and better education, they considered themselves in direct competition with Blacks.

This was a different political thrust from that of the Redeemers, former slave holders or their children, who never considered Blacks as a threat to their own secure social and political position. Their attitudes—apart from their destructive economic policies of retrenchment—had been shaped by a kindly paternalism. Now, these aristocratic Bourbons were being shouldered aside by new men of more humble origins who had risen to power by their own efforts and political acumen. In their politics, there was no room even for paternalistic benevolence toward the Blacks. After a brief interlude of interracial harmony, which came to an end with the failure of the Populist bid for power, hopes for equal educational opportunity and integrated schools faded.

Given the general condition of the South's poverty and the Blacks' fall from political power, segregated schools inevitably meant inferior schools. Increasingly, funds intended for Black schools were diverted to white ones, and these manipulations were particularly prevalent in the predominantly Black counties which were at the mercy of a power structure in the hands of a fearful white minority.

When general school funds were cut, the Black schools suffered the most severe slashing. Governor James K. Vardaman of Mississippi, one of the new politicians, articulating the prevailing view of Black education, said in his message of January 9, 1909: "Money spent today for the maintenance of public schools for Negroes is robbing the white man, and a waste upon the Negro . . . in an effort to make [him] what God Almighty never intended should be made, and which man cannot accomplish. . . ."

The changing political climate throughout the nation had left Southern Blacks without any effective allies even outside their own region. With the exception of the continuing efforts of a few philanthropists, Northerners had turned away from the issue and gone back to their own immediate concerns. Nobody spoke for the Southern Black as the caste and color line hardened into repressive law. This tragic development eventually culminated in the Supreme Court's decision in *Plessy v. Ferguson* in 1896 which froze school segregation into a mold that was not to be broken—and then only slowly—until its historic reversal in 1954.

The North generally gave sanction by its silence and even its occasional encouragement. Southern states enacted more segregation laws. Lynching and terror reached new peaks, and many conservatives, frightened by Populist gains, began to disenfranchise the Black. In 1894, Congress wiped from the federal statutes a mass of Reconstruction laws for the protection of equal rights. In September 1895, Booker T. Washington, the politically most powerful Black leader of the day, delivered an address that came to be known as the Atlanta Compromise and was widely interpreted as a sign of acceptance of an inferior status by the Black American.

Washington addressed himself to Blacks and whites alike. His theme was the importance of Black cooperation with white friends, an attitude that sprang largely from his own capacity to get along with prominent whites and to make deals with them, which at the time may well have given him and his followers as much as could rationally be expected—but which also has exposed him to the subsequent charges of submission to white supremacy.

Black education, Washington said, should be devoted to the practical business of earning a living, without any opposition to segregation. Holding up his hand, with its fingers spread wide apart, he exclaimed: "In all things purely social we can be as separate as the fingers, yet one as the hand in all things essential to mutual progress."

The address was widely hailed as a triumph of reason and common sense. President Grover Cleveland sent Washington a personal message of congratulations. But a reporter from *The New York World,* who had covered the occasion, wrote that, at the conclusion of the speech, "most of the Negroes in the audience were crying, perhaps without knowing just why."

Actually, there was little in Washington's speech that was new; but his timing, and the white South's enthusiastic response, gave it extraordinary importance at the precise moment when Blacks were being deprived of virtually all those civil rights which had been promised to them so recently. It seemed to prepare the ground for the events the following May, when Justice William Billings Brown, a Northerner, delivered the Supreme Court's opinion, in *Plessy v. Ferguson,* which upheld the "separate but equal" doctrine of public accommodations, thus confirming the principle of segregation as lawful under the Constitution. The case had actually involved a Black's refusal to sit in the rear of a streetcar.

"Legislation," Justice Brown held, "is powerless to eradicate racial instincts." He echoed the earlier ruling in the case of *Roberts v. City of Boston* which had turned down Charles Sumner's plea for equal rights in school attendance. The court, supporting established practice and social prejudice, maintained that the sponsors of the Fourteenth Amendment "could not have intended to abolish distinctions based upon color, or to enforce social, as distinguished from political, equality." In fact, the majority of the court, with its political ears to the ground, was indeed contradicting the intent of the amendment. It conveniently ignored the fact that the South had already blocked the Blacks' claim to political equality quite as effectively as any alleged claim to social equality, which no Blacks of the day had expressed. "If one race be inferior to the other socially," the court said, "the Constitution of the United States cannot put them upon the same plane."

The two opinions in support of segregation, it should be noted, were written by Northerners from Massachusetts, Justices Shaw and Brown. The dissent was the work of a Southern aristocrat,

Justice John Marshall Harlan, who held that the court was in direct conflict with the Thirteenth and Fourteenth Amendments. "In view of the Constitution, in the eye of the law," Harlan wrote, "there is in this country no superior, dominant ruling class of citizens. There is no caste here. Our Constitution is color-blind. . . ."

The judicial and social philosophy in *Plessy* became the foundation for the entire structure of the South's dual school systems, as demeaning and far more dangerous to the nation's future than the separate rest rooms, drinking fountains, and other public accommodations. As its opponents knew from the start, segregation of the races did indeed produce second-class opportunities, including second-class education, for second-class citizens. On the average, for example, about twice as much money was henceforth to be spent on the education of white pupils as on Blacks in Southern schools. And, with the neglect of the Black children's schooling, white supremacists found it easier to "prove" their theory of innate Black inferiority.

Booker T. Washington, who considered himself so successful a manipulator of white power, may well have been naïve in his belief that his compromise might, by agreeing to separation, buy white support for adequate Black schooling. But there can be no question that, according to his own lights, Washington had an abiding faith in the power of education and its importance to Black Americans.

Born a slave, he knew poverty, filth, and the struggle to learn how to read and write against the odds of a hostile environment. Yet, like so many members of minority groups, white as well as Black, who "made it" by their own stamina and intelligence, Washington viewed the future in the typically middle-class Horatio Alger tradition, despite all the humiliations to be suffered along the way.

Washington's "entrance examination" to Hampton Institute had consisted of sweeping the recitation room. After graduation, upon the recommendation of General Armstrong, the institute's founder, he was offered the job of starting a normal school for teachers in Tuskegee, Alabama.

"There were not a few white people in the vicinity of Tuskegee [a school for teachers] who looked with some disfavor on its establishment," Washington wrote in his autobiography, *Up From Slavery*. "They questioned its value to the colored people and had a fear that it might result in bringing trouble between the races. . . . [They] feared the result of education would be that the Negroes would leave the farms and that it would be difficult to secure them for domestic service."

On July 4, 1881, when Tuskegee opened, Washington recalled,

> thirty students reported for admission. I was the only teacher. . . . It had been decided to receive only those who were above 15 years of age and who had previously received some education. The greater part of the 30 were public-school teachers. . . . Some had studied Latin and one or two Greek. This they thought entitled them to special distinction.

Washington felt that many of the students did not want to work with their hands, considering such labor to be beneath their dignity, perpetuating (in Washington's view) the caste distinction between ordinary slaves in the fields and house slaves.

To make his point, Washington occasionally worked in the fields alongside his students as a means of shaming them into acceptance of such labor. Once, he reported, a Black worker in the vicinity looked at him with shock and surprise, explaining that "you sholy ain't gwine clean out de hen house in de *day* time?"

Despite much supine acceptance of all the limitations which the climate of the day imposed on Black youth, Tuskegee's early years were a time of privation and struggle. Solicitation for funds from the surrounding community often brought five cents, some sugar cane, and an old quilt. One Black woman wrote: "I ain't got no money, but I wants you to take dese six eggs, what I's been savin' up, and I wants you to put dese six eggs into de eddication of dese boys an' gals." (During its early days, it should be noted, Harvard College was supported by bushels of wheat and corn.)

Washington's work in founding Tuskegee was typical of the struggle that attended the creation of what came to be a network of Black colleges—a subsystem of American higher education that has often been overlooked. Yet it is a chapter of social and educational history that is intensely American in its optimism in the face of what ought to have seemed insuperable obstacles. To the future of Blacks, at a time when national policy and public sentiment had erected an iron curtain against their entry into the world of scholarship, the professions and, more generally, the middle-class mainstream, these institutions were the only way to beat the system.

The importance of the Black colleges can best be gauged from the fact that virtually all of the civil rights leaders and important Black public figures of the crucial era of the 1960s, including Dr. Martin Luther King, Jr., were their alumni.

In the wake of their integration into the mainstream of higher education which was not to begin in earnest until the 1960s, Black colleges have been subjected to rather rigorous scrutiny by white education leadership. Even such sympathetic observers as David Riesman and Christopher Jencks in their book, *The Academic Revolution,* called the typical privately financed, small Black colleges a "disaster area" and questioned the feasibility of bringing them up to the standards demanded of contemporary colleges. Such appraisals tend to underrate the task these institutions performed, not by choice but because of the realities that confronted Black youths for so many years.

By Harvard standards, writes Allan Ballard in *The Education of Black Folk,* the Black colleges were, of course, inferior. But the fact is, he continues, that "for generations, no other colleges admitted Black students. And many of these graduates became the leaders of their people."

In fact, neither the Riesman nor the Ballard view does full justice to the Black colleges' problems in the light of their history. Thomas Sowell, a Black economist and observer of Black education, recalled in the Spring 1974 issue of *Daedalus* that most of the Black colleges began their existence with predominantly or exclusively white faculties, administrators, and trustees. They were, in short, white-run institutions for Black students.

Progress was necessarily slow. By the time of World War I about half of the faculty and administrators of the Black colleges were Black, and during the "Black renaissance" of the 1920s demands for Black control of Black institutions became more insistent. A decade later such control had become a reality.

In assessing the consequences of that development, Sowell tends to support the Riesman–Jencks judgment of the Black colleges' problems of academic quality. The rapid Black takeover at a time of meager Black scholarship, he writes, led to a decline in academic standards.

Black administrators, Sowell continues, held onto tenure with desperation and established a near-tyrannical rule that was criticized by Black intellectuals from W. E. B. Du Bois to Ralph Ellison. Intellectual values often were undermined by a leadership of small intellectual capacity. Du Bois encountered hostility on more than one Black campus. "A list of Negro scholars alienated from the successive administrations at Howard University over the years would read like a *Who's Who* of Black academic scholarship," Sowell writes. ". . . The shaping of institutions was largely in the hands of more tractable, but less able men."

The explanation for such reliance on mediocrity was not difficult to find. It was that men who would not rock the boat were needed to give security to Black administrations which usually were responsible to white trustees, white foundations, and white state legislatures.

Inevitably, any critical view of the Black institutions' place in contemporary higher education will arouse some suspicions of elitism. In long-term projections of the academic future, however, critics are probably right in predicting that it will be increasingly difficult to maintain Black colleges against the academic competition of the mainstream—particularly if the trend toward equality in admissions, without racial discrimination, continues to open the doors to the formerly white campuses.

But in the broader historical context the need for, and the contributions made by, the Black colleges can be appreciated only against the background of the difficulties Blacks faced in gaining acceptance by the established institutions of higher education. The history of Blacks at Harvard is a case in point.

Although Blacks had served in menial jobs at Harvard for nearly a century after the Revolution—mainly as "scouts" or personal servants to white undergraduates—it was not until 1850 that three Blacks, sponsored by the Massachusetts Colonization Society, were actually enrolled as students, not at the college but in the Medical School. (The first Negro was admitted to the college fifteen years later, in 1865.)

Their presence was resented by some white students, who appealed to the university authorities for their dismissal. Even though a greater number of whites actually opposed that anti-Black petition, the faculty voted on December 26, 1850, to notify the Colonization Society that no more Blacks would be admitted. The following March, five months after they had entered, the three Black students were dismissed from the university.

One of the three young men, Isaac H. Snowden, who persisted in his medical studies under the tutelage of a prominent surgeon, reapplied to Harvard two years after. Seventy-five members of his former class petitioned the faculty in his support and made it clear that his presence would in no way offend them. Yet the faculty heeded the petition of only eight students who opposed Snowden's admission. He was turned down.

Anti-Black prejudice had a history among Harvard students, the majority of them representatives of the social elite. Lorenzo J. Greene, a Black historian, reports in *The Negro in Colonial New England:*

> According to the racial philosophy of the Puritans, Negroes and Indians were an inferior race. . . . Not only was the Negro regarded as a sub-species, but as late as 1773 a member of the graduating class of Harvard University, debating the legality of enslaving Africans, justified the institution partly on the ground that the Negro was a "conglomerate of child, idiot, and madman."

It was not until 1870 that Richard T. Greener was to be graduated from Harvard College, the first Black student to achieve that distinction. Greener, who took an extra year for graduation, largely because of his early difficulties with mathematics, was considered an "experiment" by the Harvard authorities. He subsequently became a high-school principal and, after graduation from law school, served as dean of Howard University Law School, and eventually as American consul at Bombay and Vladivostok. But at Harvard—and other American elite universities—the acceptance of Blacks still faced an uphill struggle.

It is against such a background that the founding and the work of the Black colleges ought to be viewed. Most of them—particularly the private ones—established themselves and struggled for continued existence in an atmosphere of hostility, contempt, and callousness. The majority were founded after the Civil War in the South, where ninety-two percent of all Blacks then lived.

In 1900, the total Black enrollment in all predominantly white colleges was less than 800. It rose to 7,000 in 1920 and jumped to about 100,000 in 1950. By the 1970s all American colleges enrolled 470,000 Black students—six percent of the total student body—and 160,000 of them were still attending the Black colleges, even though the percentage of Blacks they enrolled had declined from 65 percent in 1960 to 34 percent in 1970.

Out of an original estimated 200 Black colleges, 100 survive—51 of them private and 34 public four-year institutions and the rest two-year colleges.

W. E. B. Du Bois, the Black leader who never conceded an inch in the demand that Black Americans must rise to the highest standards of excellence, wrote movingly about the mission of Black schools and colleges in his book, *The Souls of Black Folk*. "The teachers in these institutions," he told young Blacks,

> came not to keep the Negroes in their place but to raise them out of the defilement of the places where slavery had wallowed them. The colleges they founded were social settlements; homes where the best of the sons of the freedom came in close and sympathetic touch with the best traditions of New England. They lived and ate together, studied and worked, hoped and harkened in the dawning light. The actual formal content of their curriculum was doubtless old-fashioned, but in educational power it was supreme, for it was the contact of the living soul.

Everything considered, Ballard concluded in 1973, "Du Bois, Washington, and those 'tyrannical Uncle Tom presidents' built better than they knew."

Booker T. Washington's role in the early stages of the Black colleges' history was, of course, only part of his pervasive, often controversial, impact. For about two decades, which ended with his death in 1915, he was the acknowledged Black spokesman, not only in education but in all other areas of life. This was not so much a tribute to his genius, according to historian C. Vann Woodward in an assessment of the era, "as to the remarkable congeniality between his doctrines and the dominant forces of his age and society. . . . The man who abjured 'social equality' in the South moved in circles of the elite in the North and aristocracy abroad that were opened to extremely few Southern whites."

A reappraisal of Washington's views and actions from the perspective of the militant civil rights movement of the 1960s may deprive him of much of his earlier prestige. His humility, though clearly a virtuoso act that made his political power palatable to the white power structure of his time, today may seem a cowardly way to achieve peace without honor. His compromises often may have blurred the line between a shrewdly expedient bargain in the best interests of his people and a cynical trade-in of others' claim to true equality in return for his own prominent place among the rich and the powerful.

Such hindsight judgments, which ignore the realities of a different age, are simplistic and misleading. Washington's outlook and policies were based openly and unashamedly on the middle-class assumption that his leadership was exercised in a society that regarded the work ethic as the admission ticket to the American way of life. He understood, much as it grieved him, that Blacks lacked powerful allies. Under the circumstances, accommodation (but always with the goal of exerting power from within the existing structure) may not have been heroic; but an assessment of his accomplishments should be made in the context of his time.

Even in his time, however, Booker T. Washington was not without opposition from within the Black community, and his critics were able to cite as their choice of Black representation William E. B. Du Bois, a man of extraordinary courage, independence, and charisma. If Washington was the pragmatic politician, Du Bois was the ideologue and philosopher—the Thomas Paine of his people. As such he may have scorned Washington's concern for the mundane and immediate needs of America's downtrodden precisely because they lacked, not middle-class skills and veneer, but fundamental human and American rights.

"So far," Du Bois wrote in 1902, "as Mr. Washington apologizes for injustice, North or South, belittles the emasculating effects of caste distinction, and opposes the higher training and ambition of our brighter minds, so far as he, the South, or the nation does this —we must unceasingly oppose him."

To Washington, the question for the Black, particularly in the South, was how to gain the white man's acceptance. It was through education, of a kind that would cultivate the Black man's virtues and thus win the white man's respect, that he wanted to solve that problem. And, while Du Bois rejected Washington's philosophy of accommodation and assimilation, he too placed almost unlimited faith in the power of education.

In contrast to Washington's humble beginnings and his personal struggle against poverty and ignorance, Du Bois was born a free Black in Massachusetts and enjoyed a first-rate education which culminated in a Harvard doctorate. Perhaps because he had grown up in the company of whites and had nevertheless tasted the bitterness that came with being a Black in privileged white surroundings, he rebelled against the very idea of accommodation and compromise. Whatever privileges the accommodations of others had gained for him clearly did not seem enough, and since current policies failed to give any indication that the white power structure would willingly grant equal rights to Blacks, the only honorable and—in the long term—effective way was the uncompromising mobilization of Black power, or withdrawal into separatism and even secession.

Du Bois, aristocratic in his view of leadership, found little to be admired in the middle-class ways that so attracted Washington. While Du Bois cared deeply about the lot of all Blacks, he never wavered in his belief that the "talented tenth" among the Blacks, as among all other races and peoples, must form the elite that would lead their sons and daughters forward to greater power and a better life. His was a Jeffersonian faith in an aristocracy of talent.

If middle-class America allowed its prejudices to deny to this proud man the fruition of his dream of creating a Black aristocracy of talent, then it was quite natural that Du Bois would turn against an Establishment which Washington continued to serve. In 1910, he left a teaching post at the University of Pennsylvania and went to New York to become research director for the newly founded National Association for the Advancement of Colored People and editor of its magazine, *Crisis*. Gradually, as the

N.A.A.C.P. assumed the leadership in the battle for Black rights, Du Bois moved away from what he considered its too moderate position, and he finally broke with the organization in 1948.

Booker T. Washington's faith in education had sprung from the same basic sentiments that had inspired wave after wave of immigrants with the hope that they could learn how to assimilate, adjust, and gradually gain acceptance by a society that considered itself superior and whose superiority they acknowledged, as long as they could expect gradual admission to it—perhaps if only for their children and grandchildren. Du Bois, by contrast, was imbued with an intellectual's and an aristocrat's confidence in his inherent right to be part of the elite of talent. He placed most of his trust in higher education, and he believed that his white peers simply could not justify any denial of equal rights to any member of an educated elite, regardless of color.

Du Bois's standards were high. He demanded as much of his Black followers as of whites, and he had only contempt for the vulgarities of both. "The greatest meetings of the Negro college year like those of the white college year," he said in 1930 as Howard University conferred an honorary doctorate on him,

> have become vulgar exhibitions of liquor, extravagance, and fur coats. We have in our colleges a growing mass of stupidity and indifference. I am not counselling perfection; as desperately human groups, we must expect our share of mediocrity. But as hitherto a thick and thin defender of the college, it seems to me that we are getting into our Negro colleges considerably more than our share of plain fools.

It was only as his hopes for an America willing to accept Blacks on terms of equality and merit began to fade that Du Bois's bitterness made him turn to other ways of achieving equality, and he espoused communism and socialism. He replied to the racism of American society with the countermovement of Black racism, even as many of his closest associates, who had shared all his dreams, continued the battle within the ranks of the N.A.A.C.P., with education and integration as their banners.

It was not easy for those who fought for Black rights to keep such faith. The years between *Plessy* and the 1954 Supreme Court ruling against school segregation were bleak. But it was also a period of dramatic changes in the Blacks' place in America. A vast black migration was under way, with wave after wave moving from the rural South to the Northern cities. Between 1919 and 1940, for example, the Black population of New York City grew from 60,000 to 450,000. Although there was little difference in the Blacks' conditions of rural and urban poverty, there was, in the cities, no barrier to the exercise of the franchise. With the power of the ballot box came the beginnings of the kind of political power that Southern Blacks had enjoyed only briefly and lost so quickly during the Reconstruction.

Education was once again the great hope. The Swedish sociologist Gunnar Myrdal, in his classic study *An American Dilemma*, pointed to "the trend toward a rising educational level of the Negro population." Education, he wrote prophetically in the 1940s,

> means an assimilation of white American culture. It decreases the dissimilarity of the Negroes from other Americans. Since the white culture is permeated by democratic valuations, and since the caste relation is anything but democratic, education is likely to increase dissatisfaction among Negroes.

Yet, important as education was to America's Blacks, their children remained in inferior segregated schools in the South and often in neglected ghetto schools in the urban North. The very fact that the history of the era contains little descriptive material of the nature of these schools underscores their problem: they were, in Ralph Ellison's apt word, invisible.

Despite Myrdal's prescience about the consequences of the gap between the ideals taught in school and the grim realities of life outside, even he overlooked many of the Black children's grievances in the North's mixed classrooms, let alone the predominantly Black ghetto schools. Malcolm X, in his *Autobiography*, poignantly described the Black experience in white schools, so often romanticized by white observers. Raised in a Midwestern community, Malcolm X was the only Black boy in a white school. Throughout, he had been the outstanding scholar, emerging as the president of his class. But when he informed his English teacher that he wanted to become a lawyer, he was told: "A lawyer—that's not a realistic goal for a Nigger."

Sporadic protests against segregation in Northern ghetto schools had occurred long before the civil rights movement led to massive urban attacks on, and boycotts of, such schools. Several local boycotts took place in East Orange, New Jersey, between 1899 and 1906, in Alton, Illinois, between 1897 and 1908 and in Springfield, Ohio, between 1922 and 1923. But lack of unity among Black protesters, the gap between the more militant young people and their fearful and acquiescent elders, and the political impotence of Blacks undermined the effectiveness of these actions. It was not until the New Deal, World War II and the greater political consciousness of Black Americans that their power became an effective force against segregated and inferior education.

In 1941, Richard Wright, the Black novelist, wrote:

> Deep down we distrust the schools that the Lords of the Land built for us and we do not really feel that they are ours. . . . Many of them say that French, Latin, and Spanish are languages not for us, and they become angry when they think that we desire to learn more than they want us to. They say that "all the geography a nigger needs to know is how to get from his shack to the plow."

Over all the dissatisfaction with the schools hung the greater gloom of an economy still largely closed to Blacks intent on using educational achievements to gain access to better jobs. In 1890, Du Bois had cited these injustices, following a study of Blacks in Philadelphia. In 1939, a similar study in Chicago showed that most of the railroad station's redcaps were Black college graduates. Historian David Tyack, who reported the results of that survey, commented: "I have found few cases where schoolmen tried to convince employers to practice what the American creed preached. And if educators did accept racism in employment, they could comfort themselves with many scientific studies demonstrating that black folk had no aptitude for white folks' work."

Indeed, schools had largely responded by setting up separate and unequal curricula for Black pupils. Schools enrolling mainly whites were offering vocational training in printing, aviation, retailing, and cosmetology; the Black schools offered bricklaying, carpentry, automobile repair, and sewing.

Black schools in the South, moreover, had deliberately and systematically been turned into an essentially conservative force, even though their maintenance required a constant combination of heroism, patience, and sacrifice.

In many instances, white officials took funds appropriated for Black schools and turned them over to white schools instead. Although the situation was not quite as bad in the cities as in the rural "Black belts," it was far from fair. Atlanta, for instance, though a prosperous city, made little effort to support Black education, even though Blacks constituted one third of the population. Du Bois charged in 1908 that Atlanta supported its Black schools with $65,000 taken from the state aid appropriation, while it used for white schools the entire $350,000 raised for education from local taxes, including the taxes paid by the city's Blacks. Ray Stannard Baker, the muckraking journalist, wrote after a visit to Atlanta in 1906: "The Negro is neglected. Several new schools have been built for white children, but there has been no school for colored children in 15 or 20 years. . . ."

Despite their arduous duties, often in double sessions, Black teachers in Atlanta were paid less than white teachers "all of whom taught only one set of children in a single, school-day session." (Atlanta, it should be noted, was the scene of an early battle by the N.A.A.C.P. for better teachers' salaries in 1916–1917.)

In rural communities, however, Myrdal wrote in 1940, Black teachers were more independent than they appeared. "This," he explained, "is solely because the white superintendent and the white school board ordinarily cares little about what goes on in the Negro school. There are still counties where the superintendent has never visited the majority of his Negro schools." They remained invisible.

In one of the few available eyewitness reports of these invisible schools, Myrdal wrote:

> I once visited such a school in a rural county of Georgia, not far from Atlanta. The building was an old Rosenwald (Northern philanthropy-donated) school, dilapidated but far better than many other school buildings in the region. The students

were in all age groups from 6 to 7 years upward to 16 and 17. There was also an imbecile man of about 20 staying on as a steady student veteran. . . . The teacher, a sickly girl about 20 years old, looked shy and full of fear; she said she had high school training.

The students seemed to enjoy the visit and it was easy to establish human contact with them. No one could tell who was President of the United States or even what the President was. Only one of the older students knew, or thought he knew, of Booker T. Washington. He said Washington was 'a big white man,' and intimated that he might be the President of the United States. . . .

"When telling such a horror story," Myrdal concluded the report, "it must, at once, be added that it is not typical. . . . It should also be said that there are a few white schools in some regions of the South which do not reach much higher. I recollect that some white school children in Louisiana believed that Huey Long was still living (in the fall of 1938) and was President of the United States."

While there were a few outstanding Blacks of the period who managed to attend such institutions as Harvard, the number was minute. Though change was in the wind, it was perceptible only to the exceptional and fortunate few whose extraordinary talents put them in the vanguard.

In actual fact, there had been a few other pioneering colleges ahead of Harvard. The first Black to get a degree from a white college was graduated from Bowdoin College in Maine, in 1826. By 1910 almost 700 Blacks had graduated from white institutions. Oberlin was in the lead; in keeping with its abolitionist principles, it had 50 Black alumni before 1890. By 1910, Dartmouth had graduated 14 Blacks, Harvard 41, the University of Pennsylvania 29, the University of Kansas 60, and Yale 37. Oberlin had remained in the undisputed lead, with 149 Black graduates. But the overwhelming fact remained that Black students seeking a higher education continued to look primarily to the Black colleges, mostly in the South.

Somehow, the power of education within the American philosophy of life was too strong to be thwarted, even when—as was surely the case in the South—the political instincts of those in power and even of those powerless poor whites who feared the Blacks as a competing force in the search for a better life wanted to shut the Blacks out. "The great wonder is," wrote Myrdal, "that the principle of the Negroes' right to public education was not renounced altogether" and that "the Negroes' statutory right to public education remained unassailable in the South."

It was from the Blacks' recognition of the importance of education and their demand for more of it that much of the drive for equality continued to gain its strength. In the South as well as in the North, the fight for educational equality was the generator of much of the power and the anger that fueled the civil rights drive of the 1960s.

Ironically, while Du Bois, who was often so despairing of American politics and power, saw the road relatively clear for a strong education drive to avert disaster, it was Myrdal who issued prophetic warnings which, had they been heeded, might have prevented much grief and even bloodshed in the Northern cities. The North, he wrote, would continue to get wave after wave of "untutored and crude" Black immigrants from the South. What was needed therefore, he continued, was an education that would make the Black child adaptable to the American culture—but it would have to be an education that paid greater attention to the Black child who, because life will be far more difficult for him, needed education more than his white contemporary.

So enlightened an approach, later to be called compensatory education, was still more than a generation in the future. The intervening generation had yet to win the battle against segregation which had made the Black schools of the South inherently unequal and had made the Black children, both in the South and in the growing Northern ghettoes, virtually invisible. It was a battle in which the stakes were almost as high as in the Civil War, and, as the level of Black educational consciousness rose in the South, the segregationists knew it. Senator Vardaman, who had earlier sensed the growing force of the tide, said: "What the North is sending South is not money but dynamite; this education is ruining our Negroes. They're demanding equality."

The Depression and World War II submerged the demands of Black Americans under the flood of national emergencies. The

New Deal, despite its concern with human problems, had remarkably little to say about Blacks, except almost peripherally in the Fair Employment order of 1941. Yet by greatly increasing the people's power and by initiating policies which gave voice to the poor, the long years of Franklin D. Roosevelt's Presidency nevertheless paved the way for dramatic change.

The symbol of, as well as the key to, such change was the Supreme Court's ruling in *Brown v. Board of Education* in 1954. The cases demanding an end to school segregation had not come to the court suddenly, without prior warnings and pressures. In 1950, for example, in *Sweatt v. Painter,* a Black student had petitioned the court because the University of Texas Law School had denied him admission in 1946 solely because he was a Black. The court took a look at the newly opened Black branch of the law school, with its five faculty members and twenty-three students, and found that it was, while separate, clearly not equal to the institution available to whites. It ruled that the Fourteenth Amendment required the petitioner's admission to the school that had excluded him.

But the court was not ready to go all the way and reverse *Plessy.* Chief Justice Vinson, who delivered the opinion, said merely that earlier standards had been violated, but that he could not agree with "the petitioner's contention that *Plessy v. Ferguson* should be reexamined in the light of contemporary knowledge respecting the 14th amendment and the effects of racial segregation."

Yet, to political observers it seemed that the court had not been keeping up with changing political and social realities. In 1947, one year after its creation by President Harry S. Truman, the Civil Rights Committee said that "discrimination imposes a direct cost upon our economy through the wasteful duplication and many facilities and services required by the 'separate but equal' policy."

Thus, the way had been prepared when five separate cases challenging school segregation reached the court in 1953, and the petition of Oliver Brown against the Topeka, Kansas, Board of Education was placed on the docket because it was alphabetically the first. Other petitions had come from South Carolina, Virginia, and Delaware.

In three days of argument, a great array of legal and sociological talent came before the court. Thurgood Marshall, later to be a Justice of the Supreme Court, pleaded the desegregation case as chief counsel of N.A.A.C.P. Kenneth B. Clark, a prominent Black psychologist, provided much of the social science data that documented the psychological and pedagogical harm done to Black children who are barred from integrated schools. The chief spokesman for the South was John W. Davis, who had been the Democratic nominee for President of the United States in 1924.

"Candor requires recognition," argued Marshall, "that the plain purpose and effect of segregated education is to perpetuate an inferior status for Negroes which is America's sorry heritage from slavery. But the primary purpose of the Fourteenth Amendment was to deprive the states of *all* power to perpetuate such a caste system."

Speaking for South Carolina, Davis reverted to the traditional Southern position, holding that the separation of the races is part of the natural order. He invoked Disraeli, whom he quoted as saying: "No man will treat with indifference the principle of race. It is the key to history." He asked dramatically whether, if three white children were added to twenty-seven blacks in a classroom, this "would make the children any happier. Would they learn any more quickly? Would their lives be more serene?"

Equal education, Davis (who was a New Yorker) concluded, in South Carolina was a reality, "not promised, not prophesied, but present. Shall it be thrown away on some fancied question of racial prestige?" Let us not, he implored, return to "what we have called 'the tragic era' "—meaning Reconstruction.

The court was not impressed. Undoubtedly, the Justices's minds went back to Justice Harlan's dissent from *Plessy*. "In my opinion," Harlan had said, "the judgment this day rendered will, in time, prove to be quite as pernicious as the decision made by this tribunal in the *Dred Scott* case."

"The destinies of the two races, in this country," Harlan had warned, "are indissolubly linked together, and the interests of both require that the common government of all shall not permit the seeds of race hate to be planted under the sanction of law."

Now, fifty-eight years later, the Supreme Court took note of the following statement by the plaintiffs in Kansas:

Segregation of white and colored children in public schools has a detrimental effect upon the colored children. The impact is greater when it has the sanction of the law; for the policy of separating the races is usually interpreted as denoting the inferiority of the Negro group. A sense of inferiority affects the motivation of the child to learn.

In a unanimous ruling delivered by Chief Justice Earl Warren, the court responded: "Whatever may have been the extent of psychological knowledge at the time of *Plessy v. Ferguson,* this finding is amply supported by modern authority. Any language in *Plessy v. Ferguson* contrary to this finding is rejected."

And in a reversal of the historic Southern doctrine, the court held: "We conclude that in the field of public education the doctrine of 'separate but equal' has no place. Separate educational facilities are inherently unequal."

Although the opinion could not have been clearer in the matter of principle, it failed to spell out the requirements. It was only one year later in *Brown II* that the court required the defendants to "make a prompt and reasonable start toward full compliance" and set down the definition that such compliance must proceed "with all deliberate speed."

It was to be a controversial decision. While those familiar with the mood of the court understood that the phrase merely acknowledged local complications in undoing systems and customs of long standing, the segregationist forces interpreted it as a loophole—an invitation to inaction.

On May 18, 1954, *The New York Times* had hailed the ruling. "Probably no decision in the history of the Court has directly concerned so many individuals," the newspaper said. "At the time of the Brown case, segregation in the schools was required by law in 17 states and the District of Columbia. In this area there were over 8,000,000 white and 2,500,000 Negro school children enrolled in approximately 35,000 white schools and 15,000 Negro schools."

Desegregation often placed an enormous burden of courage on the Black children, but they and their elders bore the new challenge with remarkable strength. Dr. Robert Coles captured the mood and the meaning of the scene in his book *Children of Crisis.* A grandmother, talking about desegregation in New Orleans, said:

"Tessie was the first Negro child to step into that white school. There were three of them, 'the three little niggers,' they were called, but Tessie stepped into the building first. I saw it with my own eyes, and I won't forget it. . . . The way I see it Tessie and I can be cursed every day, and it will only mean we're nearer our freedom."

A teacher said: "We were as nervous as they were. . . . You could hear a pin drop. Those children just sat there and they looked as if at any moment a frightful disaster, a tornado or something, might come upon them. It was obvious that none of them wanted to sit near the Negro child, and yet they were so curious you could read it all over their faces. I'll have to admit it, I was, too. How were we to know what might happen?"

It was not only in the classroom that the Black children were tested. Dr. Coles went to a basketball game with a Black boy named John, the only Black in the audience. "After the game, as we started leaving," Dr. Coles recalled, "one heckler after another confronted us. . . . Their language was awful, the behavior threatening. Were it not for quick action by hastily summoned police, there might well have been a riot."

Afterward, Dr. Coles asked the boy how he could bear up under such treatment. He replied: "You see, when I grew up I had to learn to expect that kind of treatment; and I got it, so many times I hate to remember and count them. Well, now I'm getting it again, but it's sweet pain this time, because whatever they may say to me or however they try to hurt me, I know that just by sticking it out I'm going to help end the whole system of segregation."

Yet the cure was not to come fast or easily. Ten years after the landmark decision, the Southern Education Reporting Service disclosed how effective the South had been in slowing down the desegregation process. Only 2.4 percent of the Black school children in the Deep South were attending integrated schools.

A wave of opposition and reaction had been the response through much of the South. On March 12, 1956, a group of Southern Senators and Representatives issued "The Southern Manifesto," which called the *Brown* ruling an "unwarranted decision" and an example of the dire consequences "always produced when men substitute naked power for established law." The document, which was largely the work of North Carolina Senator Sam J. Ervin, Jr., maintained that matters in the South had been entirely satisfactory until *Brown,* a decision which "is destroying amicable relations between the white and Negro races that have been created through 90 years of patient effort by the good people of both races. It has planted hatred and suspicion where there has been heretofore friendship and understanding."

Apart from painting an idyllic picture of the South, the manifesto lashed out against "outside agitators" and meddlers and expressed hope that a majority of the American people would reaffirm faith in "the dual system of government which has enabled us to achieve our greatness" and would uphold states' rights against "judicial usurpation."

Despite angry rhetoric, however, the manifesto concluded with a pledge "to use all lawful means" to prevent the use of force in the ruling's implementation.

Not all the means employed proved to be lawful, however. On September 3, 1957, Governor Orval Faubus of Arkansas called out the National Guard to block access of nine Black children who had been admitted to Central High School in Little Rock. It was the first instance of open defiance.

Three weeks later, President Eisenhower dispatched federal troops to force the Governor to comply with the court order. Behind the paratroopers' protective bayonets, nine children entered school. In a televised address to the nation, President Eisenhower remained essentially neutral on the issue of school integration, but warned: "A foundation of our American way of life is our national respect for law."

Most of the subsequent skirmishes involved higher education. In 1962, James Meredith, a Black, applied for admission to the University of Mississippi and in 1963 two Blacks, Vivian Malone and James Hood, wanted to register for the University of Alabama summer session. In Mississippi, Governor Ross Barnett had himself appointed University Registrar in order to block Meredith's way. In the ensuing violence, President John F. Kennedy acted swiftly and with strength, using federal marshals and the federalized National Guard to enroll Meredith.

The following year, when Alabama's Governor Wallace dramatically placed himself "in the schoolhouse door," President Ken-

nedy again moved quickly to uphold the law and Black rights. In
both instances, he spoke directly to the American people on television. "I hope that every American, regardless of where he lives,
will stop and examine his conscience about this and other related
incidents. This nation was founded on the principle that all men
are created equal, and that the rights of every man are diminished
when the rights of one man are threatened."

Despite the initial show of resistance, the integration of the
Southern universities, in the wake of the extraordinary courage
shown by the first Black students who defied local hostility and
harassment, proceeded more easily than had been anticipated. It
was in the public schools that resistance proved harder to break.
In 1964, the Supreme Court was faced with another crucial test in
Griffin v. Prince Edward School Board. The entire county in Maryland had responded to *Brown* by closing the public schools. White
children had continued their schooling in newly founded "academies" which, though described as private, were actually paid for
with public funds. Between 1959 and 1963, no Black child was
able to attend any school whatsoever.

The court reacted angrily. Justice Hugo L. Black, speaking for
the majority of seven, ordered the public schools to be reopened
on a desegregated basis. What the case had shown, Black said, was
that there had been "entirely too much deliberation and not
enough speed."

"In 1954, when the *Brown* decision was handed down," said
Kenneth Clark,

> desegregation and integration were the priority of the civil
> rights movement and Negroes generally. Fifteen years later,
> many militants have proclaimed the death of the civil rights
> movement and have denied the value of integration itself,
> and specifically have questioned the significance of the *Brown*
> decision and the truth of social science findings on which it
> rested.

Black nationalism, Clark warned, would increasingly adopt an
imitation of white racism, "with its hallowing of race, its attempt
to make a virtue out of color, its racist mystique." This is precisely
what did happen, particularly in the Northern cities, where school

integration lagged and faltered, as white middle-class families left the inner cities for the suburbs, to be replaced by a steadily growing influx of poor, uneducated Black families. Thus, by the end of the 1960s, for example, whites actually constituted the minority of about forty-five percent in New York City's public school system. Increasingly, the demand for integration, which had been largely ignored or responded to with evasive or half-hearted tactics, gave way to Black separatist demands for community control, with power and jobs in the hands of Black administrators and teachers.

By the late 1960s, extremes of white resistance to integration and Black insistence on separatist control had seriously damaged the liberal, integrationist movement. Some liberals, fearful of being considered racists if they opposed the Black separatist drive, began to rationalize that such an assertion of Black independence and manhood was an essential therapeutic prerequisite for ultimate peaceful coexistence.

Yet, even in the face of that new wave of Black separatist sentiment, many Black leaders continued to hold fast to their integrationist views and hopes. Kenneth Clark resigned from a white college board when the trustees authorized the establishment of segregated Black dormitories.

The election of Richard Nixon to the Presidency in 1968 confirmed the new conservative tide. Administration spokesmen suggested that the cause of the Blacks could best be served by some "benign neglect." While those who urged such a policy insisted they merely wanted to soften the rhetoric, many who had tired of the civil rights movement took it as a welcome message of general retreat.

Sensing the new mood and capitalizing on growing fears of white parents in Northern cities that court-mandated busing would send their children to schools in Black neighborhoods, Nixon declared war on busing, one of the strategies of desegregation. Conservatives in Congress needed little encouragement. The House repeatedly rushed to approve stringent anti-busing legislation. While the more liberal Senate managed to take the sting out of most provisions, the overall effect was to regroup segregationist forces and to give heart to local opponents whenever the courts, exasperated by recalcitrant local school boards, ordered busing as the only remaining remedy.

The issue exploded into the national limelight in 1974 when massive and violent opposition by the predominantly Irish, lower-middle-class residents of South Boston tried to block the transfer of Black children into their local high schools. President Gerald Ford, expressing the prevailing mood, condemned the violence, but simultaneously expressed his disapproval of busing.

At a superficial glance, the "busing issue" seemed entirely irrational. Nearly 20 million children had been going to school by bus (not counting those who used regular public transportation) before it was proposed that busing be turned into a desegregation device. Catholic parochial schools took their demand to be allowed to participate in free school busing all the way—and victoriously—to the Supreme Court, thus raising questions about the motives of those who subsequently opposed busing as being detrimental to the children's health and safety. Indeed, Black spokesmen pointed out that the school bus had been used regularly by segregationists to transport Black children past the nearby schools to keep them lily-white.

Still, it would be misleading to characterize all opposition to busing as racist. When used as a haphazard means of simply scrambling the school enrollment in a random fashion, the policy gave some weight to charges that the courts were engaging in social engineering, without sufficient concern for the educational outcome. The case of South Boston, for example, suggested the futility of sending Black children away from their own schools, inadequate as they were, into equally poor schools populated by intensely clannish whites, made hostile to any outsiders by their own economic and social insecurity. (While "Southies" stood on the barricades, the overwhelming majority of Boston's schools accepted the busing order without disruption.)

Granted that the courts were driven to drastic busing orders by the frustrating passive resistance of anti-integration school districts, there was little doubt that the opposition's fears might readily have been allayed by a credible policy of improved educational opportunities for all children, Black and white, with an assurance that no child would be transported to an inferior school. Boston, where long years of neglect had led to school deterioration, was a case in point.

Not even the most rational explanations of the growing resistance to integration can obscure the fact that the pendulum of popular feeling toward civil rights had once again swung to the side of self-centered reaction.

In 1973, Vernon E. Jordan, Jr., director of the National Urban League, asked with bitterness: "Is this the end of the second Reconstruction?" "It's interesting," Jordan wrote "that in 1972 the only state legislature in this country that passed anti-busing legislation was *not* Alabama, *not* Mississippi, *not* Georgia, *not* Louisiana—it was New York. I think that says something about where we're going."

Despite these legitimate doubts in the face of serious setbacks suffered by the integration movement in the late 1960s and early 1970s and despite the unquestioned growth of hostility between Blacks and whites in the Northern cities, the drive toward educational equality for Black Americans had accomplished much and had created a situation that was no longer comparable to conditions prior to 1954.

At the summit of the educational pyramid, in 1970, Blacks constituted 12 percent of the freshman class at Yale; 10 percent at Harvard; 16 percent at Princeton; 22 percent at Barnard; and 17 percent at Radcliffe. The drive to get a higher education had become compelling among increasing numbers of young Blacks. "Even in the worst Northern ghettoes, where the progress of the past 10 years was least felt, young men and women are working in menial jobs during the day so they can attend college at night," Representative Andrew Young, a former aide to Dr. Martin Luther King, told *The New York Times* in August 1973. "Ten years ago these blacks couldn't get a college education."

Despite initial resistance and calculated misinterpretation of the court's "deliberate speed" requirement, by 1973 forty-four percent of the 3,676,000 Black pupils in the seventeen Southern and border states were enrolled in "majority white schools." (In the Northern and Western states, somewhat ironically, the equivalent proportion was only thirty percent.)

Perhaps the extent of the change was best indicated by what may seem a small incident sixteen years after *Brown*. In September 1970, Governor Linwood Holton, Jr., of Virginia took his thirteen-year-old daughter by the hand and personally escorted her to the doors of the hitherto all-Black John F. Kennedy High School on the first day of its court-ordered integration. As the Governor's daughter and other white students gingerly approached the school, Gregory Thomas, a Black student leader, welcomed them, smiling. "This is now your school, too," he said.

8

MASS-PRODUCING THE AMERICAN DREAM

*F*ROM ITS BEGINNING, AMERICAN
higher education has been at war with itself, fighting an internal
battle between tradition and revolt, between conservatism and
innovation. The conflict is also the mirror reflection of America's
ideological tug-of-war between the forces of expansive egalitarianism and of restrictive elitism.

Often, those opposing views of society were at least partially
reconciled by a pragmatic approach to higher education policies.
No matter how new and daring the experiments, they never
seemed to burn the bridges to the past. For example, the more
novel the attempts to reshape the American college may have appeared at times, the further they usually reached back into the
reservoir of the intellectual values of the Western heritage. The
most radical experiment in the wake of the explosive student
revolt at Berkeley in 1965 was an attempt to create a college within

the college where a small group of students and faculty members, renouncing all ties and obligations to the established disciplines, would shape their curriculum around the study of such concepts as liberty, justice, and morality. Like so many radical experiments, this one sought to return to the origins of learning and civilization.

It may occasionally seem as though the new and unconventional is too readily swallowed up by the old routines—the experiment at Berkeley, for example, lasted only a few years. Such a process may well be part of a rhythm of renewal and rejuvenation alternating with stagnation and reaction. It is a spiral form of progress which, though exasperating at times, is an antidote to change by revolution.

In the minds of nostalgically backward-looking alumni, there is a tendency to romanticize the "good old days" of their own collegiate experience and to conclude therefore that everything worth preserving, or bringing back, had its origins in some glorious golden age of the distant past. In fact, American colleges and universities, rather than being the descendents of such a legendary past, have always reflected—even before the Revolution—the diversity of American life. Their one constant is the lack of uniformity; but as a result, the campuses are subject to all the contradictions of the society at large—Towers of Babel rather than ivory towers. Far from being, or ever having been, isolated enclaves for sheltered scholars, American colleges and universities were the creation of so many diverse groups and interests that there was almost always something for everyone, a situation that is anathema to academic as well as social purists.

The growth of America's institutions of higher learning, public as well as private (a distinction that is not always easy to explain or to maintain), has been closely linked to the business of nation-building. The result was—until the 1970s—a constant stress on growth, despite a frequent lack of consensus concerning intellectual and academic goals. The recurring debate has never stopped: Should the campuses be elitist, serving primarily the ruling classes, or should they assure upward mobility in an antielitist republic? It is a debate which, perhaps luckily for the good of a diverse nation not committed to either extreme, has never been resolved. Alongside heated arguments, colleges and universities usually ended up by serving both, the elitists and the egalitarians, without fully satisfying either.

The founding of Harvard College in 1636 was an extraordinary achievement. Established by a legislature that was only eight years old, Harvard symbolized the self-confidence of an infant country. (An even more daring attempt to found a college during the 1620s in Virginia had failed.) What made the venture feasible was that there was among the early Puritan settlers a high proportion of university-educated men anxious to perpetuate their traditions, not only in the ministry, but in law and in general community leadership as well. Piety, civility, and learning were to be institutionalized in the new world. Under such circumstances, it was natural that Harvard was to be modeled, as much as conditions allowed, on contemporary Oxford and Cambridge.

It was not easy to transplant either the institutions or the ideas on which they were founded. Without a sense of mission, to serve God as well as its fellow men, it is doubtful that Harvard could have survived. It was, in the beginning, a fragile promise indeed, planted in the harsh soil of the New World. There was a chronic lack of funds; tutors were poorly paid, young, and transient; an entire class would consist of between fifteen and twenty students. The largest class to graduate from Harvard before the Revolution was that of 1771 whose total of sixty-three was not to be reached again for forty years. Up to 1700, Harvard graduated only 543, an average of less than eight a year, half of them clergymen.

The young and struggling Colonial college had to look to the community at large for support, and the new relationship had all the aspects of a marriage of convenience. Even into the nineteenth century, Harvard, which later was to become the symbolic spokesman for independent higher education, was supported with public subsidy from the Massachusetts General Court. In 1652–1653, the court donated land to the college, and in the following year levied a tax for its support. In times of special need, moreover, the state increased its subsidy. At one point, during the administration of Nathaniel Eaton, shortly after Harvard's founding, the college was so hard-pressed that the court launched an investigation and actively intervened by temporarily closing the college and dismissing Eaton. (Actually, Eaton, who was the institution's presiding officer when Harvard was, according to E. J. Kahn, Jr., "little more than a finishing school for presumptive ministers," was remembered as a mean man who stole money and beat a tutor almost to death.)

In the midst of a heated public debate in 1969, when dissident students threatened to take their demands to the courts, one faculty member, familiar with Harvard's past, rose to warn the undergraduates that the Massachusetts General Court might well take matters back to the days when it wielded the kind of power neither the students nor the faculty would like to see revived. As late as the decade from 1814 to 1823, Harvard was aided by the Commonwealth of Massachusetts to the amount of $100,000 in annual $10,000 installments. (Ever since World War II, it should be noted, the impact of government-sponsored research has led to a federal subsidy that frequently constitutes about half of the university's total budget.)

But the myth of the independent university, representative of free enterprise and therefore superior to the publicly funded institution, persisted and formed the basis of much of the private sector's rhetoric. In 1873, Harvard's president Eliot, while opposing the creation of a tax-supported university, ignored Harvard's own past, when he stated flatly: "Our ancestors well understood the principle that to make a people free and self-reliant, it is necessary to let them take care of themselves, even if they do not take quite as good care of themselves as some superior power might." Yet, if Harvard had always been forced to take care of itself without aid from "some superior power," it—as well as Yale and Columbia—might not have survived until Eliot's days.

Since the public treasury in Colonial times often lacked the cash to support fledgling institutions of higher learning, many states gave their blessing to the operation of lotteries to provide the funds. Others offered gifts of land. Necessity, moreover, was also the mother of greater tolerance for sectarian views and differences. This was a matter of considerable importance, since it had been the original tendency among the Puritans and other true believers to be uncompromising in the matter of orthodox teaching. Thus, for example, Harvard's president Henry Dunster was forced to resign over his opposition to infant baptism.

But changing conditions of American life made it increasingly difficult to enforce such orthodoxy. New religious movements, inspired by the Great Awakening in the middle of the eighteenth century, led to the founding of Princeton, in New Jersey, in 1746. A new note of toleration became evident when its charter stated that the college would not be allowed to discriminate against students on the basis of their religion. Such liberalism might not have been so readily accepted had it not also been a considerable asset in the appeal for badly needed financial support from a greater variety of donors. When the College of William and Mary was chartered, not without opposition, in 1693, the state's Attorney General, informed that the new institution would be useful in the saving of souls, grumbled: "Souls! Damn your souls! Raise tobacco!"

Colonial colleges were founded and supported for many different reasons: to train a literate ministry and an educated leadership; to develop a sense of unity among Anglo-Americans separated from the homeland by an ocean; to combat the kind of restlessness that might undermine order and obedience; to install loyalty and inspire responsible citizenship; to teach men the knowledge useful to a changing world. Thus, long before the Revolution, a diversity of mission and aims had been built into the concept of American higher education.

Many of the conditions of the old English universities simply could not be reproduced in a frontier setting. American colleges were founded by their communities, not by groups of scholars intent on isolating themselves from the communities around them. Making a virtue of necessity, the new Americans thus created the tradition of lay control in the governance of their colleges and universities.

This is not to suggest that the composition of these new boards was "democratic" or egalitarian. These bodies were firmly in the hands of what was termed "the better sort" of the contemporary establishment—the landowners, merchants and, of course, the clergy. In places such as Harvard, William and Mary, Yale, and King's College (later to become Columbia) the dominant ecclesiastical groups kept their control as inviolate as circumstances would allow. But other colleges, founded by the dissenting groups, needed to promote themselves as "catholic, comprehensive and liberal." While still rigid by modern standards, they were indeed flexible and liberal in the terms of their day and in comparison to their European prototypes. In their search for support, in the harsh and spartan climate of the New World, they had to adopt a relaxed attitude toward all orthodoxy and accept a mixed clientele.

Thus, the pattern of higher education's response to the needs and the views of the surrounding communities was established, not as a result of any conscious policy but as a fact of life and in response to the problems of survival in the wilderness. In the eyes of purist critics, the goals of such responsive institutions often appeared confused and contradictory. The fact was, and remained, simply that the colleges—and later the state universities—could not ignore the culture that nurtured them.

From the outset, higher education has had to struggle against strong conservative opposition to the extension of its benefits to those who had not, by reason of class or wealth, been considered entitled to them. In a sweepingly antieducational statement, Sir William Berkeley, who was Governor of Virginia from 1660 to 1677, said: "Thank God there are not free schools nor printing, and I hope we shall not have these in a hundred years; for learning has brought disobedience and heresy . . . into the world, and printing has divulged them . . . God keep us from both."

When the first colleges of the Colonies were founded there was little about them, in fact or in philosophy, to suggest that they might eventually become a vital part of the American social scene. If there was any concern about the colleges' future, it tended to be that their value might be deflated if their benefits were extended too freely. Since even what today is known as "secondary" education was then still a rare privilege, such worries were clearly premature. Altogether, in 1776, there were an estimated 3000 living graduates of American colleges.

In 1770, a South Carolina newspaper editor worried that, if the state allowed a college to be established, "learning would become cheap and too common, and every man would be for giving his son an education."

He need not have worried. It would be a long time before every man might think of giving his son, let alone his daughter, an education. Colonial colleges had been strongly influenced by aristocratic traditions. They still served primarily the elite. The frontier moreover was both a promise and a threat as a source of material wealth, and the traditional curriculum seemed to have little relevance to the new search for success. In the middle of the seventeenth century, President Charles Chauncey of Harvard was able to comment sadly about all those who had "waxed fat" and subsequently scoffed at supporting education, a complaint college presidents were to repeat with every subsequent generation.

The Revolution proved something of a watershed for higher education. Many of the university administrations, having been the defenders of the status quo, found themselves under attack. At King's College, a Tory president had to leap over the back fence in "scanty" attire to seek refuge on an English ship bound for asylum in the mother country. An angry college mob was held back by Alexander Hamilton, class of 1774. Yale's President Ezra Stiles commented around 1780: "The Diadem of a President is a crown of thorns."

But the physical damage done to the colleges by the war proved symbolic rather than real. In the self-confident air that followed the Revolution, the climate was favorable for growth. The nine colleges, established in the Colonies, were ready for change.

Given the aristocratic style of the Colonial colleges—even though some sons of farmers who aspired to the professions had begun to attend them—it was to be expected that the nature of those changes would be a subject for continuing debate. There was growing consensus, though vague and ill-defined, that education was of great importance to the new nation. Benjamin Rush wrote: "The business of education has acquired a new complexion by the independence of our country. . . . It becomes us, therefore, to examine our former habits upon this subject, and in laying the foundations for 'nurseries of wise and good men,' to adapt our modes of teaching to the peculiar form of our government."

But when it came to specifics—Rush wanted the inclusion of science and such modern languages as French and German in the curriculum—there was less agreement. Former habits die hard. The traditional curriculum of Latin and the classics was firmly ensconced, despite pressure for change. At best, the old and the new would sometimes exist side by side, often not very comfortably, But, as they did, American higher education's capacity for diversity—and confusion—was established.

The creation of a national university was briefly advocated, but soon abandoned. What was lacking was any general agreement about such an institution's aims, curriculum, or location. And, though such sentiments were not yet clearly articulated, the American preference for institutions independent of any central, national control and sponsorship appeared already strong.

As early as 1800, Thomas Jefferson had been thinking about a University of Virginia that would provide "for the state an University on a plan so broad and liberal and *modern* as to be worth patronizing with the public support, and be a temptation to the youth of other states to come, and drink of the cup of knowledge and fraternize with us." Along with the Declaration of Independence and the Virginia statute of religious freedom, the university was one of the three accomplishments for which Jefferson wanted most to be remembered.

To some extent, the University of Virginia represented Jefferson's reaction to the personal defeats sustained in his efforts to reform education. His comprehensive school plan for the state never gained acceptance. His modernizing proposals for William and Mary had been rejected. Only in a new institution, therefore, could his ideas be tested.

The University of Virginia was as much the fruit of Jefferson's political astuteness as of his idealism. In 1818, the Rockfish Gap Commission on the search for a university site, set forth what would be the benefits of such an institution. While "some good men" believed that "education, like private and individual concerns should be left to private and individual effort," the report said, "this would leave us then without those callings which depended on education, or send us to other countries. . . ."

But, the document went on, legislators are

> sensible that the advantages of well directed education, moral, political, and economical, are truly above all estimate. . . . Education, in like manner engrafts a new man on the native stock, and improves what in his nature was vicious and perverse, into qualities of virtue and social worth; and it cannot be but that each generation, succeeding to the knowledge acquired by all those who preceded it, adding it to their own acquisitions and discoveries . . . must advance the knowledge of mankind.

Aware of the political difficulties the founding of a university would encounter, Jefferson wrote reassuringly to James Madison that he wanted "political orthodoxy" to be maintained and wished that the faculty would teach the prevailing doctrines of the Republicans. But the University of Virginia was, from the beginning, a new kind of institution. It was a campus with a wide range of academic offerings, with an elective system of subjects and without fixed terms of attendance for the students. It was a noble experiment, generations ahead of its time—so far ahead that many of its original ways (which were again and again to be rediscovered by subsequent reformers) were soon modified and brought in line with more traditional higher education customs of the day.

In the battle for his university, Jefferson could not always suppress his understandably human feelings of bitterness and of fierce, and even parochial, competition with the Northern colleges. "Even with the whole funds," he wrote at one point, "we shall be reduced to six professors, while Harvard will still prime it over us with her 20 professors."

The immediate post-Revolutionary period was a time of great expansion. "Colleges were founded," wrote historian Frederick Rudolph, "in the same spirit as was canal-building, cotton-ginning, farming, and gold-mining. . . . All were touched by the American faith in tomorrow, in the unquestionable capacity of Americans to achieve a better world. . . ."

Not all American education spokesmen shared such faith. Philip Lindsley, president of the University of Nashville, said in 1829: "Colleges rise like mushrooms in our luxurious soil. They are duly lauded and puffed for a day; and then they sink to be heard no more."

State and local pride as well as the rivalry of the various denominations provided dynamism for the great expansion. But established institutions were clearly concerned about the potential effect of the new competitors. As early as 1762, Harvard had opposed the creation of a new college in the county of Hampshire, holding that "particularly as our college, yet in its infant state, is hitherto but meanly endowed and very poor . . . founding another college would be the most probable . . . way to prevent its being hereafter endowed in such a manner as all who desire its prosperity doubtless wish to see it."

Though not always so bluntly and commercially put, this was to be the refrain repeated at each step by the established institutions as they saw themselves threatened by higher education's expansion. During the midnineteenth century, the oldtime private colleges were equally adamant in opposing the founding of Cornell. In 1948, the private sector in New York lobbied desperately to prevent the creation of a state university system or, failing that, to limit its growth, and the initial efforts to protect the older monopoly were so successful that the original charter of the new public institution allowed it only to "supplement" the existing private ones. In the subsequent drive toward higher education's dramatic post–World War II expansion, these restrictions were ignored.

During the Republic's early days, however, the institutional insecurity so eloquently set forth by Harvard may perhaps have been justified. Nearly all the struggling new colleges were on the frontier. Their development followed no discernible pattern or plan. Much of the rhetoric about their future was overly ambitious, and many of the starts indeed proved false. Worst of all, there was a shortage of students.

The inevitable result was that lofty academic goals were quickly modified to meet the demands of the marketplace and match the capacities of the clientele. President Francis Wayland of Brown University complained in 1850 that the only significance of the bachelor's degree was "a residence of four years, and the payment of the college bills. . . . We have produced an article for which the demand is diminishing. We sell it at less than cost, and the deficiency is made up by charity. We give it away, and still the demand diminishes."

A century later, during the depressed years of the late 1930s, when even the most prestigious colleges had to hustle to get enough students, Eugene S. Wilson, dean of admissions at Amherst College, said of the selection of freshmen: "If the body is warm and the check is good, you're in."

In the early part of the nineteenth century, the future of many small colleges, and their relationship to the political power of the state, remained cloudy. An important legal battle was to do much to clarify the issues and strengthen the position of independent higher education in America.

The founder of Dartmouth College, a missionary named Eleazar Wheelock, had left the presidency of his institution to his son John. A bitter church quarrel caused the younger Wheelock to attack the college trustees in a pamphlet, in the hope that the legislature might step in to bolster his position. In 1816, the dispute became the central issue of the New Hampshire gubernatorial campaign, which led to the defeat of the state's Federalists by the Jeffersonian Republicans. The newly elected Governor, William Plumer, proposed a state takeover of Dartmouth's management.

This was not an unusual practice at the time. The period of the Revolutionary War had seen attempts to turn the University of Pennsylvania and Columbia into public institutions, and to place Harvard and Yale under a degree of state management in return for financial aid. In 1792, during the administration of Ezra Stiles, a change had been made in the Yale College charter, making several state officials members of the Yale Corporation, the governing board, as a trade-in for financial subsidy. (To this day, the Governor of Connecticut remains an ex officio member of the board.)

In New Hampshire, the legislature responded to the Governor's proposal by creating Dartmouth University and enlarging the existing governing board so as to outnumber the original trustees. For some time, both the college and the university coexisted in extreme discomfort. But as it gathered confidence, the college faction took its case to the courts.

On March 10, 1818, the Dartmouth College Case reached the Supreme Court. In a historic speech, Daniel Webster said:

> . . . It is the case of every college in the land. It is more . . . [it is] the case of every man who has property of which he may be stripped—for the question is simply this: Shall our state legislature be allowed to take that which is not their own, to turn it from its original use, and apply it to such ends or purposes as they, in their discretion shall see fit? Sir, you may destroy this little institution . . . but if you do . . . you must extinguish, one after another, all those great lights of science, which, for more than a century, have thrown their radience over the land! It is, Sir, as I have said, a small college, and yet there are those that love it.

On February 2, 1819, Chief Justice John Marshall ruled that the original Dartmouth College charter, granted by George III in

1769, was a contract which remained protected by the Constitution against any interference or encroachment by the state. Marshall's decision came to be regarded as a landmark because it safeguarded private institutions—not only colleges, but corporations as well—from legislative interference or takeover by the state.

For American higher education, it was the beginning of a sharper distinction between the private and the public sector—a distinction that was not again to the eroded until the combination of federal research subsidies of the 1940s and the fiscal crisis of the 1970s led to extensive reliance by the private sector on public subsidy. For the moment, the Dartmouth ruling had clearly established that such a college was a private institution, not subject to controls by the state, but rather to the governance of a Board of Trustees and "those that love it," who would prove their love by contributing to the college's operations and maintenance.

The Dartmouth College Case did much to place private American colleges out of the range of political passion and control; it also allowed some weak institutions greater freedom to go bankrupt. In the spirit of the day, it also set the stage for the founding of all manner of institutions, some excellent and others shoddy, all of them part and parcel of the competitive and expansive mood of the Jacksonian era.

In the wake of the Dartmouth College ruling, college promoters arrived in newly developed areas alongside the land speculators and the revivalists. Every religious sect seemed intent on the founding of at least one college of its own in each state or territory. The combination of a rising new nationalism and a religious missionary zeal made the drive almost irresistible.

The continent's size and the difficulty of travel naturally encouraged the creation of easily accessible campuses, as did fierce new state and national loyalties. A delegate to California's Constitutional Convention of 1849 said: "Why should we send our sons to Europe to finish their education? If we have the means here, we can procure the necessary talent; we can bring the president of the Oxford University here by offering a sufficient salary."

Earlier, in 1819, one argument advanced for the establishment of the University of Virginia had been that the absence of such an institution would mean the loss of tuition dollars to other states. A proponent of a state university in Minnesota argued later in the century that "not a single youth of either sex should be permitted to leave the territory to acquire an education" for want of a local college. In a similar spirit of competition, various religious denominations vied with each other. The Catholic fervor to create schools spurred the Protestants to counter what they considered "the Jesuit menace."

Zealous reformers regarded colleges as an Eastern tool to civilize the West. Many founders of the new campuses were transplanted New Englanders who wished to create in the West the images of the towns and the institutions they considered the fountainhead of culture and sound politics. It was in such a spirit that Oberlin, Grinnell, and Carleton, and others like them, began to grow in the Midwest.

Improbable alliances were often initially at work in making the new campuses possible. Oberlin, for example, was the outgrowth of crusading Whig politics and the religious zeal of evangelist Charles G. Finney and his followers. Yet it was soon to grow into one of the nation's finest colleges and into the conscience of its community. Among the first colleges to admit women and Blacks, it assumed more than local leadership in the cause of academic liberalism.

At the time of their founding, however, these colleges combined, as Daniel Boorstin described it, the "booster" and the missionary approach to bring to each Western settlement "all the metropolitan hallmarks"—a newspaper, a hotel, and a college.

The Society for the Promotion of Theological and Collegiate Education in the West, formed in 1843, was a symbol of this expansionist era. Extraordinary numbers of colleges sprang up. And even though many failed and many others operated without quality controls, the impact of their presence and the faith in their power did much to transform public thinking and aspirations. They were as much part of the scene as the churches.

What did these colleges teach? The nation was in an expansive, confident, egalitarian mood. The demand was for more democracy and the extension of the suffrage. New state constitutions were being drafted. Opportunities and nationalism grew in tandem, and the beginnings of Manifest Destiny and of Henry Clay's "American system" gave the American people a sense of adventure and optimism. It was hardly surprising that at a time of such ferment and expectations colleges would come under great pressure to change—to offer something for everyone.

Many did. Others were honestly questioning whether mechanics and farmers needed education at all, and, if so, how much and of what kind? Of what use was the knowledge of Latin and Greek to a settler in the wilderness? How important was it for a collegiate education to be immediately useful? These questions mirrored the social issues of the era, but they also opened up the kind of questioning and debate that was to continue well into the second half of the twentieth century.

It was a time of trial and skirmishes. The introduction of modern languages and the sciences into the college curriculum offended many purists. The short-lived experiment with elective courses at Virginia led others to push for similar options, and radical critics at Harvard began to point to the German universities' elective system. During the 1820s, Harvard experienced internal pressure and alienation, and in 1823 severe student riots erupted.

Julian Sturtevant, who later was to become president of Illinois College, described his own classroom experience at Yale during the 1820s. The "power" of education, he recalled,

> lay in its fixed and rigidly proscribed curriculum, and in its thorough drill. . . . The tutors were . . . excellent drill masters. They could hardly be said to teach at all, their duties being to subject every pupil three times a day to so searching a scrutiny before the whole division as to make it apparent to himself and all his fellows either that he did or did not understand his lessons. . . . It was considered no part of his [the tutor's] duty to assist his pupils in preparing for recitation. In that task the pupil was expected to be entirely self-reliant. . . .

Apparently Yale had felt the stirrings of revolt, and to scotch it, issued the Yale Report of 1828 which tried to silence the upstart critics by placing its influential seal of approval on the college curriculum precisely as it was. The two "great" qualities to be acquired, according to the report, were the "discipline and the furniture of the mind; expanding its powers, and storing it with knowledge." At Yale, the mind's furniture was to be antique, or what the college considered classical.

Speaking for higher education's traditionalists, the Yale report reaffirmed that classical education was ideally suited to aid newly created men of wealth and influence and to "enable them to adorn society by their learning, to move in the more intelligent circles with dignity, and to make such an application of their wealth, as will be most honorable to themselves and most beneficial to their country." It was Yale's conviction that college training would remain essentially elitist—for the powerful few, while "the young merchant must be trained in the counting room, the mechanic in the workshop, the farmer in the field."

In retrospect, there was irony in such an affirmation of conservatism in the very year of Andrew Jackson's election, with its intimations of a rapidly changing nation. And yet, even in this self-satisfied, stodgy document there were signs that conservatism, too, had a contribution to make. While the report still viewed foreign languages as an "accomplishment" rather than a necessary acquisition and merely tolerated science as a newfangled oddity, it did stand up against the inclusion of trivia which state legislatures or sectarian groups were trying arbitrarily to impose on the curriculum. Against pressure from such reformers as George Ticknor at Harvard, the report warned: "We hope at least that this college may be spared the mortification of a ludicrous attempt to imitate [the German universities] while it is unprovided with the resources necessary to execute the purpose."

In all probability, such caution urged the right course for the wrong reasons. The fact is that the advocacy of the German way by a small but articulate coterie at Harvard was out of touch with the needs of the country. An increasingly nationalistic generation could hardly be expected to share the academic reformers' rather uncritical admiration for institutions abroad which the large majority of academicians had never come to know at first hand. In the short run, this may have been at least a partial boon for American higher education; for the young reformers had been blind to Germany's political realities which culminated in the defeat of the liberal elements—including those in the universities—in 1848. There had been no inkling of such a course in Ticknor's enthusiastic eyewitness reports. He had written from the German scene in 1815–1816:

> The first result of this enthusiasm and learning, which imme-
> diately broke through all the barriers that opposed it, is an
> universal toleration in all matters of opinion. No matter what
> a man thinks, he may teach it and print it, not only without
> molestation from the government but also without molesta-
> tion from publick opinion.

Little more than thirty years later, the toleration had come to an
end. Many of the dissenters sought refuge in America.

In quite another way, Yale's emphasis on a traditional curriculum was welcomed by those denominational forces which were
still providing much of the energy for collegiate expansion. Many
potential benefactors had become distressed over suggestions that
higher education ought to prepare men for the needs of this world
rather than for the happiness in the next. Major religious orders
were pleased indeed to find at so prestigious a center as Yale the
philosophical underpinning for the status quo. And, incidentally,
these same shrewdly frugal elements had little doubt that the old
course of study was by far the cheapest, even if it were not necessarily the best.

Historians have differed over the motives and the importance
of the founding of over seven hundred local colleges during a
short and relatively primitive period, while the older Eastern colleges continued to thrive. True, many of the new institutions did
not survive the Civil War; but 182 did, and most of them are still
educating students today. Some of the Eastern, university-oriented
historians, such as Richard Hofstadter, scoffed at the antebellum
colleges as backward and unresponsive to the real and long-term
needs of the nation's grandiose future. But there is much to recommend the more indulgent view expressed by another historian,
James Axtell, that an infant but growing America had room and
need for both the old Eastern seats of learning and the new colleges on the frontier, "distinguished more by function and founding ideal than geography."

Writing at the beginning of the twentieth century, from the
vantage point of the English observer, Lord Bryce commented on
the "services" which small colleges in rural districts of the country have performed, often unappreciated by "his American
friends." These institutions, he said,

. . . give the chance of rising in some intellectual walk of life to many a strong and earnest nature who might otherwise have remained an artisan or storekeeper. . . . They light up in many a country town what is at first only a farthing rushlight, but which, when the town swells to a city . . . becomes a lamp of growing flame, which may finally throw its rays over the whole State in which it stands.

These institutions, despite their flaws, served a segment of American youth that had moved into the vanguard of the nation's future course. It is doubtful that the old-line colleges could have reached all, or even most, of them. Without these pioneering colleges, the expansionist tradition of American higher education might never have been established.

Debate over the college curriculum continued. Union College, ignoring the Yale Report of 1828, offered modern languages, science, and mathematics—and managed to attract a record number of students. By 1839, its enrollment was second only to Yale's.

In fact, Yale itself proved a magnet for science-oriented young men, despite its officially negative attitude toward science. Professor Benjamin Silliman, who had been appointed to teach chemistry and natural history, even though he had not actually studied those subjects, undertook to educate himself and to acquire for the college a highly regarded minerals collection. This enabled him to offer the first laboratory-type course in mineralogy and geology to be offered in an American college. But Yale thought so little of the collection that Professor Silliman carried it about in a shoebox and had to enter his laboratory by climbing down a flight of backstairs.

Nevertheless the study of science was slowly moving forward both at Yale and at Harvard, despite official inertia and condescension. (It should be noted that Oxford University remained cool toward science well into the twentieth century and largely abdicated the field to Cambridge and some of the newer universities. Classical hostility to modern science education died slowly at established universities in England as well as in the United States.) Professorships in the sciences were created and the Sheffield and Lawrence schools added at Yale and Harvard respectively. Yet at both Harvard and Yale admissions standards to these science enclaves continued to be lower than for the other disciplines. At Yale, Sheffield students were not even allowed to sit with the regular classical scholars in chapel. Looking back on his days at Harvard, Henry David Thoreau wrote: "To my astonishment I was informed on leaving college that I had studied navigation! Why, if I had taken one turn down the Harbour I should have known more about it."

In terms similar to those applied later to the schools by John Dewey, Thoreau criticized the college's lack of realism. Students, he said, "should not *play* life, or *study* it merely, while the community supports them at this expensive game, but earnestly *live* it from beginning to end. How could youths better learn to live than by at once trying the experiment of living? Methinks this would exercise their minds as much as mathematics."

It was mainly at the United States Military Academy, established in 1802, that scientific study was encouraged. In 1850, Henry Philip Tappan, the reform-minded president of the University of Michigan, was able to say: "The single academy at West Point has done more toward the construction of railroads than all our . . . colleges united."

Gradually, critics of the old ways became more outspoken. In 1842, Brown's president Wayland published *Thoughts on the Present Collegiate System of the United States,* calling for a complete reexamination of that system. Unfortunately, even though Wayland's instincts were sound, his high moral principles seemed often to becloud his understanding of how institutions worked. For example, he subscribed to Adam Smith's view that endowed faculty salaries and student scholarships were morally wrong and harmful to academic stamina as well as to educational quality. (Smith's academic economics had also appealed to Thomas Jefferson and George Ticknor.)

In 1850, Wayland asked for a curriculum report, to be submitted to the Brown Corporation, which would "benefit all classes" but would pay special attention to the rising middle class. The old course of studies, Wayland felt, simply was no longer suitable for self-reliant citizens bent on developing a strong and prosperous America.

Regrettably, Wayland's concept of the future was less carefully formulated in his mind than his shrewd sense of dissatisfaction with the status quo. In 1856, he was replaced by Barnas Sears, who quickly let it be known that he was no reformer.

If Brown, as one of New England's bastions, was not ready to move toward a more worldly curriculum, neither was the University of Michigan prepared to subscribe to the German-inspired system advocated by Tappan. By the 1850s, the Midwestern university was second in size only to the University of Virginia. It had miraculously overcome even its original, unpronounceable name, Catholepistemiad, with which its founders had saddled it in 1817.

Tappan had noble visions of Michigan's future as a cultural center along with highly practical goals of making the university responsible also for the development of the lower levels of education, reminiscent of Jefferson's early plans. But the newly settled state was not an ideal testing ground for the development of a sophisticated European-style university.

Tappan, whom his critics considered arrogant and unbending, advocated the right course in the wrong context of his time. The controversies of the day—particularly slavery—and the nativist Know-Nothing hysteria doomed his European-model reforms, at least for the moment. He was forced out of office, but his successor was able to say of him: "Tappan was the largest figure of a man that ever appeared on the Michigan campus, and he was stung to death by gnats."

Despite early setbacks, the growth, the questioning, and the search for reforms continued. In 1850, a committee established by the Massachusetts General Court asked Harvard to proceed with changes in its curriculum in order to prepare "better farmers, mechanics, or merchants." In New York, the Board of Education ordered city authorities to create a college that would not exclusively be committed to serving the needs of the traditional professions. A Georgia newspaper warned in 1857: "We are now living in a different age, an age of practical utility, one in which the State University does not, and cannot supply the demands of the state. The times require practical men, civil engineers, to take charge of public roads, railroads, mines, scientific agriculture. . . ." The Superintendent of Public Instruction in California asked in the 1850s: "For what useful occupation are the graduates of most of our colleges fit?"

In the late 1850s Edward Everett, then president of Harvard, appealed to the state legislature for funds. He was aware of the growing importance of science, and it was during his term that the Lawrence Scientific School was opened. Everett was eloquent. It was the "prayer" of the colleges that legislatures would appropriate to them some fixed proportion of the revenue from public lands.

Everett stressed, not the university's intellectual mission or its exalted prestige, but its potential service to business, the economy, and the future prosperity of the state. Pointing to American scientific progress, from Franklin to Morse, Everett said that, while occasionally an uneducated genius or chance may have contributed to such progress, "the grand result is the product of cultivated mind, strained to the tension of its powers. . . ." With all the conviction of what was to become a new breed of educational philosophers who believed in the close connection between an expansionist, egalitarian society and easier access to higher education, he concluded: "It is not for the rich that public aid is wanted. They will obtain good education, if they desire it, in one place if they cannot in another; although it is a serious evil"—an aside to the chauvinism of the day—"to have to seek it abroad. As far as individuals are concerned, it is the poor student that needs cheapened education. If he cannot get that near home, he cannot get it at all." The appeal fell on deaf ears. Massachusetts, having discontinued aid to private colleges in 1823, was not prepared to offer it now.

Private institutions, for their part, perhaps in occasional desperation, did not always confine their lobbying to mere high-minded appeals. At a time when Horace Mann was advocating the rapid expansion of normal schools for the training of teachers in Massachusetts, the private colleges, under the leadership of friends of Harvard, Amherst, and Williams, used their political muscle to block the use of public funds for that purpose. They saw the proposed teacher-training institutions largely as competitors for state subsidies they sought for themselves. It was one of the early signs of the division between the private and public institutions that was to mar the peace and unity of the American academic scene through much of the next century, often to the detriment of both sectors.

Meanwhile, state authorities often resented the colleges for wanting subsidy but resisting regulation. Typically for such feelings, New Hampshire's Governor Plumer had said earlier in connection with the Dartmouth College case, that whenever these institutions want aid from the legislatures, they are "public"; but when the legislature enacts laws for their "better regulation," they are private corporations, exempt from interference or control. Colleges, Plumer believed moreover, were too denominational—seminaries for "priests"—and therefore too rigid in their course of studies to educate a young man for a secular career. Nevertheless, Plumer—who was a self-educated man—appeared sufficiently impressed with Harvard's prestige to send his son there.

The only safe generalization about American higher education before the Civil War is that it reflected all the existing religious denominations and the sociopolitical currents of the time. Colleges were created without any discernible pattern. The question of who was to be educated and what was to be learned echoed the larger questions of who was to hold power and govern, and to what social purpose.

Historians will continue to debate the significance of the defeat of John Quincy Adams (who, incidentally, conducted anything but an aristocratically clean campaign) at the hands of Andrew Jackson in 1828. But old-line collegiate interests were dismayed, particularly when, despite the misgivings of many of Boston's Brahmins, Harvard awarded Jackson an honorary degree after his second inauguration. The university's president, Josiah Quincy, privately let Adams know that he considered the President "utterly unworthy of literary honors" but that the college, having awarded a degree to James Monroe, could not pass over Jackson lest it be accused of favoritism toward one party.

Adams refused to attend the ceremony. "I would not be present," he growled, "to see my darling Harvard disgrace herself by conferring a Doctor's degree upon a barbarian and savage who can scarcely spell his own name."

During the actual convocation, Jackson apparently charmed his audience—but without being able to forestall the subsequent growth of a legend among Boston's and Cambridge's conservative upper crust that the President had responded to the Latin charge by rising and responding with a flood of wild Latin gibberish. The purity of academic life clearly was not above the partisan level of contemporary politics.

Internally too, colleges were subject to all the pressures and prejudices of their communities' political, social, and religious divisions. The idea of academic freedom for professors or students was still many years in the future, and the colleges were no more tolerant of dissent than the environment in which they operated. Local towns, having established a college, often at considerable material sacrifice, were not likely to relax their paternalistic control over it, and this was reflected in the hiring and firing of faculty as well as in the selection of students. The compensating factor was that there were enough colleges to insure safety in numbers—a dissenter from one campus could find a congenial haven in another.

Nevertheless, there were those who considered the narrowness of local campus bias a threat to the future of higher education. Thomas Jefferson wrote to his friend Thomas Cooper in 1822 about the dismal effects of religious intolerance. The University of Virginia, in a dramatic departure from the norm, had no professor of divinity. Not surprisingly, "a handle has been made of this," wrote Jefferson, "to disseminate the idea that this is an institution, not merely of no religion, but against all religion." To remedy this situation, he went on,

> we suggest the expediency of encouraging the different religious sects to establish, each for himself, a professorship of their own tenets, on the confines of the university, so near as their students may attend their lectures there, and have the free use of our library, and every other accommodation we can give them: preserving, however, their independence of us and of each other. . . .

Sectional strife and the slavery controversy which had begun to tear at the nation's fabric also engulfed the colleges. Oberlin, for example, had become firmly committed to the abolitionist cause. Illinois College opposed slavery in the setting of a hostile, conservative community. In the South, Benjamin S. Hedrick was discharged by the trustees of the University of North Carolina for publicly announcing his support of Republican John C. Frémont for President in 1856.

At Michigan, despite the Regents' stand against sectarian prejudice, their tolerance did not extend to politics. A professor was fired for appealing to the doctrine of "the higher law"—the abolitionists' way of justifying their antislavery stand, which, at that time, conflicted with the law of the land.

At the other end of the spectrum, Nathan Lord resigned from the presidency of Dartmouth in 1863, after he found that his defense of slavery had made his position untenable. While the trustees had refused to remove Lord, they managed to express their disapproval of his position in such strong terms that he felt it necessary to leave voluntarily.

Regional parochialism was mixed with what today would be considered outrageous prejudices, as when Ralph Waldo Emerson, the Sage of Concord and the quintessential New Englander, managed to lash out simultaneously against white Southerners and American Indians. "The young Southerner," wrote Emerson,

> comes here a spoiled child, with graceful manners, excellent self-command, very good to be spoiled more, but good for nothing else,—a mere parader. He has conversed so much with rifles, horses and dogs that he has become himself a rifle, a horse and a dog, and in civil, educated company, where anything human is going forward, he is dumb and unhappy like an Indian in a church.

Francis L. Hawks, a protestant clergyman and graduate of the University of North Carolina in 1815, later became the first president of the University of Louisiana. During his years in the North, he found that Emerson's attitudes were not confined to the Boston area. ". . . The truth," he wrote, "is they [the Northerners] looked upon us as *inferior*, morally, physically, intellectually. They thought our children could not learn to read but for Yankee teachers."

Simplistic interpretations of American educational history tend to point to the Civil War as the watershed—the dawning of a new era in which the university replaced the oldtime college. Such a picture is misleading. "Oldtime" colleges did not disappear and were not even bypassed. What really happened was the beginning of the large, multipurpose university, founded to respond to the diversified needs of an industrial society, existing alongside the small liberal arts college.

How firmly entrenched the small residential college had become in the American culture was shown when Yale and Harvard, after they had been transformed into universities, found it necessary to invent the "house system"—small colleges within the university which would assure the parents that the campus role as a substitute parent had not been relinquished.

If nothing else had protected the continued prestige and popularity of the small college, the nostalgia of its famous alumni alone would have guaranteed its survival. In 1871, a relatively little known Republican politician addressed an alumni dinner at Williams College, his alma mater. "The ideal college," he said, "is Mark Hopkins on one end of a log and a student on the other." The speaker was James A. Garfield, later to become President of the United States, but nothing he said in the White House was to be as long remembered as his praise of the liberal arts college's romanticized intimacy.

Not all graduates of the small, old-line colleges were as rhapsodic about their education. Andrew White, president of Cornell and one of the leading university builders after the Civil War, described his years at Yale, with the exception of praise for a few outstanding professors, as "everything of gerund-grinding and nothing of literature."

With the end of the Civil War, it had become evident that popular government was going to endure, despite early doubts by elitist skeptics in the United States and abroad. Lincoln's faith had been justified. The nation would survive as a union. Its resources seemed unlimited, as did its space, and the railroads allowed both to be conquered. Renewed faith in progress and growth inevitably formed the basis for a new and unprecedented expansion of the American universities.

It might be said—facetiously but not without foundation—that the Civil War's most important impact on higher education was that it so distracted popular attention as to make possible the passage of the Morrill Act of 1862. For almost half a century, there had been a succession of schemes and plans for the expansion of higher education, including the suggestion of a national university and a host of ideas for federal support of agricultural and mechanical training.

Reformers, including Horace Greeley, had long been advocating the use of federal land to allow states to finance new colleges to respond to changing economic needs. But it was Representative Justin Smith Morrill who, for the first time in 1857, introduced a bill in Congress that, amid a variety of reform proposals for technical education, aimed to "promote the liberal and practical education of the industrial classes in several pursuits and professions of life."

During the debates, educational goals were rarely, if ever, mentioned. When the bill was nevertheless approved, President Buchanan vetoed it. Morrill tried again after the South had seceded and Lincoln had become President. The new version, submitted in conjunction with the Homestead Act, was passed in 1862, in the midst of the Civil War. Although enacted as a sideshow during a national crisis, the new law was to have vast effects on the future of higher education and the country. When the *New York Tribune* summarized important legislation passed by Congress that year, the Morrill Act was not even on the list.

The birth of the land-grant colleges has been romanticized as an example of farsighted educational and social planning in the grand American tradition. Given the success of these institutions and their inestimable impact on the nation's growth, such hindsight embellishment is easy to forgive. But, in the interest of historical fact, it should be recalled that the actual story tells less about Congressional sense of educational purpose than about its sound instincts.

In the course of the debate over the Morrill Act, questions were raised about its constitutionality. That objection and others did not disappear with the act's passage. The sentiment of many Northern and Western farmers and workers was eloquently summarized by a Minnesota Senator who grumbled: "We want no fancy farmers; we want no fancy mechanics."

Passage of the Morrill Act thus should not be viewed as evidence of overwhelming popular commitment to higher education. In fact, Morrill himself at one point shrewdly advanced his cause by insisting that the land-grant colleges were ideally suited to help keep young people on the farms where they belonged. Even though the move to cities was already gathering momentum, land-grant advocates argued that the local college would make farms so prosperous that they would be able to compete with the cities for the "best talent of the land." And, while it is true that land-grant colleges began by making their impact felt on American farming, by creating an enterprise of unprecedented efficiency and success, they were eventually to transform American higher education rather than just improve American agriculture.

At the time of these institutions' modest beginning, they were able to rely on the long-established precedent under which states had set aside public land for the establishment of schools and colleges. It was this vague and imprecise tradition that gave shape to the Morrill Act's provision that each state would establish at least one college, whose main objective would be "to teach such branches of learning as are related to agriculture and the mechanic arts" and that this should be accomplished "without excluding other scientific or classical studies." Each of the states was to receive public lands or scrip in lieu of land to equal 30,000 acres per senator and representative as of the apportionment of 1860.

When the act was first approved, the issue of land made available to the states may well have overshadowed its educational implications. Historian Carl Becker's interpretation stresses the measure's impact as a means of distributing land. It gave Eastern states, such as New York, what they regarded as their due, and they voted for it, in Becker's view, "less because it gave them colleges than because it gave them land." The Western states, worried about land speculators, often saw the act as the culmination of a necessary effort to save public land.

It is against such a background that some of the controversies of the era must be viewed. This perspective, for example, makes it easier to understand the charges that were leveled against Ezra Cornell when he labored to establish the university that would bear his name. At various stages in his endeavor, Cornell was accused of being a common land speculator, a conspirator intent on robbing the state, and a scoundrel out to enrich his own family. Cornell and Andrew White, a member of the State Senate and later Cornell's distinguished first president, had to suffer being called "monopolistic" and "swindlers." At a moment of exceptional frustration, Cornell turned to White and sighed: "I am not sure but that it would be a good thing for me to give half a million to old Harvard College in Massachusetts, to educate the descendants of the men who hanged my ancestors." (Cornell was born a Quaker.)

Though remembered for his pledge, "I would found an institution in which any person can find instruction in any study," Cornell found it necessary to defend himself again and again against charges that he was planning an aristocratic college. At the same time that he faced the accusations of the egalitarians, he also had to suffer the jealous opposition of the establishment—New York's existing colleges, including Hamilton, Hobart, Union, and Genesee (later to become Syracuse University), who sent lobbyists to Albany to obstruct the chartering of the new college, urging instead that the Morrill funds be divided among themselves. It was a battle that foreshadowed many subsequent skirmishes between the old-established private and the upstart public colleges—skirmishes which erupted again, most recently in the 1970s when fiscal problems sharpened the competition between the two sectors.

Sectarian groups also attacked Cornell University and what it stood for. Its nonsectarian and voluntary chapel was denounced as a mockery of religion. Andrew White was called an atheist. White fought back, ridiculing the denominational colleges' standards and their lack of discrimination in the selection of students.

In the end, Cornell and White prevailed. The new institution's principles of uniting practical and liberal learning under nonsectarian control and its encouragement of scientific studies—all part of the Cornell blueprint—were to leave an indelible impression on the New York higher education scene.

Not all land-grant colleges started out as auspiciously as Cornell. The act's provisions left much leeway for local initiative, and an infinite variety of institutions sprang up across the nation. Some states, particularly in the East, used the funds to expand or merely support the existing private colleges. The Sheffield School at Yale, Brown University in Providence, Rhode Island, and Dartmouth became land-grant institutions, as did Rutgers, the State University of New Jersey, whose neighbor at Princeton looked down politely on the "excellent college at New Brunswick, managed by a few Dutchmen."

Many Eastern academic leaders continued to take a dim view of the governmental infusion of funds and potential power. President McCosh of Princeton lobbied actively against increased federal support and Harvard's President Eliot spoke out against the principle of federal endowments. Since no similar largesse from Washington was forthcoming to support the older colleges, their leaders were easily persuaded to make a philosophical principle of the importance of their institutions' fiscal autonomy and academic independence.

Despite such opposition, the land-grant colleges continued to grow. A number of states, among them North Carolina, Missouri, Minnesota, and Wisconsin, turned the funds over to existing institutions and asked them to work out plans of how to serve the agricultural and mechanical interests. Other states, such as South Dakota, Oklahoma, Texas, and Washington, established new campuses which would compete with other institutions for public funds. In 1890, a second Morrill Act provided for regular annual appropriations for land-grant colleges. By 1961, a total of sixty-nine colleges were supported with such funds in some fashion.

Predictably, the initial stages of the new educational thrust were marked by confusion and disagreement. How much Latin, philosophy, and history was compatible with a practical curriculum? Who could teach the relevant facts of farming, an entirely new discipline without a pool of trained teachers, and what facts were essential? The first president of one of the new Midwestern campuses was heard to pledge that his faculty would devote itself to "the education of a man as man, rather than that which equips him for a particular post of duty." But a member of a state board of agriculture was able to ask with quite as much conviction: "What are they going to do about hog cholera?"

Farmers, moreover, had to be persuaded that their sons really needed a college education to become more productive. There were solid grounds for apprehension that higher education might make the farms' youths increasingly more inclined to trade in the rural life's "greener pastures" for the excitement of cities.

Initially, enrollments in many of the new colleges was disappointingly low. A frantic search for students often made the academic requirements far from demanding. But gradually the scene changed. Mechanical courses were added; the faculty became better trained; scientifically agricultural courses started to pay off in terms of demonstrably bigger and more lucrative crops; experimental agricultural stations, established by the Hatch Act of 1887, were linked to the colleges. The new institutions gradually overcame popular and legislative indifference. By 1890, the land-grant colleges, in sharp contrast to the traditional campuses, offered something for everybody.

The particular spirit of these revolutionary campuses was captured by Willa Cather in her novel *My Antonia* when she described the students at the University of Nebraska who

> came straight from the cornfields with only summer's wages in their pockets, hung on through the four years, shabby and underfed, and completed the course by really heroic self-sacrifice. Our instructors were oddly assorted; wandering pioneer schoolteachers, stranded ministers of the Gospel, a few enthusiastic young men just out of graduate schools. There was an atmosphere of endeavor, of expectancy and bright hopefulness about the young college that had lifted its head from the prairie only a few years before.

The concept of an unprecedented expansion of higher education, as symbolized by the land-grant movement, had yet to assert itself against a great deal of ingrained distrust of the academic gown and the sheepskin in a pragmatic and often anti-intellectual setting. The question in parents' minds was then, as it will always be, whether a college degree is worth the investment in time and money, and the matter of "worth" tended to be figured in hard cash.

Big business, though anxious to be assured of a supply of skilled manpower, did not necessarily allow its enthusiasm for such skills to spill over into the realm of more general education as embodied by a university's curriculum or at least its goals. Andrew Carnegie, whose financial legacy did so much for higher education after his death, expressed the view of the captains of industry of his day when he said in 1889: "While the college student has been learning a little about the barbarous and petty squabbles of a far-distant past, or trying to master languages which are dead, such knowledge seems adapted for life upon another planet than this."

Leland Stanford told a correspondent from *The New York World* on October 15, 1892, that of all the young men who come to him from the East with letters of introduction, "the most helpless class are college young men. . . ." It was to respond to that situation and to equip young men for a useful life that Stanford wanted to found his dream of a university in the West. It would be "different" and it would accomplish that goal by emulating Cornell.

As late as 1915, the magazine *School and Society* reprinted a satiric verse that had wide currency as an attack on the statewide expansion of higher education in Wisconsin. Its refrain was:

> Education is the rage
>   In Wisconsin
> Everyone is wise and sage
>   In Wisconsin;
> Every newsboy that you see
> Has a varsity degree
> Every cook's a Ph.D.
>   In Wisconsin.

The startling success of the land-grant college movement which literally transformed the history and the meaning of higher education in the United States, and subsequently in many other parts of the world, makes it easy to overlook the uphill struggle faced by the new idea. It may well be that, more than the recognition of the land-grant colleges' own promise, it was the inherent deficiency of many of the existing institutions that had paved the way for a new departure. The pre–Civil War rush to dot the landscape with sectarian colleges virtually assured the inadequate quality of many of these thinly disguised academies or prep schools.

Few historians have given adequate recognition to the heroic nature of the new university leaders' task in competing with the established order in an atmosphere of pervasive sectarianism. Writing about the "Age of the University" or the "Dawn of a

New Era," they rarely took full account of the continuing strength and magnetism of old views and ways or of the dilemma of the pioneering new university presidents who had to compete with the most provincial form of religiosity, without appearing to be the apostles of the devil.

It was no accident that well beyond the Civil War virtually all references to students mention only the education of "young men." Prejudice and inertia constituted a powerful roadblock to equal opportunity for young women or, more accurately, to any opportunity at all. The traditional Colonial view of women as by nature neither physically nor intellectually the equals of men remained strongly embedded, even though a great deal of stamina and mental fortitude was routinely expected of women in a pioneering society.

In 1783, the authorities at Yale had examined a twelve-year-old girl and ruled her to be "fully qualified, except in regard to sex, to be received as a pupil of the Freshman class. . . ." Such blindly antifeminine views began to be challenged by some who understood the changing needs of society. Benjamin Rush actually advocated the education of women because they were expected to help their husbands make their fortunes and educate their sons to participate in the affairs of government. "It is incumbent upon us," Rush wrote, "to make ornamental accomplishments yield to principles and knowledge, in the education of our women."

Subsequently, more general pressures for progressive reforms—abolition of debtors' prisons, extension of the suffrage, abolition of slavery—also gave some strength to the movement for women's rights to higher education. In the face of powerful barriers against entry into the established men's colleges—particularly in the East —the initial resort was largely to a special form of the "separate but equal" doctrine. Female seminaries were founded in New York by Emma Willard in 1821 and in Massachusetts by Mary Lyon, the institution that was later to become Mount Holyoke College. In 1837, Oberlin College enrolled four women and thus was credited with laying the foundation for coeducation which was later to become the prevailing mode of education in America.

In 1849, summing up the sentiment of her time, Harriet Martineau wrote:

> We find it taken for granted that girls are not to learn the
> dead languages and mathematics, because they are not to exer-
> cise professions where these attainments are wanted; and a
> little further on we find it said that the chief reason for boys
> and young men studying these things is to improve the quality
> of their minds.

It was not until the phenomenal expansion of the nation and of public education after the Civil War that the drive for women's education gained momentum. In the East, the new trend led to the founding of such women's colleges as Vassar, Smith, and Wellesley; in the West coeducation became the dominant trend.

It would be misleading, however, to suggest that the women's colleges in their early history were enclaves of militant feminism. The nineteenth-century women's campuses rarely condoned, and hardly ever encouraged, feminist ideas. A number of women who actively supported the movement of women's higher education—largely because society needed teachers, and women were considered best suited to the task—opposed women's suffrage. As recently as 1917, Mabel Newcomer, who was then a young instructor, was reprimanded by the head of her hall at Vassar for having taken some students to a suffrage rally on the eve of New York's approval of the amendment to give the vote to women. In straw votes at Mount Holyoke in 1895 and at Wellesley in 1912, the majorities of students voted against women's suffrage. Perhaps the first high-level support of feminism in American women's college administrations came with the appointment in 1894 of M. Carey Thomas to the presidency of Bryn Mawr.

It must have seemed heresy to many educated women of the day to hear Miss Thomas speak out against the glorification of women's teaching and maternal roles when she bluntly said that "of all things taking care of children does seem the most utterly unintellectual." More than half a century before such views began to gain widespread currency, this feminist crusader told her timid contemporaries in the women's colleges that women should have the right to choose whether or not to marry and, if they married, to choose to limit their families, become self-supporting, and employ others for "household drudgery"—and that "all women, like practically all men, must look forward after leaving college to some form of public service . . . paid . . . or unpaid."

The West's early coeducational colleges were concentrating on the training of ministers for the frontier, and the women who were admitted would be the helpmates on that evangelical mission. Oberlin College aimed for just such a goal, but not apparently without some practical male thoughts in mind as well. According to Jill K. Conway, the first women were admitted to Oberlin largely because the college needed them to do the domestic chores. In order to make time for the woman students to launder and mend the men's clothes, Miss Conway reports, no classes were held on Mondays, but no such free time was made available for the girls to take care of their own housekeeping. It was the women, too, who daily did the cooking and serving of the meals, as in fact students did at many of the early colleges and universities.

The case for coeducation at Oberlin in its early days moreover was bolstered by the argument that the women's presence was good for the men—it "enkindles emulation; puts each sex upon its best behavior . . . and develops in the College all those humanizing, elevating influences which God provided in the well ordered association of the sexes together." Though perhaps condescending toward women in the modern context, the stress on the civilizing influence of coeducation was nevertheless a distinct sign of liberalism on the collegiate scene of the time.

Even then, true equality of opportunity was a long way off, and it is doubtful that it has been achieved even now. Mrs. Mary Bunting, former president of Radcliffe College, remembers that she was the one woman on a National Science Foundation committee to try to introduce more talented high-school students into scientific careers. The committee found that more than ninety-five percent of the top students in the high schools who did not go on to college were girls. "Nothing was done about it," Mrs. Bunting reported, "even though the country needed new talent in the sciences." That was when she realized that there were "hidden dissuaders" in American education to keep women out of the professions. Based on her experience, she eventually established the Radcliffe Institute in the 1960s in an effort to encourage able women to continue their academic, creative, and professional activities.

Many of the apparently "trivial" issues during the early days of women's higher education, though long ignored, have assumed a strange flavor of timeliness in the light of the modern women's movement's concerns a century later. For example, the use of the word "female" in the college's original name made Sarah Hale demand indignantly of Matthew Vassar: "What female do you mean? Not a female donkey? . . . Why degrade the feminine sex to the level of animals?" In 1867, the designation was officially dropped.

Other critics of male domination of that day debated whether first-year women students ought properly be referred to as fresh-men—shades of the semantic revolution that, a hundred years later, led to the coining of the term "chairperson."

More serious by far was the incipient women's college movement's need to fight against strongly entrenched intellectual preju-dice. In a typical example of traditional male chauvinism, an article in the *Saturday Review* stated flatly in 1860: "The great argument against the existence of this equality of intellect in women is that it does not exist. If that does not satisfy a female philosopher, we have no better to give."

Women, it was still widely believed, simply could not bear up under the physical strain of higher education. The declining birthrate of native-born whites during the nineteenth century was a cause for great anxiety, particularly among the middle- and upper-class families whose daughters were potential college students. Doctors and educators shared concern over what was feared to be the threat of physical deterioration of urban women among the social and economic elite, and many physicians were convinced that excessive education for "females" would leave them with "monstrous brains and puny bodies; abnormally active cerebra-tion and abnormally weak digestion; flowing thought and con-stipated bowels; lofty aspirations and neuralgic sensations. . . ."

Conventional medical wisdom of the day held that a young girl's vital energies should be devoted to the development of her reproductive organs. The body was believed to command only a limited amount of vital force, and whatever part of it was drained off for mental exertions would be lost to the potential strength of the reproductive equipment.

Writing in the September 1973 issue of *The Journal of American History*, Carroll Smith-Rosenberg and Charles Rosenberg describe the impact of a medical theory that considered it impossible for the brain and the ovaries to develop at the same time. A doctor of that era condensed the anxieties of his time in the simple question: "Why spoil a good mother by making an ordinary grammarian?" It was a view that, according to the Rosenbergs, was shared by most of the early leaders of American gynecology.

Thus, motherhood and education were placed in an adversary position—to opt for the one was to weaken the other, and the mood of the time clearly favored motherhood as the woman's mission, usually to the exclusion of higher (or even academic high school) education. In 1877, Regents of the University of Wisconsin declared that, although education is "greatly to be desired," it is

> better that the future matrons of the state should be without a University training than that it should be produced at the fearful expense of ruined health; better that the future mothers of the state should be robust, hearty, healthy women, than that, by over study, they entail upon their descendants the germs of disease.

"Our great-grandmothers," wrote William Goodell in *Lessons in Gynecology* in 1879, as he bemoaned the growth of women's colleges in the East and of coeducation in the state universities of the Midwest and the Pacific Coast,

> got their schooling during the winter months and let their brains lie fallow for the rest of the year. They knew less about Euclid and the classics than they did about housekeeping and housework. But they made good wives and mothers, and bore and nursed sturdy sons and buxom daughters and plenty of them at that.

In response to such views, women's colleges took great pains to insist on compulsory physical education activities and hygiene lectures—requirements that were often ignored by the men's colleges.

In 1873, a prominent Boston physician wrote a book to prove that, if women were exposed at all to higher education, it must be administered in small doses to prevent serious harm.

The establishment of most of the nation's women's colleges in the East was the logical consequence of that region's greater reliance on private preparatory schools and colleges rather than on extensive public school and university systems. By contrast, it was in the Midwest and the West that the coeducational high school had first taken root. Thus, ironically, it was true that prior to 1888 only Black girls in Baltimore could have passed college entrance examinations since only the segregated Black schools were then coeducational.

Land-grant colleges, too, already in considerable trouble over the need to shape a curriculum for farmers and mechanics, faced some initial opposition to coeducation. In the East, particularly in New England, moreover, land-grant funding went primarily to existing men's colleges and thus reinforced single-sex higher education. It was left to Cornell, which represented the wave of the future in so many other ways, to give visibility and impetus to coeducation in the East. If Ezra Cornell was to redeem his pledge that the new institution would enable anyone of ability to study there, he could not deny admission to half of the population. Persuaded of the argument's logic, a benefactor donated the funds for a women's dormitory, and the pattern was established. Yet, even Ezra Cornell was sufficiently a creature of his time to protect himself against future criticism by quietly slipping into the capsule in the dormitory's cornerstone a memorandum explaining to future historians why coeducation might fail.

Whether in women's colleges, coordinate institutions (such as Barnard and Radcliffe) or on coeducational campuses, women gradually dispelled the public's doubts about their capacity for, and rights to, higher education. They pitted their accomplishments and subsequently their power against recurrent objections, whether they were quietly raised by conservative voices or hurled from the pulpit, as in the case of the minister who asked: "Must we crowd education on our daughters, and for the sake of having them 'intellectual' make them puny, nervous, and their whole earthly existence a struggle between life and death?"

The answer to such conservative doubts was to be given only

much later—in the 1960s. Symbolically, Yale, which in the eighteenth century had turned down a female applicant for no reason other than her sex, was to be among the first of the Eastern men's colleges in the twentieth century to admit women.

The last quarter of the nineteenth century is customarily described as the dawn of the age of science—an era of progress and liberal thinking. By past standards, this is not an inaccurate picture, and the glimmer of a new vision of higher education within the incipient land-grant movement justifies such optimism. But the old order was reluctant to move out of the way. Fundamentalists and others who felt threatened by Darwin and modernity were still trying to hold the line. In 1876, on the hundredth anniversary of the nation's birth, the following statement was read to a national teachers' convention in answer to those who wanted to stand in the way of progress and growth:

> But we are told that there are too many colleges; and that this result is due to the voluntary system. In a free country, how can this be helped? There are just now too many banks, too many railroads, too many ships, too much iron; but the law of supply and demand is the only possible corrective for the evil. If a college attracts to itself patronage and endowment, it has a right to live; if it does not, it will die. The law of natural selection applies to colleges as well as to the animal and vegetable world. A college that does good work creates its own patronage by its elevating influence over the community around it. Time alone can determine whether a college has a right to live.

This was the answer to the more conservative, elitist objectors to the new expansion. It was social Darwinism. It was the application of the theory of the survival of the fittest to the growth and development of American institutions. Expansion and the laissez-faire were the new prospectus—in commerce, manufacture, agriculture, and education.

Science had come to be recognized as a new driving force, and universities were the natural breeding and proving ground for the new engine of progress. College presidents may still have had a secret hankering for the old days of a more classical curriculum;

but they adjusted to the new fact that contributions were increasingly linked to the potential benefits derived from scientific and mechanical development. It was an adjustment that often led to a deliberate balancing act of retaining as much as possible of the traditional religious orientation, while at the same time opening the doors to science. The accommodation of science and religion became a major ideological concern. (Even in the 1950s, when Nathan M. Pusey took over the presidency of Harvard, he devoted much of his intellectual energies to the effort of making science and religion compatible—in part by placing new emphasis on the revival of the Divinity School.)

Eliot, White, and Daniel Coit Gilman, at Johns Hopkins, were evolutionists. But since Darwinism, which by that time was espoused by most scientists and many of the academic spokesmen, offended the more conservative and religious community, caution was in order. Gilman hedged his bets by telling students that he had no objections if they wanted to buy a bust of Darwin, but he suggested that they also get and display likenesses of some less controversial scientists. Yale's president Noah Porter was said to have posted a notice outside his door: "At 11:30 on Tuesday Professor Porter will reconcile science and religion."

These anecdotes should not obscure the serious aspects of a very fundamental conflict. The debate over evolution involved nothing less than the question whether a new view of the world would prevail over the entrenched old order, whether the forces of the intellect would be allowed to free themselves from the bonds of a repressive form of piety, whether crucial issues of society would henceforth be decided by fixed dogma or on the basis of scientific inquiry and evidence. In 1906 Woodrow Wilson became Princeton's first secular president. Arthur T. Hadley was the first layman to preside over Yale in 1904.

The expansion of higher education in the wake of the Civil War paralleled the growth of the nation itself. Such men as White, Gilman, Eliot, and James Angell of Michigan were captains of academia in much the same way as Rockefeller and Carnegie were captains of industry. Higher education's new importance reflected the American explosion of wealth and living standards, the rapid urbanization and the population's social as well as logistical mobility.

New wealth meant a flow of funds to the universities. Such names as Rockefeller, Carnegie, Duke, Stanford, Tulane, and Vanderbilt became synonymous with the growing concept of private support for higher education. Yet there was no standard pattern either for benefactions or for the growth and development of the system.

The spirit of the age may well be mirrored most accurately in the founding of one of the nation's least typical major institutions, the University of Chicago. It involved the enormous Rockefeller fortunes, on the one hand; but it also depended on the drive of one man, William Rainey Harper, a young Baptist scholar who literally created the great university from scratch. Going far beyond what Rockefeller had dared to imagine, Harper cajoled money and land from Chicago industrialists and put together the new academic complex with a toughness of mind that any industrial empire-builder might have envied.

It was not only money Harper pursued with singleminded fervor. To assemble a first-rate faculty, he mercilessly raided other campuses. As a mitigating factor in his defense, it must also be said that many eminent scholars turned down his offers with condescending references to the "Standard Oil Institution" he was building.

The brutal laws of social Darwinism were as harsh on the smaller institutions of higher learning as on the weaker oil companies and railroads. Harper, having set his mind on pirating Clark University's faculty, returned from his triumphant raids not only with much of his human loot including five Yale professors, but with an additional booty of several former college presidents.

The evening before the University of Chicago officially opened its doors on October 1, 1892, Harper confided to a friend that he was worried whether a single student would show up to enroll. He need not have fretted. Students from thirty-three states and fifteen foreign countries clamored to be admitted. What awaited them was the model of an entirely new kind of university. The year was divided into four academic quarters, instead of the traditional two semesters. Students were given the option of enrolling for three quarters a year or for an accelerated program of four quarters. (It was an innovation that was to be rediscovered as a revolutionary approach by some colleges during the 1950s.)

A system of major and minor studies allowed students to concentrate on one subject area, while giving relatively less time to another, secondary field. As a result of the continuous sessions, the custom of annual graduation was eliminated. The faculty was under considerable pressure to produce and make a name for itself and the institution. Harper believed in the "publish or perish" doctrine and never hesitated to let his views be known. He was building a university with the same obsessive singlemindedness with which others built railroads or industrial empires. Scholarly research and investigation were his currency of power.

John D. Rockefeller, far from resenting the university's almost insatiable appetite for funds, boasted: "It is the best investment I ever made in my life." Moreover, he was willing to give Harper and the faculty the greatest degree of independence. By contrast, Stanford University, which was founded with Leland Stanford's profits from the Southern Pacific Railroad, was to be constantly aware of its benefactor's interference in the affairs of "his" university. One of the consequences was that Stanford was not to become a first-rate university and graduate school until the airplane helped to break its isolation.

The combination of the expanding nation's affluence and needs, along with the explosion of interest in science and technology, called for the kind of academic changes that would provide a hungry economy with manpower of a wide variety of talents. The elective system, briefly tried at the University of Virginia prior to the Civil War, had been quickly abandoned. Its time had not yet come. Now, amid the nation's postwar expansion, the climate was ripe for its introduction on a massive scale.

The leading spokesman for the elective curriculum was Charles W. Eliot. A Harvard graduate and subsequently a professor of mathematics and chemistry who had traveled extensively in Europe, Eliot had presented his views in writings on "The New Education" in the *Atlantic*. During his forty years as president of Harvard, he transformed the nation's first college into a truly national university.

Eliot reformed and upgraded the law and medical schools. He opened the windows on the academic world outside the United States and let its influence, particularly German scholarship and specialization, rush in. Instead of the prescribed program of Latin, Greek, grammar, mathematics, and logic taught in the traditional manner of classroom recitation, a student now was allowed to select those courses which he thought would make him an expert or a scholar in a particular field or discipline. It was a revolutionary rejection of the idea of the unified, classical curriculum that had so long dominated American higher education.

In the context of its time, the elective system, with its variety of crowded lectures, was considered the essence of academic liberalism. It was hailed as an escape from the straightjacket plan of studies that had traditionally been dictated by academic authorities and handed on from one generation to the next. It was the elite institutions' parallel to the pragmatic developments of the land-grant universities.

Higher education had not been attracting a large enough number of young people to satisfy the national need for college-educated manpower. The youth of a pragmatic country seemed to question whether getting a college degree was worth the effort. During the 1870s, attendance at twenty of the leading colleges rose only 3.5 percent, while the population had increased by twenty-three percent. In 1885, not quite one fourth of the members of Congress were college graduates, compared with thirty-eight percent a decade earlier. Michigan's president Charles Kendall Adams wrote: "The sad fact stares us in the face that the training which has been considered essential to finished scholarship has been losing ground from year to year in the favor of the people."

In comparison with the virtually unlimited opportunities that beckoned to a young man in an expanding economy, life on the campus seemed to many sixteen-year-olds dull, if not outright repressive. President Francis L. Patton, Woodrow Wilson's predecessor at Princeton at the turn of the century, actually denied that students had a claim to even the civil rights enjoyed by criminals. "Do not tell me," he said, "that a man is innocent until he is found to be guilty, or suppose that the provisions of the criminal suit will apply to college procedure."

It is not surprising that in such an oppressive atmosphere the elective system was seen as a promise of liberation. At Harvard, all course requirements for specific subjects were abolished for seniors in 1872 and for juniors about seven years later. By 1884, not even sophomores had to enroll in required courses, and by the turn of the century the only subjects prescribed for freshmen were English and one foreign language.

The reforms were an instant success. Harvard's endowment grew from $2 to $20 million, and its faculty of sixty expanded to one of six hundred. This impact is doubly remarkable because many of the powerful forces at Harvard remained highly critical of the new approach. In 1885, Eliot's job seemed actually in jeopardy as the alumni and the overseers questioned his ideas.

Outside Cambridge, however, Harvard's example launched many of the nation's colleges on a new course. In 1901, a survey of ninety-seven colleges showed that thirty-four percent of them offered courses of study that were seventy percent elective, while another twelve institutions placed between fifty and seventy percent of their courses on a similar basis.

Most of the rest, or more than half of the colleges sampled, were still slow to move in the new direction. Among those who defended the old order were Yale and Princeton and many of the small New England colleges. In the South, too, tradition continued to prevail, largely because few of its institutions could afford to offer the dazzling array of elective courses. But the public universities of the West and the Midwest moved rapidly toward the adoption of free electives.

The emerging university represented the peculiarly American mix of idealism and concern for worldly success. It was dedicated to the mission of helping its graduates succeed in American life and as leaders in their communities. Academic spokesmen still stressed the concept of service—a loose adaptation of the old ideal of the educated gentleman's obligations to society. But there was now a new class of experts who devoted their energies to a different kind of service—such as the building of railroads and bridges.

Among the academic leaders who refused to be won over to the new ways was Princeton's president Woodrow Wilson. While opposed to the elective system, he tried for reform in a different direction. He sought unsuccessfully to abolish the snobbishly aristocratic eating clubs which dominated social life on campus. In scholarly matters, however, he remained an eloquent defender of the classics and a skeptic about the benefits science would bring to human affairs. "Science has bred in us a spirit of experiment and a contempt for the past," Wilson wrote in "Princeton in the Nation's Service" in 1896. "It has made us credulous of quick improvement, hopeful of discovering panaceas, confident of success in every new thing."

When others saw the United States as the land of unlimited opportunity, Wilson warned that "the days of glad expansion are gone." He wanted the university to "illuminate duty by every lesson that can be drawn out of the past."

The concept of service, but of a more utilitarian kind than Wilson had in mind, as the university's mission, came into full flower during the era of Progressivism. Michigan's President Angell, who had been highly critical of what he considered the isolation of the older colleges from the larger community, boasted in 1898 that the Secretary of State, an Assistant Secretary of War, and the chairman of the Senate Foreign Relations Committee were all Michigan alumni.

But it was the University of Wisconsin which embraced Progressive ideals. Charles Van Hise turned his inaugural address as the institution's president into a statement on progressive thought in higher education. The doors of the university, he said, must be open to the "industrious poor" as well as to the rich, and the two must work together in complete equality. Nothing short of such opportunity is just, for each has an equal right to find at the state university the advanced intellectual life adapted to his needs. Any narrower view would be indefensible.

Two roads to such noble ends were cleared with great success. The first was to attract scholars and experts in both practical and academic subjects, with the aim of having them serve the state and the nation. The other was the creation of extension programs, which for some time managed to translate Van Hise's ideals into terms that were pertinent to the lives of every family in the state.

In 1909, Lincoln Steffens was able to write:

> In Wisconsin the university is as close to the intelligent farmer as his pig-pen or his tool-house; the university laboratories are part of the alert manufacturer's plant; to the worker, the university is drawing nearer than the school around the corner and is as much his as his union or his favorite saloon.

It would have been difficult to say as much for Princeton or for the universities anywhere in the Western world outside the United States. It was the reflection of an optimism that more democracy and more scientific and technological progress would solve all of mankind's problems.

Not all the changes in collegiate affairs were academic. At about the same time as the elective system was transplanted from Germany, rugby was imported from England and the seeds were sown for what was to become the national mania of college football. A game between Princeton and Rutgers in 1869 is credited with the official inauguration of the collegiate sport. Not every academic leader greeted the new arrival with enthusiasm. Cornell's Andrew White, though alert to the winds of change in so many other ways, responded to a challenge to let his team play the University of Michigan with the icy reply: "I will not permit thirty men to travel 400 miles merely to agitate a bag of wind."

The game nevertheless caught on and proved irresistible. Interest in it engulfed all sizes and types of campuses. Some might reject the elective system, but almost all embraced football. Football became so important that for the first time colleges began to consult with each other. The Ivy League came into being as a football association.

The impact on the social scene was equally electrifying. Around the turn of the century, New York was thrown into a virtual frenzy by games between Yale and Princeton. Hotels were jammed. Clergymen cut short their services to get their parishioners to the game on time.

As popular involvement grew, so did the game's brutality. Eighteen students died on the football fields in 1905. After the front pages of newspapers featured pictures of badly mauled players, reformers who were already busy fighting against impure drugs and food and corrupt political machines took on the crusade to clean up football. In October 1905, Theodore Roosevelt summoned the coaches of Harvard, Yale, and Princeton to lunch at the White House. Flavoring his observations with the day's moralistic overtones, the President told his guests: "Brutality and foul play should receive the same summary punishment given to a man who cheats at cards." However, the Rough Rider was too much of a believer in the manly arts of combat to support President Eliot's effort to abolish football at Harvard. In fact, when pressed for an opinion, Teddy had to concede that he did not "in the least object to a sport because it is rough."

Part of the new game's extraordinary attraction then was, and has remained, the fact that it tended to unite the campus, no matter how fragmented life in the fraternity houses and dormitories might otherwise have been. Intellectual professors and gung-ho alumni could share in the ritual, the cheering, and the drive for victory.

As the game drifted more and more out of the hands of the students and was increasingly taken over by the near-professional athletic associations, some of the academic leaders began to express concern over the moral contradictions. Eliot wrote in 1892: "There is something exquisitely inappropriate in the extravagant expenditure on athletic sports at such institutions as Harvard and Yale, institutions which have been painfully built up by the self-denial, frugality, and public spirit of generations. . . ."

But the gridiron, and to a lesser extent other team sports, also played an important role as the great social equalizer of the campuses. Particularly at the Eastern colleges, which had been the preserve of rich men's sons, it was through heroic visibility on varsity teams that new arrivals, such as the Irish and the Poles, managed to gain acceptance. Yale's President Arthur Twining Hadley was guilty only of slight exaggeration when he claimed in 1906 that football had taken hold of "the emotions of this student body in such a way as to make class distinctions relatively unimportant" and that "the students get together in the old-fashioned democratic way."

More than any other activity, too, football made the general public aware of the universities. The game became a boon to higher education's image and to the universities' capacity to spread their public relations message, and with it to appeal more effectively for funds. State universities were quick to discover that the legislatures' generosity rose in direct proportion to the triumphs of the football team.

College stadiums became symbols of institutional success. Construction of these arenas reached its peak during the prosperous twenties, with their cult of Flaming Youth and Joe College. In

1923, Michigan built a field house big enough to house football in any weather, and in Los Angeles and Pasadena private promoters erected the Colosseum and the Rose Bowl to accommodate huge crowds of spectators. By 1927, Michigan's stadium at Ann Arbor could boast of seating almost 90,000 fans comfortably, and in 1948 the university was able to report that its $4 million athletic plant had been paid for with the profits from football.

Even though overemphasis on collegiate football has periodically come under fire, few colleges have been able to resist demands for victorious teams. In 1973, *Columbia College Today,* the university's alumni publication, brushed aside more weighty academic concerns to report: "The Columbia football program is in another period of crisis. The Lion team performed poorly this fall, so poorly that Coach Frank Navarro submitted his resignation before the season ended." And the anguished report concluded: "Since athletic achievements contribute to the quality of life and prestige of a college, Columbia should have an athletic program in which its students and alumni can take pride."

The development of highly organized and standardized collegiate sports, however, was only one of the consequences of the phenomenal growth of higher education. With expansion came bureaucratization. A once relatively simple structure, dominated by a president as something of a lonely potentate, gave way to what came to be known as "administration." Prior to the Civil War, most colleges had managed with a treasurer and a part-time librarian assisting the president and the faculty in keeping academia going. But as the colleges and universities grew and their teaching and research functions became more complex, the table of organization expanded, too. Moreover, as in the country at large and in the public schools—often with advice from leading university presidents—the bureaucratization of leadership reflected the new faith in industrial-style efficiency and management.

College admission itself had grown into a sufficiently large enterprise to call for a more orderly and organized approach. Part of the thrust for organization and security came from the secondary schools. Prep schools like Andover, which had a great stake in knowing exactly what colleges required Latin or French or some other subjects, as well as some public schools anxious to compete for college places, were urging colleges to define their purposes in ways that their own teachers and curriculum planners could understand. Since high school and college educators tend to consider each other worlds apart, the admissions issue offered an opportunity to narrow the gap.

It was through a combination of such pressures from below and leadership at the university level by such recognized education spokesmen as Eliot at Harvard and Nicholas Murray Butler at Columbia that the College Entrance Examination Board came into being. College admissions standards, moreover, had begun to be a powerful lever of academic reform and the arbiters of scholastic quality in the lower schools. The prestigious Committee of Ten, appointed during a meeting of the National Education Association in 1892, began to address itself to the college admissions problem.

One of the very first discussions of the matter, during a meeting of the Association of Colleges and Secondary Schools of the Middle Atlantic States in 1899, led to a classic and recurring argument. President Eliot had been invited by Butler to state the case for standardization. President Ethelbert D. Warfield of Lafayette College spoke for the opposition. He denounced proposals for standardized entrance tests as a step toward a dehumanizing uniformity. Students, he said, who failed to pass Lafayette's own entrance examinations but were nevertheless admitted often turned out to be top scholars of their class. His institution, he warned angrily, "does not intend to be told by any Board whom to admit and whom not to admit. If we wish to admit the son of a benefactor, or of a Trustee, or of a member of the Faculty, and such action will benefit the institution we are not going to be prevented. . . ." (No subsequent agreements, it should be added, have ever prevented colleges to make precisely such exceptions in the case of favored candidates—not least of all of potential athletes whose intellectual capacity often was minimal.)

Eliot, who saw Harvard as the nineteenth-century equivalent of the university world's General Motors Corporation, replied that Warfield could, if he wished, admit candidates on the strength of their character, "or on their promise of usefulness, or on their capacity to go on with the work of the college" or—after a pause for the desired effect—"on their good looks."

Despite this clash of presidents, the CEEB was established and has governed admission to the nation's prestige colleges for better or for worse ever since—and not without its share of subsequent criticism and argument. The organization sponsored the College Entrance Examination Board tests which made standardization more effective, or objectionable—depending on the observer's point of view.

The thrust toward standardization, however, transcended the matter of college admission. It had its roots in the same concern for order and efficiency that had made the quest for "the one best way" the dominant ideological force in the public schools. It was in part a necessary and beneficial reaction to a system that had grown with little attention to quality controls and discernible goals; but it was also a simplistic attempt to apply to education the same yardsticks of efficiency that appeared to make the railroads so successful.

The bureaucratization of higher education inevitably affected the university presidency. The oldtime president had been a force of awesome power and responsibility—superfather to students and faculty alike. In 1814, Princeton's president Ashbel Green had recorded in his diary: ". . . I took the examination of the senior class on belles lettres and wrote letters to the parents of . . . dismissed students. The Faculty met in the evening and a pistol was fired at the door of one of the tutors. I ought to be very thankful to God for his support this day."

In loco parentis was the dominant doctrine. William T. Sherman—better known for his march through Georgia than for his brief career as president of a military college which later became Louisiana State University—described the concept in 1860, when he said: "The dullest boys have the most affectionate mothers and the most vicious boys here come recommended with all the virtues of saints. . . . Of course, I promised to be father to them all."

As higher education entered into its period of dramatic expansion after the Civil War, college presidents soon found it impossible to remain fathers to all their students. The *in loco parentis* role now was inherited by the "administration" as the collective father—the deans, registrars, advisers, and a growing army of other surrogate parents.

Even those presidents who nostalgically inclined toward the parental role were pulled off into quite different directions. Many were in a true sense of the word stars on the national scene and educational leaders beyond their campuses and even beyond higher education. The expansion and new fiscal complexity of their own institutions called for a businessman's organizational and fund-raising skills and often, particularly in the case of the public universities, a shrewd way with politics.

University presidents found themselves in situations for which neither their experience nor their temperament had prepared them. David Starr Jordan, Stanford's first president, an ichthyologist who at his previous post as a teacher had known all his students by name, complained that in his new capacity as head of a major university he found that, every time he recalled the name of a student, he forgot the name of a fish.

As time went on, more and more of the uncomfortable new presidents could no longer remember the names of either their students or their fish. They became estranged from both their students and their disciplines. Often, they relinquished their paternal role on campus for celebrity status in the nation. Above all, they had to learn the art of passing the hat—and with it the precarious skill of balancing the interests of their campuses with efforts not to offend their many conflicting support groups. "The most universal faker and the most variegated prevaricator that has yet appeared in the civilized world," was Upton Sinclair's uncharitable description of the new species.

Over the years, changes in American society had been reflected in similar transformations of the role and image of the college professor. In an earlier age, the academic had been romanticized as a dedicated, selfless, somewhat impractical character. Unfashionably attired in a much-worn muffler and obsolescent hat, underpaid and absent-minded, he was the butt of gentle ridicule, but never without an underlying reverence. If not actually a minister himself, the professor was imbued with ministerial devotion and disinterest in worldly wealth or glamour. He self-effacingly shouldered the burden of transmitting the ideals of a Christian gentleman.

Since the days of Adam Smith, it had been considered good and proper for faculty salaries to be low, not unlike the pay of the clergy. Even in a nation that increasingly prized material wealth, the professor was still thought to be happily and appropriately part of a different breed of men to be rewarded on a different scale of values. Such myths made it easy for university trustees and state legislatures to keep professorial salaries low, without feeling any pangs of guilt.

Putting his seal of approval on such practice, President Eliot said in his inaugural address in 1869: "The poverty of scholars is of inestimable worth in this money-getting nation. . . . The poor scholars and preachers of duty defend the modern community against its own material prosperity. Luxury and learning are ill bed-fellows."

In 1883, *The New York Times* editorialized: "No professor worth his salt ever devoted himself to learning for any other reason than that he loved learning." In an era of high living and low thinking, professors were expected to redeem the sins of their surroundings by devoting themselves to high thinking and low living. There were, to be sure, some dissenters from this view of the professor's place in contemporary America. Frederick Jackson Turner, one of the academic stars of his day, told the University of Wisconsin that he would stay only if he were to be assured of an enlarged staff, adequate fellowships, permanent funds for the purchase of books, a leave of absence, and provisions for the publication of historical studies. Yet even a man of Turner's stature had to plead for "permanent" funds for such academic necessities as books.

Toward the end of the nineteenth century, while low pay and the austere life remained in effect, the role of the professor had nevertheless begun to undergo important changes. The college teacher had been both disciplinarian and babysitter—the man who listened to the endless rote recitations of his students but who also, largely because of the lowly status reflected by his meager pay, did the parents' bidding in watching of their children's welfare.

Now, however, the rise of the degree of Doctor of Philosophy —the Ph.D. that was later to become the union card of academic respectability—marked the thrust toward a new professionalism. Once again the American university world borrowed from the German experience of scholarship and research; but, whatever the source, the effect was to give professors the standing that had earlier been denied to them.

Today it may be tempting to be critical of the Ph.D. as the prerequisite of academic status and power. Yet, some of the early attacks on the degree as part of the move toward faculty professionalization might properly be viewed with skepticism—as the ploy of those who had become used to exploiting the downtrodden professor. At Harvard, for example, Charles Townsend Copeland, the famous Copey, kept students enthralled not only in the classroom but also at open house "Wednesday evening after ten" for almost forty years; yet Copeland had to wait eighteen years before his colleagues, who cherished scholarship above teaching, were willing to promote him to assistant professor.

With professionalization came the drive toward organization, bureaucratization, and standardization that had been so dominant in the reform of the public schools. Professors, who had been individualists ministering to their students and their scholarship, increasingly felt, and were made to feel, a stronger bond to the institution as a whole. The hierarchy of which they were a part, and to which they had to look for their advancement, became more systematically ordered and graded. The threat to "publish or perish" entered the academic scale of values. Newly founded learned societies and their journals became at once more specialized and more influential in the professors' careers.

While it is tempting to be critical of these developments, it would be unrealistic not to recognize their crucial role in creating an academic profession equal to the enormous task of making possible the imminent vast expansion of higher education in response to the demands of the technological age. The days of the old professor as surrogate parent had drawn to a close. The university was preparing for a new role at the center of vast transformations of American society: the mobilization of an army of teachers —to exceed half a million by 1970—for the most extensive higher education system ever created called for a new kind of professor, as much at home among the councils of the powerful as in the classrooms.

This new professoriat would become embroiled in great national issues and thus be placed into situations of controversy, and potential recriminations, making the question of academic freedom a matter of real rather than merely theoretical concern. Contrary to much of the modern rhetoric, academic freedom is not a deeply rooted tradition. Freedom on the nation's campuses had more often been little more than an adjunct to the freedom, or lack thereof, in the adjacent community. A scholar's right to express himself without fear of retribution generally reflected the mood of the country rather than any powerful unwritten code of special academic privilege.

The professors' generally vulnerable position could not be divorced from their economic station in American society. Low salaries and paternalistic attitudes toward a teacher–servant are not conducive to independence of mind. The early tradition of the professor as a man with the "right" religious and moral views substantially reinforced such limitations on the professor's capacity to claim special protection for freely expressed unpopular opinions.

Describing the prevailing view at Columbia in the 1870s, G. Stanley Hall said that many who taught philosophy did not feel the need "of a larger and freer atmosphere. . . . Many who were seeking academic positions expected to be questioned on their religious beliefs as part of their credentials." What would be condemned as a sign of inbreeding today was believed to be a virtue that would assure for new faculty members the benefits of a congenial atmosphere among the like-minded.

With growth came standardization of requirements as well as privileges, along with the first demands for security and tenure. In academia as in business, growth meant the introduction of rules, aimed at dealing more fairly with both employer and employee. The process of hiring, promotion, and firing had to be governed increasingly by uniform regulations, with recourse by the aggrieved to appeal against injustice.

The changes shocked many—often even those who stood to gain most from them. As usual at a time of upheaval, the conditions of the past tended to be seen through the rosy glasses of nostalgia. As shrewd an observer as John Dewey was able to let a cloudy vision of the good old days mislead him into writing: "The old-fashioned college faculty was pretty sure to be a thorough-going democracy in its way. Its teachers were selected more often because of their marked individual traits than because of pure scholarship. Each stood on his own. . . . All that is now changed."

What Dewey overlooked was that what he thought he remembered as democracy "in its way" had often been a not altogether voluntary agreement within a homogeneous community. Its apparent equality rested on its sameness in religious belief and socioeconomic background and was subject to the opinions of trustees who had deliberately built and perpetuated just such a homogeneity. It was usually a community that accepted not only an agreed-upon curriculum but also a strict code of behavior determined by the moral standards of the governing board, the administration, and the outside world.

As the colleges grew and the demands diversified, the pursuit of knowledge and the need for a wider-ranging scientific inquiry brought about inevitable and liberating changes in the professors' extracurricular role and status. Initially it had come to be expected that faculty members would shoulder these new responsibilities and still act as quasifathers toward their students; pursue the truth in library and laboratory and remain that legendary perfect gentleman whom an elderly dowager capable of a major donation would be glad to invite to tea.

During the era of the universities' original formation and gradual growth, the cohesion of the campus had been maintained rather easily, moreover, because the entire community was recruited from the "nonlaboring" classes. Students and professors were separated by age, but not by origin or basic values. A philosopher under consideration at the University of Texas was said to be required to be "a person one would meet socially with pleasure." A letter of reference in that era described the candidate as "a gentleman, a scholar, a man of good appearance" who "possesses some property and voted for Mr. Cleveland in 1884."

It was a cozy, if somewhat limiting, environment. Although department chairmen went through the motions of supervising their colleagues—at Columbia, in 1909, chairmen were asked to rate their faculty members on a form similar to a report card—few would, in this setting, have the stomach to apply blunt criticism to the work or talents of a fellow gentleman.

As the bureaucracy made itself felt on the growing campuses, it chipped away at the inbred clubbiness. Professors began to demand status and security instead. The old style had often been that of the domineering masters. For example, Turner could recall the days "when the members of the Board of Regents of Wisconsin used to sit with a red pencil in consultation over the lists of books submitted by the professors, and strike out those that failed to please their fancy, with irreverent comments on 'fool professors'." Under the new bureaucracy, the ultimate domination by those at the top of the power structure remained the same, but the procedures became more subtle and routine.

These procedures still showed little concern for academic freedom. The concepts of either *Lehrfreiheit* (freedom to teach) or *Lernfreiheit* (freedom to learn) which had played so large a part in the philosophical discussion of the German universities, and among their American imitators, were little more than a myth in the days before the growing power of the professoriat in the 1940s.

According to Howard Beale, the first loyalty oaths for teachers date back to the Revolutionary War. Educated labor, however, was still in such short supply that little, if any, attention was then paid to such "patriot test oaths." It was not until some years later that fears about dangerous beliefs became widespread, leading to the passage of the repressive Alien and Sedition Acts. In 1798, a French passage was dropped from Harvard's commencement program lest the sound of that foreign tongue create suspicion and disorder. Indeed, Harvard eliminated a course in French language and literature, which had been instituted in 1787, when the French were friends and allies, and allowed it to lapse until students petitioned for its restoration in 1806.

Many of the earlier conflicts, extending well into the nineteenth century, involved issues of religious as well as academic freedom. Religious toleration in those days had meant little more than the right of divergent sects to enjoy the freedom of operating their own colleges.

Gradually, in the course of the nineteenth century, the focus of the controversy shifted to political issues. In 1812, the Reverend Henry Ware, a professor at Harvard's Divinity School, founded an antislavery society. Public pressure demanded that he be fired, and students baited him and pelted him with nuts, charging that his actions were damaging to Harvard's reputation. But Harvard's President Josiah Quincy, who previously had been mayor of Boston, considered the demands an attack on the university's freedom and refused to let Ware go.

Later in the century, the storm over Darwinism shook many campuses. Yale's President Noah Porter, though himself by no means a doctrinaire opponent of Darwin's views, was nevertheless uneasy over the fact that William Graham Sumner, the respected sociologist, used Herbert Spencer's textbook in his undergraduate classes. "I feel assured," Porter wrote to Sumner, "that the use of the book will bring intellectual and moral harm to the students, however you may strive to neutralize or counteract its influence. . . ." Sumner replied with a vigorous defense of the work, but eventually concluded that the adverse publicity of the dispute would destroy the course's usefulness, and he withdrew the book.

Looking back on that era, historian Richard Hofstadter interpreted the Sumner–Porter episode as proof that the newfound power of the professor had made possible this "appeal" to justify controversial classroom procedures. It is not easy to maintain such a sanguine view of the state of academic freedom when the fate of other, less prominent, professors of the time under similar circumstances is examined. For example, Professor Alexander Winchell was dismissed from the faculty of Vanderbilt University for his evolutionist views. A strong fundamentalist position remained firmly entrenched on many campuses for much longer than many historians have acknowledged.

As the business community grew stronger—and it was from that sector that the university trustees were largely chosen—it became difficult for all but the exceptional professors to speak out for unpopular causes and to take public issue with the main currents of contemporary politics.

Edward W. Bemis, an economist, was dismissed from Chicago for a verbal attack on the railroads. When the president of Brown University declared for free trade, he soon found his office untenable. Edward A. Ross, the sociologist credited with coining the term "social control," had to leave Stanford University after he expressed his disapproval of "coolie labor." In 1894, after a severe depression, populist victories and Coxey's march on Washington, all partisan political meetings were banned from Harvard Yard.

At issue was not so much a deliberate effort to stamp out unpopular or dangerous views as the constant pressure felt by university administrators from the surrounding community. Caution was the better part of valor. If professors merely confined their suspect views to their classrooms, they might escape the administrators' concern and censure; but, when those views became a matter of public dispute, toleration soon wore thin.

After a period of relative calm, academic peace was shattered by World War I. Columbia became the first university to institute a full-fledged "loyalty" investigation. President Butler announced during the 1917 wartime commencement ceremonies: "What had been tolerated before becomes intolerable now. What had been wrongheadedness was now sedition. What had been folly, was now treason."

Butler, the prototype of the imperious higher education establishment of his day, then added an ominous threat: "This is the University's last and only warning to any among us, if such there be, who are not with whole heart and mind and strength committed to fight with us to make the world safe for democracy."

Among those whose conscience would not allow them to submit to Butler's dictate was James McKeen Cattell, a noted psychologist and veteran of many previous bouts with the university administration. Cattell was dismissed by the trustees for petitioning three Congressmen to oppose sending draftees to fight in Europe. Also fired was Henry Wadsworth Dana, a professor of literature, who had urged students to protest the draft bill while it was still before Congress for debate.

These dismissals and other autocratic procedures eventually precipitated the resignation of Charles Beard, the historian. Beard, whose basic conservatism later became a favorite target of radical historians, charged in his letter of resignation that Columbia was "under the control of a small and active group of trustees who have no standing in the world of education, who are reactionary and visionless in politics, narrow and medieval in religion." Despite much publicity, the protest by one of the academic giants had little impact on the university and its governing structure. Complaints very much like those lodged by Beard against the Board's composition and outlook were to be voiced again in only slightly modernized, and occasionally profane, terms by rebellious students in the 1960s.

Although Columbia's jingoist disregard for academic freedom was typical of much repressive action on campuses, it did not tell the full story of higher education's posture. Following a rumor that a wealthy alumnus had threatened to withdraw his bequest unless a pro-German professor were dropped from the faculty, the Harvard Corporation issued a statement to the effect that the university "cannot tolerate any suggestion that it would be willing to accept money and abridge free speech, to remove a professor or to accept his resignation." In contrast to Butler, Harvard's president Lowell included in his annual report this ringing defense of academic freedom:

> It is sometimes suggested that the principles are different in times of war; that the governing boards are then justified in restraining unpatriotic expressions injurious to the country. But the same problem is presented in war time as in time of peace. . . . There is no middle ground. Either the university assumes full responsibility for permitting its professors to express certain opinions in public, or it assumes no responsibility whatsoever, and leaves them to be dealt with like other citizens by the public authorities according to the laws of the land.

Increasingly, however, the professoriat began to understand the risks involved in entrusting the defense of faculty rights to university presidents. In 1915, the American Association of University Professors was created as an organizational response to the need to define and protect the principles of academic freedom and professional rights. But it was not until twenty-five years later that this incipient faculty union—the suggestion that it might eventually have to match actual unions would have been considered absurd and odious at the time—had become strong and self-confident enough to codify the protection of academic freedom.

The intervening years were marked by many disconcerting episodes. Higher education could not escape the fallout of the nation's political traumas, particularly recurring Red scares. "A majority of the college professors in the United States are teaching socialism and Bolshevism," millionaire oilman Edward L. Doheny told a press conference during the 1920s. History, however, re-

members Doheny primarily as one of the leading members of the
cast of characters in the Teapot Dome scandals of the Harding
administration. Harding's Commissioner of Education expressed
his determination to eliminate "communism, bolshevism, and socialism" from the schools. (The myth of the radically contaminated
campus died slowly, if at all: In the 1950s, William F. Buckley,
in his book *God and Man at Yale*, once again alerted the populace
to what he considered rampant leftism in academia.)

Calvin Coolidge, then Harding's vice-president, authored a
three-part magazine series on the question, "Are the 'Reds' Stalk-
ing Our College Women?" Deploring student radicalism, he
warned of the Red taint at Mount Holyoke, Wellesley, and Bryn
Mawr—all bastions of respectability.

With the perennial anguish of conservatism and advancing age,
Coolidge complained: "Children rebel at the authority of teachers
and parents, teachers rebel at the authority of school boards, college faculties rebel at the authority of presidents and trustees. . . ."

As time went on, the furor of the early 1920s over the radical
menace was eventually calmed by what turned out to be a far
greater menace to the nation's health—"normalcy." The fearful
vision of revolutionary students gave way in the public mind to
the image of Joe College—the vapid and pleasure-oriented symbol
of flaming youth, more akin to the subsequent era of the panty
raids than to that of the 1960s student rebellion.

The Great Depression of the late 1920s put an end to the care-
free air. Enrollments declined. Professors had difficulties finding
jobs. But, with the coming of the New Deal, the place of professors entered a new era of prestige and high-level activity. As had
been the case during the Progressive era, academicians and experts
were drafted into government service.

The professoriat rode high during Franklin D. Roosevelt's years
of economic recovery, and its stock skyrocketed during World War
II and the nation's dependence on technological and scientific superiority. It may well have been part of the penalty for this prominence that the Red hunt of the McCarthy era turned with such
venom on the professors and the campuses. As Cold War hysteria
gripped the country, national frustration over what seemed to be
a rising tide of communism and Soviet power in much of the

world once again singled out the exposed world of academia as a convenient scapegoat.

The attack was powerful. It may have been blunted a little by the fact that in 1940 the American Association of University Professors had issued its statement on academic freedom and tenure. Fundamental to its effort to create a sense of political as well as economic security was its insistence that "academic tenure in its freedom aspect is fundamental for the protection of the rights of the teacher in teaching and of the student to freedom of learning."

It was a far from radical definition. In fact, it clearly aimed at reassuring those who tended to see Red at the idea of unlimited professorial freedom. Thus, the statement said that "the teacher is entitled to freedom in the classroom in discussing his subject, but he should be careful not to introduce into his teaching controversial matter which has no relation to his subject"—an oddly purist, if not archaic, view of university instruction. Written at a time of considerable insecurity, it was a good deal less sweeping than the guidelines set down by Jefferson when he had written, in a letter to William Roscoe, in 1820: "This institution [the university] will be based on the illimitable freedom of the human mind. For here we are not afraid to follow the truth wherever it may lead, nor to tolerate any error so long as reason is free to combat it."

In the 1940s, however, a great many Americans appeared to be afraid that the truth might threaten their peace of mind. Between 1945 and 1950, the A.A.U.P.'s committee on academic freedom had to deal with 227 major cases of attacks on, or violations of, campus freedom. In his final report to Harvard's Board of Overseers, President James B. Conant found it necessary to write:

> There are no known adherents of the Communist Party on our staff, and I do not believe there are any disguised communists either. But even if there were, the damage that would be done to the spirit of the academic community by an investigation aimed at finding a crypto-communist would be far greater than any conceivable harm such a person might do.

Although such political rabble-rousers as the late Senator Joseph R. McCarthy led the witch-hunt, the danger to academic freedom sprang in large measure from more deep-seated fears and prejudices even among highly educated Americans.

The popular tide of reaction and suspicion challenged the foundations of academic autonomy most severely at the public universities. In 1940, Bertrand Russell, the eminent British philosopher, was appointed to the faculty of the College of the City of New York by unanimous vote of the Board of Higher Education. But William T. Manning, the politically powerful bishop of the Protestant Episcopal Church, denounced Russell as "a recognized propagandist against both religion and morality, and who specially defends adultery." Other clergymen and politicians, including the city council, joined the fight against Russell, and Mrs. Jean Kay, a taxpayer, allowed her name to be used in a suit before the State Supreme Court.

Judge John E. McGeehan, representing the prejudices and provincialism of the day, declared the appointment illegal on the astonishing grounds that Russell was an alien and that the board had no right to appoint any faculty member who had not been subjected to a competitive examination. To underscore his displeasure, Judge McGeehan accused the board of having created a "chair of indecency" by appointing a man whose books he considered filled with "immoral and salacious doctrines." To make matters worse—illustrating the power of these behind-the-scenes pressures—the city's corporation counsel, who had been charged by the board with Russell's defense, suddenly deserted the cause and scuttled all efforts to appeal the case.

Although more grotesque than other assaults on academic freedom, the Bertrand Russell case was merely the beginning of a decade of similar trouble. A classic, but by no means isolated, battle was fought at the University of California at Berkeley, where President Robert Gordon Sproul, trying to appease a legislative committee, submitted to the demands for the imposition of a loyalty oath. The issue split the faculty and led to a counterrebellion by Berkeley's Chancellor Clark Kerr, a strong-minded civil libertarian with an unassailable Quaker conscience, who refused to dismiss faculty members for refusal to sign the oath.

Eventually, the forces of freedom prevailed. The oath requirement was rescinded after Governor (later Supreme Court Chief Justice) Earl Warren redressed the liberal–conservative balance of the Board of Regents. One year after it had been eliminated, the California State Supreme Court declared the oath requirement unconstitutional. Before the dismal chapter was closed, however, a number of prominent and able faculty members had left the Berkeley campus in protest.

While President Pusey stood his ground at Harvard, backed by his trustees and three hundred years of high visibility and esteem, other institutions, less self-confident and in fear of losing financial support, caved in. Faculty members were dismissed or suspended, pending the outcome of investigations by a variety of committees.

Not all threats to academic freedom during the 1950s came from the self-appointed superpatriots. The universities had allowed themselves to be excessively dominated by governmental research policies, many of which demanded a secrecy that is incompatible with the free exchange of ideas. On many campuses, the federal portion of the budget had come to amount to more than half of the total, and in the case of such research-oriented universities as the Massachusetts Institute of Technology it had grown to nearly eighty percent.

It was in the strong institutions, however, that the academic leaders were generally better able to resist undue official interference. Harvard's President Conant had been among the few academic leaders who had never been easy about secrecy on campus—perhaps because of his experience as an academic scientist intimately involved with atomic energy research in World War II. In his 1946 annual report, Conant warned: "In time of peace I think it highly inadvisable for a university to undertake the type of work which was done during the war, namely, secret research or development. All such research in peacetime should be done in government establishments or by contract with industry."

When the Massachusetts legislature tried to force M.I.T. to dismiss a professor with alleged Communist sympathies, Dr. J. A. Stratton, the provost, replied that, "despite actions that we find impossible to condone, despite an apparent insensitivity to the good name of the Institute," the professor in question would be kept in his post.

Tenure, Dr. Stratton insisted, remained a vital foundation of academic freedom, and the principle was so crucial that it had to be upheld "at the price of retaining in our midst an occasional member whose opinions may be unpopular and at times distasteful." Reminiscent of Jefferson's original definition, Dr. Stratton warned that, even in the face of considerable risk, such tenured appointments must be upheld "as a monument to the safety with which error of opinion may be tolerated where reason is left free to combat it."

It was not until the 1970s, when conservative forces once again tried to gain the upper hand and economic crisis forced the reduction of university staffs, that tenure was subjected to new attack. This time moreover the assault was joined by some left–liberal voices who saw tenure as an obstacle to the more rapid admission of racial minorities and women to faculty positions. But, once again, efforts to undermine the professoriat's security were opposed by spokesmen for some of the nation's leading institutions. And many university administrators, who viewed with some alarm the fact that about ten percent of all university faculty members had, by the 1970s, joined teachers unions, were afraid that any weakening of protective tenure would speed teacher unionization. Tenure to them suddenly seemed the lesser evil.

Between the expansionist creation of the land-grant colleges and the next period of dramatic growth following World War II, higher education had stabilized sufficiently to engage in the luxury of experimentation. Dissatisfaction had been building up for some time, but without any sharp focus. In the early 1900s, a Yale undergraduate commented on his lecture courses: "Instead of being a person . . . I am now merely a suit of clothes pinned together by four of five seat numbers." (The cyclical nature of dissatisfaction and reform in American education becomes evident when it is recalled how much that student's complaint resembles the angry charge of his successors at Berkeley in 1964 who compared themselves to numbers on computer print-outs.)

Even at Harvard, the cradle of the elective system, President Lowell expressed concern, at the beginning of his term in 1909, that students seemed neither intellectually nor socially as well-rounded as might be wished.

Almost by way of a preview, Columbia gave premature academic expression to the new search for intellectual cohesion in 1919 when it launched a course in Contemporary Civilization as a means of bringing all students together—an incipient challenge to the concept of the elective systems. Ironically, the program had grown out of a special course on "war aims," a mixture of intellectual propaganda and genuine concern for social goals. "As early as possible," the prospectus had said, "young men should be acquainted with the facts and problems which are the common property and common responsibility of their generation. . . ." It was a course and a requirement that eventually was to become the model for general education programs throughout the country.

The precise origins of the counterrevolution are not clear. There were, however, signs of a growing feeling, particularly during the period of disillusionment after World War I, that, whatever the elective system had offered by way of greater freedom, it lacked in providing a sense of direction. Intended to free students from the tyranny of a prescribed curriculum, it left them without any clear understanding of their own place in the larger scheme of things, expert only in their own specialty and strangers to the goals and activities of those around them. The collegiate experience opened up a peephole instead of a panorama. The malaise of what came to be known as the Lost Generation, adrift in the aimless affluence of the twenties, suggested serious flaws in society that were reflected in a collegiate system that had provided both leaders and followers wanting in intellectual stamina and purpose.

The counterrevolution against the elective system did not begin from any organized center of new thinking. It flared up almost simultaneously in many different parts of the country, and it took a wide variety of different forms of rebellion against similar conditions. Most had in common a search for a new, shared purpose and philosophy.

In 1931, Robert Maynard Hutchins earned for himself a reputation as education's "boy wonder" when he took over the presidency of the University of Chicago at age thirty. Hutchins was sharply critical of the American high school which, he felt, unlike the model of the German *Gymnasium,* failed to give students a thorough grounding in the humanities on which to base subsequent specialization. Attacking the old problem with a new strategy, he opened the doors of the undergraduate college to students who had completed their sophomore year in high school and offered them an integrated liberal education, thus making the last two years of high school concurrent with the first two years of college. The two upper years subsequently were devoted to specialization at the university.

While the concept of the early admission to college and the unified, prescribed curriculum was radical in terms of academic administration, the content of the two Hutchins-dominated years was, in fact, ideologically a conservative return to more classical learning. It was based on the rediscovery of the great books and foundations of Western civilization—an attempt to generate a sense of history and belonging. A shared knowledge of the past was to create in the young the capacity for original ideas in the future.

The elective system had given students an almost completely free hand. Some had been merely interested in a degree, a chance to get by with "gentlemen's grades" in a collection of snap courses. Others concentrated on turning themselves into experts in narrow specialties. Now the Chicago plan, expanding on the single Columbia course in Contemporary Civilization, demanded extensive work in a common core of prescribed studies.

Within a few years, the revolt moved east. In 1937, Columbia expanded its earlier experimentation into a two-year requirement in general education. (It was to become a nationwide model until it fell victim to the next counterrevolution in the 1960s.) St. John's College in Annapolis, Maryland, revised its entire plan of study, basing its curriculum primarily on the Great Books. Whereas the teachers and the books were old, the methods brought to the approach were, if not new, clearly different from those of the nineteenth-century tradition. The seminar and individual tutorial became central to the student's activities, supplemented by lectures and experimentation in laboratories. It was essentially a rediscovery of Aristotle, Plato, and the Oxford–Cambridge tradition.

Elsewhere, the revolution took a different course. The so-called "progressive" colleges—such as Bennington and Goddard, in Vermont; Antioch, in Ohio; Sarah Lawrence, in New York; Reed College, in Oregon; and a number of others—were equally outspoken in their opposition to prevailing practice; but instead of turning to the classics and to long-forgotten traditions, they adopted the ideas of the man who had changed the course of elementary and secondary education—John Dewey.

Even though the tactics of Chicago and St. John's differed almost militantly from those of the progressive colleges, it is possible in retrospect to trace convergences between the two reform currents which were not apparent to their original advocates. Two quotations illustrate this point:

"The St. John's curriculum," wrote its founders,

> is seeking to convey to the students an understanding of basic problems that man has to face at all times. In doing that it may help the students to discover a new kind of historical perspective and let them perceive through all the historical shifts and changes the permanence and ever-present gravity of human issues.

Compare that prospectus with this passage from Dewey's *A Common Faith:*

> The things in civilization we most prize are not of ourselves. They exist by grace of the doings and sufferings of the continuous human community in which we are a link. Ours is the responsibility of conserving, transmitting, rectifying and expanding the heritage of values we have received that those who come after us may receive it more solid and secure, more widely accessible and more generously shared than we have received it. . . .

At Chicago and St. John's reformers believed that the main task was to put an end to fragmentation. They looked for unity and cohesion. But they also felt that each student would bring to the task so much individuality that peaks of originality would naturally rise out of the common ground of scholarship.

The progressives, on the other hand, aimed at much the same results—a balance between independence and cohesion—by starting out from the opposite direction. The stress was on the new mechanics of teaching. Initially, at least, hostility to the lecture was almost pathological. Instead of introducing all students to the same areas of scholarship and expecting each to emerge with individual conclusions, the progressives hoped that each student would follow an individual path to the same conclusion of basic values and principles.

In another interesting progressive and characteristically American, departure, Antioch applied Dewey's theory that life experience and school learning should not be kept apart. This stream of the reform movement led to two important concepts: the total educational experience in a self-governing college community, with the students assuming substantial powers and responsibilities in the management of the campus; and the merging of academic learning with practical experience in the off-campus world of work. The device used to accomplish this was variously known as the "field period," the "cooperative plan," or the "work-study" program.

It was no accident that Antioch stood in the forefront of the educational reform movement. Its first president, from 1853 to 1859, had been Horace Mann, the New England pioneer of public education, who had left Massachusetts determined to carry his ideals west into the heartland of America. It was at Antioch that he gave visibility to his daring concepts of education and of society—not only in strictly academic terms but also through a display of an egalitarianism that was still radical in his time. Long before such principles were widely adopted, he welcomed to Antioch students without regard to sex, creed, or color. He appointed women to the faculty and assured them of full equality with their male colleagues—well before the impact of the first feminist reform groups and even ahead of the founding of most of the women's colleges.

Mann had deliberately created a college community where the total intellectual and physical progress of each student was to be judged more important than grades and credits. Before his death, he admonished the last of his graduating classes: "Be ashamed to die until you have won some victory for humanity."

Like progressive schools, progressive colleges have always been subjected to a measure of hostility. The progressive label, instead of being appraised on educational grounds, has often aroused suspicions of political radicalism. "Permissiveness," associated with the progressive approach, is a red flag to conservative bulls. Yet, despite the strident rhetoric against progressive ideas, and particularly against Dewey, many of the progressive colleges' specific tactics—particularly their stress on seminars and independent study —subsequently became part of all American higher education.

The main thrust of the reform movement that began with Columbia's early effort to recreate a shared purpose and intellectual common ground, however, still had to await action by traditional elite universities. In 1946, Harvard published its report on *General Education in a Free Society,* to be known in academia as the Red Book for the color of its binding rather than for its radical intent. As a blueprint, it did little by way of pioneering, but it had the total effect of making the general education movement respectable. "General and special education are not, and must not be placed in competition with each other," the report said, thus spelling out a classically conciliatory approach to two perpetually opposite views.

The Harvard approach was a compromise between the progressive and the Chicago–St. John's reforms. Specialization was still served by elective courses, while general education came to be safeguarded by such courses as "The Great Texts of Literature" in the humanities, "Western Thought and Institutions" in the social sciences, and similar broad courses in the sciences. More important than the specific course offerings themselves was the invention of the "distribution requirement"—making each student include a certain number of courses from each of the three major areas, the humanities, the social sciences, and the natural sciences. Harvard, which had given birth to the elective system at an earlier reform stage, now created a diplomatically disguised merger of requirements and electives.

Harvard's imprint gave general education the respectability that the progressive reforms never managed to achieve. During the 1950s, general education became accepted throughout the country, and within a decade the counterrevolution had become the standard pattern. Before long, the new movement faced the eternal dilemma of all successful reforms—respectability. Imitation of an initially sound scheme led to its gradual reduction to a level of mediocre routine. General education came to mean "generalized." Faculty members, absorbed with their specialized research, let the general education courses deteriorate. What had begun as an effort to pull together the scattered knowledge of electives often ended up as a smattering of ignorance.

In the large universities, new requirements were often relegated to the listlessness of large lectures, followed by reluctant rehash in "sections" presided over by the academic slave-labor of graduate assistants. Thus they furnished an ideal target for the disaffected student rebels of the 1960s. Amid demands for a socially and ideologically "relevant" education, it was natural that stale requirements would become symbolic of the need for a new, more radical reform movement.

Symptomatic of a shift in the intellectual center of gravity, the search for new answers this time was led, not by Harvard nor even by rebels in the East, but by Berkeley, symbol of the national trend to giant campuses—Clark Kerr, as Berkeley's Chancellor, had coined the descriptive term "multiversity." When the battle smoke cleared, after the massive student uprising at Berkeley in 1964, the document that achieved a ceasefire by promising reforms would best be described as a carefully camouflaged return to the elective system, with pledges of an institutional open mind to experimentation and to student participation in the decision-making process. The memories of few campus observers stretched back far enough to realize that what was being hailed as a leap into the future seemed in fact merely another example of the cyclical nature of higher education reforms.

Although much reform rhetoric attacked the impersonality of large institutions, a small but poignant episode at Berkeley suggested that the counterrevolution against Bigness was never powerful enough to recapture the lost Shangri-la of an earlier day. Joseph Tussman, a professor of philosophy at Berkeley, responded dramatically to the chorus of complaints about modern education's remoteness from humane values. Together with a small group of other faculty members, he created a college within the liberal arts college within the giant university with its 27,000 students. Under the Tussman plan, the first two collegiate years of this small, voluntary group of some 150 students would be spent entirely in an in-depth exploration of such ideas as liberty, war, peace, and the traditions of justice. Though a communal arrangement, the controls of scholarship were to be firmly in the hands of senior faculty temporarily divorced from all departmental responsibilities and all research demands.

Once again, a reformer had borrowed heavily from the classical tradition of scholarship, from the cozy cohesion of a St. John's and from the communal concept of the progressives. But, despite initial enthusiasm, the strong pull of academic departments and the lure of the more cosmopolitan modern academic world preordained the experiment's failure within a few years of its inception. As the brave scheme folded, despite the loyalty of many of its sponsors, Professor Tussman surveyed the scene and said: "What students are now asking for [in terms of relevant courses] is largely bunk, but they'll win and get it."

The essentially conservative experiment at Berkeley had failed. The academic departments' response to the dissatisfied students was what Tussman had predicted. Requirements were dropped by way of appeasement. A decade after the revolt in California and its subsequent spread eastward, toward the end of the sixties, as far as Harvard, the cycle had run its course—and so had the golden age of the universities.

For several decades, universities had been in the center of the great issues of their time. They had made possible great scientific and technological revolutions. They helped propel the United States into the atomic age and toward the conquest of space. They had finally responded to the demand by the radical minorities for educational equality.

Toward the end of the 1960s the scientifically and socially compelling demands on the universities had begun to subside. More than two decades of steady expansion—marked first by the enrollment revolution of the post–World War II G.I. Bill of Rights and subsequently by the postwar baby boom—had come to an end. Like the closing of the frontier, the prospect of a long period of no-growth, so foreign to the American psyche, sapped the optimism and self-confidence of the academic community. A conservative political current, given ideological and administrative expression by President Richard M. Nixon, together with a faltering economy, sent the universities into the tailspin of an intellectual as well as financial depression.

Within a few years, the egalitarian exuberance that spawned a brief vision of a triumphant "greening of America," without much need for competitive academic rigor, gave away to fears that economic retrenchment would once again place a high premium on competition for achievement, grades, and jobs. The humanitarian revulsion against a cutthroat contest had, during the post-Berkeley reform era, replaced competitive grading with such substitute devices as pass–fail or credit–no credit. But a new generation, faced with a scarcity of jobs, grudgingly rediscovered the work ethic and the need for competition.

The absence of strong leadership figures in higher education—the lack of an Eliot, a Harper, a Hutchins, or a Conant—may have contributed to the shortening of the reform cycle. The changes that had taken place were largely the result of pressures by the amorphous mass of students and by outside forces, rather than of reforms planned by charismatic personalities or persuasive educational philosophers. The dearth of national leadership in politics—the lack of any figure of the stature of a Woodrow Wilson or the two Roosevelts, let alone a Lincoln or a Jefferson—was reflected in academia. Committees had replaced individuals. The trauma of the student rebellion and of the subsequent fiscal crisis had ushered in the age of the crisis managers in the university presidency.

John W. Gardner, one of academia's last strong personalities, before he turned his attention to the political arena, had complained of the menace of an "antileadership virus." Improvisation replaced reform. The system of requirements and of general education had given way, under the gun of the student revolt, to something chaotic resembling the elective system. Then, in the 1970s, with pressure from a faltering economy, requirements began to seep back, but this time without any discernible effort to create new patterns or even a superficial rationale for deliberate change.

In general, the last quarter of the twentieth century began in an academic atmosphere of uncertainty and even fear. Following the Harvard-dominated Administration of John F. Kennedy, with its liberal–intellectual tinge, and the expansionist populism of Lyndon B. Johnson's "Great Society," universities found themselves relegated to a minor and defensive role when President Nixon aimed his appeal at the supposedly anti-intellectual "silent majority."

Johnson's dramatic adoption of the civil rights slogan "We Shall Overcome" had briefly given new impetus to the egalitarian drive. In 1970, in the aftermath of racial confrontations, the giant City University of New York, the largest of all urban universities, with sixteen campuses and over 200,000 students, announced that it would henceforth open its doors to all high-school graduates, regardless of their grades. Open admission became the latest in a long history of tests of American mass education.

The new policy was introduced amid heated and continuing controversy. To opponents, the plan was tantamount to the destruction of academic standards. Its advocates hailed it as a decisive step toward equality and social justice.

In reality, open admission was not a new concept. Until the 1950s, many of the mid-Western state universities had operated under a legislative mandate to admit all high-school graduates. California had, for almost two decades, practiced open admission of all its high-school graduates to a network of university centers, state colleges, and two-year community colleges.

New York's new venture, however, differed from the earlier versions on two counts: the university committed itself to a large measure of remedial education designed not only to admit great numbers but to help them succeed—a far cry from the Midwestern "revolving door" admission that often was almost as quick in pushing students out as in taking them in; and New York's new liberal commitment was unmistakably aimed at opening the doors to the nonwhite minorities. As a result, objections to the plan came both from traditionally anti-egalitarian conservatives and from those who feared inundation by Black and Puerto Rican students. (In fact, open admission brought into the university a greater number of underprepared whites from the lower socioeconomic strata than had been anticipated.)

Even as the controversy concerning the effects of the latest extension of higher education opportunities continued to rage, it became apparent that across the nation the expansionist era was drawing to a close. Nixon shrewdly exploited the new anti-intellectual current. At least for the foreseeable future—well into the 1980s—the prospects were for retrenchment. As the economy ran out of resources and optimism, assumptions of unlimited growth were challenged on all fronts. The population curve itself appeared to make it inevitable that higher education would have to adjust to a new era of no-growth. In 1973, the nation's elementary school enrollment had declined by 2.2 percent. Thus, the handwriting was on college walls as well.

Throughout most of the 1960s, scholarly meetings had been the scenes of frantic shopping for academic talent. Deans and department chairmen had virtually fallen over each other trying to bag promising new Ph.D.'s for their faculties, while university presidents raided each others' campuses for the cream of the professoriat, as Chicago's Harper had raided rival campuses in an earlier era of scarcity.

By the beginning of the 1970s the professor's and Ph.D.'s seller's market had evaporated. The talent hunt was over. Ph.D.'s were a glut on the market. Part of the reason was the amazing success of the academic production line. In 1959, the universities' total output had amounted to 9,400 Ph.D.'s; ten years later, annual production had risen to 26,000.

By that time, universities had begun to drift into what the Carnegie Commission on Higher Education was to call their "new depression." Deficit-ridden and with declining federal support and decreasing research contracts, universities were faced with the immediate need to cut expenditures. The Carnegie Commission warned that, in order to avert disaster and massive bankruptcies, colleges would have to trim their expenses by almost $10 billion by 1980, while still having to find about $16.5 billion in "new" revenues to keep abreast of inflationary costs. At least $12.5 billion would by that time have to be contributed by the federal government, compared to the approximately $3.5 billion appropriated by Washington at the time these estimates were made.

Moreover, a shrinking pool of applicants had, by 1973, begun to revive the competition between private and public colleges and universities. During the late 1940s and 1950s, when the postwar push for expansion had caught the campuses unprepared, the public sector responded enthusiastically. Obscure teachers colleges had turned themselves into university centers. States created networks of higher education systems. For the first time in American higher education history, enrollment in public institutions outnumbered that of the private sector. Although private institutions expanded as well, they did so at a much slower pace, limited both by resources and by a generally more selective approach to applicants. Before World War II, 80 percent of all students were on private campuses; by 1974, almost 80 percent were enrolled in public institutions.

As long as the oversupply of students lasted, relations between the public and private sectors had remained tolerably pleasant. But, by the beginning of the 1970s, old feuds erupted again, reminiscent of the days when the early land-grant colleges had to brave the social and intellectual snobbery of the established institutions, the majority of them privately financed.

This time, however, the issues were financial rather than social. Relatively low-tuition public campuses—and the still tuition-free City University of New York—seemed to the increasingly costly private institutions to be guilty of the sin of cutthroat competition. Spokesmen for the private sector lobbied for increased tuition in the public colleges as a means of closing the gap.

While there was widespread agreement that generous scholarships ought to continue to keep the college doors open to the poor, the threat of rising tuition now began to arouse the fears and political anger of the lower middle class. The continuing trend toward egalitarianism had all but drowned out the earlier, pre–World War I plaint that "every cook's a Ph.D. in Wisconsin"; but once again there were echoes of the warning sounded by Wisconsin's Van Hise almost a century earlier—that the university's gates must be open to the "industrious poor" so that they may be educated together with the sons and daughters of the rich.

Against the threatened closing of the educational frontier, amid pressures of ever higher tuition, social critics and educational planners sensed a challenge to the dream of a society in which education would be—in Horace Mann's words—the great equalizer between classes. While the social conscience of the rich and powerful still promised to protect the demands of the poor for equal access (demands now underscored by the newly developed political sophistication of the poor themselves), there was growing apprehension that "the industrious poor"—the children of the lower-middle-class blue-collar workers—would be squeezed out of the colleges by retrenchment and inflation.

In the 1970s such a retrogressive trend was a particularly

bitter pill for those who had barely and only recently risen above poverty. They found it harder to pay for their children's college education, just as the poor had finally managed to gain admission. But, though a divisive issue for the moment, a long view of history and politics makes it unlikely that such a threat would be allowed to go unanswered for long.

The expansive thrust may seem temporarily to have run out of steam and funds; but there is no reason to believe that the masses of that embattled lower middle class will ease up their pressure to keep the egalitarian ideal alive—for their own children. And, even though they may momentarily often be at odds with the poor, the goals of those two factions—so close to each other on the socioeconomic ladder—are essentially the same. Together, they command sufficient power to make it safe to predict that in the long run the seesawing battle between higher education's elitism and egalitarianism will not be lost by the many to the few.

9

STUDENTS: UNCERTAIN VANGUARD

$\mathcal{C}$OLLEGE STUDENTS CONSTITUTE THE most neglected, least understood element of the American community," Frederick Rudolph observed during the midsixties.

> They flow rather aimlessly in and out of our picture of the past—wholesome and frolicsome young men and women of no very certain purpose, in the process of being rounded in mysterious ways, living on the whole rather safe and uninteresting lives, conforming to rather dull standards of undergraduate thought and behavior, capable of nothing more imaginative than such a stunt, say, as leading the village cow up the stairs of the chapel tower.

Until the violent student revolt of the 1960s, Americans had alternated between ignoring and romanticizing youths. While the revolution was at its height, the history of student activism be-

came instantly conceived as a concoction of myth, wishful thinking, and ideology. Implicit was the assumption that, throughout
American history, there had been a consistent pattern of student
involvement in political, social, and economic affairs. Youth-
oriented observers suddenly discovered a trend of undergraduate
progressivism and social consciousness dating back to President
Dunster at Harvard in the seventeenth century.

The view of student life as an unbroken chronicle of riots, rebellions, and religious revivals bears little resemblance to historical reality. The sudden discovery of such a trend is the result of a
sense of guilt over the long neglect of the students' existence on
the national stage. Just as misleading as the notion of a perennial
collegiate drive for social progress is the opposite portrait, painted
by embattled traditionalists, who saw the 1960s ferment as an
unprecedented threat to campus civility. Archibald Cox was almost instantly proven wrong when, as the chief investigator of
Columbia's violent student uprising in 1968, he observed con-
descendingly that no such disgrace could ever have happened at
Harvard. (It did happen less than two years later with similar fe-
rocity.)

Equally wrong is the judgment of those who magnify modern
flare-ups by ignoring the largely unrecorded or forgotten earlier
episodes of strife. In the nineteenth century, for instance, Harvard's President Quincy "was plagued with the problem of nonconformity of dress by the students." Indeed, Quincy on one occasion called the police to deal with rebellious students, and at
least one observer complained that even then the police were
"often guilty of needless brutality and lack of tact" in dealing
with students.

That charge was repeated almost verbatim in 1970 when Harvard's president Pusey called in the police to drive student rebels
from their stronghold in the occupied administration building.
Defenders of police action in Quincy's days, moreover, sounded
not at all unfamiliar when they complained that "students make
it a point to wantonly insult and exasperate the peelers [then the
equivalent of "pigs" as a description of the lawmen] on every occasion when it can be done with safety."

It is as dangerous to generalize about students' political involvement in the past as it is in our time. Some insight into undergrad-

uate realities of an earlier age is offered by O. A. Brinsted, an undergraduate at Yale during the 1830s who had attended Cambridge and visited other European universities as well. "The majority of highly educated young men under any government," he wrote,

> are opposed to the spirit in which that government is administered. Hasty and imperfect as the conclusion is, it certainly does hold good of many countries. . . . [The student] sees the defects in the government of his country; he exaggerates them with the ardor of youth, and takes that side which promises to remedy them, without reflecting at what cost the remedy may have to be purchased.

Students on the Colonial campuses were frequently younger than today's undergraduates. Harvard's records indicate that some boys were admitted as young as thirteen years of age. A speaking and reading knowledge of Latin and familiarity with Greek vocabulary and grammar were prerequisites. College rules were strict. In the 1640s harsh discipline was thought necessary "for the perpetual preservation" of the scholars' "welfare" and "government." The religious orientation of the colleges and parental demands that their children's spiritual as well as physical needs be catered to served to buttress such discipline.

As recorded in Josiah Quincy's *History of Harvard,* some of these rules were spelled out as follows:

> Everyone shall so exercise himself in reading the Scriptures twice a day, that they be ready to give an account of their proficiency therein. . . .
> . . . They shall honour as their parents, magistrates, elders, tutors and aged persons, by being silent in their presence (except they be called on to answer). . . .
> None shall, under any pretence whatsoever, frequent the company and society of such men as lead an ungirt or dissolute life. . . . Nor shall any, without the license of the overseers of the college . . . his parents or guardians go out to another town. . . .
> No scholar shall buy, sell or change anything, to the value of sixpence, without the allowance of his parents, guardians, or tutors. . . .

The scholars shall never use their mother tongue, except
in public exercises of oratory, or such like, they be called to
make them in English. . . .

"Dunster's rules," as they were called, were accompanied by
a long list of fines for every transgression from tarrying out of
town without leave, fetching prohibited liquors, and rudeness
during meals to firing guns or pistols in the college yard.

Although thought to be modeled after their English counter-
parts, early American colleges never truly attained the ideal of a
community of scholars. The campus was closer to the restrictive
atmosphere of an old-fashioned boys' boarding school.

For some time, flogging remained an accepted means of discipline. When flogging was replaced by the "gentler" device of
boxing in 1718, the measure of such progress was that the offender
was to kneel at the feet of his tutor to allow himself to be slapped
on the side of his face. The custom was finally dropped from the
regulations in 1767.

The gradual elimination of physical punishment reflected a
change of spirit from stern Calvinism to a mood of greater freedom
in a society where young men could make their way in the world
without attending college if the campus seemed too oppressive.
Parents, too, fell in line with the new mood. In 1718, a father told
that his son had been flogged, reacted in anger: "I rather have my
son abused as a man . . . [than as] a beast."

If the colleges were to survive, they would have to adjust to
society's changing attitudes. As Samuel Eliot Morison suggests
in his description of early Harvard: "The beginnings of the college were not happy. Nathaniel Eaton, the first head, had every
qualification on paper for a successful president; but he used the
rod more freely than college students were willing to put up with
even in those rough days. . . ."

Throughout the Colonial period and continuing until after the
Civil War, records show periodic student uprisings, frequently
sparked by atrocious food. Henry Thoreau's grandfather is reported to have confronted a tutor with the demand: "Behold our
Butter stinketh and we cannot eat thereof. Now give us we pray
thee Butter that stinketh not." In 1822, Augustus Torrey, an un-

dergraduate, wrote: "Goose for dinner. Said to have migrated to this country with our ancestors."

Food was not the only source of complaint. During the early period, student dissatisfaction, with occasional bursts of rebellion, arose from the severity of existing behavioral restraints, including the always implicit and occasionally explicit prohibition against involvement in the outside world.

Perhaps because campus life was essentially grim and oppressive—faculty members who tried to be friendly with students were subject to contempt and suspicion—undergraduates created their own customs and rituals to brighten the daily routine by way of customs outside faculty control.

"Fagging" was one such custom. Imported from England, it required freshmen to act as unpaid servants to upperclassmen, reminiscent of the use of batmen by army officers. Apparently, the system was still in force at Yale during the 1790s when Lyman Beecher recalled that, shortly after his arrival, he was "sent for to a room so full of tobacco smoke you could not see across it. There I was asked all manner of questions, in English and Latin and received all manner of solemn advice. Then Forbes, a big fellow, took me as his fag."

Gradually, fagging faded away, but long after some college authorities had tried unsuccessfully to abolish it during the early Colonial era. At Yale, it was finally eliminated in Timothy Dwight's administration at the end of the eighteenth century, signifying perhaps the advent of a more democratic social order.

More durable was another collegiate ritual—hazing. This practice of subjecting freshmen to all sort of indignities and endurance tests has survived in some places until today, even though it periodically turned dangerous enough to worry the college authorities to the point of outlawing it. Loosely defined as an initiation rite, hazing has ranged from trivial practical jokes to elaborate ceremonial tributes. Time and again, the practice has degenerated into rough and even sadistic treatment of newcomers, resulting in serious injuries and even death. Although more familiar in the twentieth century as part of fraternity initiations, hazing in the early days tended to be associated with more general admission into a new class.

Writing about those early days from the "modern" vantage point of 1900, Henry Sheldon commented on the ritual in *Student Life and Customs:*

> Usages so rough that they would not for a moment be tolerated elsewhere continued to flourish in institutions which were expected to send forth the intellectual leaders of the next generation. . . . It is difficult now from the evidence at hand to estimate just how much physical injury was wrought by these customs, because it was to the interest of all parties concerned in such affairs to keep the evidence below the surface.

College administrators, aware of the dangers involved in student-run hazing, often institutionalized the ritual into organized contests between the freshmen and sophomores, and sometimes local noncollege youths joined in the fray. In its more genteel and sporting form, such annual initiation fights have survived until today as a means of creating campus spirit and class pride.

In the battle against boredom and the search for inspiration and intellectual as well as spiritual stimulation, American students have traveled back and forth between profane and sacred escapism. The first half of the nineteenth century, for example, saw repeated outbursts of evangelical "revivals" among undergraduates. The diary of a student at Amherst in the 1850s offers this testimony: "Many are giving up the foul feasts of tobacco, and instead of the curse from almost every room may now be heard the voice of prayer. It is wonderful to perceive the holy calm that reigns around us." (The pendulum has never stopped swinging between curses and piety. After the rebellious 1960s, with their delight in verbal obscenity, students on many campuses in the early 1970s threw themselves with similar abandon into an endless variety of religious revival movements, giving rise to the new designation of "Jesus freaks.")

For religious nonconformists, life on the early campuses could often be a severe trial. Not to be "converted" at a time when the mass of students had espoused prayer and piety was as difficult as being a country boy among a majority of city sophisticates. Rutherford B. Hayes, later to become the nineteenth President of the United States, found himself one of only ten students at Kenyon College in 1839 who had not yet "changed." In a depressed letter home, he wrote: "Every single one of my best friends are 'gone' as it is called. I have but little hope I shall be among them. If I am not, I fear I can never spend as happy a time in Kenyon as I have."

It was, of course, not merely the students' pressure that then created an atmosphere of religious compulsion. Although the "revivals" were often sponsored by undergraduate religious societies, teachers considered compulsory chapel one of the best ways to exercise moral and spiritual supervision, and the practice survived well into the twentieth century. At so secular an urban institution as New York University, students in the 1930s were known to "hire" stand-ins for 25 cents a session to fill their seats during compulsory chapel.

Thus, it is hardly surprising that these religious requirements flourished in the early nineteenth century. Historian Dixon Ryan Fox describes the practice at Union College:

> . . . [The] ringing of the Chapel bell called sleepy boys to "repair in a decent and orderly manner" without running violently in the entries or down the stairs, to prayers that were to open the day. We can see the college butler on a cold pitch-black winter morning at his post beside the pulpit stairs, when the officers file in, holding his candle high so that the president may safely mount to read the scripture lesson from the sacred desk, to petition the Almighty on behalf of the little academic group, and to address to his charges such admonition as in his judgment they require,—such of each lad's attention, on penalty of a four-cent fine. . . .

But undergraduates in search of stimulation did not rely only on the physical hijinx of hazing and the spiritual solace of piety. They also sought entertainment and enlightenment in literature, perhaps to make up for a curriculum barren in the humane letters. Undergraduate literary societies flourished until well after the midnineteenth century.

Despite their exalted label, these societies were, in fact, often debating clubs. Mastery of public speaking, which often played a crucial role in students' future careers, was given little support and encouragement in classroom exercises usually confined to rote learning and repetition.

It was largely left to the literary societies and their libraries (which often contained more books than those operated by the colleges), the clubs, the journals, and, in Rudolph's words, the "organizations which compensated for the neglect of science, English literature, history, music and art in the curriculum" to serve the intellect. This vast developing, student-initiated extracurriculum was the students' response to the deficiencies of an outmoded classical curriculum. "It helped," concluded Rudolph, "to liberate the intellect on the American campus."

Although students were first to sense the need for change, the trend was inevitable. The cloistered view of the campus was challenged not only by the weakening hold of religion but by the growing notion that college should be useful in a young man's professional career. Though a long way from the days, in the 1950s, when advertisements would spell out how many extra dollars over a lifetime a college could promise, the seeds of a utilitarian view of higher education had already been sown.

But the American view of college, with its rustic atmosphere and its intimations of privilege, had always focused on more than study and curriculum; it was conceived as a social ladder. Social advancement was often considered at least as important as scholarly and professional achievements. As Oscar and Mary Handlin put it,

> The education administered by the college was neither totally religious nor totally professional, it was connected with the desire to adjust the individual to the society within which he would play a part. . . . Precisely how the process of socialization operated depended not only on the college as an institution, but also upon the changing structure of the society into which the individual would move and on the changing conception the individual held of himself.

Although many of the major universities, such as Columbia, Yale, and Harvard, now seem essentially urban institutions, they were founded as predominantly rustic communities before the cities began to surround and engulf them. As late as 1880, Daniel Coit Gilman found that the urban setting of Johns Hopkins University was often used as an argument against the development of an undergraduate college. To counter such objections, he urged parents to look for themselves so that they could discover "that most of the temptations to which youths are exposed may be found in the neighborhood of country colleges as well as large towns."

Yet, a romantic belief in the intrinsic educational value of rolling hills and green pastures persists to this day and is part of the literature of college fiction and college catalogues. Neither the academic success of such urban institutions as the City College of New York nor the fact that by 1920 census statistics showed that the majority of Americans lived in cities has been able to dispel the romantic myth of pastoral college life.

Somewhat ironically, it was Henry Wadsworth Longfellow who, among a minority of those who doubted the superior virtue of the rustic campus, asked: "Where should the scholar live? In solitude, or in society? In the green stillness of the country, where he can hear the heart of Nature beat, or in the dark gray town, where he can hear and feel the throbbing heart of man?" And the poet, who at the time taught at Harvard, answered "in the dark gray town." In the midnineteenth century, President Eliot exclaimed: "In spite of the familiar picture of the moral dangers which environ the student, there is no place so safe as a good college during the critical passage from boyhood to manhood." And Yale's President Noah Porter, a staunch advocate of college life, believed in its advantages even when the student's academic gains left much to be desired. Porter wrote in 1870:

> The effects [of collegiate living] are so powerful and salutory that it may well be questioned whether the education they impart does not of itself more than repay the time and money which it costs, even to those idlers at college who derive from their residence little or nothing more than these accidental or incidental advantages. . . . To many who persistently neglect the college studies, the college life is anything rather than a total loss. Even those who sink downward with no recovery, find their descent retarded.

A few years later, President Alice Freeman Palmer of Wellesley College put the romantic theory of education-by-osmosis even more succinctly: "Merely for good time, for romance, for society, college life offers unequalled opportunities." "Good times," in those days, however, were not all play. In keeping with the views of Henry F. Durant, the college's founder, all the Wellesley students were responsible for domestic work in the dormitories and kitchens—from mopping floors to hulling strawberries. Such labor, Durant believed, was "a character building device, and introduction to community life, and a curb upon any tendency to laziness or luxurious living."

Other observers were not as sure of the colleges' magic powers. President Lindsley, of the University of Nashville, said in 1848: "This is certain: that parents need never look to a college for any miraculous moral regeneration or transformation of character." But, among the majority of academic spokesmen, faith in the moral uplift provided by college life persisted throughout most of the nineteenth century. It was a faith undergirded by the notion that mental discipline was provided by a complex of theological, moral, psychological, and behavioral factors whose vagueness was more than offset by the power of popular convictions.

Briefly stated, it was the purpose of a formal collegiate education to develop the faculties of will, intellect, and emotions—attributes of a healthy soul—and keep them in proper balance.

The students' academic regimen bore this out. A typical class at Yale during the 1860s was portrayed by this description:

> In a Latin or Greek recitation one [student] may be asked to read or scan a short passage, another to translate it, a third to answer questions as to its construction, and so on. . . . The reciter is expected simply to answer the questions which are put to him, but not to ask any of his instructor, or dispute his assertions. If he has any enquiries to make, or controversy to carry on, it must be done informally, after the division has been dismissed. . . . The advance [lesson] of one day is always the review of the next, and a more perfect recitation is always expected on the second occasion; a remark which is not confined to the languages but applies equally well to all the studies of the course.

College discipline extended even to the laundry. In 1885, Princeton's faculty resolved: "That should any students continue to have their washing done in town as heretofore, it must be done under the supervision of the College Office." Only the most complete vigilance could assure an end product of moral perfection.

Even for an era when men's lives in the real world were hard and often strictly regulated by custom and religion, the paternalism that dominated the students' conduct seems oppressive. Princeton's James McCosh was led to confess: "I abhor the plan of secretly watching students by peeping through windows at night, and listening through key-holes." Long lists of required student behavior continued to be memorized and enforced, still resembling the earlier commandments that governed life at the original Harvard. But times were changing. Many professors began to find their disciplinary duties irksome and, at Yale (which for some time had required students to swear a loyalty oath to the administration) many of the rules, though still on the books, were widely ignored.

At any rate, the mental and moral discipline imposed by the colleges of that era cannot be judged by modern standards. Most of the academic leaders were clergymen. The prevalent philosophy of the day held that the harsh discipline demanded of the students would open the doors to worldly and heavenly rewards. Professions and vocations of the time also imposed strict rules of personal conduct on all their members and employees. Colleges were not institutions apart; they were the training ground for America's elite.

It is hardly surprising, under such circumstances, that there were signs of an incipient rebellion against the boredom of such oppressive attitudes. During the first half of the nineteenth century, nearly every campus experienced some flash of student revolt of varying degrees of seriousness. All involved some form of collective and organized action, either on the part of a class or even of the entire student body. No section of the country was immune. At Princeton, violence erupted in 1817 and, as one account has it, "crackers were fired, the walls were scrawled on, there was clapping, hissing, and screaming in the refectory." Those commentators of the 1960s who reacted to their decade's student unrest as if a new form of insurrection and incivility had just been invented, might have been better equipped for the events of their time had they bothered to look back at an earlier chapter in American students' history. Indeed, they might have discovered that during the 1830s and 1840s a professor was killed and armed police were required to restore order on Thomas Jefferson's idyllic campus of the University of Virginia.

At Harvard, too, the first half of the nineteenth century was punctuated with recurrent rebellions, bonfires in the yard, and even explosions in lecture rooms. In 1823, the so-called "Great Rebellion" shook the campus over the expulsion of a senior. Before it was over, forty-three seniors of a class of seventy had been expelled. One of those so disciplined was a son of John Quincy Adams.

Not unlike its successors in the late 1960s, the Harvard Corporation's nineteenth century investigators, led by Justice Story, concluded that most rioting and disturbances tended to take place with the arrival of warm weather in spring, and that distinguished body wondered whether the college might not be spared future insurrections by terminating the spring semester a bit earlier, before the sun could heat up the emotions.

Somewhat more substantial were recommendations that the student body be subdivided into classes and the college organized, for the first time, according to separate departments, giving the students a choice of some subjects. But the most immediate consequence to the students was a recommendation of considerable future impact—introduction of a rigorous academic grading system.

Much adult reaction to student unrest was harsh. But wiser heads showed a new understanding. In a letter to Harvard's George Ticknor, Thomas Jefferson wrote on July 16, 1823:

> The insubordination of our youth is now the greatest obstacle to their education. We may lessen the difficulty, perhaps, by avoiding too much government, requiring no useless observances. . . . On this head, I am anxious for information of the practices of other places, having myself had little experience of the government of youth.

"Useless observances" and petty restrictions had indeed become part of an elaborate codification. In some institutions even after

1865, the listing of such regulations required eight pages of fine print. Students were prohibited from leaving the college on Sundays without special permission. They were even barred from "loitering" in groups on what was characteristically called "college property."

Students often regarded college authorities as the enemy and occasionally treated them as such. Harvard's President Edward Everett told his brother in 1846: "Dr. Ware commences his lectures to the freshman class on Wednesday. It is necessary, I understand, to send in a proctor to protect the Professor from being pelted with chestnuts." Being treated like naughty children, students acted the part. During long hours of class recitations, they often passed the time by throwing spitballs, chalk, and other missiles at their instructor.

Student discipline was rationalized by the college's *in loco parentis* role. The ideal of protective paternalism is eloquently expressed by this letter from the president of Dickinson College to a father:

> A parent cannot but be anxious when his Child is at a Distance from him & exposed to Dangers of different kinds, but as in Educkation a certain Risk must be run, in order to gain a certain Advantage, every good Parent, as well as every good Teacher ought to be satisfied when he is taking the best means for preserving the Morals of his Child, as well as for improving his Understanding. Your son is well, tho' some few of our students have been troubled with Colds and Sore Throats.

The pledge made by General William Tecumseh Sherman, during his brief stint as president of a military college, "I shall be father to them all," was still being kept. Early in the nineteenth century, a president of Brown University reassured an anxious mother: "Though I have examined the case, I cannot find that Henry is addicted to gambling. . . ." And he assured a concerned father: "I have requested your son not to contract any other debts without my knowledge; for I find that the value of Money has not yet engaged his attention."

Faculty reaction was not always so fatherly and benign. In 1855, a professor at Davidson College delivered himself of what has long

been and still remains the recurrent view of teachers at the far
end of the generation gap, when he offered this description of the
typical student:

> Indulged, petted, and uncontrolled at home, allowed to tram-
> ple all laws, human and divine, at the preparatory school . . .
> [the student] comes to college, but too often with an un-
> disciplined mind, and an uncultivated heart, yet with exalted
> ideas of personal dignity, and a scowling contempt for lawful
> authority, and wholesome restraint. How is he to be con-
> trolled?

Students told a different story—on the rare occasions that their
views were heard, usually years later, after they had become
successful alumni. Thomas Wentworth Higginson, the distinguished Boston author, who entered Harvard around 1837 at the
age of thirteen, wrote of his college years: "We were not encouraged or even permitted to do thorough work in anything. We lived
intellectually from hand to mouth or from book to mouth, which
is worse."

The relationship between students and professors was often
strained, if not outright hostile. A member of Harvard's class of
1832 recalled the antagonism, but divided the blame almost
equally between the two factions. F. A. P. Barnard, remembering
his student days at Yale, wrote that an undergraduate "scarcely
came into mental contact with a professor before his senior year."

In a commentary on Williams College, G. Stanley Hall wrote:

> The professors seemed to us to live in splendid isolation.
> There was only a "ten-foot-pole" relation between them and
> us. I never heard of a reception to students given by any of
> them. To call on them socially was unheard of; nor did they
> visit us in our rooms. Even to linger after class to ask ques-
> tions was bad form—"boot-licking," currying favor, etc. I do
> not think that I ever met one of the professors' wives. How
> the faculty, who usually taught three hours a day, spent their
> spare time was always a mystery to us for we rarely saw them
> outside of the classroom or chapel.

There is no clearly discernible pattern of student rebellion and
involvement in off-campus politics during the early years of Amer-

ican college life. Perhaps because there were isolated instances of such involvement, many observers have commented, often in contradiction with each other, about the extent and the nature of such student activism. Samuel Eliot Morison quotes an observer of the 1770s that the students "are already taken up with politics. They have caught the spirit of liberty." Yet, shortly after the Battle of Bunker Hill, a Harvard student recorded in his diary: "Amid all the terrors of battle I was so busily engaged in Harvard Library that I never even heard of [it] . . . until it was completed." At best, the case for or against the tradition of student's political activism is inconclusive.

Some American collegians did, of course, participate in the Revolution, and several colleges were damaged during the fighting and had to be closed down. An engraving in Yale's possession shows George Welles, captain of the Student Company, defending the college buildings against the invading British on July 5, 1779. However, some observers of the action maintained that the buildings were saved less by the student militia than by the fact that the British thought them too handsome to burn. After the Revolution, and lasting until the period of the Civil War, the occasional riots, however, were directed largely against the rigidities of campus discipline and dogma.

It is difficult to get sufficient insight into the political and social views of American students for any single period to generalize about them. A case in point is the extent of Northern college students' role in the abolitionist movement. Actual response differed from institution to institution and from section to section, and it depended more on the prevailing sentiments of the community than on any collegiate doctrine. The University of Michigan operated a secret underground railroad to transport runaway slaves to Canada. Before it was banned in 1835, the Amherst College Abolition Society had enlisted one third of the local undergraduates. Charles W. Eliot (Harvard, class of 1853), while a tutor at the University, took part in an unsuccessful attempt to free a fugitive slave who had been captured by the civil authorities.

As the oppressively paternalistic attitudes toward students receded after the Civil War, the majority of undergraduates seemed to concentrate on the good life and good fellowship. The relatively few upward mobile poor were too busy improving their prospects to rock the boat. If students then spoke out on current issues at all, they seemed to reflect the opinions of their families.

One area where public policy eventually clashed with some vocal student opinion was the Land-grant Act's requirement that the universities benefiting from it must institute compulsory military training. It was an issue which affected students directly. The University of Wisconsin's student newspaper insisted that to oppose militarism was in the American tradition. In 1886 a violent protest ended with a foray by students into a military storehouse and the theft of stocks and barrels to sabotage the army training program. Heated protests over the issue at the University of Illinois ended with the president's resignation.

In general, however, most students appear simply to have felt the cheerless resignation expressed later by James Thurber at Ohio State University:

> We drilled with old Springfield rifles and studied the tactics of the Civil War even though the World War [I] was going on at the time. At 11 o'clock each morning thousands of freshmen and sophomores used to deploy over the campus, moodily creeping up on the old chemistry building. It was good training for the kind of warfare that was waged at Shiloh but it had no connection with what was going on in Europe.

A generation later, during the pacifist days of the 1930s, undergraduates at New York University were to toss pebbles and empty bottles under the feet of parading R.O.T.C. detachments to disrupt their exercises and protest their military image. And, in the 1960s, the antiwar protestors literally drove the R.O.T.C. off dozens of campuses, as "Off Rotsie!" became one of the key demands of the undergraduate rebellion. (By 1973, a number of university administrations who only four years earlier had expelled the military under pressure from the student rebels invited the R.O.T.C. back to academia—though generally without the benefit of academic credit.)

The ideals of a free society were hard to reconcile with the oppressive discipline that had so long governed young Americans in the colleges—but spokesmen for the establishment tried to do just that. President Thomas Cooper of South Carolina College, for example, appears to have sensed the contradiction between his Jeffersonian principles and the college's rigid code. He came up with this quaint formula: "Republicanism is good: but the rights of boys and girls are the offspring of Democracy gone mad." (Similar arguments were to be heard again when, in the 1960s, new demands were made to define and uphold students' rights, this time on the high school level.) One of Cooper's professors, an émigré political economist, tried conscientiously to enforce the rules. In pursuit of a student carrying off a stolen turkey, he stumbled and fell into a pile of bricks. As he emerged, he muttered: *"Mein Gott! All this for two thousand dollars!"*

The gradual rejection, halfway past the nineteenth century, of the innate depravity of men—and boys—along with the growing reluctance of students to submit to the oppressive regimen—was beginning to make a difference. In a society predicated on faith in man's essential goodness, colleges could not continue to function as a mixture of reformatory and nursery. Advanced thinkers increasingly talked about a goal of harmony and community. Harvard's President Eliot was among those with a new vision: ". . . A real comradeship in scholarly adventures, no matter what subject the group may be pursuing. That intimate comradeship involves small use of the lecture method and large use of the small-class method, where the intercourse between teacher and student is conversational, intimate and stimulating to all participants."

What unfortunately beclouded these visions of the academic community was the fact that they coincided with the rapid growth of enrollments and the newly dominant model of the German universities' specialized scholarship. Neither trend was designed to further a closer rapport between faculty and students. After a tour of fourteen campuses in 1909, Edwin E. Slosson, a journalist, saw lack of personal contact as the "weak point" of the great universities and even of some of the smaller colleges.

"It is partly due," Slosson diagnosed what was to be a persistent malady for decades to come,

> to . . . the development of a new school of teachers who detest teaching, who look upon students as a nuisance, and class work as a waste of time. . . . In Harvard the adviser is supposed to make the acquaintance of the Freshmen in his

charge, but this is generally a perfunctory relation, sometimes no more personal than the interpretation of the curriculum of railroad trains to the passenger in a union station by the Bureau of Information. . . . Teacher and pupil were not even on opposite ends of the same log. They were at opposite ends of a telephone working only one way.

Half a century later, with the campuses grown to the gigantic size of a Berkeley with 27,000 students, similar dissatisfaction was expressed, through the portrayal of the student as a computer print-out: "Don't fold, spindle, or mutilate."

Although there is a strong element of constancy in the conflict between students' and faculties' basic interests, real changes were to take place in the social background and outlook of the undergraduates. In Colonial colleges, the collegiates were almost exclusively the sons of the upper and upper-middle classes, with only a token representation from below—just enough to justify the American view of the college as an instrument of social mobility. Before the Revolution, John Adams complained about the practice of "ranking" students according to their fathers' place in the community. And, although the practice was abandoned soon after, Harriet Martineau reported in the 1830s that the aristocratic dominance at Harvard was modified only slightly by "a few breezes of such democratic inspiration as issue from the schoolhouses of some of the country districts."

Pressures were nevertheless building up toward greater egalitarianism. Just as Horace Mann saw public school education as "the great equalizer," voices were being heard to demand that the campuses do their share in building a nation which, if not classless, would encourage bright and industrious young men from lowly origins to use education as the ladder on which to climb to success and status. The American college, said Lyman Beecher, the minister, must "bring the children of the humblest families of the nation a full and fair opportunity . . . giving thus to the nation the select talents and powers of her entire population."

Unfortunately, the physical arrangements of the campuses did little to provide the environment that might encourage a happy and harmonious camaraderie between divergent social groups. There was as yet little effort to provide organized recreation or sports. The prevailing atmosphere suggested a belief that boys coming together for an extended period of joint study were most readily transformed into educated men by being confined to uncomfortable and often unheated dormitories and herded into dining halls where they would be subjected to the same poorly prepared food. Thus hardened, they would go forth to take their place of leadership in their communities, vocations, and professions.

Academic leaders appeared to have closed their minds to the risk that such conditions would periodically produce riots and rebellion. They were even less aware of the fact that in such an environment the divisions of class, caste, and religion would often be aggravated. Contrary to the idyllic vision of the rich and poor forming one fraternity of young scholars, the harsh sink-or-swim social atmosphere of the campuses often prevented such blending.

A different kind of fraternity was created, not by the colleges, but by the students, perhaps as an antidote to the lack of amenities provided by the academic administration—the fraternity of the fraternities. It was a societal system that neither the administration nor the faculty had intended for the students. It was, at least in part, an answer to adults interested only in drilling and shaping young minds. Fraternities became for many students a refuge from the rigidities of their education and the drabness of their lives, leading one cynic to remark that for many undergraduates the fraternity letters were the only Greek they had ever learned.

For increasing numbers of students, the fraternity system became a substitute for education and a device for "making it" first on campus and later in the world. Initially, however, the fraternity house meant more comfortable living quarters and a measure of control over everything from diet to life style.

It is worth noting that in the nineteenth century, when eating commons were temporarily eliminated on some campuses, they were subsequently restored for the less affluent students. Yet, when fraternities and eating clubs started to take over the functions of the commons, their high cost, along with their frequent social exclusiveness, locked out the poor, and thus barred them from the new promise of greater physical comfort, freedom—and social acceptance. As Rudolph put it, the fraternity movement placed a premium on "good friendship, good looks, good clothes, good family and good income."

With few exceptions, Eastern colleges had been the most class-bound and selective. Extremes of wealth and class declined progressively the further one moved westward. Although the Western colleges, too, soon imported fraternities, their influence tended to be less dominant and less socially divisive. But, even on those traditionally more egalitarian campuses, changes became apparent. Many leading families had begun to send their children—most often their sons—to the Eastern colleges. Eventually, even those who continued to attend campuses nearer the home began to put on airs that came with social ambitions.

The fraternity was tailor-made for a society that gave high marks to the joiner and the conformist and for an age when nouveau riche youth longed for a sense of exclusiveness. Nor was it surprising that reports from Cornell, Stanford, and Berkeley all agreed that academic grades of fraternity men were consistently below average. More important, new lines had been drawn, establishing an undergraduate social hierarchy with subtle and often not-so-subtle distinctions. Fraternity and nonfraternity men—the Greeks and barbarians—increasingly saw themselves as belonging to two different worlds.

Divisions inherent in the fraternity system, however, were not confined to wealth. The power to exclude naturally made it easier for prejudice—racial and religious as well as social—to dominate admissions policies. The dean of the Junior College at the University of Chicago charged that the fraternities maintained a "senseless prejudice," often aimed at Jews. Gradually, the Jewish response was the establishment of Jewish fraternities, often with the same superficial yardsticks of social snobbery.

Catholic students faced somewhat less clearly visible barriers than Jews or Blacks; yet, they too, suffered from a domination by the Protestant majority that refused to admit them fully to all the privileges of the inner circle. They, too, failed to meet the test implied in the question: "Would you want your sister to marry one?" However, unlike the push for integration and acceptance that was to characterize the Jewish and Black response, Catholic reaction was more often one of deliberate separatism. Many Catholic churchmen and parents still viewed the universities as godless institutions and a threat to their faith. Discrimination against their children strengthened their case for urging them to attend Catholic colleges.

Differences in attitudes and customs between the Eastern seacoast, on the one hand, and the American heartland as well as the West, on the other, were reflected on the nation's campuses as well. In the East, the clubby lines of snobbery and discrimination had been drawn sooner and more sharply—and this may well be the reason why it was also in the East that those barriers were ultimately first to be challenged. But, in their time, these barriers were formidable. In 1867, Oscar Strauss, later a member of Woodrow Wilson's cabinet, wrote about his undergraduate days at Columbia:

> I was under many disadvantages, comparatively poor, not as well dressed as most of my classmates, with no social standing and a Jew. For the latter offense I was even excluded from the literary society of the undergraduates. Often was the day I returned home with a heavy heart, because of some slight on the part of some of the other of my classmates, which I could only resent by excluding myself entirely from their social gatherings.

Agnes Meyer, later a powerful social critic and wife of the publisher of *The Washington Post,* reported that, during the first decade of the 1920s, Jewish girls were not eligible for membership in Barnard's sororities.

Fraternity discrimination should not be judged narrowly as a collegiate problem. On the contrary, apart from the students' understandable desire to make the campuses more livable and congenial, the creation of these enclaves of social privilege simply reflected similar efforts in the larger society to shore up the power and prerogatives of the established elite against the onrush of a mass of outsiders.

Expansion of educational opportunities had made Jefferson's vague ideal of an aristocracy of talent swim into sharper focus. There were those who, viewing themselves as the bastion of the existing aristocracy, wanted, at the very least, to control access to the establishment. Fraternities helped to keep these controls in socially approved hands, with genteel discretion—the old-boy network that prevented the "wrong" new elements from flooding or taking over the positions of power in communities, clubs, industry, and government.

It was not until World War II that old barriers began to fall. Discriminatory restrictions which had become the hallmark of the fraternities' public image came under attack—often in the courts. The early idealism of the civil rights movement of the 1960s, often led by students, also turned against campus enclaves of unearned and unjustified privilege.

One by one, local fraternity chapters, either to ward off the legal threat to their existence or in an honest reply to the pangs of a newly gained social conscience, forced their national headquarters to eliminate restrictive clauses or disassociated themselves from the central control. In some places, particularly in the East, where the prestige of the campuses was often almost inseparably interwoven with the prestige of the fraternities, efforts were made to allow fraternities to have their cake and eat it, too—by mandating 100 percent pledging. This was an administrative device to enforce social justice by requiring the fraternities to invite all freshmen to join.

As might have been expected, this bureaucratic response to a deeper social problem failed. It satisfied neither the old supporters of the fraternities as bastions of exclusivity nor the proponents of an open society. More radical remedies were sought. Just as students, in their earlier revolt against the dismal conditions of collegiate life, had created the fraternities as an antidote, so it was again students who led the campaign against fraternities. In keeping with the more admirable traditions of *noblesse oblige,* the privileged undergraduates of such elite colleges as Williams stood in the vanguard of that battle.

In 1962, undergraduate leaders at Williams, in cooperation with the administration, said in effect that the problems created by the fraternity system, with its inherently undemocratic attitudes, could not be cured by cosmetic changes. Abolition was demanded as the only effective and honest remedy. Fraternity properties, which over the years had become intertwined with the college's residential and feeding requirements, were to be bought by the institution and henceforth operated as facilities open to all students, like all college dormitories and dining halls.

Entirely predictably, these student-led reforms aroused the ire, not of undergraduate fraternity members, but of older alumni. These adult members of the established order saw elimination of the fraternities as an assault on their own world and on the legitimacy of their own preferred status. Some oldtimers took the matter to court, in an attempt to block the sale of fraternity houses and thus force the continued operation of the system of special privilege. They failed. The courts upheld the student leaders' drive toward greater equality for themselves and their peers.

Although few campuses followed Williams' radical lead, the fraternities' hold over undergraduates—and the cruel pressures of pledging—went into decline everywhere, though less dramatically in the West, where the fraternities had arrived much later and with far less social snobbery.

It was not until the early 1970s that fraternities were making a comeback, once again reflecting the changes of the atmosphere in society at large. The student rebellion of the 1960s, with its political and moral concern for social justice and racial equality, had run its course. A new student generation, worried about a sluggish economy, once again turned inward in search of personal security and promising careers. Conservative currents washed across the national stage. The earlier drive toward racial integration had, at least temporarily, been slowed. All of these factors, in addition to students' renewed interest in nonideological and "simple" diversions, contributed to a revival of fraternities and sororities.

Fraternities were not the only mark of elitism and discrimination on the collegiate scene at the turn of the century. Viewed from the vantage point of the 1970s, the Eastern college establishment was a bastion of WASP influence and mores, although some of the region's urban universities by 1900 did accept a sprinkling of selected Catholics, Jews, and, as the somewhat exceptional history of Harvard shows, even Blacks. At the time, 40 percent of all college students were women. Considering that the women's colleges had been founded relatively recently and even the state universities were still comparatively new institutions, this astonishing proportion is the only indication that the extreme power of the establishment's conservatism had begun to lose its grip.

A president of Bowdoin College summed up the general quality of the era's college life as "excessively gregarious." Something far different from the romantic vision of the scholarly community emerges from this description:

> Men herd together so closely and constantly that they are in danger of becoming too much alike. . . . The same feverish interest in athletics, the same level of gossip, the same attitude to politics and religion, tend to pass by contagion from the mass to the individual and supersede independent reflection.

The homogenizing influence of the era's campuses was similarly recalled by William Lyon Phelps: "It is impossible to exaggerate the intensity of class spirit. We never thought of any man in college except with his class numerals; it was always Peter '86 or Doggett '85."

For those who did not "belong," the environment was anything but congenial. A junior who, before he had arrived at Princeton, had heard much talk about that institution's democracy wrote in 1907:

> . . . But after I came I soon found that generally speaking that democracy applied . . . only to athletes. . . . To make a good club a man can't . . . entertain ideas much in advance of, or much different from those generally entertained by the student body, or his social aspirations will have vanished forever. In short, he has constantly so to be on his guard, so to conduct himself, as not to deviate in the slightest degree from the smooth, somewhat monotonous affable, acquiescent manner and thought which is required as the standard for club making.

And an observer at Harvard recalled:

> Ever since I have known anything of the college the worst feature of student life has been the solemn feminine importance attached to two-penny social distinctions. I was subject to it enough, God knows, and the shame at remembrance

makes me the more bitter against it now. Men are often valued not because they are clever or generous or gay or brave or handsome or strong, not because of their heads or their lungs or their belly or their legs, but because they are "the thing."

By comparison with his Eastern counterpart, the Midwestern and Far Western collegian remained less sophisticated and, in this sense, more democratic. There were fewer extremes of wealth or poverty; the contrast was more often between students from farm backgrounds and those from the town or city. At Michigan in 1902, a poll of the occupations of students' fathers revealed that thirty percent were businessmen (including merchants and manufacturers), twenty-two percent were farmers, 17 percent practiced a nonacademic profession (e.g. law, medicine, engineering, or pharmacy), whereas only 5.21 percent were mechanics, craftsmen, or skilled laborers.

Midwestern beginnings, moreover, had been more robust and earthy. During the early days at Michigan State Agricultural College, a dean who recalled the prevailing doubt about what academic subjects ought to be taught remembered that "upon one point there was general agreement—the student should be required to work with his hands under the instruction of men who had no previous teaching experience . . . but who knew only the imperative necessity for clearing the heavily wooded land which now comprised our farm and campus." For the first thirty years, each student had to do manual labor three hours a day—felling trees, clearing swamps, building fences and bridges, in addition to caring for the livestock. Under such conditions, there was little time—or tolerance—for the foppish conformity of many Eastern collegians.

Actually, even though Harvard was also swept along by the current of socially approved, mediocre conformity, the nation's first university did show even then a greater tolerance for occasional nonconformity, and it managed to nurture such dissenting intellectuals as John Reed, Randolph Bourne, Van Wyck Brooks, Herbert Croly and Walter Lippmann. Reed, who undoubtedly represented the minority of those who were strongminded enough not only to resist the homogenizing pressures but to encourage others to use the university's hidden potential to good advantage, offers this account of his undergraduate years from 1906 to 1910:

> All sorts of strange characters, of every race and mind, poets, philosophers, cranks of every twist, were in our class. . . . So many fine men were outside the charmed circle [of the social elite] that, unlike most colleges there was no disgrace in not being a "club man." What is known as "college spirit" was not very powerful; no odium attached to those who didn't go to football games and cheer. . . . No matter what you were and what you did—at Harvard you could find your kind.

But for the overwhelming number of students the uses of college were more nearly embodied by the more superficial goals, described by Rudolph:

> . . . What mattered for so many young men was not the course of study but the environment of friendships, social development, fraternity houses, good sportsmanship, athletic teams. The world of business was a world of dealing with people. What better preparation could there be than the collegiate life outside the classroom—the club room, the playing field, where the qualities that showed the stuff a fellow really was made of were bound to be encouraged.

The prototype of the highly qualified outsider who faced this frivolous, tight circle of insiders with great frustrations and handicaps was the Jewish student. In his description of Princeton, historian Laurence Veysey writes: "A student of Jewish origin might find it impossible to gain acceptance, no matter how acquiescent his manner. When such a boy was hazed, he did not initially connect it with anti-Semitism, but as he found himself systematically ostracized he began to lose his innocence." A Princeton alumnus wrote to Woodrow Wilson in 1904: "Both you and I know that it is the fashion (among students) to look at the Jew unsympathetically, simply because he is a Jew."

Part of the irony of the colleges' hostility to "foreign elements" —and their periodic denials of prejudice, bolstered by statistics of how many Jews, or Catholics, or Blacks, etc. they had admitted— is that the resistance of the admissions offices generally stiffened when newcomers seemed different from the mold. The classic description of the "Jewish problem" at Harvard offers an insight into that phenomenon. "The first German Jews who came," writes Samuel Eliot Morison, "were easily absorbed into the social pattern; but at the turn of the century the bright Russian Jewish lads from the Boston public schools began to arrive. There were enough of them in 1906 to form the Menorah Society, and in another fifteen years Harvard had her 'Jewish problem.' "

Prejudice against Jews had, of course, existed long before the discovery of that "problem." When John Finley, then at Princeton, was offered the presidency of New York's City College, a colleague on the faculty, trying to fill him in on his prospects, said: "I think a large percentage of the students are of foreign parentage and that a great many of them are Hebrews." At institutions such as Harvard and similar elite colleges, on the other hand, there had previously been too few Jews to raise the issue. Most of those few who were admitted had resembled in socioeconomic and educational background, as well as in their outlook on American society, the ways and mores of the dominant WASPS. Their successful assimilation had given them a protective coloration that shielded them from open attack and exposed them only to the more subtle slights, such as being barred from admission to the more exclusive fraternities and eating clubs.

As the twentieth century wore on, social discrimination intensified—in clubs, resorts, residential neighborhoods, and other "restricted" preserves of the Protestant upper middle class. At the same time, new waves of immigration brought great numbers of Jews from Russia and other Eastern European countries, many of them the victims of centuries of oppression that had barred them from access to middle-class or professional status. A sizable Jewish proletariat was added to what had been in the past a predominantly middle-class Jewish population. But it was a proletariat committed to the American dream of assuring its children's future success by sending them to school and college.

The Jew, said *The Nation* in 1923, "sends his children to college a generation or two sooner than other stocks, and as a result there are in fact more dirty Jews and tactless Jews in college than dirty and tactless Italians, Armenians, or Slovaks."

Dirty and tactless were, of course, the disapproving terms that the established order always reserves for newcomers. (Similar characterizations were used to describe the Black influx following the great civil rights battles of the 1960s.) The new Jewish college applicants could not help but come into conflict with the clubby life and the self-satisfied gentleman's C of a secure generation of youths whose future success was easily assured by virtue of their social origin. By contrast, newly arrived Jewish students seemed pushy grinds. Clearly they had come to college with neither the social standing nor the economic resources that permitted them to look on the four undergraduate years as just a pleasant interlude. College was the engine that would propel them out of lower-class poverty. Thus, when they violated the unspoken but widely accepted "taboo of scholarship," these students caused resentment among the establishment that viewed with distaste the prospect of ungentlemanly academic competition.

An old-line Protestant described his feelings: "My own background was middle-class, Protestant, non-competitive, like that of most Roxbury Latin boys. I had always taken for granted that I should go to Harvard because my father in his time had gone there. . . . That Harvard could be the goal of anyone's ambitions never occurred to me."

With equal honesty, this prototype of the favored majority went on to say that, quite naturally, "we despised the industry of those little Jews. . . . They hated us in return with the accumulated resentment of the past and because they knew that the way for us was easier."

It could not be charged that the new Jewish undergraduates might be a threat to academic standards—usually the colleges' defensive argument against the admission of any new element. On the contrary, the Jewish intruders were "curve-raisers," and they were resented in the same manner in which unions object to faster workers who might create pressures for increased productivity.

Many adult leaders within the Eastern college establishment shared the students' uneasiness over the new scholastically oriented, success-hungry group. A member of the Harvard faculty said haughtily: "Many Jews have personal and social qualities and habits that are unpleasant. . . . They come in large measure from the social isolation to which they have been subjected for centuries, by prejudice and ignorance of Christian communities. Most

Jews are socially untrained, and their bodily habits are not good."
In a pattern that was to be repeated with the arrival of each
strange new group, most recently the nonwhite minorities, blame
was placed on past prejudice—not to help eradicate the disadvantages but to justify present prejudice. The president of Tufts University rationalized: "The social characteristics of the Jews are
peculiar. The subtle thing which we call manners, among them
differs from the manners of Americans generally."

More than manners was involved. Reactionary forces were
strong in the 1920s. The colleges' genteel objections to foreign
influences were more than matched by the political xenophobia
that led to the enactment of stringent immigration quotas.

At Harvard, too, a Jewish quota was introduced. Yet, it would
be unfair to single out Harvard, simply because it was more
forthright. Most other prestige colleges had already embarked on
the same course, even if they did so without official announce-
ments.

Despite public denials of quotas, Jewish enrollments suddenly
declined during the 1920s. At Columbia, for example, a two-year
period saw a sharp decrease of Jewish students, from 40 to 22
percent. At New York University, a dean explained: "We do not
exclude students of any race or national origin because they are
foreign, but whenever the student body is found to contain elements from any source in such proportions as to threaten our
capacity for assimilating them, we seek by selection to restore
the balance."

No academic policy on so crucial an issue could be fully understood without an account of Harvard's attitudes and actions. The
situation was complex. President Lowell represented all that is
best and worst in the New England tradition of high principles
and deeply rooted prejudices. He was said to have been displeased
by much that had been done during Eliot's administration. Not
only more Jews, but more Catholics, Blacks, and Chinese had been
admitted. Eliot's wide-ranging interests moreover had made him
a champion and a reformer of *public* education.

A man of purist tastes and conservative standards, Lowell saw
the old values threatened. Yet Lowell was not a villainous reactionary or bigot; his record on academic freedom was, for his time,
quite extraordinary. When the late Harold Laski, then a relatively

obscure British scholar, got into trouble with the university's Overseers for having defended Boston's striking police, Lowell threatened that if they "ask for Laski's resignation, they will get mine." It was more than a lofty gesture: Lowell himself had supported Calvin Coolidge, then governor of Massachusetts, in his effort to suppress the strike, and he had even urged Harvard students to join the strike-breaking police forces. (Some two hundred students did.)

In fact, students had been far less fair-minded in their own conservatism than their president. *The Harvard Lampoon,* the undergraduate humor magazine, published a violently anti-Soviet issue which claimed to have discovered that Lenin owned 148 personal automobiles and Trotsky fifty-two, while Laski had been sent to Harvard as one of the Bolsheviks' secret emissaries. The journal also accused the visiting lecturer of being an ardent advocate of free love. (Later, in 1935, the *Lampoon*'s editors officially apologized to Laski for their predecessors' vicious attacks.)

But it was not only in the matter of academic freedom that Lowell had shown himself a man of principle. Some time before he became Harvard's president, he had publicly expressed disapproval at finding the college's wealthy students segregated in posh apartments, known as the Gold Coast. Among his early acts as president were reforms which compelled all freshmen to live in dormitories.

Yet Lowell also remained a prisoner of prejudices which his intellectual sense of fairness could not conquer. He democratized freshman living; but he could not bring himself to include Black students in that egalitarian scheme. In barring Black students from these otherwise all-inclusive dormitories, Lowell said that he believed it unwise "for a Negro to apply for a room. . . . It has nothing to do with the education he receives; that, of course, was furnished equally to a man without distinction as to race, color or previous condition of servitude." The edict was rendered all the more curious by the fact that, until that time, Harvard had admitted Blacks on the same terms as whites, and they had eaten in the same commons, roomed in the same dorms, used the same athletic facilities. In fact, during the nineteenth century, many Southerners were reported to have avoided Harvard for precisely that reason.

Despite some protests, Lowell would not budge. In a letter to a Black freshman's father, he wrote:

> . . . I am sorry to have to tell you that in the Freshman Halls, where residence is compulsory, we have felt from the beginning the necessity of not including colored men. To the other dormitories and dining rooms they are admitted freely, but in the Freshman Halls I am sure you will understand why . . . we have not thought it possible to compel men of different races to reside together.

Compounding the irony of this correspondence was the fact that the Black boy's father was himself a graduate of Harvard. Like his son, the father had prepped at the fashionable Exeter Academy.

Perhaps the apparent irrationality of Lowell's approach to both the Black and the Jewish "problems" is best explained by an equally irrational arrogance: Lowell's ingrained belief that whatever policies a Harvard—or a Lowell—wanted to impose would have to be accepted on those terms, without apology or explanation. This was precisely why Lowell chose not to join his fellow university presidents in discreetly imposing, and publicly denying, anti-Jewish quotas. He saw no conflict between prejudice and candor. He felt no need to explain or apologize for actions which he considered in keeping with the demands of his time and his class, and which clearly were in complete agreement with the underlying anti-Semitism of his constituency.

And so Lowell spoke the hitherto unspoken, when he was quoted in the *New York Times* of June 23, 1922: "To shut the eyes to an actual problem of this kind and ignore its existence, or to refuse to grapple with it courageously, would be unworthy of a university." What was the "problem"? Simply, the growth of Harvard's Jewish enrollment from six percent in 1908 to twenty percent in 1922.

Lowell's statement evoked a storm of protest. He stood firm. In a public letter on the issue, he elaborated:

> There is perhaps no body of men in the United States . . . with so little anti-Semitic feeling as the instructing staff of Harvard University. . . . There is, most unfortunately, a

rapidly growing anti-Semitic feeling in this country . . . fraught with great evils for the Jews, and very great perils for the community.

The quotas, in other words, were designed supposedly not to hurt Jews but to reduce anti-Semitism.

The debate went on, but the problem remained: Jews had come to be viewed as a threat to the mystique of a college life that placed genteel social traditions and customs so far above all other values that it could not brook the imposition of more demanding intellectual goals and standards—at least not quite yet. Just as institutions were to argue three decades later that a certain percentage of nonwhites constituted the "tipping point," the hidden fear then was that if the proportion of Jews were to reach forty percent—at Harvard, but presumably on any other campus as well —the college's character "would be completely changed."

These labored alarms stood in odd contrast to the realities, as underscored by the critic Malcolm Cowley, who looked at Harvard's Jewish students in 1916 and saw them not as a threat but as a group of young scholars "backed by a whole generation of rabbis versed in the Torah and Talmud, representatives of the oldest Western culture now surviving." He saw young men already mature with "memories of an exciting childhood; street gangs in Brownsville and . . . all the emotions, smells and noises of the ghetto." And yet, he marveled (as later commentators were to marvel again at young Black men and women, some of them the product of the very same Brownsville ghetto) that these students were willing to devote four years to read "Keatsean sonnets about English abbeys, which [they] had never seen, and nightingales that [they] had never heard."

Protected by the defenders of the status quo against the onslaught of foreign intruders, the social and clubby air prevailed at Harvard and other elite colleges well into the 1930s. It was not until after World War II that social restrictions began to recede. An increasing number of Irish Catholics entered Harvard. Jewish recruitment and acceptance grew markedly. Academic competition now was keen, and it was taken for granted and no longer considered a sign of upstart bad manners. By the 1960s, in a complete reversal, social status, once virtually the only mark of distinction, had become something of an embarrassment.

It is easier to describe the changing trends of undergraduate social and intellectual life than to assess the impact of higher education on successive student generations or to gauge the influence students brought to bear on social and political issues of their time. Conservatives have often charged that radical college faculties indoctrinate impressionable youths; radicals denounce the university establishment as a reactionary force that conditions young minds; liberals want to believe that students inevitably represent the progressive wave of the future. A more accurate conclusion is that the students' outlook as well as the atmosphere of the institutions they attended were affected in constantly changing ways by the environment and the currents of the time.

At the turn of the century, students became active in the urban settlement houses. Young women graduates, in search for an altruistic outlet for their energies, founded the College Settlement Association to "unite all college women, and all who count themselves our friends, in the trend of a great modern movement." The settlement work was depicted as "a graduate school in life" for women "whose university is the outer world." For some, it was the introduction to a lifetime of public service.

Both before the Spanish American War and before World War I, some opposition to American involvement developed on the campuses. Distinguished faculty members openly voiced their objections. Students organized meetings to discuss the issues. But it would be a distortion of the facts to suggest that these mild hints of disagreement over official policy were akin to the student protests over the war in Vietnam during the 1960s. In fact, once American troops entered the hostilities most of the opposition fell silent. The campus mood was generally supportive of those wars, and it was to remain so even throughout the war in Korea in the 1950s which students of draft age faced with stoicism, though without enthusiasm.

In general, the American undergraduate tradition is not one of political activism or firebrand radicalism. In 1886, only a few months after the Haymarket bombing, a student editorialist at

Harvard explained the lack of political excitement among his classmates on the grounds that it was a calm age.

In the early 1900s, college journalism, in addition to being of mediocre quality, was generally noncommittal, avoiding a stand on any major issues of the day. Although a mild progressivism eventually registered itself in some college circles, support for Populism or other movements further to the left was extremely rare. Conventional patriotism was all but universal.

In assessing the priorities of a typical editor of the Harvard *Crimson,* Arthur M. Schlesinger, Jr., wrote: "His editorial range was wholly conventional, displaying the earnest senior's concern for the football team, the Harvard cheering section, boardwalks in the Yard in winter, and more fire extinguishers in the dormitories." The editor so described was Franklin D. Roosevelt.

The decade before World War I did see the introduction of socialism to the campuses, but the number of students involved was small and even fewer turned out to have been permanently affected. John Reed, a founding member of the Harvard Socialist Club, wrote:

> What's wrong with Harvard? . . . Numbers of letters from alarmed alumni pour into President Lowell's office every day, asking if Socialists and Anarchy are on the rampage among undergraduates. . . . Old graduates shake their heads mournfully and agree the place is going to the dogs. . . . The idea [of the club] was to stir up criticism, revolt, discussion, opposition, not only of the present state of things in the outside world, but of the state of things at Harvard. They wanted to make undergraduates take sides on every issue that concerned them: to what they wanted to learn, and demand of the Faculty that the "dead wood" among the teachers be cleared away. . . .

In its early days, Reed estimated, the club may have had fifty members, with perhaps twice as many others interested. In 1908, the group actually campaigned for such local issues as housing in Cambridge and Boston—issues which once again came to the fore in the 1960s—but such political activism proved shortlived.

Randolph Bourne, complaining about the tame quality of such radicalism, wrote in *The New Republic* in 1916:

> The real trouble with middle-class radicalism today is that it is too easy. It is becoming too popular. . . . Let the college man or girl . . . join the Intercollegiate Socialist Society or some similar institution, and discover how discouragingly respectable they are.

Respectable or not, a mildly questioning spirit had at least made its appearance on the campuses. At Princeton, F. Scott Fitzgerald observed, the general air of conservatism was ruffled when students around small tables in the Nassau Inn discussed "sex and socialism" and "the social barriers as artificial distinctions made by the strong to bolster up their weak retainers and keep out the almost strong." But, in what Fitzgerald called a "fury of righteousness," 180 students resigned from their clubs.

Even before World War I, changes in American mores had begun to influence undergraduate life—far more directly than any political activism or any innovations in courses of study. These changes, though still unnoticed by most contemporary observers, soon gained momentum. As early as 1911, writing in *The Atlantic Monthly,* Cornelia Comer lamented the decline of religion, the questionable impact of certain developments and attitudes in the news and entertainment media, and the new pressures of the peer group. In terms similar to later complaints about the influence of television, she wrote:

> How can anything avail to refine children whose taste in humor is formed by the colored supplements of the Sunday paper. . . . "I don't approve," your fathers and mothers say anxiously, "but I hate to keep Tom and Mary at home when all the others are allowed to go." . . . When these young people adopted a philosophy, it was naive and inadequate. They talked of themselves as "socialists."

In part, of course, these words reflect the perennial despair of the older generation over the ways of the young. But more was involved. Old customs of a social order were being challenged. Describing the period of 1914 to 1932, historian William Leuchtenburg wrote:

> The assault on the authority of the older America would have created terrible problems in the best of times. The experience of World War I made matters much worse. . . . [The war] reinforced the conviction that evil came from outside America and from alien sources within, and evil became identified with the groups demanding change. The war destroyed much of the traditional confidence in the ability of American society to assimilate all manner of men. . . . The period brought everything that had been festering in the pre-war years into the open. Much of it was ugly, but it had been no less ugly when it was concealed. For the first time, the United States came face to face with the swift pace of economic change, technological innovation and the rapidly rising standard of living.

Traditional living patterns were coming apart under the assault of the new technology. One invention to have a revolutionary impact on student life was the automobile. Princeton's Dean Christian Gauss was among the first who realized that a newly motorized student body would soon break out of the confinement of the residential college and elude adult supervision. Cars would soon mean more than mobility—they offered independence and privacy, and gave young people at least the appearance of an earlier maturity.

The combustion engine was not the only technological break with the past. "The most popular amusement today," Dean Gauss also noted, "is the cinema; it, too, has had its effect. The boy or girl who comes to the college, and who has been attending the movies for the past six or eight years, has seen far more life than the ordinary undergraduate of 1895 ever dreamed of. . . ." Few of Dean Gauss's academic colleagues were aware of the impact of the new technology—just as few educators in the 1960s acknowledged the far-ranging changes wrought by television.

The trend-setting communication and entertainment system of the movies changed personal behavior and attitudes at a hitherto unimaginably rapid rate. This was the era of the flapper, with short hair and shorter skirts—both scandalous to old-fashioned observers—and a new freedom in the relationship between the sexes. Moreover, the Volstead Act made law-breaking glamorous and hypocrisy a way of life for young and old. The hip flask and the automobile may not have been solely responsible for the assault on sexual taboos, but statistical evidence of the 1920s, according to Kinsey, shows a quantum jump in the proportion of women who engaged in premarital sex. The percentages were not again to increase among the female college population until the next phase of the sexual revolution in the 1960s.

For students of the twenties, little seemed left of the Puritan ethic. All around them was easy money and easy living. Honesty and chastity had come to be viewed as platitudes. Democracy was reserved for the insiders—the immigrants, the poor, Jews, Blacks, Italians, Poles were outside the charmed circle. But, for those inside, the world was filled with pleasure and opportunity.

At least, such was the superficial mood. Even then—as was to be the case again during the activist 1960s—much routinely hard work undoubtedly went on unaffected by the much-publicized nihilism, hedonism, and bohemianism. Many Americans, including some of the young, took their stand with Bryan's thundered warnings that godless commercialism and a blasphemous neglect of religious values were undermining the colleges along with the rest of America. Many others agreed with Vice President Calvin Coolidge that "the attempt to open the colleges to undirected radical influences is going on. . . ."

"Are they missing the one true aim of all education," Coolidge asked, "the development of character? In their scramble to teach commercialism have they forgotten that character does not come from economic development? Sound economic development comes from sound character."

Threadbare as they were, such platitudes nevertheless found a hearing among many undergraduates of Coolidge's day. The old age, though dying, was not yet dead. During his student days in 1927, David Riesman recalls, national politics played only a minor role at Harvard. "A plurality of my classmates," he writes,

> were for Herbert Hoover in the election of 1928, and the great majority in the election of 1932. But this was a matter

of reflex, of family and class. And there was very little social consciousness of the contemporary sort; some of us mocked Roger Baldwin and Corliss Lamont when they worried about the wages of Harvard scrubwomen.

In the 1920s, great numbers of students poured into the colleges. The pressure of numbers constituted a challenge to the old amenities. A professor at Wisconsin, describing the new collegiate life in much the same words that rebellious undergraduates were to use in their attack on the universities in the 1960s, wrote:

> The student is admitted by thousands, registered by a vast clerical machine, assigned to a course, divided into sections, lectured to, quizzed, tested, examined; he is warned by his instructors, warned through his parents . . . he is limited in the number of semester hours, limited in his elections, limited in his student activities, limited in his social life; he is recorded, card-indexed, filed, questionnaired, statisticized, and his documentation is kept in a safe.

(All that was to be added later was the efficiency of the computer.)

If society's larger issues occupied the students' minds at all, little evidence appears in the chronicles of the era. The Sacco and Vanzetti case, the most controversial radical issue of the twenties, does not appear to have aroused massive student reaction. Harvard's undergraduates were, of course, aware of the trial, which took place in the Boston area. A three-man committee appointed by the Governor and chaired by President Lowell concluded that the two anarchists were guilty. Yet, there was little indication of more than routine interest in the affair on the campuses.

Rather than search for political or social significance among that generation of students, one might accept as typical the summary provided by a young prototype at Pomona College, in California, in 1924, who wrote:

> I have made more friends than I ever thought possible in four years. It is a great opportunity for a man to round out his personality, and to develop the ability to meet other men and leave a good impression. I hate to think of saying goodby to the old friends, but I have the consolation of feeling that

some day I am going to call a lot of congressmen and college presidents names that don't sound like Doctor and Honorable.

Here were the overtones of the recurring American preoccupation with the "well-rounded" which believes—not without good reason —that "it isn't what you know but whom you know."

The Great Depression scuttled the smug optimism. At the end of the spring term of 1930, one thousand students, short of funds, withdrew from the University of Michigan. Faculty salaries were cut. A student editor, commenting on the situation, said that the professors had, as a result of the shared adversity, "come a lot nearer to a common feeling with the students. Now everyone on the campus can admit quite freely that he is broke."

Economic realities shaped a new generation of students. A college education suddenly had become an expensive luxury, and in the view of many hard-pressed families quite expendable. More and more students had to leave college to look for work; all of them shared a sense of common hardship—in sharp contrast to the easy-going, fun-loving generation that had so recently populated the campuses.

It was an unsettled and unsettling time in which to grow up. Old theories came under attack. Some students turned to political activism and protest, and they challenged a wide variety of old rules and customs, from compulsory chapel attendance to the economic and political doctrines that had seemed inviolable during more optimistic days. They seemed useless and even odious now.

Political anger seethed at some urban universities. At the City College of New York, open warfare broke out between the students, most of them poor and many the sons of immigrants, and President Frederick B. Robinson, who had expressed admiration for some of Mussolini's policies. In 1933, undergraduates tried to stop Dr. Robinson and some visiting celebrities on their way to the college's Great Hall. The demonstration turned ugly. "An umbrella was the weapon used yesterday by Dr. Frederick B. Robinson . . . to disperse a crowd of about 400 militantly pacifist students," *The New York Times* reported, omitting the fact that the police may have been more effective than Dr. Robinson's umbrella in repelling the attack. Robinson subsequently tried to deflate the crisis by testifying that he had recognized only one of the assailants as a student and that the others "were probably Communists from outside."

Many faculty members—threatened by the same economic disaster as their students—sympathized with the protesters. Occasionally, this bond of understanding offered a glimpse of the humane concern that often becomes submerged in large and impersonal institutions. When the City College's dean, Morton Gottschall, a legendary figure among generations of undergraduates, was told by excited aides that demonstrators were staging a sit-in strike—one of the first in undergraduate history—outside his office, he calmly ordered them to rush to the supply rooms of the Reserve Officers Training Corps and collect blankets "so the boys won't catch cold sitting on the stone floor." As assistants arrived to distribute the blankets, the students were so embarrassed by the dean's concern over their welfare that they abandoned the sit-in.

Dean Gottschall, however, was hardly typical. The response by college administrators to student protests ranged from harsh penalties, including summary expulsion, to confusion and disbelief. At Fordham, a dean tried to isolate his own campus from the nation's conflicts. "I don't care," he said, "whether they are demonstrating at other colleges here in this city today. They are making fools of themselves. We are common-sense here. What war are they worrying about anyway?" A dean at Columbia, trying to placate a group of alumni who protested the undergraduate newspaper's apparent radicalism, said: "You fellows are, I think, color-blind. What you mistake for red is simply green."

It is futile to assess, in retrospect, the extent of actual communist influence on student publications, organizations, and opinion. The young communists' voice was more impressive than their actual numbers. Whatever hold they had on the students' idealism and conscience—during the grim years of depression, Fascist takeovers in Italy and Germany, and the horrors of the Spanish Civil War or the bombing of Ethiopian villages by Mussolini's air armadas—was to be short lived. The left-wing alliance of the Popular Front was shattered by the 1939 Nazi-Soviet Pact. In the early days of World War II, a strident communist propaganda campaign that depicted Franklin D. Roosevelt and Winston Churchill as imperialist warmongers isolated the hardcore Communists from the rest of the radical and liberal student movement.

While idealistic pacifism had earlier helped to create a sizable common front of communist and noncommunist students, held together by peace strikes and other protests, Stalin's cynical readiness to join forces with Hitler torpedoed the naïve faith in the Soviets' claim to superior international morality.

Surveys of the extent of student radicalism in the thirties produce an uncertain, often contradictory, picture. One study, published by Purdue University, insisted students were more radical "because they are facing a less secure world in 1931." A 1936 *Fortune* magazine survey suggested that the Depression had created a new seriousness of purpose. It found a declining interest in the colleges' social activities, while "students have been flocking to history, economics, and sociology courses. . . ."

The observation was to be applicable almost verbatim to the early 1970s, marked by a return to academic competition and interest in the traditional subjects. In both instances, an unfavorable economy and a declining job market (though clearly not as threatening during the 1973 turndown as in the Depression) appear to have been largely responsible for the changes in the campus mood. Similarly, in both of these troubled eras, student activism was estimated to have involved only between five and ten percent of all undergraduates. It should, however, be added that radical or activist movements rarely are embraced by a larger percentage of the adult population.

World War II virtually emptied the campuses. Except for women and some special collegiate programs sponsored by the armed forces, the universities might have been faced by total shutdown. The students' response to the war movement was overwhelmingly supportive. While the worldwide conflict was marked by none of the earlier wars' jingoism of flags and marching bands, the threat of fascist aggression had unified the nation, and its youth, in a quiet resolve.

The interlude of campuses deserted by their male youth was instantly followed, at the conclusion of the war, by the greatest tidal wave of students ever to hit this, or any nation's, colleges and universities. On June 22, 1944, Congress enacted the G.I. Bill of Rights, a historic innovation of rewarding veterans not with patriotic oratory but with a gift of free higher education. In the twelve years that followed, nearly eight million former servicemen availed themselves of the offer and studied in colleges and universities, in vocational schools and on-the-job training programs, in factories and on farms.

In fact, the G.I. Bill turned out to be a milestone in educational progress, not because of its planners' foresight but rather because the American people caught a ball that was rather offhandedly thrown to them—and ran with it. Not unlike the Land-grant Act, the Servicemen's Readjustment Act of 1944, as it was officially called, was favored by the political leadership with little actual concern for education. The motivation was, as Keith W. Olson of the University of Maryland documents in a concise and unsentimental article in the December 1973 issue of the *American Quarterly*, almost entirely economic.

President Roosevelt and Congress feared widespread unemployment following the demobilization of the huge World War II forces. The veterans, F.D.R. said in a fireside chat on July 28, 1943, "must not be demobilized into an environment of inflation and unemployment, to a place on the bread line or on a corner selling apples." Other voices, particularly those of American Legion commanders, recalled that returning soldiers of World War I had led the Bolshevist and fascist uprisings. When the Senate Finance Committee unanimously recommended enactment of the bill, it warned that, "if the trained and disciplined efficiency and valor of the men and women of our armed forces can be directed into the proper channels, we shall have a better country to live in than the world has ever seen. If we should fail in that task, disaster and chaos are inevitable."

Neither the Veterans Administration nor the organized university leadership reacted with enthusiasm. The bureaucratic response of the former was that an extension of the act's educational provisions, which was being lobbied by the veterans' organizations, would not be in keeping with the bill's original intent. Many educators, on the other hand, responded to the prospect of an influx of "new" students exactly as their predecessors had on every similar occasion—with warnings that only a few are capable of withstanding the academic rigor and with dire predictions of declining academic standards.

Robert M. Hutchins, then president of the University of Chicago, called the bill "a threat to American education," termed its provisions "unworkable," and warned that the colleges, in order to collect the veterans' tuition, would be tempted to hold on to them longer than necessary and regardless of their ability. (Similar objections would be raised twenty-five years later against the subsidized admission of nonwhite minorities.) Harvard's president Conant called the G.I. Bill "distressing" because it failed to "distinguish between those who can profit most by advanced education and those who cannot." He moved for the adoption of a measure that would have selected a few highly qualified veterans lest "the least capable among the war generation [be] flooding the facilities for advanced education."

The educators' initial doubts were not purely academic. The thought of independent and—ultimate of horrors!—married students with pregnant wives made them shudder. A University of Chicago dean asked: "What will we do with married students? . . . How will we house them? . . . Will we be embarrassed by the prospect of babies and by their arrival?" At Columbia, a senior professor said bluntly: "If there is a baby, college is almost out of the question for any reasonable man. . . ."

If they were wrong about the veterans' capacity to benefit from higher education and about the colleges' capacity to survive a new breed of students, both the bureaucrats and the educators were even more seriously in error in their predictions of the veterans' response to the G.I. Bill. Governmental surveys anticipated that no more than eight percent of the demobilized soldiers would want to return full-time to school or college. Educators thought that a total of 640,000 veterans might be expected to attend college under the bill, with no more than 150,000 actually studying in any one year.

The Establishment's mood of skepticism, opposition, and defeatism was clearly not shared by the American people, least of all by the veterans. By the time the act's education title had run out, 37 percent of all eligibles had availed themselves of their rights. During the height of the act's effectiveness, in 1947–1948, over one million veterans were crowding the nation's campuses. John

S. Allen, New York State's Director of Higher Education, wrote: "When the G.I. Bill was made a law of the land it is probable that no one in his wildest flights of imagination anticipated that veterans would attend college in such numbers. . . ." Altogether, 2,232,000 veterans ultimately went to college under the bill, at a cost of $5.5 billion.

Once conservative objections had been swept aside by the tide of new students, the academic response was, on a whole, comparable to the nation's earlier industrial crash programs in answer to the need for instant war production. Quonset huts rose virtually overnight on previously serene campuses. Veterans, often with their wives and babies, transformed the social as well as the intellectual climate of higher education. What they lacked in academic preparation they made up in maturity and motivation. Faculty skeptics were quickly won over by the new students. "They have brought to the campuses an atmosphere of serious purpose and a sense of responsibility," was a typical comment.

Two years after his alarm over the veterans' threat to academic quality, Dr. Conant called them "the most mature and promising students Harvard has ever had." A study by the Carnegie Foundation for the Advancement of Teaching found that veterans were getting superior grades. Regular students at Stanford University afforded the veterans the unintended compliment of referring to them as D.A.R.'s—Damned Average Raisers. But, while historians subsequently confined their accounts largely to the G.I. Bill's landmark success as an example of sound governmental policy, Olson is closer to the mark when he concludes that "rarely has the implementation of an Act of Congress combined such high degrees of both success and surprise." On the whole, it was a triumph of the people's faith in education over the policy-makers' limited vision guided by purely economic concerns.

The G.I. Bill turned out to be more than a temporary postwar measure. It was another stage in a continuing revolution of expanded opportunities that gradually transformed higher education from an elite into a mass enterprise. In 1946, *The New York Times* reported:

> Several college presidents suggested that the G.I. Bill, which
> provides free educational opportunities for the veterans, is

partly responsible for the greater number of women who are seeking admittance. Because the veterans do not have to pay for their college education, many families can now afford to send their daughters to a college or university, using funds that would have gone in normal times for their sons.

In the long run, an even more fundamental change was in the making. The G.I. Bill had shown that the traditional definition of "college material" had been too narrow. Old criteria—most of them defined by class rather than intellectual merit—were obsolete. Not only the sisters but the friends and cousins of the veterans now clamored for admission to higher education. Expansion could no longer be contained. Before World War II, total college and university enrollments had been 1.5 million; by 1973, they had skyrocketed to over eight million. (In 1900, the total stood at 237,600.)

Numbers alone could not describe the changes that were taking place. Veterans were intent on making up for lost time, anxious for successful careers. While they themselves wanted to get on with the job of civilian living, they also imbued the new generation of young students who went to college side by side with them, with a postwar spirit of idealism. The evil of totalitarianism and aggression had been defeated and purged. The new generation was inspired by the prospect of world cooperation and peace.

The world soon dashed these hopes. The cold war between the United States and the Soviet Union, with its fallout of McCarthyism at home, shattered the students' idealism and exposed those who clung to their hope for a peaceful brotherhood of nations to the wrath of the new wave of jingoists. The Korean War sealed the fate of the peace movement.

The students' response was one of withdrawal. The college generation of the 1950s was to be labeled as "silent." Its doctrine was described as privatism—introspective and self-centered. It was not a time for great controversy or deep thinking. During his brief tenure as president of Columbia, before assuming the Presidency of the United States, Dwight D. Eisenhower may well have struck the note symbolic of the era when he told the new freshman class: "I don't care how much they talk to you about geology and geography, but I hope the day never goes by that you don't have some fun, that you don't enjoy life."

In their quiet, withdrawn, isolated way, those postwar generations did enjoy life. They married young, moved out of the cities into the suburbs, built their split-level homes, bore the largest crop of babies, barbecued tons of steak, commuted to work, created the two-car yardstick of American prosperity, rose in the corporate hierarchy, and adjusted to the "system" without rocking the boat.

It was the generation that made the Youth Culture the dominant social and commercial force in America. To be young and informal was to be "in" with modern America. Distrust for "eggheads" —the new term for intellectuals and college professors—prevailed, and in the 1952 election the nation sought security in the Eisenhower father image.

A different kind of appeal eventually aroused youthful idealism and activism, and reawakened the social conscience of a new student generation. A little-known Southern minister in Alabama had challenged the segregationist establishment when, in response to the arrest of a tired seamstress who had refused to move to the back of the bus, he aroused the entire Black population of Montgomery to boycott the city's buses until he had forced Jim Crow to surrender. The passive resistance lasted for more than a year, but by the time the bus company at last capitulated, Dr. Martin Luther King, Jr., had become a national hero.

King's pledge, "We shall overcome," was to be the password for a new generation of student activists. The quiet courage of Black college students in North Carolina who, though threatened and spat upon, sat in nonviolent defiance at "whites-only" lunch counters until that barrier fell, too, provided the model and the inspiration. The nonviolent student movement spearheaded the integrated Freedom Riders and the civil rights marchers. Students across the nation had found a cause that won praise and support from their liberal elders, and even grudging admiration from conservatives. Faced by what seemed like an unyielding, law-defiant force that was often backed by the power of the state—by armed troopers and sheriffs' guns and dogs—students drew strength from what had been the dream of rebellious youth through the ages: to be on the side of righteousness and, at the same time, justified to ignore, challenge, and even break the laws.

Other young people heard a new call from Washington. A youthful John F. Kennedy had been elected President in 1960, and in his inaugural address he proclaimed that the torch had been handed on to a new generation. Youth looked to him for inspiration and guidance as it had not been looking to a President since the days of Franklin Roosevelt.

During a visit to the University of Michigan in Ann Arbor, almost by way of an aside, Kennedy suggested that young men and women might serve their country and the world by forming a peaceful army ready to aid people in underdeveloped nations. Spontaneously, students picked up the idea and literally besieged the President with pleas to send them on just such a mission. The Peace Corps was born. Thousands of young men and women, with an enthusiasm reminiscent of the post–World War II quest for a world of international friendship, flocked to the Corps' campus recruiters.

Neither the challenge of the civil rights battle nor opportunities to serve in a peaceful army abroad, however, engaged the imagination and interest of all, or even the majority, of students during the early sixties. Conventional campus frivolity was slow to die. The pent-up tensions of the silent, withdrawn generation, coupled with the aimless adolescence of the Youth Culture, still constituted an explosive force.

In 1963, more than a thousand students at Princeton staged what came to be known as the first of a series of "rah-rah riots." For hours, they rampaged through the town. Property damage was substantial. Although New Jersey's Governor Richard J. Hughes tried to shrug it off ("It's spring, and the sap is beginning to rise"), Princeton President Robert F. Goheen expressed anger over the incident, particularly because it came at a time of "the deeply somber [civil rights] struggles at Birmingham."

Like so many faddish college incidents, the Princeton rah-rah riot was almost instantly imitated on dozens of campuses. A riot at Yale ended tragically, when one student was severely beaten by overreacting police. A panty raid carefully planned by Columbia students against neighboring Barnard was prevented by more sophisticated police action from turning into a riot. Symbolic of the range of public reaction to these playful undergraduate excesses, one police officer overheard at the scene said contemptuously: "These are the future advisers to Presidents." A second officer suggested a more indulgent explanation: "There are a lot of pretty girls secreted in those dorms, and these guys here want to unsecrete them."

Less than a decade later, the unsecreting process at Columbia, Barnard, and the majority of colleges across the country had been routinely completed by the widespread acceptance of coeducational dormitories—and others that had turned coeducational, or cohabitational, without official sanction.

Many undergraduate outbursts seemed unrelated to anything other than undirected exuberance. During an earlier riot at the Massachusetts Institute of Technology in 1957, in protest over the quality of the food, one of the first demonstrators to be arrested had been—a visiting Yalie. A rampage of over 1000 Harvard undergraduates was started in alleged anger over the replacement of the traditional Latin diplomas by English ones.

At the height of the 1963 rah-rah excesses, the *Cornell Daily Sun,* expressing chagrin that peace reigned on its own campus, editorialized: "Rioting, as any prison warden will tell you, is a wonderful safety valve for accumulated tension." Some observers of the campus scene and the Youth Cult were reminded of the motion picture *Rebel Without a Cause,* whose hero and teenage idol, the late James Dean, had kept repeating the imploring refrain: "Tell me what to do, Dad, just tell me what to do."

Commencement 1964 was still a scene of serene optimism. For the first time, substantial improvements in the job opportunities for Black graduates were reported by the campus placement offices. The class of '64 was hailed as "the brightest ever" in commencement speeches. A record number went on to graduate schools—or to well-paying jobs. Early marriage still was the order of the day.

A minority of concerned students had long departed from the happy-go-lucky Joe College role and were deeply involved in the fight for racial justice and the battle against poverty abroad—but they were pursuing their idealistic goals away from the campuses, without much impact on the collegiate scene.

But beneath the surface all was not serene. Critics complained of the universities' feverish chase after research contracts. The academic research enterprise had risen from $40 million in 1940 to more than $2 billion by 1963. M.I.T. alone, during that year held $70 million in defense contracts. Meanwhile, complaints—not unfamiliar in collegiate history—were becoming insistent that the undergraduate was "the forgotten man."

Ironically, it was Clark Kerr, former chancellor of Berkeley and by then president of the University of California system, who had issued the most urgent warnings. The giant "multiversities," he wrote, were in danger of becoming "knowledge factories," whose neglect of students could easily turn undergraduates into an alienated "class"—and the universities into Latin American–style political fortresses. "When the extremists get in control of the students, the faculty, or the trustees, with class warfare concepts," Kerr warned, "then the delicate balance of interests becomes an actual war."

Before 1964 had ended, "war" broke out at Berkeley, the University of California's flagship campus, the envy of educators. In surveys of academic quality, the great public university had begun to run neck-and-neck with Harvard. The institution, with its 27,000 students, had an abundance of Nobel laureates—but also of inexperienced, preoccupied teaching assistants, to be exact, over 700 of them.

The explosion came over a squabble with the administration about the students' right to set up political propaganda tables on a narrow strip between campus and city streets. Out of the dispute, the Free Speech Movement was born, and a new generation of radical student leaders declared war on the authorities—academic and civil alike. When police entered the dispute, great masses of students—in accordance with the dissident leaders' scenario—allowed themselves to be radicalized.

Ultimately, the student rebels were to lose much credibility and sympathy. But, initially, their cause appeared to many observers, and particularly to undergraduates across the country, as just and reasonable. Charles Powell, who, as president of Berkeley's student government at the time of the uprising, represented moderate undergraduate opinion, said nevertheless with indisputable satisfaction: "Student government leaders all over the country report that they have never been listened to as seriously by their college presidents as since the Berkeley crisis."

As the conflict lingered and the students' demands became more erratic, often tinged with the off-campus radicalism of the "street people," new questions arose about the rebellion. Neil Smelser, a sociologist and one of Berkeley's hastily assembled emergency administrators, suggested the dimensions of a problem created by students who want complete freedom from restrictions but, at the same time, "want to be clutched to the bosom of their professors." It was, he said, comparable to the conflict between a longing for free love and the security of a faithful life within the family.

Ultimately, tensions grew between students' demands for more attention and faculty self-interest in their own scholarly research. When students barged into a faculty committee meeting, a professor, giving vent to his feelings, may have spoken for many of his colleagues when he shouted: "I've had my fill of students!"

The debate seesawed, not only at Berkeley but throughout the country. Universities had, in fact, grown too impersonal as they grew in size. "We know we want to grow," said a faculty member at Berkeley, "but we lack the resources of mind to do it right." One of his colleagues sympathized with freshmen who, having just come to know and trust a specific faculty adviser, find at the start of the next semester that he has gone off in the pursuit of his own projects. To many students, whose vision was confined to their own special interests, these haphazard incidents of neglect seemed like deliberate betrayal, giving birth to the slogan: "Never trust anybody over thirty."

The more mature students—and no more than ten percent of the nation's undergraduates were ever on the rebellion's barricades—might have agreed with a Berkeley professor who theorized that some students wanted to crawl back into "a kind of monastic shell which they knew only in their nostalgic dreams." But students also knew that many of their grievances were real. At Berkeley, they could cite a symbolic incident: In the midst of the upheaval, after the name and the picture of Mario Savio, the leader of the rebellion, had appeared on the front pages and covers of national newspapers and magazines, a faculty member asked for Savio's personnel file to bring his grades up to date. The bureaucrat in the registrar's office looked up in routine detachment and asked: "How do you spell the student's name?"

Despite the trauma at Berkeley, with its subsequent scramble for instant reforms, the emerging armistice was prematurely hailed as the end of the crisis. Commencement 1965 seemed once again devoted to serene self-satisfaction. Jobs were still plentiful. Columbia's President Grayson Kirk described the universities as "filled with young people whose natural idealism is as yet untempered by the patience and tolerance of maturity." He called for "self-imposed restraints."

Yale's President Kingman Brewster, Jr., was more alert to the gathering storm. He warned of the social crisis of contemporary America, while deploring the "impatient anti-intellectualism" of the student activists. Yale (followed soon by several other universities, including Cornell) moved to give students a voice in the granting of faculty tenure. The step represented a significant departure from the tradition of supreme faculty power in such matters. It was the consequence of complaints which were summarized in one undergraduate report by one sentence: "We are strangers being graded by strangers." While similar complaints might have been pertinent a hundred years earlier, it was only now that students had achieved power to do something about it.

In the years immediately following revolt and pacification at Berkeley it sometimes appeared as if the students might withdraw from the general academic issues and turn once again inward to deal with their personal problems. The focus of adult concern shifted from quasipolitical rebellion to experimentation with drugs. In 1966, Cornell's President James A. Perkins broke the silence about that issue when he said: "A lot of us have been sweeping the problem under the rug, and the rug is getting pretty lumpy." Critics of a drug scene that rapidly escalated from glue-sniffing to marijuana to LSD and eventually to heroin, blamed a combination of permissive homes and the steady acceleration of young people's experiences in an affluent society.

For the colleges, the problem was compounded by the fact that their old *in loco parentis* role had been abandoned under fire. Neither sexual mores nor such personal behavior as drug use were readily, or at all, regulated by any dean. It was a long way from the time when even professors were judged by rigid standards of their "moral" rectitude.

In what may have been the last publicized flurry of excitement over such issues as students' sexual behavior, Barnard College in 1968 expressed concern at finding that one of its students had been sharing an off-campus apartment with a young man who was enrolled as a student at another institution. Barnard's president asked in a letter to the young woman: "At what age and for what reasons did they [your parents] grant you the freedoms you now enjoy?" The girl's father, apparently trying to answer for his daughter, said he had not granted such freedoms but did not know what to do about it.

On the whole, the college decided to let sleeping coeds lie. In a response that would have seemed all but incomprehensible to earlier college administrators, a joint faculty–student committee, assigned to the case, penalized the student by depriving her of the use of the college cafeteria and snack bar and prohibiting her from attending social events in the dormitories.

Such tempests in college teapots were already being overshadowed by a new round of student unrest. Berkeley had not been, as some academic observers had hoped, an isolated incident. By 1968, the phenomenon had become worldwide. Perhaps it was an indication of American students' new prominence in the world of undergraduate affairs that the rebellion spread literally across the globe. From Berkeley to Tokyo and from Warsaw to Madrid, in democracies and totalitarian countries, often for totally different reasons, students were engaged in protests, boycotts, and political activism.

In London, a student charge was indistinguishable from those that had been uttered at Berkeley: "Professors come to lecture, not to discuss." In France, where the rebellion was to clash head-on with President Charles de Gaulle, dissatisfaction was based on even more demonstrably solid ground. At the University of Paris, it had not been unusual for a professor to lecture, standing-room-only, to 2000 undergraduates. In Prague, Warsaw, and Madrid, students risked their freedom, even their lives, by speaking out in demand of political and civil rights.

The start of the second round in the United States was marked by an uprising at Columbia in 1968 when some 300 students, led by the radical Students for a Democratic Society, out of a total enrollment of 17,500, charged the university with a long list of omissions and commissions—neglect of students, complicity with the war in Vietnam, disregard of the rights and needs of the poor and predominantly Black community adjacent to the campus. During twelve days of conflict, students occupied five academic buildings, captured and held the president's office, drove the administration into a basement redoubt, kept a dean hostage for twenty-six hours, and refused to negotiate on any terms other than the administration's unconditional surrender, including total amnesty for the rebels. In the end, a police raid broke the impasse. The insurrection was thus put down, but President Kirk and several top members of his administration had to resign.

Within a year, the scene at Columbia was reenacted on dozens of campuses, including Harvard, where the S.D.S. occupied University Hall; Cornell, where Black students brandished guns in the takeover of the student union; City College of New York, where students set fire to a building to underscore their demand for open admission for all high-school graduates. University presidents, including Pusey at Harvard, went into early retirement.

Richard Hofstadter, the historian, who was pressed into service to preside over Columbia's commencement to prevent tempers from being newly aroused by President Kirk's presence, saw the situation as a "crisis point in the history of American education and probably that of the Western world." Others were not so sure. Arthur M. Schlesinger, Jr., bringing a different historical perspective to the issue, took a less cosmic view. He warned students against the growing belief among the New Left that "one should feel and act first and think later."

Never before had the motives and views of American students been subjected to as much debate and analysis. Yet there was little agreement concerning the causes of unrest. The quest for social justice and the earlier experience of the civil rights fighters in their defiance of Southern segregationists and sheriffs—now applied to university administrations—undoubtedly played an important part. The aimlessness of much in their academic curriculum led students to make "relevance" one of their battle cries. But ultimately it was the war in Vietnam and the disorder in American society at home that fanned the students' sense of alienation and rage. They had seen their heroes—President Kennedy and his brother Robert, and Martin Luther King, Jr.—assassinated. Although Kennedy's Indochina policy had led to the full-scale war in Vietnam, the students lashed out at Presidents Johnson and Nixon for escalating and continuing the war.

In the midst of their confusion, students expressed immature impatience with what they scornfully termed "procedural liberalism," calling instead for participatory democracy which one faculty observer defined as Thoreau spiked with Maoism.

Radical students were primarily the sons and daughters of the well-to-do, dabbling in revolution but secure in their own social and economic status. Author John Hersey reported on the backgrounds of one such "action collective" at Yale and found that its eighteen members included four sons of Yale alumni and six prep school graduates; they were the sons and daughters of six heads of small companies, two high-ranking executives of large corporations, two lawyers, a doctor, and four distinguished university figures. Only one student in the group could be said to have come from a background of modest means.

Youthful rhetoric resorted to its own pseudopsychology. "You might want to know what is wrong with this society," said Mark Rudd, Columbia's rebel leader, to President Kirk, "since after all you live in a very tight self-created dream world." To shatter that world—which in its way was no more unreal than the world the students tried to construct for themselves—undergraduate rebels hurled what only a decade earlier would have been unspeakable obscenities at college administrators.

This, too, was a cry for attention. When Harvard Law Professor Archibald Cox, as chairman of a commission of inquiry, diagnosing what had gone wrong at Columbia, said: "The faculty as a body and most of its members as individuals failed to speak out upon matters of intense student concern." Susannah Wood, an undergraduate who spoke at Radcliffe's baccalaureate, following the uprising, said: "We do not feel like a cool, swinging generation—we are eaten up inside by an intensity that we cannot name."

No student generation had been more eloquent in trying to come to grips with its own confusion. Commenting on the occupation of Harvard's administration building, a *Crimson* commentator wrote: "What was most euphoric, however, was us and what we were to each other. For those few hours we *were* brothers and sisters . . . you had to realize, whatever your politics and whatever your tastes, that we were very beautiful in University Hall, we were very human, and we were very together." Another student commentator wrote: "Emotions are our guts; without them we are but thinking machines, and the destruction of which such machines are capable has left its scars on all of us."

The mass culture of the universities and of society had left students feeling lonely. The age of mass communications seemed to many young people to make personal communications more difficult. Issues crowded in from all sides, but the capacity of the individual to respond to them seemed to atrophy. Resisting a hateful war gave students a sense of the heroic—but also a deep feeling of guilt over the knowledge that others, mainly the poor, were fighting in Vietnam while they, the war protesters, were safe in the sanctuary of the campus.

The tragic climax came in the spring of 1970 when the American invasion of Cambodia enraged students—and many of their teachers—across the nation. During one such uprising at Kent State University in Ohio, ill-trained, tired, and trigger-happy National Guardsmen opened fire and left four students dead. The combination of Cambodia and Kent State led to the closing down of an estimated three hundred campuses by student strikes. President Brewster, at Yale, himself an early ally in the students' protests against the war, pleaded to avert a national student strike. There must be, he said, a better way to show distress over national policies than by "curtailing education." A delegation of university presidents, led by New York University's James M. Hester, called on the White House. "We share these [students'] apprehensions," they said. "We implore you to consider the incalculable dangers of an unprecedented alienation of America's youth. . . ."

The traumatic era ended almost as suddenly as it had begun. The end of the draft, even before American military involvement had come to a formal close, defused the anger. The threat of an economic recession caused students once again to focus on their personal problems—their academic work, their grades, their chances for jobs and careers. From what had seemed an unending period of plenty and unlimited opportunities for college graduates, the nation slid into a new economic pessimism.

Symbolically, the death of an innocent graduate student, as a result of a bomb planted by radicals at the University of Wisconsin's mathematics center, hastened the disenchantment with violence-prone rebels. The rebellion had run out of steam. A new generation of students had arrived on the scene.

In their own "morning-after" appraisals, many students seemed to question both the propriety and the productivity of lashing out against universities when their grievances in fact originated in Washington. But, in a more general sense, they had also grown tired of the emotional pitch of the radical dialectic—of being, as Yale's Kingman Brewster put it, "exploited and herded by contemporary demagogues." The more the radical activists talked about violence as a routine tool of their revolution, the more deliberately the majority of students pulled back. One radical student, who personally deplored these defections, told the *Columbia Spectator* in 1970: "We never did enough propaganda and education—but anyway, middle-class kids probably couldn't relate to violence as a tactic."

In 1974, a nationwide survey of youth attitudes, conducted by the Daniel Yankelovich research organization, found students were once again ready to reconcile themselves to society, in hopes that they would be able to function constructively within the system. Also in 1974, five years after colleges across the country had abandoned annual proms as irrelevant and outdated, students at Yale turned out again in formal attire to dance to the tune of a fifteen-piece orchestra playing waltzes and fox trots. "It's all coming back and I'm so happy," said Eddie Wittstein, the eighty-nine-year-old bandleader who, until the revolution called a halt, had played at Yale proms for fifty-two years. "The last time," recalled Wittstein, "we even had girls in blue jeans with American flags sewed on their behinds . . . to mock the whole thing." Now the girls were back in their evening gowns. "This is a revival of a tradition that people can enjoy and not feel guilty about anymore," said one student.

To underscore the new combination of fun and egalitarianism—with a nod to the economic squeeze—ticket prices had been lowered from $25 to $8 a couple, and nobody bid $100 for a table near the dance floor any longer. "Nobody has that kind of money or snobbish sense of prestige anymore," a student said. Even at the low price, the proceeds were going to charity. Altogether, a student said, "it was okay to dance again."

Such rapid swings in taste and behavior could easily lead to the conclusion that all student views and actions are erratic and therefore best to be ignored. A long-term look at the history of student life, however, suggests something quite different. While student attitudes do fluctuate, they also reflect quite accurately the concerns of contemporary society. If the young are naturally more volatile, they also tend to react with fewer inhibitions, and thus with greater honesty, to shortcomings in the adult world. They signal the need for revised academic standards and a relaxation of unreasonable and counterproductive pressures for grades and examinations. Students are infected by the same idealism and the same virus of corruption as their elders. To pay no attention to the students' voices and mores is to ignore one of society's best indicators of what lies ahead.

10

THE
UNFINISHED
PROMISE

*E*DUCATION HAS BEEN AMERICA'S IN-
visible frontier. It has enticed generation after generation of young
people to move forward into territory that had been strange and
forbidding to their parents. The promise of that open frontier
liberated the young from the confinement of their past, but in the
process it also often severed them from their roots. For some, the
frontier was temporarily shut down by prejudice and politics; but,
as soon as those barriers were lifted, those who had been held back
surged forward by taking full, often almost compulsive, advantage
of education.

Jefferson's ideal of an "aristocracy of talent" may have seemed
an impossible dream in his time, but it remains crucial to self-
government. The "diffusion of knowledge" cannot be said to have
failed when the diffusion of contemporary American leadership is
compared to the narrow base from which such leadership used to

emerge, and still does in many other nations. Public schools and the great network of state universities have responded to the technological society's insatiable demand for managers, executives, and planners. Graduates of this vast public education system have long since joined the earlier cozily homogeneous cadre of leaders until today they outnumber them. Whatever might once have been considered the American equivalent of the playing fields of Eton as the training ground for policy-makers has long since been replaced by the public high school. Even the elite colleges themselves—the only remaining bastion of the Old Boy Network—now draw the majority of their students from that egalitarian pool and contribute directly to the diffusion of status and leadership.

Social critics and radical reformers have not had to look far to be able to focus on American education's specific flaws and failures. Many historians, and virtually all history textbooks, have ignored the pervasive influence of education on the shaping of American thought and the ordering of American society. Thus, the field was wide open for revisionist critics to evolve a succession of devil theories—tales of conspiracies enlisting the schools in evil purposes. In this distorted view, education becomes a tool to enslave; schools are an instrument of oppression; the colleges, an assembly line that produces a standard-model ruling class; universities, blind servants of the military–industrial complex. The entire educational enterprise thus emerges as a giant, efficient machine created to assure conformity to an approved political scenario and servility to capitalist technocracy.

Such theories are seductive. They gain support because they single out some real weaknesses which, at a particular moment, are of serious and justified concern. For example, schools have indeed allowed themselves, time and again, to be used by conservative establishment forces to impose unthinking obedience to a special brand of Americanism; the ruling elite has sought to perpetuate itself by trying to turn some colleges into finishing schools for its brand of gentlemen; the universities have, at times, done the government's bidding without sufficient concern for the morality and wisdom of the government's policies. Public school educationists have, on many occasions, been guilty of some of the follies of which they have been accused. American pedagogues have espoused theories that failed to teach; condoned policies of exclusion and neglect which, by shutting out large groups of children, violated public education's own basic principles. At other times, they have embraced vapid academic standards which temporarily jeopardized the nation's intellectual stamina.

It is not difficult to show that, at one point or another, American educators have been smug (rejecting all criticism with the standard reply that the schools were better than ever), or arrogant (insisting that, if only the lay public kept hands off, the professional pedagogues could cure all of society's ills), or defensive (attributing the children's failures exclusively to circumstances beyond the schools' control).

It is not that the critics are wrong about any specific observation; it is rather that they train their telescope on an isolated part of the landscape and, on discovering a patch of dry rot, conclude that they have seen a panoramic vision of doom. Insularity compounds these distortions. Measured against a utopian ideal, for example, the American school is indeed often autocratic and oppressive; compared to existing models, say, in France or Germany, the same schools are oases of liberation.

American education has often been under severe stress. Whenever it ignored its own principles and goals, as it did in condoning the "separate but equal" doctrine that violated both the spirit and the letter of the Constitution, the educational leadership undermined the foundations on which the public school pioneers wanted to build a new interdependence between school and society.

But the major strands of education's fabric have stood the test of time remarkably well. Faith in education remains a unifying force. It is as strong in today's urban ghettoes as it was among a different population of similar ghettoes throughout the nation's history. It is a faith that even slavery could not erase; it remains the faith that still transcends all lines of color and national origins. Black militants, who charged that schools which failed to teach their children were guilty of "educational genocide" expressed the Black parents' traditional American belief that the difference between educational success and failure is the difference between life and death.

Such grass-roots faith in the magic of education placed a heavy burden on schools, which had no magic answers to the problems they were expected to solve. But, despite its flaws and setbacks,

American education has been remarkably successful in giving a high measure of social and political cohesion to a diverse population without any common ethnic or historic heritage. If schools have failed to wipe out poverty and to eliminate conflicts of wealth and status, they nevertheless prevented those social and economic strata from becoming frozen. Education may not have emerged as the great equalizer envisioned by Horace Mann; but American education more than any other force has kept society fluid and upwardly mobile. The rise, within one generation, from unskilled labor to the professional class, for example, is still commonplace. For each new group of first-generation collegians, the campus remains the staging area for economic achievement and social elevation.

While reality belies the myth of a classless America, education continues to be an effective escape hatch that reduces the danger of explosive class warfare. Radical leaders, including those of the 1960s student rebellion, have repeatedly failed to rally the poor and the deprived to their cause, in large measure because of the continuing faith in the evolutionary power of education. The promise to improve the schools and colleges, or to remove barriers to educational opportunity, proved highly magnetic; but those who threatened to bring the educational institutions to a halt, or to tear them down as part of a revolutionary strategy, soon found themselves without followers. In July 1974, only two years short of the Revolution's bicentennial, James Alexander Harris, one of six children of a welfare family, was elected president of the National Education Association which, he recalled, twenty years ago had still conducted much of its business in two separate compartments—"For Whites" and "For Colored."

America's educational origins were elitist and restrictive. To give the poor any schooling at all was a matter of charity. But the founders instinctively sensed the inevitability of conflict between an elitist social order and the egalitarian politics of a self-governing republic. Jefferson's proposal to make available free schooling from first grade through the university to a few of the ablest youngsters, regardless of family background, was a small beginning; but it started a trend that eventually made one fourth of the nation either learners or teachers.

Over the years, support for mass education became overwhelming. The demand by each new generation of parents was irresistible. What often remained vague was the strategy to accomplish those goals or an understanding of education's limitations. The debate over what constitutes the most effective curriculum, begun by Jefferson and Franklin, still continues. The conflict between the advocates of utilitarian training and the supporters of broad, general knowledge has never been resolved, with the result—probably essentially beneficial—that the two streams continue to mingle and modify each other. When James B. Conant appealed for the comprehensive high school in which vocational training could coexist with intellectual studies, he was actually pleading for the retention of the kind of republican egalitarianism in which youths are not separated at an early age into those who work with their hands and those who work with their heads.

This view of schooling contains a vital political safeguard. It lowers the barriers between blue- and white-collar workers; it reduces the likelihood that an excessively specialized education will, at times of economic recession, give birth to an alienated intellectual proletariat ready to seek totalitarian solutions simply because there are no jobs for its narrow competence.

The American decision not to sort children at an early age for different types of schooling which would in turn predetermine their future economic status in society was a sharp break with a tradition that in many European countries still remains dominant. Readiness to keep options open is more than a pedagogical tactic; it is an ideological commitment. Some have scorned the commitment as an anti-intellectual threat to academic standards; but experience has shown that those nations which established academic hurdles between elementary and secondary school find themselves trapped in a selection process that is more responsive to economic and social class than to talent and potential. An affluent, verbal, and book-oriented environment (often shored up by private tutoring and parental influence) tends to give privileged children an unfair advantage, thus hardening the mold of a stratified society.

Although American education has instinctively opted for the open access, it has found no perfect solution for the attending problem: how to sort children for the purpose of giving them the most suitable instruction, without shunting them into "tracks" which would subtly recreate elitism and divisions. This danger has been underscored by some consequences of school integration, when deprived children were transferred to schools with a predominantly affluent, middle-class clientele. Under such circumstances, "tracking" without sufficient attention to individual children's strengths and weaknesses has often created segregated classrooms within nominally integrated schools.

Such examples show the complexity of an ideal that seemed so simple when Horace Mann predicted that rich and poor would send their children to the same public schools, thus wiping out all differences of class. The goal has remained both unchanged and elusive. Reflecting a deeper change in the nation's mood, the earlier easy optimism has been dimmed.

No rational assessment of American education is possible without an understanding of the close link between the nation's mood and the schools. The optimism of the frontier, the fear of foreign (un-American) dogma, the dream of an open society, the conviction that there are pragmatic solutions for all problems, the trust in efficiency and productivity, the faith in the triumph of the new over the old—all of these often conflicting currents of thought have shaped American schools. They did so not because educators recommended it but because society willed it. Those who are convinced that they have discovered sinister conspiracies to use the schools for evil ends fail to understand the intricate American connection between school and society: schools' tactics and actions have indeed often been at odds with the spirit of the American ideal; but, instead of reflecting secret planning of deliberate plotters, these aberrations usually mirrored the vacillating resolve and changeable mood of the American people.

In the broadest sense, the progress of American education has been guided by two opposites—the Organizers and the Romantics. Both are inextricably part of the American way, and while they usually confront each other as deadly enemies, they ultimately and unwittingly complement each other in the shaping of institutions and the implementation of ideas.

Educational reform movements bear the stamp of one or the other of these strains. The romantic vision of a world of reason and a society freed from the tyranny of inherited privilege was indispensable to the creation of a system of universal schooling and constantly expanding access to higher education. But the romantic dream could not have been transformed into concrete policy without the organizers' pragmatic leadership.

The search for administrative solutions is a reflection of the American myth that all problems can be "fixed" by the application of efficiency and organization. Decentralized urban schools during the era of mass-immigration reflected the then prevalent faith in the political ward as the answer to the problems of the newly arrived and disoriented poor. In the absence of an organized state or a federal social welfare system, the concept was more realistic than it seems in self-righteous hindsight.

But, as the ward system began to drown in corruption and chaos, centralization was the obvious answer. The massive expansion of public education called for systematic planning and unified leadership. It was natural that the organizing tactics of industry and railroads would provide the model for a nation fascinated with these dynamic enterprises.

The creation of a schoolhouse with separate classrooms for children of different ages represented a distinct improvement over the old one-room schools (even though the nongraded schools of the 1950s reformers disinterred some of the original togetherness). Similarly, consolidation of school districts too small to maintain adequate facilities and staff was a step toward better education; but the compulsive pursuit of bigness that ultimately led to schools with thousands of students which could only be managed by the imposition of quasi-industrial or military administrative devices was as much a reflection of the American obsession with size as of the administrators' love affair with the corporate model. It was only as the cost-effectiveness commitment to bigness began to arouse the ire of educational counterreformers that the giant structures were challenged—as in the subdivision of schools into "mini-schools" in the late 1960s.

With the American penchant for standardized answers to all problems, school administrators have been bent on the search for "the one best way." Find the correct answer—to the teaching of reading or the schools' architectural design—and administrators throughout the nation would follow, show teachers how to lead their children to the promised land of graduation, and satisfy parents and politicians alike with end-of-the-year balance sheets of achievement.

Accountability and productivity are the organizers' controversial goals for the schools of the 1970s. Although teachers' unions and associations, including the National Education Association, view these goals with deep suspicion as a shorthand code for "more work at less pay," the quest is hardly new. In 1911, the N.E.A. had established a Committee on Economy and Time in Education. (In 1911, it should be added, the N.E.A. was dominated by the "one best way" organizers—the school administrators. In the 1970s, having virtually expelled the administrators from the association's ranks, the teachers were in the driver's seat. Teachers' unions and professional associations had become a powerful force within the Establishment, and their concern with job security and due process often clashed head-on with dollar-conscious seekers of efficiency and productivity.)

Administrative rigidity has been, without question, the grave-yard of many educational reforms which initially depended for their success on effective organization and leadership. But obses-sion with administrative solutions is deeply rooted in the Ameri-can character. British airmen in World War II used to quip that, when a four-man American bomber crew bails out of a crippled craft, they immediately form a committee and, before hitting ground, have already elected a chairman, vice-chairman, treasurer, and recording secretary.

Schools, particularly in times of stress, were affected by the same national drive to organize and administer. Not unlike railroaders and industrialists, new captains of education pushed the frontiers of universal education forward—successfully, until their single-minded devotion to the one best way and the perfect table of or-ganization began to reawaken the romantic strain in the American character. Exasperated by the pedantic managerial domination of the schools, the heirs of Emerson and Rousseau time and again counterattacked. Charging that the administrators had, in effect, been guilty of destroying sound ideas by pinning them, like dead butterflies, on the organizational charts and the lesson plans, romantic critics at such junctions served notice that the schools had been established for the benefit of the children, not for the convenience of administrators.

As the progressive cycle ran its course, it would fall victim to its own excesses. Just as organizers would inevitably regress from rational order to obsessive standardization, the countermovement would eventually slide from liberation to chaos, from rebellion against repressive order to a sentimental glorification of disorder.

Although these swings between opposite extremes may appear to represent an irrational state of affairs, with one neutralizing the other, the long-term historical effect appears quite different. Cyclical reforms and counterreforms are indeed repetitive; but the pattern is not so much one of mutual nullification as of balance. Without attention to organization, the continentwide mass education system could not have been created; without recurrent reliance on the administrators' skills, the system probably would not have survived. On the other hand, without periodic challenge by the romantics, humanists, and intellectual rebels, the tyranny of the one best way would have broken education's spirit.

As New York City's public schools were driven by the reformers of the late 1960s into decentralization, proponents of the status quo—school administrators and, by now, teachers' unions and their allies—pointed to the chaos that had engulfed the schools during their earlier period of decentralization. Such objections failed to take into account the cyclical nature of progress in American school and society. The American folly is the expectation that knowhow, money and a new policy can easily "fix" all problems; the American genius is readiness to abandon earlier blueprints for new improvisations, even if it means backtracking to a previous policy. The Organizers and Romantics have both repeatedly tried to impose their orthodoxies on American education. But as soon as one or the other appeared to gain too much power, the basic American distrust of orthodoxy so far has managed to call a halt. Reformers of every stripe have at times been infuriated precisely because this distrust of orthodoxy frustrated their appeal for total and unquestioning support; but, in the long run, the nonideological nature of the American people erects an invaluable barrier against irreversible educational as well as political folly.

It is easy to parody and ridicule the excesses of both conservative and progressive educational reformers. At the conclusion of each reform cycle, analysts tend to focus narrowly on the failure of the particular approach. At the height of the student revolt in Berkeley, the sociologists followed the rebels with tape recorders and tried to unlock the inner secrets of a generation by listening to the high pitch of a local skirmish.

A broader view suggests that new ideas in each cycle have had a more lasting influence on the total enterprise than is generally acknowledged. Often the benefits are not recognized until a new generation of educators and parents encounters them under new auspices and different labels, their original goals freed from political and ideological connotations. The open classroom of the 1970s has had its supporters and detractors, but not even ultraconservatives attacked it with the venom that their predecessors showered on John Dewey. Yet the open classroom movement is clearly Dewey rising again—not from Dewey's ashes but from a social and educational soil fertilized by his ideas.

The continuing battle between the elitists and the egalitarians should be viewed from the same perspective. Americans as a whole have always been ambivalent about how self-evident is the truth that all men are created equal; but most individual Americans believe that they are equal to their neighbors and stand ready to cut down those who lay claim to superior privileges. National clichés often contain a kernel of truth. It is not irrelevant that, whereas German army privates were inspired by the belief that each of them carried a marshal's baton in his knapsack, American boys (and in the future, one must hope, girls as well) viewed themselves as potential Presidents.

College alumni carry on their shoulders the chip of elitism—the notion that the hurdles they cleared ought to remain at least as forbidding for those who come after them. Qualities that earned them their diploma henceforth become the qualities by which all standards should be measured. Privilege—whether inherited or earned—is one of the building blocks of conservatism.

The elitist wall in America is a reality, but it is not central to the national structure. It acts as a dam that slows, but cannot permanently block, the egalitarian push out of the confinement of lower socioeconomic origins. The expansionist trend in American education, with its attending rewards of economic and social status, has been continuous, frustrating skeptics and confounding the conservative prophets of academic doom. And still—as in the case of the balance of power between the organizers and the romantics in the reform cycles—the elitist strain has performed a useful task in preventing the anti-intellectual forces from permanently capturing the egalitarian movement. For example, when Dewey's anti-intellectual followers scuttled all quality controls and tried to establish that soccer and Socrates were academic equivalents, elitists ultimately manned the barricades and stopped the egalitarians' rush to intellectual disaster.

The system is not fail-safe. Whenever the elitist strain in the American character has allowed itself to be captured by the forces of prejudice, the resulting barriers that excluded some children from the benefits of the open society did grievous harm. The distortion of elitism into white supremacy was truly the great American tragedy; its aftereffects still pose the most serious threat to the future of American democracy. The belated discovery that this society cannot survive half open and half closed has once again assigned to education the task of building a more perfect union.

Nation-building has always been American education's mission. The delicate distinction between the creation of cohesive values and the imposition of chauvinistic dogma has often been blurred. In times of political confusion, the schools have occasionally strayed from the spirit of building a *free* nation. The "fix-it" approach to social and political problems moreover has repeatedly saddled public education with the impossible task of rooting out unpopular thoughts and ideas.

By the same token, naïve social reformers have tried to enlist the schools in grandiose schemes of sociopolitical change, without realizing that no society will allow its educational institutions to be used as a revolutionary or heretical force to dismantle the establishment that supports them. The American school is deeply rooted in the society it serves. Those who wanted to use the schools to build a new social order were ignorant of the fact that, throughout their history, the schools have reflected the ideals and follies, the strengths and weaknesses of their environment. Neither the conservative administrators' and unions' lobby nor the radical romantics can have their way for very long before a new anti-doctrinaire consensus flashes the red light.

Three powerful factors have given education in America a

special role above and beyond the transmission of knowledge—making education, in fact, an instrument of extraordinary importance for the continued renewing of society.

The first of these forces is the dynamism of educational reformers. Generally cool toward philosophical and intellectual abstractions, this pragmatic nation has nevertheless shown extraordinary interest in the work and the prescriptions of educational theorists. To these theorists, and to the activists who translated their proposals into classroom practice, fell most of the burden of humanizing childhood in America.

It was not an easy task. America is not as child-centered as the self-congratulatory myth suggests. Children have all too often been regarded primarily as either economic assets or liabilities, and treated as such, with little regard for their individual sensitivities and feelings. Even the best-intentioned adults, including parents and teachers, are chronically afflicted with what Dr. Bruno Bettelheim calls "childhood amnesia"—an inability to recall their own view of the world from a child's perspective. Few human and civil rights have traditionally been extended to children. Children are often deprived of justice during the very years when they are expected to learn about its importance. The long and dreary history of child labor provides ample testimony that America has often fallen short of the utopian dream. For the babes of poverty, from Nick the Chicken Boy to today's ghetto children, the dream was often a shattering nightmare.

Again and again, it was left to the education reformers to shake the insensitive adult establishment—including the educational establishment—out of its indifference. More than an academic debate was at stake when Horace Mann challenged the Boston Latin masters' harsh and unimaginative pedagogy or when Dewey tried to turn the school into an embryonic society of joyful living, or when Jerome Bruner enlisted the instruments of psychological research in the quest for ways of making learning both more effective and more humane. It is a measure of the need to extend to children the benefits of a democratic society that leading legal scholars and educational psychologists in 1973 joined in a determined campaign to outlaw the neglect, abuse, and exploitation of children.

The second factor that has given education in America an extraordinarily vital mission is its capacity to act as a compensating and modifying force, when the dynamics of the nation call for major readjustments. During the era of nation-building, schools performed their homogenizing assignment. Had the Americanization course of the schools been inflexible, the consequence, once the nation was built and its self-confidence established, might well have been an escalation of superpatriotism. The danger signals of such a trend were, in fact, clearly discernible—in the elevation of the American way of life to something of a religious credo, in the creation of "un-American activities" as a punishable offense, in the gradual application of "the one best way" to the teaching of history, economics, and civics, in the adamant, often cruel manner with which the schools tried to sever the ties between the "un-American" heritage of the parents and the new American children.

But under new pressures, the system proved capable—not without resistance—to reverse or at least modify its course. The demands of excluded minorities, whose own history and culture had been ignored, reminded the nation that pluralism is as much an American reality as the sharing of national goals and institutions. It was through the schools that the legitimacy of group differences and the importance of ethnic roots were brought into focus.

The third factor that confirms the extraordinary link between school and society is the impact of the Supreme Court on educational policy. Historians have never questioned, and even the general public has been made aware of, the court's role in keeping the Constitution relevant and in adjusting American institutions to the changing demands of American life. Far less attention has been paid, at least until the 1954 *Brown* decision against school segregation, to the continuous relationship between the court and the schools. As that tribunal has gradually—and not without occasional backsliding—tipped the scales toward egalitarianism, it has given aid and comfort to the social and humanistic school reformers.

The American dream of utopia is predicated on individuality and freedom; in the every-day reality, by contrast, the American way of life often drifts into a self-satisfied pattern of uniformity that stifles dissent. As a result, neither the liberating nor the regimenting current of American school and society can be considered separately, without the risk of distorting the nation's goals, achievements, and shortcomings.

The perennial conflict between liberal reformers and the conservative establishment is rendered more complex by the fact that new answers invariably lead, not to definitive solutions, but to new questions or a restatement of old, but forgotten ones. Positions shift. Good intentions lead to reforms which, in turn, become standardized procedures, and thus eventually unresponsive to changing needs. Progressives whose major goal initially was to thaw or shatter the frozen mold of conservatism eventually freeze their own progressive approach into another unchangeable creed. Teachers' unions, once committed to fight the oppressively standardized rule by the administrator–bosses, turn into another special-interest establishment, wedded to the benefits of the centralized power they used to denounce. The unions' slogan, "Teachers Want What Children Need," gradually changes from a public-service reform banner to a deceptive commercial. The extreme of child exploitation through child labor gives way to the new extreme of child uselessness, reinforced by liberal opposition to a lower minimum wage for teenagers that results in the elimination of jobs. Universal education, the triumph of the American reform movement, is increasingly viewed as a meal ticket by armies of organized professionals who begin to neglect the individual needs and rights of their captive audience—until a new countermovement threatens their professional security by challenging the very constitutionality of compulsory education.

Cynics, time and again, sound the same note of ridicule and contempt for the reformers. "Every year," H. L. Mencken wrote in 1922, "sees a craze for some new solution to the teaching enigma, at once simple and infallible. . . . There is no sure-cure so idiotic that some superintendent of schools will not swallow it. . . ."

The Establishment, time and again, sounds a familiar note of defense. New York City's Superintendent of Schools William Maxwell wrote in his 1906 annual report:

> The opponents of modern educational methods who would abandon the present rich courses of study and return to the barren instruction of sixty years ago . . . have for a long time been deploring the alleged fact that children today do not

spell and cipher as well as did pupils half a century ago . . .
The truth [is] that children in the eighth year of the New
York City's elementary schools are better in spelling and
arithmetic than were much older pupils in the high schools
of sixty years ago.

Mencken and Maxwell are both typical of the continuing,
cyclical attack and defense. And, in their way, they are both right.
Educational reform movements are reflections in the same mirror
of society that shows political problem-solving phases such as the
New Deal, the Fair Deal, the New Frontier, and the Great Society. They are often just as simplistic, naïve, gimmicky—and
necessary.

Most of the highly advertised reform thrusts contained within
themselves the certainty of failure, simply because they promised
too much; yet most of these crusades moved society and its schools
toward greater egalitarianism. Whenever the immediate side-effects
were sufficiently disturbing, they helped to rally the reactionary
countercurrents; but, on the long-term tally sheet, liberal entries
dominate. The egalitarian push has often been slowed, but never
fully contained for long, by the elitist dam.

Critics who despair of the moral and political state of the union
want to dismantle the educational edifice as a prelude to the similar
dismantling of the entire political and economic power structure.
But the late Chief Justice Earl Warren, himself the son of an immigrant railroad worker, urged his countrymen two months before his death in July 1974 never to tear down good buildings because they are inhabited by some bad tenants.

Growing up in America is infinitely less onerous and more indi-
vidually promising today than it was two centuries ago. The dichotomy between privilege and deprivation has not disappeared,
but the nation's consciousness about such injustice has been raised,
and education deserves at least a share of the credit. Equal access
to education is on the way to becoming a right under the Constitution.

It would be entirely wrong to conclude that the nation, because
it is infinitely better schooled, is therefore wiser, and thus safe
from political folly and ethical lapses. Two centuries of experience
have shown that it is no contradiction to say that education has

been immensely powerful in shaping American society and yet impotent in its efforts to influence the nation's day-to-day political decisions. The best that can be said is that American education and social progress reflect a remarkable determination to disprove the elitist credo that "more is worse." But it remains for future generations to prove that more is better—or even good enough.

Education has been enormously successful in expanding opportunities for great masses of Americans—far beyond the boldest dreams of the early pioneers. But the triumph of such egalitarian expansion of opportunities alone is not sufficient cause to proclaim the ultimate triumph of the diffusion of knowledge as the guarantor of a free society. The options are yet to be used so that they may be translated into a just and harmonious way of life.

ANNOTATED BIBLIOGRAPHY

General

It would be impossible, within the scope of this volume, to list every book, source, or study used in our research. We have tried to acknowledge our debt to the work of others in the course of the narrative and wherever possible in these notes as well. The major aim of the listings that follow, therefore, is not to be definitive but rather to serve as a starting point for those who wish to pursue a particular subject in greater depth. We have sought to strike a balance between general works and the readings necessary for more specialized study. Whenever the issues have involved controversy, it has been our aim to include authors representing varied, and often opposing viewpoints, enabling readers to form their own opinions.

As far as feasible, this listing indicates whether books are available in paperback editions and whether journal articles appear in relatively accessible collections. Because of the difficulty in obtaining them, only the few most important theses consulted have been included here.

To supplement this guide, we also point to the best available bibliographies relating to subjects covered in this book, particularly in the areas of more recent scholarship, e.g., women's role in education, childhood in America, college students, Black education, etc., along with other useful materials, even if their basic focus lies elsewhere.

Two series have been particularly helpful: the Teachers College Classics in Education (books of this series will be designated TC) and the Arno Press reprint series *American Education: Its Men, Ideas and Institutions* (to be designated AP, plus the particular work's original date of publication). Both of these series in their entirety represent such a wealth of topics and variety of content that the interested reader is well advised to check the listings of their offerings. In addition to the articles and bibliographies specifically cited below, periodic listings in the *History of Education Quarterly* and the *American Quarterly*, as well as other journals mentioned in connection with specific subjects, should be considered as generally useful for further reading.

For additional reading toward a general scholarly background in the history of education, there are several excellent bibliographic studies which discuss both the earlier "Whig" interpretation and the new conceptualizations of educational historians.

Bernard Bailyn: *Education in the Forming of American Society* (1960)

Lawrence A. Cremin: *American Education: Some Notes toward a New History* (1969)

———— *The Wonderful World of Ellwood Patterson Cubberley* (1965)

Marvin Lazerson: "Revisionism and American Educational History," *Harvard Educational Review,* XLIII (1973)

David B. Tyack: "New Perspectives on the History of American Education," in Herbert Bass, ed., *The State of American History* (1971)

Laurence R. Veysey: "Toward a New Direction in Educational History: Prospect and Retrospect," *History of Education Quarterly* (Fall 1969)

In addition, there are many outstanding historical works which treat what has been called "intellectual" or "social" or "cultural" history and include some aspects of American education during different periods or from different individual, institutional or sectional viewpoints. These include Daniel Boorstin's three-volume work, *The Americans,* all volumes of which have sections dealing directly with education and others which treat closely related subjects; Merle Curti, *The Growth of American Thought;* Henry Steele Commager, *The American Mind;* Max Lerner, *America as a Civilization;* Richard Hofstadter, *Social Darwinism in American Thought* and *Anti-Intellectualism in American Life;* David Potter, *People of Plenty.*

Chapters 2 and 3   School on the Hill and Pragmatic Visionaries

The seminal essay by Bernard Bailyn, *Education in the Forming of American Society: Needs and Opportunities for Study* (1960) offers an excellent short introduction to the study of education history during the formative period. *American Education: The Colonial Experience* by Lawrence A. Cremin (1970) provides a definitive treatment of this period in American education. Scholars will find Cremin's bibliographic essay of particular interest.

Books which were also useful were Russel B. Nye, *The Cultural Life of the New Nation* (1960), Chapters 7 and 8; Robert Middlekauff, *Ancients and Axioms: Secondary Education in Eighteenth Century New England* (1963); Samuel Eliot Morison, *The Puritan Pronaos: Studies in the Intellectual Life of New England* and *The Founding of Harvard College* (1936); Louis B. Wright, *The Cultural Life of the American Colonies* (1951) and *Culture on the Moving Frontier* (1961).

Paul Leicester Ford's edition of *The New England Primer* (TC 1962 reissue) gives an introduction to the primer and its style and flavor. It was written in 1897.

The following books provide a good basic introduction to Thomas Jefferson's contributions to American education. *Crusade against Ignorance: Thomas Jefferson on Education,* edited by Gordon C. Lee (TC) contains some selections of his writings on education and an introductory essay. This short volume describes the range of Jefferson's thinking and includes notes and suggestions for further reading. Lawrence Cremin's lecture *The Genius of*

American Education (1965) is a perceptive discussion of how Jefferson's ideas permeated the philosophies of those who followed him, particularly Mann and Dewey. See also Roy Honeywell, *The Educational Work of Thomas Jefferson* (1931); C. F. Arrowwood, *Thomas Jefferson and Education in a Republic* (1930); and James B. Conant, *Thomas Jefferson and the Development of American Public Education* (1962).

No one can hope to understand Benjamin Franklin's life or his views on education without reading his *Autobiography*. An excellent supplement to this is Carl Becker's concise sketch in the *Dictionary of American Biography* (VI, 1931). For specific attention to Franklin on education see John Hardin Best, *Benjamin Franklin on Education* (TC), and Thomas Woody, *Educational Views of Benjamin Franklin* (1931).

For background on other important men see: Ervin Showmaker, *Noah Webster, Pioneer of Learning* (1936), Henry Steele Commager, ed., *Noah Webster's Spelling Book* (TC 1963). H. G. Good, *Benjamin Rush and His Services to American Education* (1919), Dagobert D. Runes, *Selected Writings of Benjamin Rush* (1947). See also John Locke, *Some Thoughts Concerning Education; John Locke on Education* by Peter Gay (TC 1964); Merle Curti, "The Great Mr. Locke, America's Philosopher," an essay in *Probing Our Past* (1955); Hyman Kuritz, "Benjamin Rush: His Theory of Republican Education," *History of Education Quarterly* (Winter 1967).

General books about education during this early period which are helpful include the following: Dupont de Nemours, *National Education in the United States of America* (1923); Oscar Allen Hansen, *Liberalism and American Education in the Eighteenth Century* (republished 1965); Frederick Rudolph, ed., *Essays on Education in the Early Republic* (1965); David Madsen, *The National University: Enduring Dream of the USA* (1966).

Chapter 4   The New Americans

One of the most important and useful document collections for this chapter and the several following is *Children and Youth in America: A Documentary History* (5 vols; 1971), by Robert Bremner, et al. Despite the difficulties posed by its organization, it is an indispensable collection. Hector de Crèvecoeur's *Letters from an American Farmer* and Alexis de Tocqueville's *Democracy in America* both provide valuable insights into how Americans viewed themselves and how this is reflected in the schools. Also useful for this topic is the previously cited book by Louis B. Wright, *Culture on the Moving Frontier* (1961).

McGuffey's fifth and sixth readers have been reprinted in paperback by Signet Books; excerpts are found in numerous anthologies. See also Mark Sullivan, *Our Times* (Vol. II), and Henry Steele Commager, *The American Mind* (pp. 38–40). The cultural values implicit in nineteenth-century American textbooks are described by Ruth M. Elson in her well-documented study *Guardians of Tradition*. Other useful works on American schoolbooks include: Clifton Johnson, *Old Time Schools and Schoolbooks* (1963 reprint), and Monica Kiefer, *American Children through Their Books, 1700–1835,* which has a useful bibliography (1948); J. Merton England, "The Democratic Faith in American Textbooks, 1783–1860," *American Quarterly* (Summer (1963).

Specific scholarly studies of the establishment of schools in the West are David B. Tyack, "The Tribe and the Common School: Community Control in Rural Education," *American Quarterly* (Spring 1966), and, by the same author, "The Kingdom of God and the Common School: Protestant Ministers and the Educational Awakening in the West," *Harvard Educational Review* (Fall 1966); Timothy Smith, "Protestant Schooling and American Nationality, 1800–1850," *Journal of American History* (March 1967). See also Ray Billington, *The Protestant Crusade (1800–1860).*

Some works which treat the immigrant's problems in urban schools include: Allan Schoener, *Portal to America: The Lower East Side 1870–1925;* Selma Berrol, *Immigrants at School 1898–1914* (unpublished Ph.D. thesis CUNY); Moses Rischin, *The Promised City* (1962); Diane Ravitch, *The Great School Wars* (1974); Marvin Gettlemen, "John H. Finley at CCNY—1903–1913," *History of Education Quarterly* (Winter 1970).

General books which furnish an overview of the immigrant in school and society are Oscar Handlin, *The Uprooted* (1940); John Higham, *Strangers in the Land: Patterns of American Nativism* (1955), which includes material on how discussions of hereditary intelligence influenced immigration restriction in the 1920s; Barbara M. Solomon, *Ancestors and Immigrants, 1860–1925* (1956); Nathan Glazer and Daniel Moynihan, *Beyond the Melting Pot;* Michael Novack, "White Ethnic," *Harper's* Magazine (September 1971).

A paperback collection of famous Supreme Court cases, which includes many on education, is John Garraty, ed., *Quarrels that Have Shaped the Constitution* (1966). The cases presented are discussed in historical context, as is the Pierce case in David Tyack's "The Perils of Pluralism," in the *American Historical Review* (October 1968). Howard Beale, in *Are American Teachers Free?* (1936), deals with the issue of academic freedom, as does Robert W. Iversen in *The Communists and the Schools* (1959). In many instances, it is necessary to go directly to the cases themselves. For a comprehensive approach to the impact of the courts on education, with particular emphasis on the growing interplay between the law and sociology, see *Educational Policy and the Law* (1974) a casebook by David Kirp and Mark Yudof—a volume made particularly useful by its presentation of a wide variety of views and reactions concerning the meaning and consequences of court rulings affecting American education.

Chapter 5   Blackboard Politics

It is virtually impossible to list one or two works which will provide an introduction to this complex area. We have tried below to suggest, by topic, some introductory books as well as specialized scholarly studies. Some books, however, are particularly helpful for long time periods or coverage of wide subject areas. Merle Curti's *Social Ideas of American Educators* takes a biographical approach and places leaders of American education in their historical contexts. (The paperback issue for 1959 contains an updated introduction.) Excellent insight into urban schooling is found in David Tyack's *The One Best System: A History of American Urban Education* (1974). In *Popular Education and Democratic Thought in America* (1962), Rush Welter emphasizes the relationship between education and politics. Henry J. Perkinson, in his book *The Imperfect Panacea: American Faith in Education, 1865–1965* (paperback), describes the tendency to call on the schools to solve societal problems. An interesting and valuable collection of source materials from Horace Mann's time to the present has been assembled by Michael Katz in *School Reform Past and Present* (Beacon paperback).

A good beginning for the pre–Civil War period is found in Lawrence A. Cremin, *The American Common School: An Historic Conception* (1951) and *The Republic and the School: Horace Mann on the Education of Free Men* (1957), which contains selections from Mann's annual reports to the Massachusetts Board of Education (TC series). The earlier interpretation is found in Ellwood P. Cubberley's influential *Public Education in the United States,* first published in 1919. Recent revisionist scholarship for this period is best represented by Michael Katz, *The Irony of Early School Reform.*

For further background, see also Maxine Greene, *The Public School and the Private Vision* and Jonathan Messerli's biography of Horace Mann and his article, "Localism and State Control in Horace Mann's Reform of the Common Schools," *American Quarterly* (Spring 1965). See also Henry Barnard, *Memoirs of Teachers, Educators* (Arno Press).

More technical economic and demographic material for this era can be found in Albert Fishlow, "The American Common School Revival: Fact or Fancy?" in *Industrialization in Two Systems: Essays in Honor of Alexander Gerschenkron,* Henry Rosovsky, ed. (1968). Criticisms are offered by Maris A. Vinovskis, "Trends in Massachusetts, 1829–1868," *History of Education Quarterly* (Winter 1972). Earlier economic thinking is found in Frank Tracy Carlton, *Economic Influences upon Educational Progress in the U.S., 1820–1850* (1966; TC reprint).

By far the best account of the impact of the progressive education movement in the United States is Lawrence Cremin's *Transformation of the School* (1961). Recent scholarship has aimed at reinterpreting that era; Cremin's book remains the outstanding work, both scholarly and readable.

A good introduction to the writings of John Dewey is Martin S. Dworkin, *Dewey on Education* (TC series, 1959). See also Oscar Handlin, *John Dewey's Challenge to Education* (1959); Douglas Lawson and Arthur E. Lean, *John Dewey and the World View* (1964). An extensive collection of his works is found in Joseph D. Ratner's *Intelligence and the Modern World: John Dewey's Philosophy* (1939).

Valuable supplementary studies for the progressive era include Raymond

Callahan, *Education and the Cult of Efficiency* (1962); Patricia A. Graham *Progressive Education: From Arcady to Academe, A History of the Progressive Education Association* (1964); Robert Wiebe, "The Social Functions of Public Education," *American Quarterly* (Summer 1969); Moses Stambler, "The Effect of Compulsory Education and Child Labor Laws on High School Attendance in New York City, 1898–1917," *History of Education Quarterly* (Summer 1968); Selma Berrol, "William H. Maxwell and a New Educational New York," *History of Education Quarterly* (Summer 1968); William M. Landes and Lewis C. Solomon, "Compulsory Schooling Legislation: An Economic Analysis of the Law and Social Change in the Nineteenth Century," *Journal of Economic History* (March 1972).

The Shaping of the American High School by Edward Krug (2 vols.) is a solid straightforward presentation: Volume I covers the period from 1880 to 1920, and there is an excellent bibliographic essay (especially section IV, which gives a guide to the various pedagogical journals of the period); Volume II, from 1920 to 1941, does not contain a bibliographic essay.   Krug edited *Charles W. Eliot and Popular Education* (TC 1961), a collection of documents which describe Eliot's involvement, particularly with the Committee of Ten. Theodore Sizer offers documents and commentary on the pre–Civil War academies in *The Age of the Academies* (TC 1964) and James McLachlan discusses the growth and development of *American Boarding Schools.*

Much recent scholarship has focused on urban schools and the growth of school bureaucracy since the end of the nineteenth century. The approach varies greatly, ranging from objective scholarship to ideologically oriented polemics. Books about New York City include: Sol Cohen, *Progressives and Urban School Reform* (1963); Carl F. Caestle, *The Evolution of an Urban School System: New York City 1750–1850* (1973); Diane Ravitch, *The Great School Wars* (1974). The Boston schools are treated by Joseph Cronin in *The Control of Urban Schools: Perspectives on the Power of Educational Reformers* (1973); Marvin Lazerson, *Origins of the Urban School: Public Education in Massachusetts 1870–1915;* Stanley K. Schultz, *The Culture Factory: Boston Public Schools 1789–1860* (1973). See also Sheldon Marcus and Harry Rivlin (ed.), *Conflicts in Urban Education,* and Joel Spring, *Education and the Rise of the Corporate State;* Michael Katz, *Class, Bureaucracy and the Schools* (1971). *History of Education Quarterly* (Fall 1969) has essays by David Tyack, Sol Cohen, and Michael Katz on this subject.

Some current works which deal with the relationship of school funding to broader social problems are: *Financing American Education,* published by the National Council for the Advancement of Education Writing (revised edition, May 1973); George A. Kinzler, "Federal Aid to Education: 1945–1963," *History of Education Quarterly* (September 1970); John E. Coons, William H. Clune III, and Stephen D. Sugarman, *Private Wealth and Public Education;* Samuel Bowles, "Unequal Education and the Reproduction of the Social Division of Labor," in Martin Carnoy, ed., *Schooling in a Corporate Society: The Political Economy of Education in America* (paperback). See also Kirst and Wirt, *The Political Web of American Schools* (1972).

For the period since World War II, there are many books which focus on the problems of maintaining both quality and quantity in a mass system. Required reading in this area is James B. Conant's *The American High School Today* (1959) and *The Education of American Teachers* (1963). In addition, see Robert Bendiner, *The Politics of the Schools* (1969); Martin Mayer, *The Schools* (1961); Arthur Bestor, *Educational Wasteland* (1953); Hyman G. Rickover, *Education and Freedom* (1959). Conant's *American High School Today* was written in response to these more extreme critics, as were the valuable books by Paul Woodring, *One Fourth of a Nation* (1957) and *Let's Talk Sense About Our Schools* (1952).

Another area of contemporary concern is the question of greater equality in the schools and improving the conditions of individual pupils. See Charles Silberman, *Crisis in the Classroom* (1970); Herbert Kohl, *36 Children* (1967); John Holt, *How Children Fail* (1964); Harold H. Hart, ed., *Summerhill: For and Against*, E. Z. Friedenberg, *Coming of Age in America* (1965); Christopher Jencks, *Inequality: A Reassessment of the Effect of Family and Schooling in America* (1972); Ivan Illich, *DeSchooling Society* (1970); and Colin Greer, *The Great School Legend* (1972).

Chapter 6 American Childhood: The Utopian Myth

For much of the documentation of this chapter, we are again indebted to Robert H. Bremner, et al., *Children and Youth in America: A Documentary History*. It contains a useful introductory bibliography, notes, and suggestions for further reading. Detailed scholarly bibliographic material is offered by C. John Sommerville in an essay, "Toward a History of Childhood and Youth," originally published in *The Journal of Interdisciplinary History* (Autumn 1971) and also available in a paperback collection, *The Family in History* (Harper Torchbooks).

No reading about childhood history would be complete without Philippe Ariès's *Centuries of Childhood* (1961), even though his work does not deal with American children. The work of Lenore and Peter Opie, particularly *The Lore and Language of Schoolchildren* (1959), also fits into this category. An introduction to the major writings of social scientists and historians on culture and personality and on the American character since 1940 is offered by Michael McGiffert in "Selected Writings on American National Character" in the *American Quarterly* (Summer 1963); Parts I and II provide an excellent introduction to this area.

A good survey collection of theories about child-rearing from Locke and Cadogan to Freud and Piaget can be found in William Kessen, ed., *The Child* (1965). A survey history of American youth which emphasizes older children is Oscar and Mary Handlin's *Facing Life* (1971). See also H. S. Commager's *The American Mind* and Frank Luther Mott's *A History of American Magazines, 1885–1905*, both of which have sections on changing American child-rearing theories. See also the Arno Press reprint series, *Children and Youth: Social Problems and Social Policy*, Robert H. Bremner, ed.

An area of recent historical interest of obvious importance to the history of childhood is the history of the family. There is no major single work which provides a conceptual framework. The work of Peter Laslett, which is summarized in his introduction to *Household and Family in Past Time* (1972), is helpful. This essay collection contains some work on America; Laslett's best-known work is *The World We Have Lost* (1965). A short American overview is offered by John Demos, "The American Family in Past Time," in the *American Scholar* (Summer 1974). In spite of its age and its old-fashioned approach, Arthur Calhoun's three-volume study, *A Social History of the American Family* (1917), remains useful (especially I:4,6,9,17; II:3,6; III:3,7,14). Recent work in progress on the history of the family is reported in the *History of the Family Newsletter* (Tamara Haraven, ed.) from Clark University. See also the Arno Press reprint series, *Family in America*, David J. Rothman and Sheila M. Rothman, eds.

Bernard Wishy's *The Child and the Republic* (1968) surveys the literature for and about children until the end of the nineteenth century and has an excellent bibliography. Helpful books for the Colonial period are: Edmund S. Morgan, *The Puritan Family* (1966); Alice Morse Earle, *Child Life in Colonial Days* (1899), John Demos, *A Little Commonwealth* (1970); "Childlife in New England" (pamphlet published by Sturbridge Village, Massachusetts); Stanford Fleming, *Children and Puritanism* (1933); Philip Greven, "Family Structure in Seventeenth-Century Andover, Massachusetts," in *The American Family in Social-Historical Perspective* (paperback collection). An expanded version of the last work appears in Greven's book, *Four Generations: Population, Land and Family in Colonial Andover, Massachusetts* (1970). See also Michael Zuckerman, *Peaceable Kingdoms: New England Towns in the Eighteenth Century* (1970).

Views of nineteenth-century classrooms can be found in: Warren Burton, *The District School as It Was* (AP, 1850); Herbert A. Falk, *Corporal Punishment: A Social Interpretation of Its Theory and Practices in the Schools of the United States* (TC, 1941); B. J. Finkelstein, "Governing the Young: Teacher Behavior in American Primary Schools, 1820–1880" (TC, unpublished Ph.D. thesis), Peter A. Soderbergh, "Old School Days on the Middle Border, 1849–1859: The Mary Payne Beard Letters," *History of Education Quarterly* (Winter 1968).

Other nineteenth-century views of children include Robert Sunley, "Early Nineteenth-Century American Literature on Child Rearing," in *Childhood in Contemporary Cultures*, Margaret Mead and Martha Wolfenstein, eds.; Ann L. Kuhn, *The Mother's Role in Childhood Education: New England Concepts 1830–1860* (1947); Charles Strickland, "A Transcendentalist Father: The Child Rearing Practices of Bronson Alcott," *Perspectives in American History* (Vol. III, 1969): Richard Rapson, "The American Child as Seen by British Travellers, 1845–1935," *American Quarterly* (Spring 1965); G. R. Clay, "Children of the Young Republic," *American Heritage* (April 1960); John C. Crandall, "Patriotism and Humanism in Children's Literature 1825–1860," *American Quarterly* (Spring 1969); Daniel Calhoun, *The Intelligence of a*

People (1973); Bernard Farber, "Family and Community Structure: Salem in 1800," reprinted in *The American Family in Social-Historical Perspective,* from Chapter 4 of that author's *Guardians of Virtue: Salem Families in 1800* (1972); Michael Zuckerman, "The Nursery Tales of Horatio Alger," *American Quarterly* (May 1972).

For further reading on child labor, see Walter Trattner, *Crusade for Children* (1970), which provides a detailed history of the Child Labor Committee; Forest C. Ensign, *Compulsory School Attendance and Child Labor* (AP, 1921); and Jeremy Felt, *Hostages to Fortune* (1965).

Some recent studies of specialized areas for the late nineteenth century include Anthony Platt, *The Child Savers* (1969); Joseph Hawes, *Children in Urban Society* (1971); Peter Gregg Slater, "Ben Lindsey and the Denver Juvenile Court: A Progressive Looks at Human Nature," *American Quarterly* (Summer 1968). Robert Bremner's *From the Depths* (1969) and David Rothman's *The Discovery of the Asylum* (1971), which both contain sections on childhood.

An introduction to the work of G. Stanley Hall can be found in C. S. Strickland and Charles Burgess, eds., *Health, Growth and Heredity* (1965) in the TC series. Hall wrote *Life and Confessions of a Psychologist;* and Dorothy Ross has written a recent biography, *The Psychologist as Prophet* (1972).

For an historical interpretation of adolescence see Joseph Kett, "Adolescence and Youth in Nineteenth Century America," in *The Family in History;* Kenneth Keniston, "Psychological Development and Historical Change," from the same collection; and David Bakan, "Adolescence in America: From Idea to Social Fact," *Daedalus* (Fall 1971).

For child-rearing in the early twentieth century see Celia B. Stendler, "Sixty Years of Child-Training Practices," *Journal of Pediatrics* (1950), an examination of the changing theories of child-rearing as demonstrated in the major women's magazines of this period; L. Emmet Holt, *The Diseases of Infancy and Childhood* (1900), is an important book by a leading and influential exponent of the "schedule." See also Richard Hofstadter, "The Child and the World," *Daedalus* (Summer 1962); V. F. Calverton and Samuel D. Schmalhausen, *The New Generation: The Intimate Problems of Modern Parents and Children* (AP, 1930); Angelo Patri, *The Problems of Childhood* (1928).

A fine introduction to the beginnings of the scientific approach to education can be found in the life and works of Edward L. Thorndike. *Psychology and the Science of Education: Selected Writings of Edward Thorndike,* edited by Geraldine Jonich Clifford (TC series), has a valuable introductory essay. Her biography of Thorndike, *The Sane Positivist* (1968), is an important contribution, and its bibliographic essay will prove invaluable for studies of the early scientific approach.

Earlier quarrels provide a perspective for the contemporary controversy over intelligence testing. For an idea of the popular, scholarly, and professional interest in this topic, consult listings in *The Reader's Guide to Peri-odical Literature* (1918 through the early 1920s), frequently listed under "mental tests." Walter Lippmann's *New Republic* articles ran in 1922 and 1923. See also Joel Spring, "Psychologists and the War: The Meaning of Intelligence in the Alpha and Beta Tests," *History of Education Quarterly* (Spring 1972); Walter F. Dearborn, *Intelligence Tests, Their Significance for School and Society* (1928); Joseph Peterson, *Early Conceptions and Tests of Intelligence* (1925); John Hersey, *Intelligence: Choice and Consent* and *The Child Buyer.*

For the current I.Q. testing controversy see Richard Herrnstein "I.Q.," *Atlantic Monthly* (September 1971) and *IQ in the Meritocracy* (1973), and Arthur R. Jensen, "How Much Can We Boost I.Q. and Scholastic Achieve-ment?" in *Harvard Educational Review* (Winter 1969) (and rebuttals to the last article). A good background is provided by a series of three articles in *Change* magazine—H. J. Eysenck "I.Q., Social Class and Educational Policy," (September 1973); Leon Kamin, "The Misuse of I.Q. Testing" (October 1973), Thomas Sowell, "Arthur Jensen and His Critics" (May 1973).

A fresh perspective on I.Q. testing is provided by Samuel Bowles and Herbert Gintis in a provocative paper, "I.Q. in the United States Class Struc-ture," which has been reprinted in *The New Assault on Equality: I.Q. and Social Stratification,* edited by Alan Gartner, Colin Greer, and Frank Riess-man (Harper paperback). It also contains essays by Jerome Kagen, Noam Chomsky, David McClelland, and others, all of which challenge the assump-tion of the dominance of heredity in relation to the I.Q. scores.

As a result of frequent changes in both expert and public attitudes toward child-rearing practices, many currently widely known authors writing in these areas tend to become caught in recurring cross-currents of controversy. The peculiarly American phenomenon which produces pendulumlike swings in judgment about child-rearing almost decade by decade must be kept in mind in perusing any of the following widely read and influential commentaries: David Riesman, et al., *The Lonely Crowd* (1950); Margaret Mead, *The School in American Culture* (Inglis lecture), *And Keep Your Powder Dry* (1942), *Male and Female* 1949; Helen and Robert Lynd, *Middletown* (1929) and *Middletown in Transition* (1937); James Coleman, *The Adolescent Society* (1961); Erik Erikson, *Childhood and Society* (1950), *Identity, Youth, and Crisis* (1968); Grace and Fred M. Hechinger, *Teenage Tyranny* (1962).

More popular and more frequently subject to changes and criticism are advice books for parents since the 1950s: Benjamin Spock, *Common Sense Book of Baby and Child Care* (1946); Arnold Gesell's *The Infant and the Child in the Culture of Today* and others; the infant- and child-care bulletins published by the Children's Bureau, the books by H. G. Ginott and Lee Salk, and their advice columns in popular magazines.

For new research on how children learn, see Jerome Bruner, *On Knowing: Essays for the Left Hand* (1962) and *The Process of Education* (1960). The work of Jean Piaget has been summarized in part by J. M. Hunt in *Intelli-*

gence and Experience (1961) and by Mary Ann Spencer Pulaski in *Understanding Piaget*. D. Elkind did an introductory article, "Of Time and the Child," in the *New York Times Magazine* (October 11, 1970). There are numerous paperback collections of, commentaries on, summaries of Piaget's work, including the recent *A Brief Introduction to Piaget* by Nathan Isaacs (1974).

Other recent research of contemporary interest includes the outstanding approach to the early years by Uri Bronfenbrenner, *The Two Worlds of Childhood* (1972), and "The Changing American Child: A Speculative Analysis," *Journal of Social Issues* (1961); Martha Wolfenstein, "Fun Morality: An Analysis of Recent American Child-Training Literature," reprinted in *Childhood in Contemporary Culture* (paperback). *The Harvard Education Review* devoted two issues to "The Rights of Children" from many different perspectives (November 1973 and March 1974); of interest for this chapter are Rochelle Beck, "White House Conferences on Children: An Historical Perspective" (November 1973), and Mary Jo Bane, "A Review of Child Care Books" (November 1973), though both are merely superficial introductions to their subjects.

Although some of its conclusions and recommendations remain controversial, *Youth: Transition to Adulthood* (1974), the report of the Panel on Youth of the President's Science Advisory Committee, headed by James S. Coleman, provides a comprehensive statement of current thinking about the problems of youth in and out of school, some of it closely related to James B. Conant's earlier observations in *Slums and Suburbs* (1961).

For those interested in television and children, the best available summary of research is offered by Robert M. Liebert, et al., *The Early Window: Effects of Television on Children and Youth* (1973). References for additional reading are included at the end of each chapter.

Chapter 7   The Black Ordeal

There are, of course, sections on Black education in many of the works cited—e.g., Curti and Welter—as well as information in the Bremner documentary collection which should not be overlooked. Comprehensive general studies of Black education and history include John Hope Franklin, *From Slavery to Freedom: A History of Negro America* and *Reconstruction after the Civil War* (1967); Henry A. Bulloch, *Negro Education in the South* (1961).

For material on Black education before the Civil War see Carter Woodson, *The Education of the Negro Prior to 1861* (AP, 1919); Frederick Law Olmsted, *The Cotton Kingdom: A Traveller's Observations on Cotton and Slavery in the American Slave States* (1861).

Invaluable material on the Reconstruction, which includes the struggle for Black education, can be found in Willie Lee Rose, *Rehearsal for Reconstruction* (1964); C. Vann Woodward, *Origins of the New South* (1951) and *The Strange Career of Jim Crow* (1955); Charles Wynes, ed., *The Negro in the South Since 1865* (paperback, 1968). The work of the Freedmen's Bureau is described by George Bentley, *A History of the Freedmen's Bureau,* and LaWanda and John Cox, "General O. O. Howard and the 'Misrepresented Bureau,' " *Journal of Southern History* (1953).

Other specialized studies include: Alfred Kelly, "The Congressional Controversy over School Segregation," *American Historical Review* (April 1969): Louis Harlan, "Desegregation in the New Orleans Public Schools During Reconstruction," *American Historical Review* (April 1962); James M. McPherson, "White Liberals and Black Power in Negro Education, 1865–1919," *American Historical Review* (1969).

There is a wealth of material both about and by Booker T. Washington and W. E. B. Du Bois. Louis Harlan has written an excellent recent biography of Washington; *Up From Slavery,* Washington's autobiography, has its own unique interest; see also Harlan's article, "Booker T. Washington and the White Man's Burden," *American Historical Review* (April 1966). Important works by Du Bois include *Black Reconstruction in America, 1860–1880* (1935), and a collection of essays, *The Education of Black People: Ten Critiques, 1906–1960,* edited by Herbert Aptheker (1973).

Gunnar Myrdal's classic study, *The American Dilemma* (1944), remains an indispensable contribution. See also Ray Stannard Baker, *Following the Color Line;* Vernon Wharton, *The Negro in Mississippi* (1947); and Louis Harlan, *Separate and Unequal* (1958).

Intimate insight into the lives of Black Americans in society and in education is provided by Robert Coles in his *Children of Crisis* (1964); Martin Kilson, "The Black Experience at Harvard," *New York Times Magazine* (September 2, 1973). Among the classics in that category remain Ralph Ellison, *The Invisible Man* (1952); Richard Wright, *Native Son* (1940); and Du Bois, "The Souls of Black Folk," in *Three Negro Classics* (republished 1965).

Problems of Blacks in Northern ghettoes are treated by David B. Tyack, "Growing Up Black: Perspectives on the History of Education in Northern Ghettos," *History of Education Quarterly* (Fall 1969), which has an excellent bibliography; August Meier and Elliot M. Rudwick, "Early Boycotts of Segregated Schools: The East Orange, New Jersey, Experience, 1899–1906," *History of Education Quarterly* (Spring 1967); Edgar A. Toppin, "Walter White and the Atlanta NAACP's Fight for Equal Schools," *History of Education Quarterly* (Spring 1967); David Tyack, "Catholic Power, Black Power and the Schools," *Educational Forum* (November 1967).

In higher education, the experience of Blacks at Harvard is described by Emory West in two issues of the *Harvard Alumni Bulletin* (November 1971 and May 1972), "Harvard and the Black Man 1636–1850" and "Harvard's First Black Graduates, 1865–1890." The most recent book, with special emphasis on the Black colleges, is Allen B. Ballard, *The Education of Black Folk* (1973), which discusses and takes issue with the David Riesman and Christopher Jencks position in *The Academic Revolution* (1968). See also the *Daedalus* issue on "The Future of the Black Colleges" (Summer 1971), particularly the article by H. A. Bullock, "The Black College and the New

Black Awareness." Earl J. McGrath, *The Predominantly Negro Colleges and Universities in Transition* (TC, 1965) is useful. A sensitive article, "The Plight of Black Students in the United States," by Thomas Sowell, appeared in *Daedalus* (Spring 1974).

Since it is difficult to find books and articles which give a comprehensive view after the Brown decision, much of the information must be taken from current newspapers and periodicals. A good collection appears in a special issue of *School Review* (University of Chicago, Vol. 81, No. 3, May 1973), "The Future of Education for Black Americans." See also Kenneth B. Clark, "Fifteen Years of Deliberate Speed," *Saturday Review* (December 20, 1969) and, from the same magazine, December 20, 1969, "The Court, the Schools and the Southern Strategy." In a reform-oriented book, *A Possible Reality* (1972), Clark addresses himself to a design for high academic achievement by students in urban ghettos.

Chapter 8 *Mass-Producing the American Dream*

Frederick Rudolph's *The American College and University* (1962) is a book to which we are much indebted. Readable and scholarly, it provides an excellent bibliographic essay that includes listings of histories of specific colleges and universities. For the period during the late nineteenth century, Laurence Veysey's *The Emergence of the American University* (1965) is outstanding. (Both are available in paperback.)

Other helpful general works include Richard Hofstadter and Wilson Smith, eds., *American Higher Education: A Documentary History* (2 vols., 1961); John S. Brubacher and Willis Rudy, *Higher Education in Transition* (1968); Christopher Jencks and David Riesman, *The Academic Revolution* (1968); Oscar and Mary Handlin, *The American College and American Culture* (1970). The Carnegie Commission on Higher Education has issued a series of studies during the early 1970s which are valuable for those interested in higher education. Several are specifically cited below.

For the pre-Civil War period, see Richard Hofstadter, *Academic Freedom in the Age of the Colleges* (1955) (paperback); Theodore R. Crane, ed., *The Colleges and the Public, 1787–1862* (TC 1963); James Axtell, "The Death of the Liberal Arts College," *History of Education Quarterly* (1971); Freeman R. Butts, *The College Charts Its Course* (1939); George P. Schmidt, *The Old Time College President* (1930). Donald G. Tewsbury's *The Founding of American Colleges and Universities Before the Civil War*, written in 1932, has long been considered a standard work, despite its lack of availability. His thesis has been criticized by Natalie A. Naylor in "The Ante-Bellum College Movement," *History of Education Quarterly* (Fall 1973).

Studies of specific institutions which have been particularly helpful (this list by no means includes all of the first-rate institutional house histories available) include: Samuel Eliot Morison, *Three Centuries of Harvard* (for the Colonial era see also Morison's *The Founding of Harvard College* and *Harvard College in the Seventeenth Century*); Carl Becker, *Cornell University: Founders and the Founding* (1943); Richard J. Storr, *Harper's Uni-*

versity (1966); Robert S. Fletcher, *A History of Oberlin College from Its Foundation through the Civil War* (1943, 2 vols.); Verne A. Stadtman, *The University of California, 1868–1968* (1970). Some less formal useful contemporary sources include E. J. Kahn, *Harvard* (1969); Reuben A. Holden, *Yale: A Pictorial History* (1967); Joseph Tussman, *Experiment at Berkeley* (1969); Marvin Gittleman, "John H. Finley at CCNY," *History of Education Quarterly* (Winter 1968).

For further information on university affairs at the end of the century consult Walter Metzger, *Academic Freedom in the Age of the University* (1955 paperback); .Robert M. MacIver, *Academic Freedom in Our Time* (1955); Claude M. Fuess, *The College Board: Its First Fifty Years* (1950); Hugh Hawkins, *Between Harvard and America: The Educational Leadership of Charles W. Eliot* (1972). Nicholas Murray Butler, ed., *Education in the United States* (1900; AP reprint) is a collection of monographs which provides insight into thinking of that era.

An excellent background view of the Morrill Act appears in Carl Becker's history of Cornell cited above. For the birth and growth of the state universities, see also Earle Ross, *Democracy's Colleges* (1942); John H. Florer, "Major Issues in the Congressional Debate of the Morrill Act of 1862," *History of Education Quarterly* (Winter 1968); Allan Nevins, *The State Universities and Democracy* (1962).

In addition to the Carnegie Commission series for the current scene see: Clark Kerr, *The Uses of the University* (1963); Nevitt Sanford, ed., *The American College* (1962); "The Embattled University," the *Daedalus* theme for Winter 1970 issue (of particular interest is the article by Martin Trow, "Reflections from Mass to Universal Higher Education").

Three useful works discuss the question of professors' salaries and general academic conditions: Beardsley Ruml and Sidney Tickton, *Teaching Salaries Then and Now: A 50-Year Comparison with Other Occupations and Industries* (1955); Logan Wilson, *The Academic Man: A Study in the Sociology of a Profession* (1942); Theodore Caplow and Reece J. McGee, *The Academic Marketplace* (1958).

Two very different personal views are expressed by John Hersey, *Letter to the Alumni* (1970), and Paul Goodman, *The Community of Scholars*.

An interesting presentation of the background and influence of the G.I. Bill of Rights is offered by Keith Olson, "The G.I. Bill and Higher Education: Success and Surprise," *American Quarterly* (December 1973).

Chapter 9   Students: Uncertain Vanguard

There is material on students' attitudes, lives, and politics in many of the works cited for the previous chapter, especially in Veysey, Rudolph, Brubacker and Rudy, Jencks and Riesman, as well as in the studies of particular institutions, particularly Morison's of Harvard. However, there is a great need for further research in this area. Frederick Rudolph's "Neglect of Students as a Historical Tradition," in *The College and the Student* (Lawrence

E. Dennis and Joseph Kauffman, eds.; 1965), explains some reasons for the neglect of the subject. Oscar and Mary Handlin's two previously cited works, *Facing Life* and *The American College and American Culture,* provide a general overview, though their interpretations of the most recent period remains subject to further debate and analysis.

Some specialized, helpful historical studies include: Henry D. Sheldon, *Student Life and Customs* (1901, AP reprint); David F. Allmendinger, Jr., "New England Students and the Revolution in Higher Education 1800–1900," *History of Education Quarterly* (Winter 1971); Lois W. Banner, "Religion and Reform in the Early Republic" and "The Role of Youth," *American Quarterly* (December 1971).

The problems of minority students on campus are described by Michael Steinberg, *The Academic Melting Pot* (Carnegie Commission Study, 1974) and the changes in student life on campus after World War II are sketched by Keith Olson, "The G.I. Bill and Higher Education: Success and Surprise," in the *American Quarterly* (December 1973), cited earlier.

After the campus ferment of the 1960s, much interest was generated in student activism. Among the books which offer historical perspective are Seymour Martin Lipset, *Rebellion in the University* (1971), and Lewis Feuer, *The Conflict of Generations: The Character and Significance of Student Movements* (1969), especially Chapters 7, 8 and 9. Philip Altback, *Student Politics in America: A Historical Analysis* (McGraw-Hill, 1974) deals primarily with 1900 to 1960. Each chapter has an annotated bibliography, but the 1960s are not covered in any detail.

For a somewhat controversial psychologically oriented view of modern students, see Kenneth Keniston, *The Uncommitted* (1960) and "Social Change and Youth in America," *Daedalus* (Winter 1972). Similar ground is covered with varied viewpoints in *Students in Revolt,* edited by S. M. Lipset and P. G. Attbach (1970).

A personal, charming, instructive, and unique memoir, *The Innocents at Cedro,* by H. L. Duffus describes the early days of Stanford. See also Owen Wister's *Philosophy Four,* a novel about turn-of-the-century Harvard.

For an assessment of the postrebellion era of the 1970s, with emphasis on public opinion analysis and statistical data, see the nationwide survey on youth attitudes by the Daniel Yankelovich research organization (1974).

WOMEN IN SCHOOL AND SOCIETY

Throughout all chapters of this book, issues affecting women in American school and society, though consistently emphasized, have been deliberately treated in the context of the larger scene. Further readings in this important area may, however, be facilitated by the addition of these separate bibliographical suggestions.

Unfortunately, not many books or studies exist on the education of women in America at any level or for any period. Many of the works listed in previous chapters, particularly those on higher education and on childhood, contain valuable and interesting material. For the rest, the following should be regarded as an introduction to a previously neglected subject.

Thomas Woody, *History of Women's Education in the United States* (2 vols.) was written in 1929 and, though it is therefore inevitably dated, still contains much that is of value for the serious scholar; including extensive supplementary material and bibliography. Mabel Newcomer, *A Century of Higher Education for Women,* is a useful contribution. See also Jessie Bernard, *Academic Women* (1964) and Opal David, ed., "The Education of Women: Signs for the Future," *American Council on Education Bulletin* (1957).

A good introduction to the problems of nineteenth-century women in education is Barbara Cross, ed., *The Educated Woman in America: Selected Writings of Catherine Beecher, Margaret Fuller and M. Carey Thomas.* See also Benjamin Rush, "Thoughts on Female Education Accommodated to the Present State of Society, Manners and Government in the United States of America," in Frederick Rudolph, ed., *Essays on Education in the Early Republic* (1965).

More specialized studies of interest include Glenda Riley, "Origins of the Argument for Improved Female Education," *History of Education Quarterly* (Winter 1969) and that journal's Spring 1974 issue on the theme "Reinterpreting Women's Education." See also an excellent essay review of the Carnegie Commission's report on "Opportunities for Women in Higher Education" by Esther M. Westervelt in the *Harvard Educational Review* (May 1974).

Two stimulating historical studies not specifically on education which nonetheless contain interesting, relevant information are Barbara Welter, "The Cult of True Womanhood," *American Quarterly* (Summer 1966), which has been widely reprinted, and Charles Rosenberg and Carroll Smith-Rosenberg, "The Female Animal: Medical and Biological Views of Woman and Her Role in Nineteenth-Century America," *Journal of American History* (September 1973). See also Helen R. Olin, *The Women of a State University: An Illustration of the Working of Coeducation in the Middlewest* (1909).

For the current period, there are several collections which cover a broad range of topics on women in modern America and include education. Alice Rossi, ed., *The Feminist Papers* (1970 paperback); R. J. Lifton, ed., *The Woman in America* (Beacon Press paperback, originally an issue of *Daedalus*); Joan Huber, ed., *Changing Women in a Changing Society* (originally an issue of the *American Journal of Sociology*). These collections contain current information and listings for further reading.

Elaine Kendall's "Up from Mother's Knee: Female Education Before 1900," *American Heritage* (June 1973), is a lively popular account.

In the March 1975 issue of *Yale,* the alumni magazine, Peter Dobkin Hall suggests that Lucinda Foote, the twelve-year-old girl who in 1783 was denied admission to the university, may actually have completed her collegiate studies, possibly under president Stiles's tutelage, without ever being formally enrolled. (See reference in Chapter 8.)

ABOUT THE AUTHORS

Fred M. Hechinger, formerly education editor of *The New York Times*, is a member of that newspaper's Editorial Board. Long a leading observer of education and politics, Mr. Hechinger is the author of numerous books, including *The Big Red Schoolhouse* and, with his wife, Grace Hechinger, *Teen-Age Tyranny*.

Grace Hechinger, author and columnist for *The Wall Street Journal,* is a historian who has specialized in children and education.

Fred and Grace Hechinger live in New York City.